Criminal Costs

legal aid costs in the criminal courts

Anthony Edwards is a criminal law solicitor at TV Edwards LLP. He is a higher courts advocate and duty solicitor. He is a visiting professor at Queen Mary, University of London and a member of the Law Commission's advisory panel on criminal law.

Anthony writes and lectures widely on criminal law. He is on the editorial boards of *Criminal Law Review* and *Blackstones' Criminal Practice*, author of *Advising a Suspect in the Police Station* (Sweet & Maxwell) and *Magistrates' Court Handbook*, contributing author to *Blackstone's Criminal Practice* and *Handbook of Youths in the Criminal Courts* (all OUP), and of *Criminal defence: a guide to good practice* (with Roger Ede) (Law Society) and *Legal Aid Handbook* (with Vicky Ling, Simon Pugh and Sue James (LAG).

Available as an ebook at www.lag.org.uk/bookshop/ebooks

The purpose of Legal Action Group is to promote equal access to justice for all members of society who are socially, economically or otherwise disadvantaged. To this end, it seeks to improve law and practice, the administration of justice and legal services.

Criminal Costs

legal aid costs in the criminal courts

SECOND EDITION

by Anthony Edwards

with Colin Beaumont

 Legal Action Group
2019

This edition published in Great Britain 2019
by LAG Education and Service Trust Limited
National Pro Bono Centre, 48 Chancery Lane, London WC2A 1JF
www.lag.org.uk

© Anthony Edwards 2019

First edition Anthony Edwards 2016

Previously published as *Fixed fees in the criminal courts: a survival guide* by
The Law Society. Third edition 2013 © The Law Society.

While every effort has been made to ensure that the details in this text are
correct, readers must be aware that the law changes and that the accuracy of
the material cannot be guaranteed and the author and the publisher accept no
responsibility for any losses or damage sustained.

The rights of the author to be identified as author of this work has been
asserted by him in accordance with the Copyright, Designs and Patents
Act 1988.

All rights reserved. No part of this publication may be reproduced, stored
in a retrieval system or transmitted in any form or by any means, without
permission from the publisher.

British Library Cataloguing in Publication Data
a CIP catalogue record for this book is available from the British Library.

Crown copyright material is produced with the permission of the Controller of
HMSO and the Queen's Printer for Scotland.

This book has been produced using Forest Stewardship Council
(FSC) certified paper. The wood used to produce FSC certified
products with a 'Mixed Sources' label comes from FSC certified
well-managed forests, controlled sources and/or recycled material.

print ISBN 978 1 912273 86 7
ebook ISBN 978 1 912273 87 4
print and ebook bundle ISBN 978 1 912273 88 1

Typeset by RefineCatch Limited, Bungay, Suffolk
Printed in Great Britain by Hobbs the Printer, Totton, Hampshire

Introduction

Scope of this edition

We are concerned to explain the principles that apply to the proper calculation of costs and to identify the relevant authority for making appropriate claims. Most firms now bill electronically and computers are programmed to apply the correct regime. The rates for graduated fees are so complex that the Legal Aid Agency's or another computer program must be used. We have included the basis on which these fees are calculated but excluded the lengthier Schedules. The key is to give the computer the correct information from which to calculate the fee. We have attempted to state the law accurately at 1 April 2019.

The figures used as examples in this edition cover the following situations:
- investigation cases where the first call is referred or reported on or after 1 April 2016;
- magistrates' court cases where the representation order is dated on or after 1 April 2016;
- unless otherwise stated, Crown Court cases where the representation order is dated on or after 31 March 2016 in relation to litigators' fees; and on or after 31 December 2018 in relation to advocates' fees.

The advocacy fee rates between 1 April 2018 and 30 December 2018 appear in appropriate tables, footnotes or appendices.

The key date for legal aid purposes is the date of the unique reference number (UFN) or representation order, and the rates payable on the date of the number or order prevail for the whole length of that matter or case. If an order is transferred, it is the date of the original order, and not of the transfer, that determines the remuneration rates. It is otherwise if an old order is revoked and a new order granted.

Where dates are referred to below it is to the date of the determination of the grant of assistance, advocacy assistance or representation.

Changes of rates

In all cases for work conducted before 1 April 2016 reference should be made to earlier editions of this guide,[1] its supplements, and to the Legal Aid Agency (LAA) Manual for the various and changing rates payable.

The critical dates – *for litigators* – for the first giving of advice or of the representation order are as follows:
- **From 13 April 2013 to 29 March 2014:** Criminal Legal Aid (Remuneration) Regulations 2013 SI No 435 sets out the core rates but note that for prison law, VHCC and experts, rates were reduced from **2 December 2013** by Criminal Legal Aid (Remuneration) (Amendment) Regulations 2013 SI No 2803.
- **From 30 March 2014 to 30 June 2015:** Criminal Legal Aid (Remuneration) (Amendment) Regulations 2014 SI No 415 – 8.75 per cent reduction in fees.
- **From 1 July 2015 to 30 March 2016:** Criminal Legal Aid (Remuneration etc) Regulations 2015 SI No 1369 – further 8.75 per cent reduction in fees.
- **From 31 March 2016:** Rates before reduction of 1 July 2015 are restored. These rates are those used in the text.

For advocates *in the Crown Court* the rates are set by:
- **From 13 April 2013 to 31 March 2018** Criminal Legal Aid (Remuneration) Regulations 2013 SI No 435.
- **From 1 April 2018 to 30 December 2018** Criminal Legal Aid (Remuneration) (Amendment) Regulations 2018 SI No 220.
- **From 31 December 2018** Criminal Legal Aid (Remuneration) (Amendment)(No 2) Regulations 2018 SI No 1323.

Sources of law

For Crime Lower (police station, magistrates' court, prison law etc) reference is made to the Standard Crime Contract (SCC) 2017 as well as to the statutory regulations. The Regulations set out the law for Crime Higher (Crown Court and above).

The relevant regulations and their main implications are as follows:

---

1 Anthony Edwards, *Fixed Fees in the Criminal Courts: a survival guide*, third edition, The Law Society, 2013.

2013
- Criminal Legal Aid (Remuneration) Regulations 2013 SI No 435. The base regulations and sets the continuing rates for advocates.
- Criminal Legal Aid (General) (Amendment) Regulations 2013 SI No 2790 – changed the scope of prison law under the Own Client Crime Contract (OCCC).
- Criminal Legal Aid (Remuneration) (Amendment) Regulations 2013 SI No 2803 – reduce rates for experts and identify very high cost cases (VHCC) rates.

2014
- Criminal Legal Aid (Remuneration) (Amendment) Regulations 2014 SI No 415 – fees reduced for litigators by 8.75 per cent.
- Criminal Legal Aid (Remuneration) (Amendment No 2) Regulations 2014 SI No 2422 – additional interim payments for litigators and change of scope to remove some cases, wholly discontinued by the Crown, from fixed fees in the Crown Court for both litigators and advocates.

2015
- Civil and Criminal Legal Aid (Remuneration) (Amendment) Regulations 2015 SI No 325 – categorisation of low value shoplifting; additions to Class H and provision for civil injunctions.
- Criminal Legal Aid (Remuneration) (Amendment) Regulations 2015 SI No 882 – provide for payments to trial, not instructed, advocates.
- Criminal Legal Aid (Remuneration etc) (Amendment) Regulations 2015 SI No 1369 – further 8.75 per cent reduction in litigator fees; and rates for work on and after 1 April 2016.
- Civil and Criminal Legal Aid (Amendment) Regulations 2015 SI No 1416 – civil injunctions.
- Civil and Criminal Legal Aid (Amendment) (No 2) Regulations 2015 SI No 1678 – removal of references to committals for trial and to plea and case management hearings (PCMHs).
- Criminal Legal Aid (Remuneration etc) (Amendment) (No 2) Regu-lations 2015 SI No 2049 – delay in implementation of new costs regimes for crime lower and for fixed fees for Crown Court cases with up to and including 500 pages.

2016
- Criminal Legal Aid (Remuneration) (Amendment) Regulations 2016 SI No 313 – Repeal Criminal Legal Aid (Remuneration etc) (Amendment) Regulations 2015 SI No 1369 and restore fees to

the levels set by Criminal Legal Aid (Remuneration) (Amendment) Regulations 2014 SI No 415.

2017
- Criminal Legal Aid (Standard Crime Contract) (Amendment) Regulations 2017 SI No 311 extend advice and assistance and advocacy assistance to 'magistrates' court applications relating to police bail' as opposed to bail conditions from 1 April 2017.
- Criminal Legal Aid (Amendment) Regulations 2017 SI No 1319 restores to scope aspects of prison law.

2018
- Criminal Legal Aid (Remuneration) (Amendment) Regulations 2018 No 220 makes changes to the Advocates' Graduated Fee scheme.
- Criminal Legal Aid (Remuneration) (Amendment) (No 2) Regulations 2018 SI No 1323 makes further changes to the Advocates' Graduated Fee scheme.

Defence costs orders

In the limited situations when a defence costs order may be granted under Prosecution of Offences Act 1985 s16 the rates payable are limited to legal aid rates. It is hoped that the relevant parts of this guide will assist in the calculation of the sum recoverable for the client. Hourly rates and not standard, fixed or graduated fees apply. The Criminal Cases Unit of the LAA (CCU) publishes guidance setting out the appropriate rates.

VAT

All rates quoted in this edition are *exclusive of VAT* (SCC A5.4).

Prescribed proceedings

These are civil proceedings conducted under criminal representation orders such as applications for football banning orders, parenting orders or sexual harm prevention orders, etc. The full list appears in Criminal Legal Aid (General) Regulations 2013 reg 9.[2] Authority must be obtained on Form CRM 5 to incur fees in excess of £1,368.75. These and other civil proceedings are considered in chapter 10.

Guidance

Guidance is available on the Ministry of Justice website. The most significant are the:
- Criminal Bills Assessment Manual (CBAM): at the time of publication the most recent edition is June 2018; and
- Crown Court Fees Guidance (CCFG): at the time of publication the most recent edition is December 2018.

While the guidance is helpful it is not always wholly accurate, it is in some places wrong and has not kept up to date with developing law. It does not bind the appellate bodies (*Lord Chancellor v Purnell*[3] and, among many other decisions, *R v Sturmer*[4]).

The LAA has begun to publish 'key costs judge decisions' but it is very limited in scope.

Reference, in relation to making claims for 'crime lower' work, should be made to the LAA Guidance for Reporting Crime Lower Work. Parts are reprinted in appendix C. At the time of publication the most recent edition is June 2018.

We are indebted to Esther Pilger of LAG for her remarkable editorial work in producing this text. Any errors, however, are our responsibility alone.

Anthony Edwards and Colin Beaumont
April 2019

---

3 [2009] EWHC 3158 (QB).
4 SCCO 277/08.

Contents

Introduction   v
Table of cases   xv
Table statutes   xxiii
Table of statutory instruments   xxv
Table of abbreviations   xxxi
Index of fees table   xxxiii

1 The principles of costs and enhancement in criminal legal aid cases   1
The principles of costs   2
The principles of enhancement   9

2 Criminal investigations and freestanding advice   13
Work types and definitions   15
Investigations conducted other than by a constable and all attendances upon witnesses; freestanding advice   15
Investigations conducted by a constable in relation to both suspects and volunteers   17
Payment   18

3 Magistrates' court proceedings   35
Court duty solicitor   37
Virtual courts   38
Costs without a representation order   39
Costs with a representation order   41

4 Prison law   55
Introduction   56
Fees available   56
Calculating core costs   57
Additional payments   58
Number of cases   59

5 Crown Court work   61
Overview   63

Principles applicable to litigators and advocates in cases sent to the
     Crown Court   64
Litigators' graduated fees   92
Advocacy in the Crown Court   115

6 **Costs in relation to appeals and reviews   143**
   Part 1: Costs under the Standard Crime Contract   144
   Part 2: Claims in the Court of Appeal and Divisional Court   146
   Part 3: Costs in the Supreme Court   147

7 **Very high cost criminal cases   149**
   Definition   150
   Notification   151
   Appointment   151
   Individual case contracts   151
   Remuneration   151
   Cases ceasing to be very high costs cases   152

8 **Disbursements   153**
   Definition   154
   Prior authorities   154
   Payments on account of disbursements   155
   Travel costs and parking   155
   Transcripts   158
   Livenote   158
   Copying   159
   Experts   159
   Other expenses (including witness expenses)   162

9 **Administrative issues   163**
   Appeals   164
   Time limits, extensions and late claims   165
   Interim staged and hardship payments on account   168
   Overpayments   170

10 **Relevant civil proceedings   171**
   Part 1: Prescribed proceedings   172
   Part 2: Civil proceedings related to criminal cases   174
   Part 3: Civil proceedings in the youth court and
       other courts: injunctions and breach of injunctions   175

APPENDICES

- A Claims summary for Crime Lower 181
- B Criminal matter type code descriptions for magistrates' court work 185
- C Guidance for reporting Crime Lower Work 197
- D Police station scheme codes 211
- E Magistrates' court codes 281
- F Prison ID codes 295
- G Crown Court litigators' offence classes 299
- H Mark-ups for litigators 315
- I Advocates' rate bands and graduated fee tables 317
- J Crown Court hourly rates and Court of Appeal fees 341
- K Very high cost cases (VHCC) payment rates 345
- L Experts' fees and rates 347
- M Prescribed proceedings fees 351
- N Crime Lower police station rates 353
- O Magistrates' court fees and Crown Court fees for non-indictable offences 363
- P Payments for assigned counsel 365

Index 367

Table of cases

Barras v Aberdeen Steam Trawling & Fishing Co Ltd [1933] AC 402, [1933] All ER Rep 52, (1933) 45 Ll L Rep 199, 1933 SC (HL) 21, 1933 SLT 338, [1933] 3 WLUK 34, HL	1.42
Brown v Haringey LBC [2015] EWCA Civ 483, [2017] 1 WLR 542, [2016] 4 All ER 754, [2015] 5 WLUK 357, [2015] HLR 30	10.2
Brush v Bower Cotton & Bower [1993] 1 WLR 1328, [1993] 4 All ER 741, [1992] 11 WLUK 372, [1997] Costs LR (Core Vol) 223, QBD	1.12, 1.21
Bwanaoga v Bwanaoga [1979] 2 All ER 105, [1978] 10 WLUK 1, (1978) 9 Fam Law 60, (1978) 122 SJ 713, Fam	1.22
Devon CC v Kirk [2016] EWCA Civ 1221, [2017] 4 WLR 36, [2016] 12 WLUK 91	10.2
Environment Agency v Flanagan SCCO 215/13	5.128
Francis v Francis and Dickerson [1956] P 87, [1955] 3 WLR 973, [1955] 3 All ER 836, [1955] 12 WLUK 5, (1955) 99 SJ 891	1.23
Frempong SCCO 84/18	5.47
Goodman and Farr v Secretary of State for Constitutional Affairs [2006] EWHC 3669 (QB), [2006] 11 WLUK 270, [2007] 3 Costs LR 366	5.9, 5.25
Johnson (X2003)	5.272
King's Lynn and West Norfolk BC v Bunning [2013] EWHC 3390 (QB), [2015] 1 WLR 531, [2014] 2 All ER 1095, [2013] 11 WLUK 189, [2014] 1 Costs LO 85	10.2
Landau and Cohen v Lord Chancellor's Department (R v Abraham) [1999] 7 WLUK 731, [1999] 2 Costs LR 5	8.27
London Corp v Cusack-Smith [1955] AC 337, [1955] 2 WLR 363, [1955] 1 All ER 302, [1955] 1 WLUK 463, (1955) 119 JP 172, 53 LGR 209, (1954–55) 5 P & CR 65, (1955) 99 SJ 108, HL	1.42
Lord Chancellor v Ahmed [2013] EWHC 3642 (QB), [2013] 10 WLUK 410, [2014] 1 Costs LR 21	5.125
Lord Chancellor v Alexander Johnson & Co Solicitors [2011] EWHC 2113 (QB), [2011] 7 WLUK 887, [2011] 6 Costs LR 987	7.3
Lord Chancellor v Eddowes Perry and Osbourne Ltd [2011] EWHC 420 (QB), [2011] 3 WLUK 110, [2011] 3 Costs LR 498	5.90, 9.41

xvi *Criminal Costs / Table of cases*

Lord Chancellor v Edward Hayes LLP [2017] EWHC 138 (QB), [2017] 2 WLUK 33, [2017] 1 Costs LR 1475	5.10, 5.13, 5.32, 5.36, 5.45
Lord Chancellor v Frieze [2007] EWHC 1490 (QB), [2007] 4 WLUK 533, [2007] 5 Costs LR 684	5.76
Lord Chancellor v Ian Henery Solicitors Ltd [2011] EWHC 3246 (QB), [2011] 12 WLUK 222, [2012] 1 Costs LR 205, (2012) *Times*, January 18	5.53, 5.55
Lord Chancellor v McCarthy [2012] EWHC 2325 (QB), [2012] 8 WLUK 69, [2012] 5 Costs LR 965	5.86, 5.88, 5.117
Lord Chancellor v McLarty and Co Solicitors [2011] EWHC 3182 (QB), [2011] 12 WLUK 64, [2012] 1 Costs LR 190, (2012) *Times*, January 2	5.24, 5.172, 5.182
Lord Chancellor v Michael J Reed Ltd [2009] EWHC 2981 (QB), [2009] 11 WLUK 543, [2010] 1 Costs LR 72	5.23, 5.172
Lord Chancellor v Purnell [2009] EWHC 3158 (QB), [2009] 12 WLUK 192, [2010] 1 Costs LR 81	5.65, 5.73
Lord Chancellor v Woodhall [2013] EWHC 764 (QB), [2013] 2 WLUK 513, [2013] 4 Costs LR 527	5.76
Lowsley v Forbes (t/a LE Design Services) [1999] 1 AC 329, [1998] 3 WLR 501, [1998] 3 All ER 897, [1998] 2 Lloyd's Rep 577, [1998] 7 WLUK 591, (1998) 95(35) LSG 37, (1998) 148 NLJ 1268, (1998) 142 SJLB 247, (1998) *Times*, August 24, HL	1.42
Maclaverty Cooper Atkins v Lord Chancellor [2014] EWHC 1387 (QB), [2014] 5 WLUK 204, [2014] 4 Costs LR 629	5.23
Meeke and Taylor v Secretary of State for Constitutional Affairs [2005] EWHC 2004 (QB), [2005] 3 WLUK 800, [2006] 1 Costs LR 1	5.273
Mehmood and Horvathova SCCO 76/16; SCCO 194/16	5.299
Miller Gardner v Lord Chancellor [1997] 5 WLUK 145, [1997] 2 Costs LR 29, QBD	1.33, 1.45
Murria (Solicitors) v Lord Chancellor (R v Crossley)[2000] 2 All ER 941, [1999] 12 WLUK 399, [2000] 1 Costs LR 81, (2000) 97(3) LSG 35, (2000) 150 NLJ 59, (2000) 144 SJLB 36, (2000) *Times*, January 11, (2000) *Independent*, February 7, QBD	1.42
Perry v Lord Chancellor TMC SJ4	1.31
R (Ames) v Lord Chancellor [2018] EWHC 2250 (Admin), [2018] 8 WLUK 216, [2018] Lloyd's Rep FC 545, [2018] ACD 115	7.12
R (Law Society) v Lord Chancellor [2018] EWHC 2094 (Admin), [2019] 1 WLR 1649, [2019] 1 All ER 638, [2018] 8 WLUK 16, [2018] 5 Costs LR 937, [2018] ACD 112	5.134
R (T) v Legal Aid Agency [2013] EWHC 960 (Admin), [2013] 4 WLUK 659, [2013] 2 FLR 1315, [2013] Fam Law 805	8.4
R v AS (2015) Luton Crown Court, 22 June	5.30
R v Akinrele (Costs) [2013] 6 WLUK 617, [2013] 4 Costs LR 637	1.25
R v Alays (Mohammed) [2006] 11 WLUK 136, [2007] 2 Costs LR 321	5.59

R v Aldridge SCCO 221/13	9.21, 9.24
R v Ali TMC S12	5.179
R v Ali [2017] 6 WLUK 421, [2017] 4 Costs LO 533	5.34
R v Alwan (Hisham) [2000] 2 WLUK 321, [2000] 2 Costs LR 326	1.45
R v Andall SCCO 06/17	5.19
R v Arney TMC S24	8.44
R v Ayres (X32) [2002] 4 WLUK 607, [2002] 2 Costs LR 330	5.57, 5.57, 5.262
R v Backhouse TMC S30 [1986] 3 WLUK 1, [1997] Costs LR (Core Vol) 445	1.42, 5.181
R v Badham SCTO 621/93	5.179
R v Bailey (X16)	5.211
R v Bishop [2007] 10 WLUK 71, [2008] 5 Costs LR 808	5.275
R v Bowen [2011] 4 WLUK 467, [2011] 4 Costs LR 693	5.6, 5.89, 5.90
R v Brandon [2011] 3 WLUK 837, [2012] 2 Costs LR 424	5.182
R v Brazier (X5)	5.16, 5.22, 5.22
R v Brindle SCCO 91/11	5.95
R v Brinkworth [2005] 4 WLUK 343, [2006] 3 Costs LR 512	5.259
R v Brown [2002] 8 WLUK 155, [2002] 3 Costs LR 539	1.14
R v Brown SCCO 215/10	8.26
R v Budai [2010] 10 WLUK 590, [2011] 6 Costs LR 1073	5.55, 5.80
R v Bullingham [2010] 10 WLUK 737, [2011] 6 Costs LR 1078	5.55
R v Bury Magistrates' Court ex p Cornthwaite CO 296/95 [1995] 11 WLUK 394	5.179
R v Carlyle [2001] 8 WLUK 177, [2002] 1 Costs LR 192	5.301
R v Carty [2009] 1 WLUK 5, [2009] 3 Costs LR 500	5.74
R v Cato SCCO 155/11	5.63
R v Cevik (Bozkurt Bulent) [1998] 6 WLUK 99, [1998] 2 Costs LR 1	1.42
R v Chilton SCCO 400/14	5.38
R v Chowdhury [2009] 5 WLUK 641, [2009] 3 Costs LR 514	5.65, 5.73
R v Chubb [2002] 5 WLUK 379, [2002] 2 Costs LR 333	5.1, 5.72
R v Coles SCCO 51/16	5.55, 5.74
R v Connors [2014] 8 WLUK 387, [2014] 5 Costs LR 942	5.250
R v Cox SCCO 299/12	9.22
R v Daugnitis; R v Cvetkovas; R v Liumas SCCO 154/17; 155/17; 177/17	5.44, 5.49
R v Davis	5.122
R v Dawson (Stuart Ian) [1998] 11 WLUK 405, [1999] 1 Costs LR 4	5.72
R v Day SCCO 173/18	5.121
R v Debenham SCCO 10/12	5.20
R v Dhaliwal [2004] 5 WLUK 582, [2004] 4 Costs LR 689	5.1
R v Dhesi [2003] 6 WLUK 504, [2003] 4 Costs LR 645	1.42
R v Dinu SSCO 146/16	5.33
R v Dodd [2014] 11 WLUK 430, [2014] 6 Costs LR 1131	5.37
R v Dumbaya [2012] 9 WLUK 83, [2012] 5 Costs LR 976	9.12
R v Dunne [2013] 10 WLUK 878, [2013] 6 Costs LR 1031	1.2, 1.7
R v Duxbury TMC S2	1.12

xviii *Criminal Costs / Table of cases*

R v El Treki (X26)	5.6, 5.22
R v Evans-Southall [1998] 1 WLUK 11, [1998] 1 Costs LR 68	1.45
R v Fairhurst (X6A)	5.94
R v Fiaz SCCO 57/14	5.41
R v Finn [2006] 1 WLUK 356, [2006] 3 Costs LR 525	5.58
R v Fletcher (X6)	5.94
R v Fletcher SCCO 85/12	9.13, 9.20
R v Ford-Lloyd TMC S6	1.27
R v Forrester [2011] 11 WLUK 776, [2012] 4 Costs LR 811	5.89
R v Forsyth SCCO 155/10	5.63
R v Frampton [2004] 12 WLUK 206, [2005] 3 Costs LR 527	5.73
R v Frempong SCCO 84/18	5.47
R v French [2014] 6 WLUK 176, [2014] 4 Costs LR 786	1.8
R v Furniss (Michael) [2015] 1 WLUK 390, [2015] 1 Costs LR 151, Crown Court (Nottingham)	5.30, 5.32
R v Fury [2010] 9 WLUK 320, [2011] 5 Costs LR 919	5.93, 5.246
R v Garness SCCO 132/13	5.123
R v Geeling SCCO 40/14	5.69, 9.41
R v Gemeskel (X2)	5.79
R v Ghaffar [2009] 7 WLUK 550, [2009] 6 Costs LR 980	5.281
R v Gillett SSCO 185/14	5.40
R v Gleeson (2011)	5.22
R v Gravette (2016)	5.292
R v Great Western Trains Co Ltd [2002] 5 WLUK 383, [2004] 2 Costs LR 331	1.31, 8.42
R v Green TMC S13	5.179
R v Greenwood [2010] 1 WLUK 11, [2010] 2 Costs LR 268	5.21
R v Griffiths SCCO 277/10	5.99
R v Grigoropolou and others [2012] 8 WLUK 132, [2012] 5 Costs LR 982	9.18, 9.20
R v Halcrow TMC S14	5.179
R v Harris [2009] 5 WLUK 640, [2009] 3 Costs LR 507	5.77
R v Hart-Badger [2012] 10 WLUK 511, [2013] 1 Costs LR 181	9.14
R v Hines (X24)	5.193
R v Howitt SCCO 386/12	5.63
R v Hudson TMC SJ2	1.14, 1.16
R v Hunt [2016] 3 WLUK 673, [2016] 2 Costs LR 429	5.57
R v Hunter-Brown (X29)	5.57
R v Hussain [2010] 6 WLUK 709, [2011] 4 Costs LR 689	5.89
R v Hussain SCCO 217/13	5.65, 5.73
R v Jagelo SCCO 96/15	5.170, 5.271
R v Jalibaghodelehzi [2013] 11 WLUK 754, [2014] 4 Costs LR 781	5.37, 5.41
R v Jedran SCCO 54/18	5.121
R v Johnson (Craig) [2006] 10 WLUK 630, [2007] 2 Costs LR 316	5.227
R v Jones (X2000)	5.56
R v Karra (X19A)	5.59
R v Kemp (X15) 3633/99	5.1
R v Khan (ex Liverpool Crown Court T20117540) SCCO 316/13	5.66

Table of cases xix

R v Kholi [2010] 7 WLUK 253, [2010] 6 Costs LR 982	5275
R v Knight (X35)	5.123
R v Lafayette [2010] 4 WLUK 465, [2010] 4 Costs LR 650	9.20
R v Lawlor SCCO 444/15	8.15
R v Lee SCCO 343/13	5.37
R v Legal Aid Board ex p RM Broudie & Co [1994] 3 WLUK 252, [1994] COD 435, (1994) 138 SJLB 94, (1994) *Times*, April 11, DC	1.40
R v Legal Aid Board No 15 Area Office (Liverpool) ex p Eccleston [1998] 1 WLR 1279, [1998] 4 WLUK 78, [1999] PIQR P38, [1998] COD 482, (1998) 95(20) LSG 35, (1998) 142 SJLB 155, (1998) *Times*, May 6, (1998) *Independent*, May 4, QBD	8.44
R v Lennon SSCO 186/15	5.31
R v Lowe TMC S15	1.30
R v Luck SCCO 135/16	5.250
R v Ludic SCCO 73/17	5.47
R v MA [2018] 4 WLUK 268, [2018] 2 Costs LR 419	5.46
R v McCall [2011] 5 Costs LR 914	5.27
R v McCarthy SCCO 36/17	5.45, 5.75, 5.87
R v McCreadie SCCO 350/12	5.6
R v Mahmood and Mahmood SCCO 149/16; 155/16; 185/16	5.44
R v Marandola [2005] 7 WLUK 717, [2006] 1 Costs LR 184	5.274
R v Martini	5.115
R v Matthews TMC S26	8.3
R v Matthews SCCO 58/07	5.5
R v Maynard (X19)	5.59
R v Mira (X54)	5.115, 5.217
R v Morfitt SCCO 55/16	5.57
R v Moss TMC S16	1.17
R v Motaung SCCO 179/15	5.22
R v Muiyoro SCCO 70/18	5.47
R v Muoka [2013] 5 WLUK 61, [2013] 3 Costs LR 523	5.300
R v Muiyoro SCCO 70/18	5.47
R v Murray SCCO 233/14	5.40
R v Napper [2014] 9 WLUK 130, [2014] 5 Costs LR 947	5.31, 5.37, 5.40
R v Nassir (X13)	5.79
R v Nazir SCCO 135/13	5.171
R v Nelson SCCO 417/09	5.123
R v Nettleton [2012] 11 WLUK 398, [2013] 1 Costs LR 186	5.63
R v Nettleton SCCO 58/13	5.64
R v Newton (Robert John) [1982] 12 WLUK 57, (1983) 77 Cr App R 13, (1982) 4 Cr App R (S) 388, [1983] Crim LR 198, CA	5.57
R v Nicholson SCCO 197/14	5.41
R v Noon [2013] 5 WLUK 186, [2013] 4 Costs LR 633	1.7
R v North Kent Justices ex p McGoldrick & Co [1995] 1 WLUK 457, (1996) 160 JP 30, [1995] COD 314, (1995) 159 JPN 722, (1995) *Times*, February 6, QBD	9.16
R v Nutting SCCO 215/13 [2013] 11 WLUK 108, [2013] 6 Costs LR 1037	5.39, 5.124, 5.217

R v O'Donnell and Fawley [2011] 10 WLUK 281, [2012] 2 Costs LR 431	5.131
R v O'Rourke SCCO 10/17; 34/17; 47/17	5.48
R v Osoteko [2014] 1 WLUK 65, [2014] 1 Costs LR 190	5.23
R v Ototo SCCO 8/11	5.89
R v P SCTO 158/93	1.47
R v PW [2016] EWCA Crim 745, [2017] 4 WLR 79, [2016] 6 WLUK 583, [2016] 2 Cr App R 27, [2016] Crim LR 844	5.86
R v Parke SCCO 67/17	5.13
R v Pelepenko SCCO 186/2001	5.73
R v Powell SCCO 7/16	5.22
R v Pullum TMC S1	1.12
R v Qu [2012] 3 Costs LR 599, [2012] 3 Costs LR 599	5.10
R v Ranjit [2006] 2 WLUK 667, [2006] 3 Costs LR 541	5.274
R v Richardson [2006] 10 WLUK 15, [2008] 2 Costs LR 320	5.211
R v Riddell (X3)	5.57
R v Rigelsford [2005] 7 WLUK 77, [2006] 3 Costs LR 518	5.22
R v Roberts SCCO 112/14	5.42
R v Robertson SCCO 22/17	5.44
R v Russell (X31)	5.261
R v Sallah SCCO 281/18	5.55
R v Samoon and Baryali SCCO 24/16	5.22
R v Sana [2014] 11 WLUK 849, [2014] 6 Costs LR 1143	5.43, 5.44
R v Sandhu TMC SJ1	1.27, 1.28
R v Sanghera [2008] 6 WLUK 604, [2008] 5 Costs LR 823	5.74
R v Sarfraz SCCO 122/16	5.263
R v Schilling SCCO 22/11	5.100
R v Seivwright [2010] 7 WLUK 518, [2011] 2 Costs LR 327	5.63, 5.69
R v Sereika SSCO 68/13	5.31
R v Shaoib SCCO 142/18	5.46
R v Sharif SCCO 168/13	5.2, 5.85
R v Shoaib SSCO 68/13	5.31
R v Sibanda SCCO 227/14	5.44
R v Shields TMC S20	8.1
R v Slessor TMC S23	8.15
R v Smith SCTO 117/93	1.47
R v Somers SCCO 162/11	5.128
R v St Martin SCCO 141/15	5.121
R v Stables (X12), 1999	5.119
R v Starynskyj SCCO 9/16	5.171
R v Sturdy (Michael Lewis) [1998] 12 WLUK 452, [1999] 1 Costs LR 1 (X9)	5.10, 5.22, 5.26
R v Sturmer and Lewis SCCO 277/08 [2009] 1 WLUK 37, [2009] 2 Costs LR 364	5.98
R v Supreme Court Taxing Office ex p John Singh & Co TMC SJC	1.33
R v T; R v Burton [2018] EWCA Civ 2485	5.86
R v Tai SCCO 4/16	5.120
R v Taylor [2005] 3 WLUK 228, [2005] 4 Costs LR 712	5.18
R v Taylor [2012] 11 WLUK 905, [2013] 2 Costs LR 374	9.11
R v Teret [2016] 4 WLUK 558, [2016] 3 Costs LO 393	5.272

R v Tooth (David Christopher) [2006] 5 WLUK 127, [2007] 2 Costs LR 302	5.94
R v Tunstall SSCO 220/15	5.44
R v Turnbull SCCO 86/12	9.11, 9.20
R v Uddin [2010] 1 WLUK 126, [2010] 2 Costs LR 274	5.23
R v Varney TMC S21	1.36
R v Walsh SCCO 197/16	5.35
R v Walton (Andrew) [2011] EWCA Crim 2832, [2011] 11 WLUK 196	2.14
R v Wanklyn TMC S28	1.34
R v Ward [2012] 1 WLUK 48, [2012] 3 Costs LR 605	5.9, 5.22, 5.22
R v Wembo [2010] 12 WLUK 719, [2011] 5 Costs LR 926	5.52
R v Wortley SCCO 06/14	5.39
R v Yates SCCO 66/17	5.44
R v Zavola TMC S11	1.17
Secretary of State for Constitutional Affairs v Stork [2005] EWHC 1763 (QB), [2005] 8 WLUK 67, [2006] 1 Costs LR 69, (2005) *Times*, October 7	5.220
Secretary of State for Justice, the Lord Chancellor v SVS Solicitors [2017] EWHC 1045 (QB), [2017] 4 WLR 87, [2017] 5 WLUK 257, [2017] 3 Costs LO 331, [2017] Lloyd's Rep FC 404	5.8, 5.11, 5.13, 5.30, 5.32, 5.36
Sereika SSCO 68/13	5.31
Smith Graham (Solicitors) v Lord Chancellor [1999] 2 Costs LR 1, (1999) 149 NLJ 1443, [1999] All ER (D) 957	1.12, 8.41
Truscott v Truscott; Wraith v Sheffield Forgemasters [1998] 1 WLR 132, [1998] 1 All ER 82, [1997] 7 WLUK 670, [1997] 2 Costs LR 74, [1998] 1 FLR 265, [1998] 1 FCR 270, [1998] Fam Law 74, (1997) *Times*, October 15, CA	8.12
Tuckers Solicitors v Lord Chancellor [2013] EWHC 3817 (QB), [2013] 10 WLUK 602, [2014] 1 Costs LR 29	5.148

Table of statutes

Anti-social Behaviour, Crime and
    Policing Act 2014 c12–
    Pt 1 (ss1–21)   10.23
Bail Act 1976 c63   3.30, 5.94, 5.295
    s6   5.244
Crime and Disorder Act 1998 c37–
    s1C   5.97
    s1CA   5.97
    s51   5.9, 5.113, 5.141, 5.161, 5.282
    Sch 3   3.33
Criminal Attempts Act 1981 c47–
    s1   2.47
    s1A   2.47
Criminal Damage Act 1971 c48–
    s1(1)   2.47
    s1(2)   2.47
    s1(3)   2.47
Criminal Justice Act 1967 c80–
    s9   5.57
    s10   5.57
Criminal Justice Act 1987 c38–
    s8   5.231
Criminal Justice Act 1988 c33–
    s40(1)   2.14
Criminal Law Act 1977 c45–
    s1   2.47
Criminal Procedure (Insanity) Act 1964 c84–
    s4A   5.73, 5.248
Criminal Procedure and Investigations Act 1996 c25   8.39
Customs and Excise Management Act 1979 c2–
    s170(1)   5.125
    s170(2)   5.125

Drugs Act 2005 c17–
    s12   3.30
Homicide Act 1957
    c11   2.47
Legal Aid, Sentencing and Punishment of Offenders Act (LASPO) 2012 c10   10.18
    s2(1)   7.2
    s14   10.2
    s14(g)   10.4
    s14(h)   10.3
    s15   2.20
    s15(2)(c)   6.1
    s16   6.1, 7.2
    Sch 1 para 40   10.18
Magistrates' Courts Act 1980 c43–
    s22   3.31
    s22A(3)   3.31
    s128(7)   2.14
Mental Health Act 1983
    c20   8.33
    s41   5.114, 5.118, 5.215
Offences Against the Person Act 1861 c100–
    s4   2.47
    s18   2.47, 5.122
    s20   2.47, 5.122, 5.214
    s57   5.130
Offender Management Act 2007
    c21   5.127
Police and Criminal Evidence Act 1984 (PACE)
    c60   2.36
    s66(9)   2.6

Powers of Criminal Courts
    (Sentencing) Act 2000 c6–
    s1   3.31
    s155   5.97
Prison Act 1952 c52–
    s40B   5.127
Proceeds of Crime Act 2002
    c29   10.18
    s16   5.287
    s70   5.180, 5.285
Road Traffic Act 1988 c52–
    s1   2.47
Serious Organised Crime and
    Police Act 2005
    c15   2.22
    s74   5.97

Sexual Offences Act 2003 c42–
    s1   2.47
    s2   2.47
    s5   2.47
    s6   2.47
Terrorism Act 2000
    c11   2.36
    s41   2.47
    Sch 7   2.23
Theft Act 1968 c60–
    s8   2.47
Youth Justice and Criminal
    Evidence Act 1999 c23–
    s28   5.60, 5.82
    s38   5.292

Table of statutory instruments

Civil Legal Aid (Remuneration) Regulations 2013
    SI No 422–
        Sch 1 Pt 1   10.20
        Sch 1 Pt 2   10.20
        Sch 1 Pt 3   10.21
        Sch 2   10.22
Civil Procedure Rules 1998 (CPR) SI No 3132   1.9
Costs in Criminal Cases (General) Regulations 1986
    SI No 1335   9.16
    Pt V (regs 15–25)   8.11
    regs 16–20   8.36
    reg 24   8.11
Criminal Justice Act 1988 (Offensive Weapons)
    (Amendment) Order 2016 SI No 803   5.120
Criminal Justice Act 1988 (Offensive Weapons) Order
    1988 SI No 2019   5.121
Criminal Legal Aid (Determinations by a Court and
    Choice of Representative) Regulations 2013
    SI No 614–
    reg 8(2)   6.11
    reg 16   3.46
Criminal Legal Aid (General) Regulations 2013 SI No 9–
    reg 9   3.18, 3.31, 5.203, 10.1, 10.3, 10.4, 10.26
    reg 9(v)   10.2, 10.23
    reg 12(2)(i)   2.6
    reg 12(2)(j)   2.20
    reg 12(2)(k)   2.23
Criminal Legal Aid (Remuneration) (Amendment)
    Regulations 2018 SI No 220   5.214
    reg 19   5.5, 5.220
Criminal Legal Aid (Remuneration) (Amendment)
    (No 2) Regulations 2018 SI No 1323   5.1
Criminal Legal Aid (Remuneration) Regulations 2013   1.42, 3.47, 5.12, 5.28,
    SI No 435   5.51, 5.57, 5.105, 5.179, 5.200, 5.209, 5.233, 5.241, 6.10, 6.14, 8.4, 9.10, 9.25, 9.27, 10.4, 10.11

Criminal Legal Aid (Remuneration) Regulations 2013 SI No 435 *continued*

reg 2	5.175, 7.1
reg 2(1)	7.2
reg 4	6.9
reg 4(3)	9.10
reg 5(2)	8.22
reg 5(3)	9.10
reg 6	6.10
reg 7	6.14
reg 12(2)	7.6
reg 12A	7.6
reg 13	8.2
reg 13(3)	8.5
reg 14	8.10, 9.27
reg 16	8.28
reg 16(2)	8.31
reg 16(3)	8.31
reg 17	5.188
reg 17(2)	8.12
reg 17(3)	8.2
reg 17(5)	8.3
reg 17(6)	8.30
reg 17(7)	8.30
reg 17A	9.31
reg 18	9.30
reg 19	9.30
reg 20	9.38
reg 21	9.39
reg 25	9.41
regs 28–30	9.3
reg 28	9.3
reg 28(3)(b)	9.3
reg 28(7)	5.216
reg 29	9.4
reg 29(5)	9.3
reg 30	9.5
reg 31	9.17
reg 31(2)	9.19
Sch 1	5.3, 5.5, 5.7, 5.189, 5.220, 5.257, 5.270, 10.19
Sch 1 para 1	5.84
Sch 1 para 1(1)	5.257
Sch 1 para 1(2)–(5)	5.5, 5.7, 5.220
Sch 1 para 1(3)–(5)	5.7
Sch 1 para 1(5)	5.7, 5.44
Sch 1 para 2(1)(b)	5.257
Sch 1 para 2(2)–(7)	5.249
Sch 1 para 2(3)	???
Sch 1 para 2(8)	5.57, 5.79
Sch 1 para 3(1)(b)	5.116

Criminal Legal Aid (Remuneration) Regulations 2013 SI No 435 *continued*

Sch 1 para 3(1)(f)	5.118
Sch 1 para 3(1)(g)	5.118
Sch 1 para 3(2)	5.127
Sch 1 para 3(3)	5.127
Sch 1 para 4	5.263
Sch 1 para 12(2)	5.255, 5.257
Sch 1 para 13	5.262
Sch 1 para 13(1)(a)	5.261
Sch 1 para 13(1)(b)	5.261
Sch 1 para 13(1)(c)	5.261
Sch 1 para 13(1)(d)	5.261
Sch 1 para 13(1)(da)	5.261
Sch 1 para 13(1)(e)	5.261
Sch 1 para 13(3)	5.261
Sch 1 para 14	5.261, 5.285
Sch 1 para 15	5.258
Sch 1 para 15(2)	5.258
Sch 1 para 17	5.5, 5.269
Sch 1 para 17(1)	5.270
Sch 1 para 17(1)(a)	5.272
Sch 1 para 17(1)(b)	5.220
Sch 1 para 17(1)(c)	5.44
Sch 1 para 18	5.279
Sch 1 para 19	5.264
Sch 1 para 19A	5.255
Sch 1 para 19A(2)	5.256
Sch 1 para 20(1)	5.194, 5.199
Sch 1 para 20(2)	5.195
Sch 1 para 20(3)	5.195
Sch 1 para 20(4)	5.199
Sch 1 para 20(5)	5.199, 5.201
Sch 1 para 20(5)(a)	5.201
Sch 1 para 20(5)(b)	5.201
Sch 1 para 21	5.196, 5.261
Sch 1 para 22	5.78, 5.282
Sch 1 para 22(6)	5.261
Sch 1 para 23	5.261
Sch 1 para 24	5.257
Sch 1 para 24A	5.295
Sch 1 Pt 6 (paras 25–34)	5.50
Sch 1 para 26	5.303
Sch 1 para 27	5.117, 5.247
Sch 1 para 27(2)	5.197, 5.245
Sch 1 para 31	5.83, 5.248
Sch 1 para 32	5.292
Sch 1 para 33	5.294
Sch 1 para 34	5.292
Sch 2	5.3, 5.7, 5.96, 5.152
Sch 2 para 1	5.84
Sch 2 para 1(2)–(5)	5.7

Criminal Legal Aid (Remuneration) Regulations 2013 SI No 435 *continued*
    Sch 2 para 1(2)   5.137
    Sch 2 para 1(3)–(5)   5.7
    Sch 2 para 1(3)   5.11
    Sch 2 para 1(5)   5.7, 5.32, 5.44
    Sch 2 para 2   5.181, 5.182
    Sch 2 para 2(4)   5.57, 5.79
    Sch 2 para 2(6)   5.143
    Sch 2 para 3(1)(b)   5.116
    Sch 2 para 3(1)(d)   5.123
    Sch 2 para 3(1)(f)   5.118
    Sch 2 para 3(1)(g)   5.118
    Sch 2 para 3(2)   5.127
    Sch 2 para 3(3)   5.127
    Sch 2 para 10   5.206
    Sch 2 para 11   5.108
    Sch 2 para 13   5.145, 5.152
    Scg 2 para 13(1)   5.152
    Sch 2 para 13(8)   5.153, 7.10, 7.11
    Sch 2 para 13(9)   5.153, 7.13
    Sch 2 para 17   5.97
    Sch 2 para 19   5.97
    Sch 2 para 20   5.32, 5.168–5.179
    Sch 2 para 20(1)(a)   5.44, 5.170
    Sch 2 para 20(1)(b)   5.170
    Sch 2 para 20(3)   5.170
    Sch 2 para 21   5.78, 5.161
    Sch 2 para 22   5.78, 5.163
    Sch 2 para 23   5.184
    Sch 2 Pt 6 (paras 24–29)   5.54
    Sch 2 para 24   5.117
    Sch 2 para 25   5.83
    Sch 2 para 26   5.168–5.179
    Sch 2 para 27   5.173, 5.183
    Sch 2 para 29   1.39
    Sch 3   6.10, 6.12, 9.7
    Sch 3 para 8   6.10
    Sch 3 para 9   6.10
    Sch 4 para 2(6)   2.11
    Sch 4 para 2(7)   2.11
    Sch 4 para 4(1)   3.4
    Sch 4 para 5A   10.24
    Sch 4 para 7   10.11
    Sch 4 para 10   10.10
    Sch 5   8.28, 8.30, 8.32
    Sch 6   7.9
    Appendix 1 para 14(2)   5.260, 5.290
Criminal Legal Aid (Remuneration etc) (Amendment)
    Regulations 2015 SI No 1369   2.11, 5.2
Criminal Procedure Rules 2011 SI No 1709–
Consolidated PD III.21

Criminal Procedure Rules 2015 SI No 1490	5.11
Pt 45	9.4
PD I.3B.2	5.12
PD I.3B.3	5.12
PD I.3B.4	5.12
PD I.3B.5	5.12
PD XIII.B1	5.179
Supreme Court Rules 2009 SI No 1603–	
PD 12	6.14

Abbreviations

ABE	Achieving Best Evidence
CBAM	Criminal Bills Assessment Manual of the LAA
CCFG	Crown Court Fee Guidance published by the LAA
CCU	Criminal Cases Unit (replacing the High Cost Crime Team and the National Taxing Team)
CJA	Criminal Justice Act
CRIMLA	Decisions of the Costs Appeal Committee of the LAA on points of principle (PoP). The LAA publishes these decisions with the most recent edition being February 2017.
DSCC	Defence Solicitor Call Centre
HFL	Higher fee limit
HSF	Higher standard fee
LAA	Legal Aid Agency
LFL	lower fee limit
LSC	[former] Legal Services Commission
LSF	lower standard fee
NAE	notice of additional evidence
PPE	pages of prosecution evidence
PTPH	Pre-trial Preparation Hearing
Remuneration Regulations	Criminal Legal Aid (Remuneration) Regulations 2013 SI No 435 as amended (see Introduction)
RUI	Remain under investigation
SCC	Standard Crime Contract 2017 as amended
SCCO	Senior Courts Costs Office
SCTO	[former] Supreme Court Taxing Office
TIC(s)	[offence(s)] taken into consideration
TMC	Taxing Masters' Compendium
TONG	Taxing Officer's Notes for Guidance
UFN	unique file number
VHCC	very high cost case

References to cases in the style 'X123' are to cases quoted in the TMC. Many are referred to in CCFG Appendix K.

Index of fees tables

For matters and cases beginning on or after 1 April 2016

Fees	Paragraph	Page	Appendix
Investigations			
Telephone fees	2.27	21	
CDS direct	2.30	22	
Attendance fees	–	–	N
Hourly rates	2.41	24	
Warrants of further detention	2.68–2.69	31–32	
Magistrates' court pre-charge bail conditions	2.70	33	
Proceedings			
Court duty	3.2	37	
Virtual court	3.8	38	
Fees without representation order	3.11	39	
Hourly rates	3.35	50–51	O
Standard fees	3.36	51	O
Assigned counsel	3.43–3.45	53	P
Prison law			
Sentence fixed fee	4.4	56	
Disciplinary and parole standard fees	4.8	57	
Advice and assistance hourly rates	4.10	57	
Disciplinary and parole hourly rates	4.11	58	
Crown Court Fees: litigators			
Litigators: non-indictable	5.95	85	
Litigators: defence election	5.106	88	
Defendant multipliers	5.120	90	H2
Transfer and retrial fees	5.122	90–92	H2

xxxiv Criminal Costs / Index of fees tables

Fees	Paragraph	Page	Appendix
Litigators: discontinuances and dismissal	5.137	96	
Hourly rates for special preparation and confiscation	5.154	100–101	
Evidence provision fee	5.158	102	
Crown court fees: advocates			
Non-indictable crime	5.164–5.165	104	
Contempt of court	5.166	105	
defence election	5.175	107	
Graduated fees	5.182	108	
Supplementary fees	5.212–5.225	114–119	I1
Confiscation fees	5.235	122	I2
Retrial percentages	5.236	122	
Mitigation only	5.238	123	
Appeal cases			
Advice and assistance	6.6	129	
Case stated	6.7	129	
Crown court hourly rates and Court of Appeal	6.9	130	J
VHCC Rates	chapter 7	133–136	K
Experts Fees	8.23	143	L
Civil proceedings			
Higher Courts prescribed proceedings	10.10	157	P
Civil injunctions	10.16–10.17	159–160	
Independent Bar	10.18	160–170	
Breach of civil injunction	10.19	161	
Appendices			
Litigator defendant uplift; Transfer and retrial percentages			H
Advocacy rate bands and graduated fees Part 1			I
			From 1 April to 30 December 2018

Part 2	From 31 December 2018
Crown Court hourly rates and Court of Appeal fees	J
VHCC fees	K
Expert fees	L
Crown court Prescribed proceedings fees	M
Crime lower fees	N
Magistrates' court fees and crown court fees for non-indictable cases	O
Payments for assigned counsel	P

CHAPTER 1

The principles of costs and enhancement in criminal legal aid cases[1]

1.1	**The principles of costs**
1.2	Time recording and work logs
1.6	What is reasonable?
	Ex post facto billing
1.14	Routine letters and telephone calls
1.17	Preparation
1.34	Advocacy
1.35	Travel and waiting time
1.39	**The principles of enhancement**

1 See generally Criminal Bills Assessment Manual (CBAM) 2 and CBAM 3.

The principles of costs

1.1 Although many fees are prescribed by the fixed, standard and graduated fee schemes, it is still essential to be able to apply the principles of costs in criminal legal aid cases. These will determine whether an exceptional claim can be made for police station work; whether in the magistrates' court a fee is beyond the standard fee limit so that a claim can be made on Form CRM7; whether the escape figures have been reached in prison law; and the amount payable for special preparation and for work connected with confiscation in the Crown Court.

Time recording and work logs

1.2 Time recording and other records are vital (see CRIMLA 5 and Standard Crime Contract (SCC) Standard Terms 7.19(f)).[2] Advocates must also maintain a contemporaneous work log: *R v Dunne*.[3]

1.3 The more detail that is provided, the more likely it is that a claim will be allowed. When papers have been read, the actual times should be recorded together with the page numbers considered. When documents are dictated or prepared they should be identified and different drafts should be retained to show the development of the papers. Records of meetings with clients should set out at least an outline of the instructions received and advice given. There should be written evidence of how individual pieces of work progressed the case.

1.4 Where a case may take longer than normal, the reason of this should be clearly recorded, for example if the client has mental health issues or is very young or immature, or does not have English as a first language.

1.5 Care should be taken in the wording of file notes as those assessing bills will pay careful regard to what is said.

What is reasonable?

1.6 The fundamental rule is that payment may be claimed in respect of profit costs for all work actually and reasonably undertaken by a fee

---

2 See also CBAM 2.1 and 3.2.5.
3 [2013] 6 Costs LR 1031. A specimen work log appears at Crown Court Fee Guidance (CCFG) Appendix E but the computer printout from a time recording system will do as well as long as the nature of each attendance is entered on the system.

earner[4] (SCC Specification 8.31). Where a member of staff undertakes some fee-earning work, it is wise to designate them for the purposes of the SCC.

1.7 While rules of thumb as to the time required for different types of work are helpful, such as that it takes about two or in *R v Dunne*[5] three minutes a page to read prosecution evidence, this is a guide to test what is reasonable. The claim cannot be for longer than was actually taken to do the work. To allow only one minute a page to read additional statements, which have to be checked against earlier statements by the same witness, is insufficient: *R v Noon.*[6] While it will normally take about two units to dictate a proof or instructions, much longer will be reasonable when drafting documents such as skeleton arguments or chronologies,

Ex post facto billing

1.8 In *R v French and others*[7] the judge confirmed that the following were of assistance in assessing a claim

- The dates, times and descriptions of the work completed, and the page count of the material considered
- In so far as there are any documents produced, these should be annexed to the claim, in order to assist determination.

1.9 In handling appeals, Independent Costs Assessors apply the standard basis as defined by the Civil Procedure Rules (CPR) (SCC Specification 8.30[8]). These provide that costs will be disallowed if:

(a) They are unreasonably incurred;
(b) They are unreasonable in amount;
(c) They are disproportionately incurred; or
(d) There is a doubt whether they were reasonably or proportionately incurred or whether they are reasonable or proportionate in amount.

1.10 Profit costs may be claimed, subject to specific provisions, for the value of the work actually and reasonably done by way of:

- routine letters and telephone calls (emails and faxes are usually classified as letters; text messages as telephone calls);
- advocacy;

4 See CBAM 2.2.
5 [2013] 6 Costs LR 1031.
6 [2013] 4 Costs LR 633.
7 [2014] 4 Costs LR 786.
8 See also CBAM 2.4.

- attending an advocate at court;
- preparation and attendances;
- travel;
- waiting.

1.11 To be chargeable the item claimed must not be purely administrative work (SCC Specification 5.54). Administrative work does not go directly to the provision of contracted legal services for the client.[9] No claim may be made for opening and setting up files, closing files, the maintenance of time recording records, or preparing checking or signing a claim for costs.[10] Initial money-laundering and conflict checks are administrative but these issues are more complex once a case is underway. Some guidance is given at Criminal Bills Assessment Manual (CBAM) 10.1 but it is suggested that any work going to whether a solicitor can continue to act relates to the conduct of the case. The exercise of delegated powers and the upkeep of records of such decisions may be claimed (SCC Specification 5.55).

1.12 The work must be such as might reasonably be undertaken by a fee earner. Fee earner[11] includes anyone undertaking the fee earner work, whatever their employment status and even if at other times they are not a fee earner, including employed counsel and those appointed for a specific task for which they charge the litigator a specific fee.[12]

1.13 In determining the reasonableness of work done and whether the time is reasonable, account should be taken of all relevant circumstances of the case including the nature, importance, complexity or difficulty of the work and the time involved.

Routine letters and telephone calls[13]

1.14 Routine letters and telephone calls represent a significant element of all claims. Routine letters written are those that are not items of preparation and are more than a compliments slip.[14] Legal Aid

9 CBAM 3.1.2.
10 CBAM 3.1.4.
11 See also CBAM 2.2. An enquiry agent doing solicitors' work will be a fee earner but if their principal instructions are for enquiry agent work, they should be charged as a disbursement (CRIMLA 43).
12 *R v Duxbury* TMC S2; *R v Pullum* TMC S1; *Smith Graham (Solicitors) v Lord Chancellor* [1999] All ER (D) 957; *Brush v Bower Cotton & Bower* [1993] 4 All ER 741; CBAM 2.2.
13 CBAM 3.8.
14 *R v Hudson* TMC SJ2.

Agency (LAA) guidance in CBAM suggests a letter is routine unless outside the range of an average letter, substantial in length or complex in content. The additional guidance that letters should be more than one page in length and take more than 12 minutes to prepare does not appear to be based on authority but provides a good guide. Individual letters are chargeable even if standard[15] and each letter in similar terms to a number of different people may be charged. Client care letters may be charge separately.[16] Covering letters may be charged when sending documents.[17] Regular reports are required of all stages of a case and its preparation and should be remunerated (CRIMLA 2). Fax and text messages and emails may be charged as letters (but only one claim for each item). Where time is taken to consider a file so that a letter can be written, the consideration time should be recorded and claimed.

1.15 Routine letters received may only be charged if the reading time becomes an item of preparation.

1.16 Routine telephone calls made or received are all calls that are neither an item of preparation nor abortive: *R v Hudson*.[18] CBAM suggests that for a telephone attendance to amount to preparation, it must be of such substance as to constitute preparation and should materially progress the case. Again a requirement that it lasts at least 12 minutes is a guide but not based on principle. A call that does not get through will not meet the test for a routine call; a call that leaves a message that progresses the case will do so.

Preparation

1.17 Preparation includes:

- taking instructions, including shorter appointments when a client calls without a pre-planned meeting[19] or because a letter cannot be sent to them to preserve confidentiality or because they cannot read; attendances upon a client in custody should be remunerated and the number of attendances must take account of the limited appointments available;[20] longer periods of time

---

15 *R v Brown* [2002] 3 Costs LR 539.
16 CBAM 3.8.6.
17 CBAM 3.8.16.
18 TMC SJ2.
19 *R v Moss* TMC S16.
20 CBAM 6.11.

may reasonably be spent in attendance with those under 18 or mentally disabled than with other clients;[21]
- interviewing witnesses;
- ascertaining the prosecution case;
- advising on plea and mode of trial;
- preparing and perusing documents; this will include regular consideration of the entire file ahead of a hearing or meeting, for instance;
- dealing with letters and telephone calls (which are not routine), and with more complex letters received;
- preparing for advocacy, including identifying the history of and issues from the file;[22] work in connection with case management and for pre-trial hearings will be recoverable;
- instructing an advocate and expert witnesses;
- conferences, consultations and work done in connection with advice on appeal;
- listening to or viewing any tape or video recording of interview or evidence. This will take longer than the length of the tape itself;[23]
- advising on appeals.

1.18 It is suggested, for instance, that it is reasonable in straightforward cases to review the prosecution evidence on three occasions: 1) on first instruction to advise on plea and allocation; 2) on taking detailed instructions from a client or preparing a note for advocacy; and 3) for the main hearing in the case.

1.19 It is best practice sufficiently to prepare a case so that a fee earner may understand the file in the absence of the person primarily responsible and so that an advocate can take over the handling of the case at court.

1.20 The LAA is suspicious of claims to 'review' a file but a fee earner may refresh his or her memory of a case at appropriate stages.[24]

1.21 Dictating time is properly charged as preparation[25] and this will include the dictation of file notes that add value to the file. Acknowledging modern ways of working, CBAM 3.3 3 confirms that:

> ... if a fee-earner types his or her own work then reasonable preparation time may be allowed for time spent typing provided that this is done by the same fee-earner who saw the client (and it takes no longer

21 CBAM 3.2.6.
22 See *R v Zavola* TMC S11.
23 Detailed consideration of the time to be allowed is given in CBAM 3.7.
24 CBAM 6.8.
25 *Brush v Bower Cotton & Bower* [1993] 4 All ER 741.

than it would have taken to dictate and check). It may sometimes be more efficient for a fee-earner to input data directly whilst going through papers, rather than spending additional time dictating. In such circumstances time spent inputting data may be allowed provided that it is reasonable and is the most economic means of undertaking the work. An example of this is where a fee-earner directly inputs data into an evidential database resulting in overall savings in the time spent on case preparation.

1.22 Preparation also includes long telephone calls and letters written that are more than routine.[26]

1.23 Decisions on whether work was reasonable must be made without the benefit of hindsight.[27]

1.24 Drafting time and time spent reading and updating case papers is properly charged. This may include correcting prosecution papers if the Crown has not taken appropriate steps (CRIMLA 16).

1.25 Additional time should be allowed when a period of time has passed since preparatory work for advocacy was undertaken, and the case was adjourned, so that the case has to be prepared again.[28]

1.26 Attendance at a police station when a sealed tape has to be opened may be remunerated as may collection of tape when an undertaking has to be given, but not usually otherwise.[29]

1.27 Supervision which enables a less experienced fee earner to conduct a file may be charged, as may time spent in arranging appropriate delegation. The test is whether there is an overall saving to the fund.[30] In larger cases requiring the work of more than one fee earner, the time spent in their meeting together may be chargeable (CRIMLA 39). Duplication of work should otherwise be avoided.[31] A longer time may have to be allowed when the normal fee earner is not available because for instance a client, who is not in regular contact, attends without an appointment or there is an unexpected court hearing, such as when there is a breach of bail. Where discussion with a specialist lawyer in the firm, for instance in mental health or housing law, progresses the case, the time of both may be reasonably incurred.

1.28 Completion of LAA application forms (in the CRM series) but not billing forms (which are administrative), may be charged

---

26 *Bwanaoga v Bwanaoga* [1979] 2 All ER 105.
27 *Francis v Francis and Dickerson* [1955] 3 All ER 836; CRIMLA 38.
28 *R v Akinrele* [2013] Costs LR 637.
29 CBAM6.10.
30 *R v Ford-Lloyd* TMC S6; and see generally CBAM 3.5.
31 See generally *R v Sandhu* TMC SJ1; and CBAM 2.1.

(CRIMLA 67[32]). Two units are routinely allowed for completing an application on forms CRM3, CRM4, or CRM5 and five units for completing forms CRM14 and 15. The process of billing may not be the subject of a claim.[33] Administrative work is not recoverable (SCC Specification 5.54),[34] nor is extra work caused by a solicitor's inefficiency

1.29 Time to comply with case management requirements is recoverable including the completion of PET forms.[35]

1.30 Checking transcripts is fee earner work (CRIMLA 19, 35, 49) but transcription is not (CRIMLA 78). The collation of photocopying may be fee earning work for instance in the preparation of a jury bundle. The service of a witness summons may be fee earner work.[36]

1.31 Routine research and updating of the law is not normally work that a fee earner can charge to an individual file, but claims may properly be made for time spent in the application of the law to the facts of a particular case. In addition, research may be chargeable if it is new, developing or unusual law (see also SCC Specification 5.56 and CBAM 3.4).[37] Copies of, or references to, documents consulted should be kept on file.

1.32 Unless the client can confidently agree the detail of a prosecution summary, and where the client raises issues of police conduct, it is reasonable to watch body-worn video footage, to listen to 999 tapes and to listen or watch recordings of police interviews. Any police station file and custody record may require consideration.

1.33 The total preparation time must be justified[38] and is often best done by a case plan identifying the use of the time involved. If time is disallowed, the LAA must give reasons for doing so.[39]

Advocacy

1.34 The time that a bench or jury is in retirement is time charged as advocacy.[40] In the magistrates' court more than one advocate may

32 And CBAM 3.3.4.
33 *R v Sandhu* TMC SJ1; CBAM 2.1.
34 This would appear to include money-laundering checks and conflict checks.
35 CBAM 6.7.41.
36 *R v Lowe* TMC S15.
37 *Perry v Lord Chancellor* TMC SJ4; CBAM 3.4; *R v Great Western Trains Co Ltd* [2004] 2 Costs LR 331.
38 *R v Supreme Court Taxing Office ex p John Singh & Co* TMC SJ3. And see CBAM 3.3.7–3.3.11.
39 *Miller Gardner v Lord Chancellor* [1997] 2 Costs LR 29.
40 *R v Wanklyn* TMC S28; CBAM 6.7.37–6.7.38.

reasonably attend different defendants represented by the same firm in a single case (even though there is no conflict), if issues of presentation require it (CRIMLA 11). In the Crown Court each defendant is entitled to his or her own advocate.

Travel and waiting time[41]

1.35 Payment for travel and waiting time is rarely available under the various fixed standard and graduated fee schemes. In those cases where it can be claimed the amount of travel time must be reasonable. Apportionment is required if more than one case is undertaken. Travel between a firm's offices will rarely be claimable. Agents' and unassigned counsels' travel time is charged as if from the relevant office of the firm.

1.36 It may be reasonable to travel further if there is no more local supplier; if the client's problem is so specialised that the attendance of the particular solicitor is reasonable; and if the client is particularly well known to particular supplier; or if the local court or prison is at some distance.[42]

1.37 Fee earning work undertaken while travelling may compensate for any loss through unremunerated travel time.

1.38 Waiting time cannot be charged if lunch is being taken.[43]

The principles of enhancement[44]

1.39 Enhancement is relevant under the SCC (Specification 10.99–10.102) for proceedings billed in the magistrates' court, and under Remuneration Regulations 2013[45] Sch 2 para 29 for work in all classes except E, F and H, in connection with confiscation proceedings in the Crown Court.

1.40 An item in a bill only enhances if, taking into account all the relevant circumstances of that case, the work was done with any one or more of the following exceptionalities:
a) exceptional competence;
b) exceptional skill;

---

41 CBAM 3.6 and 3.9.8.
42 CRIMLA 21 31 and 34.
43 *R v Varney* TMC S21.
44 See generally CBAM 9.1.
45 Criminal Legal Aid (Remuneration) Regulations 2013 SI No 435 ('Remuneration Regulations 2013').

10 Criminal Costs: legal aid costs in the criminal courts / chapter 1

c) exceptional expertise;
d) exceptional dispatch;
or the case involves:
e) exceptional circumstances; or
f) exceptional complexity.

'Exceptional' means unusual or out of the ordinary when compared with the generality of criminal cases.[46]

1.41 If enhancement applies, a percentage uplift is applied to relevant items. The percentage takes account of:
a) the degree of responsibility accepted by the solicitor;
b) the speed and economy with which the case was prepared; and
c) the novelty, weight and complexity of the case.

1.42 Rates for enhanced work: because of the rule in *Backhouse*,[47] the percentage uplift is never less than 100 per cent[48] which is normally also the maximum. However, an uplift of up to 200 per cent may be paid in the magistrates' court in the now very unlikely event that the proceedings relate to serious or complex fraud. The meaning is considered in CRIMLA 74. The allegation itself need not be of fraud,[49] but the fraudulent importation of drugs is excluded from the category of serious or complex fraud.[50]

1.43 Reasons must always be given for enhancement.

1.44 Enhancement should be considered when the case has substantially increased the burden on the solicitor.

---

46 *R v Legal Aid Board ex p RM Broudie* (1994) 138 SJ 94.
47 *R v Backhouse* [1997] Costs LR 445, TMC S30. The LAA has attempted to argue that this decision is under the old Regulations and is no longer good law. However, exactly the same wording is used in the current Regulations. Under the 'Barras principle' (*Barras v Aberdeen Steam Trawling and Fishing Co Ltd* [1933] AC 402, 411) the words will continue to have the same meaning. 'Where Parliament continued to use words on which the meaning has been settled by decisions of the courts, it is to presumed that Parliament intends the words to continue to have that meaning' (*London Corporation v Cusack-Smith* [1955] AC 337, 361). See also *Lowsley v Forbes (t/a LE Design Services)* [1999] AC 329, 340; and *Bennion on Statutory Interpretation* (7th edn, p596): 'Where an Act uses a word or phrase that has been subject of previous judicial interpretation in the same or similar context it may be possible to infer that parliament intended the word or phrase to bear the same meaning as it had in that context.'
48 *R v Dhesi* [2003] 4 Costs LR 645; CRIMLA 59.
49 *Murria (Solicitors) v Lord Chancellor (R v Crossley)* [2000] 2 All ER 941.
50 *R v Cevik* [1998] 2 Costs LR 1.

The principles of costs and enhancement in criminal legal aid cases 11

1.45 Depending on the ground for finding exceptionality, each item of work should be considered separately for enhancement.[51] Enhancement will only very exceptionally apply to travel and waiting such as where the amount of time spent on these items (if in an area where they can be claimed) is wholly disproportionate to the effective work conducted.[52] Routine letters and telephone calls may be integral to the case and so worthy of enhancement.[53]

1.46 Relevant factors, considered in turn by independent costs adjudicators, include

- the character of the defendant;
- the weight and complexity of the case and the nature of the allegation;
- the degree of public interest in the case;
- the use of expert evidence – particularly if contested (CRIMLA 22);
- the length of any trial; and
- issues arising over defence witnesses.

1.47 The preparation of a case for imminent hearing may show exceptional dispatch (CRIMLA 18). The use of foreign languages by the solicitor's staff avoiding the need for interpreters may significantly improve efficiency (CRIMLA 4) and exceptional skill may be required to represent a number of defendants with different needs, though that factor alone will not be enough (CRIMLA 17). In the magistrates' court, a hearing lasting more than two days may be exceptional (CRIMLA 24). Preparation which avoids a trial may enhance[54] and cases involving child witnesses, particularly where there is sexual abuse, will often enhance, particularly in the youth court.[55] The fact that other solicitors in the same case have received enhanced payment is a relevant consideration (CRIMLA 71).The mere fact that there is a certificate for assigned counsel does not of itself justify enhancement in the magistrates' court (CRIMLA 32) but, as solicitor advocates from the same firm may not be paid as assigned counsel,[56] enhancement may allow appropriate remuneration and it is relevant consideration.[57]

---

51 *R v Evans-Southall* [1998] 1 Costs LR 68.
52 *Miller Gardner v Lord Chancellor* [1997] 2 Costs LR 29 and CRIMLA 62.
53 *R v Alwan* [2000] 2 Costs LR 326.
54 *R v Smith* SCTO 117/93.
55 *R v P* SCTO 158/93.
56 CBAM 3.6.7–13.
57 CBAM 6.7.16.

CHAPTER 2

Criminal investigations and freestanding advice[1]

2.1	**Work types and definitions**
2.4	Definition of business day and hours
2.6	**Investigations conducted other than by a constable and all attendances upon witnesses; freestanding advice**
2.6	Claims and claim codes
2.7	Payment
2.10	**Investigations conducted by a constable in relation to both suspects and volunteers**
2.10	Advice and assistance
2.11	Claims
2.13	**Payment**
2.13	Definition of a matter
2.20	Volunteers
2.22	Agreements under the Serious Organised Crime and Police Act 2005
2.23	Detainees under Terrorism Act 2000 Sch 7
2.24	Telephone-only advice
	Claim rates

continued

---

1 Provided for by Standard Crime Contract SCC Specification 9; and Criminal Legal Aid (Remuneration) Regulations 2013 SI No 435 ('Remuneration Regulations 2013') reg 8 and Sch 4. See Criminal Bills Assessment Manual (CBAM) 5.

2.27	Telephone-only cases
2.30	Attendance cases
2.31	Fixed fees
	Claiming; and claiming more than the fixed fee • Limitation on claims
2.46	Definition of duty solicitor cases and enhanced cases
2.48	Restrictions on number of claims by different firms on the same matter
	Bails to return/RUI
2.58	Escape provisions
	Value of claim • Calculating the value
2.63	Cases outside fixed fees
	Advocacy assistance
2.72	Disbursements
	Method of claiming

Work types and definitions

2.1 Record the final charge that your client faces. Where your client is facing multiple charges, you should identify the most serious charge.

2.2 A full list of offences covered by codes 1–12 appears in appendix B.

2.3 Code 12 is used when no other appropriate code exists or when the client is not subject to an investigation or proceedings or where the nature of the matter is not known.

Definition of business day and hours

2.4 A 'business day' means a day other than a Saturday, Sunday and any bank or public holiday in England and Wales; 'business hours' means from 9am to 5.30pm each business day (Standard Crime Contract (SCC) Standard Terms 1.1).

2.5 The rates for unsocial hours thus apply to any work carried out by a duty solicitor or an accredited representative handling duty work after 5.30pm and before 9 am on each weekday or at weekends or on bank holidays

Investigations conducted other than by a constable[2] and all attendances upon witnesses;[3] freestanding advice

Claims and claim codes

2.6 With regard to claims and claim codes:

> 2 Eg Department for Work and Pensions; Department for Business, Energy and Industrial Strategy; local authorities (SCC 9.113–9.140). The definition of 'constable' is at SCC Standard terms 1.1: 'Constable' means: a police officer, a British Transport Police officer, an officer of HM Revenue and Customs and any other official with a power of arrest by virtue of his or her office. It does not include other investigators, eg government departments. Local authority or Serious Fraud office even if they have power to search premises or are required by section 66(9) of the Police and Criminal Evidence Act 1984 (PACE) to have regard to the PACE Codes of Practice.
> 3 SCC Specification 9.3–9.4 states that you may only provide advice and assistance to a witness if there is a complicating factor (as specified in the Contract Guide) but this cannot override the statutory provision. The suggestion in contract guidance that the provision for witnesses is wider than the statutory provision does not appear to be correct.

- A means test applies. Care is needed to ensure that relevant evidence of means and necessary extensions on Form CRM5 are obtained. See appendix A. There must be an eligible client and valid Forms CRM1 and CRM2.
- Costs limitations apply to these claims as set out in appendix A and it is essential to plan ahead if long or further interviews may take place so that sufficient extensions are obtained on Form CRM5.
- Advice may be given to a witness in criminal proceedings requiring advice and assistance regarding self-incrimination (Criminal Legal Aid (General) Regulations 2013[4] reg 12(2)(i)). Concern will arise for instance if there is a risk of a witness providing evidence that they have committed offences such as wasting police time or attempting to pervert the course of justice. Each could lead to criminal proceedings. Claim on Form CRM6 under code INVA. Guidance on completion of the form is at appendix C.

Payment

2.7 Payment is at hourly rates, including travel and waiting, for work actually and reasonably undertaken. These rates apply to matters commenced on or after 1 April 2016.

Work	London rate	National rate
Preparation	£45.35	£42.80
Travel and waiting	£24.00	£24.00
Routine letters written and routine telephone calls	£3.51 per item	£3.38 per item

2.8 These claims are also available in criminal related matters that do not involve interrogations, eg advice in connection with restraint proceedings, when criminal proceedings have not yet commenced.

2.9 These claims apply to enquiries by the Financial Conduct Authority (FCA) and the Serious Fraud Office (SFO) unless a constable is present.

4 SI No 9.

Investigations conducted by a constable[5] in relation to both suspects and volunteers[6]

Advice and assistance

2.10 If there is no attendance at a police station or at a place where a constable is present then claims may be made on forms CRM1 and CRM2 as set out at para 2.6 above and SCC Specification 9.54–9.55. However, once such a police station attendance is made, the advice and assistance claim becomes part of the police station claim (SCC Specification 9.135) and the following rules apply.

Claims

2.11 With regard to claims:

- No means test applies to the work at the police station, but if a client is not eligible for free advice and assistance, private client fees may be claimed for work outside the police station, with the attendances in connection with the police station claimed from the legal aid fund (SCC Specification 8.41).
- Claim on Form CRM6.
- Guidance on completion of the form is at appendix C.
- A list of all police station and scheme references appears at appendix D.
- Attendance need not be at a police station provided that a constable is present This situation is dealt with by Remuneration Regulations 2013[7] Sch 4 para 2(6), which provides that:

    (6) ... where the place of attendance is not a Police Station, the place of attendance is deemed to be–
       (a) where an interviewing Constable is present–
          (i) if the interviewing Constable is normally based at a Police Station, that Police Station, or
          (ii) in any other case, the Police Station nearest to the location of the interview, or
    (7) where a Services Person is assisting with an investigation by Services Police, the Police Station nearest to the location of the interview.

2.12 Use the police station code for the relevant area.

---

5 Eg police, HM Revenue and Customs; National Crime Agency.
6 SCC Specification 9.
7 Criminal Legal Aid (Remuneration) Regulations 2013 SI No 435, as amended by the Criminal Legal Aid (Remuneration etc) (Amendment) Regulations 2015 SI No 1369.

Payment

Definition of a matter

2.13 A claim may be made for each matter. A matter includes all ancillary issues (SCC Specification 9.90) and all bail to returns, or other returns (RUI), in that matter, however many attendances there may be (SCC 9.81).

2.14 The contractual provisions as to the number of matters are complex and difficult to apply. Reference is necessary to SCC Standard Terms 1,1 for the definitions of matter and investigation and Specification 9.79–9.93).[8]

- A separate fixed fee is payable for each suspect advised and in that event time must be apportioned appropriately and each allocated a separate unique file number (UFN) (SCC Specification 9.83, 9.108).
- However if a conflict develops between suspects, while subject to the investigation, an attendance fixed fee may only be claimed for each continuing client. It is therefore important to recognise conflict as early as possible (SCC Specification 9.88–9.89).
- Once a client is charged or a matter ended in any other way, such as no further action, or diversion, any further attendance to advise must be a new matter (SCC Specification 9.82). A case remanded to the police station under Magistrates' Courts Act 1980 s128(7) will generate a new matter. If one matter is charged and there is a reasonable attendance on another on a bail to return or RUI two fees are payable (SCC B9.82). The contract requires reasonable checks to be made that the bail to return is effective (SCC Specification B9.2). There must be a substantive reason to attend (SCC Specification B9.14).
- An arrest for criminal conduct in the police station is a separate matter from the offence that caused the suspect to be in the police station (*R v Walton*[9] interpreting Criminal Justice Act 1988 s40(1)).
- An unconnected arrest creates a new matter, even if it is for a similar offence. It must be unconnected to the existing enquiry when the arrest takes place. Thus there will more than one matter where a client is arrested for theft from a shop, is bailed to return to the police station or RUI and the next day he is arrested for

---

8 The Legal Aid Agency (LAA) understanding of these provisions is at CBAM 5.9.
9 [2011] EWCA Crim 2832.

another theft from a shop; or where a client is arrested for burglary, fails to appear at court and is arrested on the street for failing to appear.

2.15 Subject to those propositions: the following test should be applied:
1) Is there more than one genuinely separate matter? If No: one matter (SCC Specification B 9.80).The starting point is that there is one matter when the client is under investigation for a number of matters.
If Yes:
2) Was advice given on more than one police station attendance? If No: one matter (SCC Specification 9.90).
If Yes:
3) There are as many matters as there are attendances on a suspect in relation to the genuinely separate matters. An actual attendance is required under the contracts (SCC B9.85) so that no fee would be due if there is a cancellation at any point before the adviser has met the suspect. However, exceptions to this rule appear below at paras 2.32 and 2.33 below (CBAM 5.11.17). Attendance is mandatory (SCC Specification 9.38–9.40) where there is to be an interview, identification procedure, other than a video identification, or a complaint of serious maltreatment. Otherwise an attendance must be reasonable Solicitors are expected to take reasonable steps, as the sufficient benefit test applies (SCC Specification 9.14).

2.16 Genuinely separate enquiries are those that arise in new and different circumstances and are not merely the widening of the original enquiry such as where a suspect is further arrested in an on-going investigation (SCC Specification 9.87). Allegations during a continuing enquiry that would amount to a series of offences at court may well be a single matter. Contract guidance gives an example of an arrest for handling a stolen credit card which is widened to include a number of allegations of fraud arising from its use. The other examples given are fact-dependent and not so clear cut.

2.17 There is one matter, however many allegations are investigated and whatever their nature, if the whole enquiry concludes on a single attendance.

2.18 The number of custody records opened is not an essential consideration, though separate records may support separate claims. Separate Defence Solicitor Call Centre (DSCC) references must be obtained to support separate claims, and each should have its own unique file number (UFN) (SCC Specification 4.40).

2.19   If there is more than one matter, this may require apportionment of the relevant attendance between the possible claims to show an attendance on the suspect was made, thus justifying the fixed fee.

Volunteers

2.20   A claim may also be made for a volunteer who attends at any place where a constable is present.[10] By definition, he or she is not arrested.

2.21   Difficult issues will apply in the application of these rules where suspects are interviewed about matters to be taken into consideration (TIC). Separate claims would appear to be proper where there is no connection or similarity between the matters subject to the original investigation and those taken into consideration, and they conclude with attendances on separate occasions.

Agreements under the Serious Organised Crime and Police Act 2005

2.22   CBAM 15 identifies that a claim under the police station scheme may be made when attending a client to advise on the basis and terms of an agreement reached under the Serious Organised Crime and Police Act 2005.

Detainees under Terrorism Act 2000 Sch 7

2.23   Such detainees are entitled to police station advice under the Criminal Legal Aid (General) Regulations 2013 reg 12(2)(k).

Telephone-only advice

2.24   This covers all telephone advice on a single matter dealt with only over the telephone (SCC Specification 9.112). A single call with a person in custody is required in order to generate a claim (SCC Specification 9.111). To assist in communication with the police, an email may be charged as a call.[11] It is necessary to obtain a DSCC reference (SCC B9.18–19; 9.21).

---

10 Legal Aid, Sentencing and Punishment of Offenders Act 2012 s15; Criminal Legal Aid (General) Regulations 2013 reg 12(2)(j); and SCC Specification 9.1 and 9.54.
11 CBAM 5.10.2.

2.25 A telephone advice fee may not be claimed separately where an attendance is made and an attendance fee is claimed for that (SCC Specification 9.112). It is however relevant both in identifying whether the escape provisions apply (SCC B9.84) and as a stand-alone payment.

Claim rates

Cases where criminal defence direct is not involved

2.26 These rates apply to matters started on or after 1 April 2016.

Location	Fee exclusive of VAT
London	£28.70 per matter
National	£27.60 per matter

Telephone-only cases

2.27 Fees for attendance at a place where a constable is present are payable if the attendance is reasonable and not excluded by the contract.

2.28 An attendance cannot be claimed for in the following matters unless an exemption applies (SCC Specification 9.8–9.13):
- detention for non-imprisonable offences;
- arrest on warrant (except where the solicitor has clear documentary evidence available that would result in the client being released from custody);
- arrest for driving with excess alcohol (driving unfit/drunk in charge/failure to provide a specimen); and
- arrest for breach of bail;

except where (SCC Specification 9.10):
- there is to be an interview or identification procedure;
- the suspect is eligible for an appropriate adult;
- the suspect is unable to communicate over the telephone (this will include a requirement for privacy);
- the suspect alleges serious maltreatment by the police;
- the investigation includes another offence for which an attendance may be paid;
- the solicitor is already at the police station (when the claim is limited to a telephone advice fee);
- the advice relates to an indictable offence; and

- the request is identified to you by DSCC as a 'special request' (SCC Specification 1.2): that is, you are asked to attend in spite of the normal rules because Criminal Defence Direct cannot handle the matter (SCC Specification 9.12–9.13).

Cases where criminal defence direct has initially been involved

2.29 The following fee, an acceptance fee for a case received though Criminal Defence Direct, is never paid as such but it may be used to calculate whether the total claim reaches the figure to escape from fixed fees (SCC Specification 9.95, 9.97). In Criminal Defence Direct cases that do not fall within the exceptions (SCC Specification 9.10) no claim may be made (SCC Specification 9.9). These figures relate to matters beginning on or after 1 April 2016.

Location	Fee exclusive of VAT
All areas	£7.30 per matter

Note 1: The DSCC and Criminal Defence Direct are separate organisations. Calls will normally come through the DSCC but only if Criminal Defence Direct is involved would this lower fee be credited.
Note 2: The position on telephone claims is summarised at SCC Specification 9.109–B9.112.

Attendance cases

2.30 Note that no claim may be made unless the case has been registered at the DSCC. You must report it if the police have not already done so (SCC Specification 9.18). The report must be made before attending the client if the solicitor is asked by a third party to attend a client already under arrest. If the client attends as a volunteer with the solicitor, or the client meets the solicitor who is at the police station, the case must be registered strictly within 48 hours (SCC Specification 9.19–9.20). This is strictly interpreted so that, if necessary, claims must be lodged over weekends and public holidays.

Fixed fees

2.31 These fees cannot be claimed for witnesses; such fees are payable as free standing advice and assistance (SCC Specification 9.4).
2.32 For a fixed fee claim to be made there must be an attendance upon a client in the police station (SCC Specification 9.85). However, CBAM 5.11.17 confirms that:

... in some circumstances, the solicitor will attend the Police Station in good faith having been contacted by the DSCC. Where a solicitor responds to a call from the DSCC but, for circumstances out of the solicitor's control, no attendance takes place, a fixed fee is still claimable. A note should be kept on the file detailing the particular circumstances.

2.33 Reference should be made to the DS4,[12] which states the principle more widely:

> A legal representative who attends by prior appointment at a police station for the purpose of giving advice and assistance is entitled to be paid for work actually and reasonably done even though the purpose of the attendance is thwarted, for example because the client does not attend or the appointment has been cancelled without notice.

2.34 Applying these principles, the LAA will pay solicitors a fixed fee for attendance at a police station where they are called out by an 'appropriate adult' to advise a child or vulnerable adult even if that person chooses not to see the solicitor. This was an important point taken by the request of the National Appropriate Adult Network. This gives effect to para 3.19 of PACE Code C.

2.35 These fees are payable, when there is a sufficient benefit in attending (SCC Specification 9.14), for each claim made *only* under the following codes:

- INVC (police station attendance);
- INVD (police station attendance: armed forces); and
- INVJ (immigration matters).

2.36 The sufficient benefit test is deemed to be satisfied where a client has a right to legal advice for example under PACE or the Terrorism Act 2000. After the first attendance the sufficient benefit test must continue. Circumstances when there is a sufficient benefit include:

a) providing advice prior to and during interview;
b) advising at an identification procedure (including a video identification procedure when the client is not present);
c) when appropriate, advising on the implications of the caution when the client is charged with an offence;
d) advising when the advice may materially affect the outcome of the investigation and goes significantly beyond initial advice;
e) advising a client who complains of serious maltreatment by the police.

---

12 LAA Points of Principle of General Importance Manual, DS4: Abortive visit to police station.

24 *Criminal Costs: legal aid costs in the criminal courts* / *chapter 2*

2.37 If none of the above is satisfied, further justification for attending should be provided on the file.

In relation to each matter the fee payable is a fixed fee *for the police station first actually attended* (from whichever scheme the work originated) *unless* the full value of the claim exceeds the escape figure.

2.38 The rates (together with escape figures) are set out in the table at appendix N.

2.39 If a fixed fee is payable, *no* separate claim may be made for:
- advice and assistance related to the investigation;
- travel;
- waiting; and
- telephone advice.

Claiming; and claiming more than the fixed fee

2.40 It is still necessary to know the appropriate claim rates because:
1) the LAA requires the claim value to be inserted on Form CRM6 even if a fixed fee results;
2) they are required to identify whether an additional claim can be made because the value of the matter exceeds the escape figure;
3) they are payable for all work in the criminal investigations class represented by the following claim codes:
    - INVE (warrants of further detention, including terrorism);
    - INVF (warrants of further detention (armed forces)(including terrorism));
    - INVH (post-charge attendance, breach of bail, warrants in cases where an attendance may be made); and
    - INVI (post-charge identification, caution, youth caution).

2.41 *Important note:* All these figures are exclusive of VAT. They relate to matters beginning on or after 1 April 2016.

Hourly rates

At the police station	London rate	National rate
Duty solicitor (unsocial hours)	£63.01	£63.01
Duty solicitor (other hours)	£51.28	£47.45
Own solicitor	£51.28	£47.45
Duty solicitor – serious offences (unsocial hours)	£73.00	£73.00
Duty solicitor – serious offences (other hours)	£59.31	£54.75

Travelling and waiting	London rate	National rate
Duty solicitor (unsocial hours: including excess travel time)	£63.01	£63.01
Duty solicitor (other hours)	£51.28	£47.45
Own solicitor	£26.28	£26.28

Fixed fees

Work type	London fee	National fee
Police station telephone advice fixed fee (including all telephone calls whether routine or fixed 'advice' (except Criminal Defence Direct cases for which no such fee may be claimed))	£28.70 per claim	£27.60 per claim
Fixed acceptance fee (former Criminal Defence Direct cases referred to a duty or own solicitor for police station attendance only)	£7.30 per case	£7.30 per case

Limitation on claims

2.42 The claim is for all time actually and reasonably spent on the matter.

2.43 However, the contracts limit the time that may be spent at the police station after charge (SCC Specification 9.16). It is not normally appropriate to remain for fingerprinting DNA samples and photographs unless the particular circumstances of the suspect require you to remain. You may remain to make representations on bail.

2.44 In escape fee cases travel time is limited, to a total of 45 minutes (SCC Specification 9.102).

2.45 There are severe limitations on giving immigration advice (SCC Specification 9.61–9.66).

Definition of duty solicitor cases and enhanced cases

2.46 This is relevant to see if the claim reaches the escape figure. A case is a duty case when allocated as such, and the duty solicitor status lasts throughout the duty period and for the duration of the suspect's first continuous period in custody beginning within that period (SCC Specification 9.98).

2.47 Enhanced (serious case) duty rates apply in those circumstances to the following offences (SCC Specification 9.99):
- treason (common law);
- murder (common law) and soliciting to murder (Offences Against the Person Act 1861 s4);
- manslaughter (Homicide Act 1957 and common law);
- causing death by dangerous driving (Road Traffic Act 1988 s1);
- rape (Sexual Offences Act 2003 s1);
- assault by penetration (Sexual Offences Act 2003 s2);
- penetration of a child under 13 (Sexual Offences Act 2003 s5);
- assault of a child under 13 by penetration (Sexual Offences Act 2003 s6);
- robbery (Theft Act 1968 s8);
- assault with intent to rob (common law);
- arson (Criminal Damage Act 1971 s1(1), (2) or (3));
- perverting the course of public justice (common law);
- conspiracy to defraud (common law);
- kidnapping (common law);
- wounding or grievous bodily harm (Offences against the Person Act 1861 ss18 and 20);
- conspiracy to commit any of the above offences (Criminal Law Act 1977 s1);
- soliciting or inciting to commit any of the above offences (common law);
- attempting to commit any of the above offences (Criminal Attempts Act 1981 s1 or s1A);
- any offence if the client is accused of possessing a firearm, shotgun or imitation firearm; and
- any offence if the client is detained under Terrorism Act 2000 s41;

provided that:
- duty solicitor rates would normally be payable;
- a duty solicitor personally attends who is in the employment or otherwise a member of the personnel of the firm or a delivery partner;
- and the firm does not have a category 3 claims assessment outstanding on a contract compliance audit.

Restrictions on number of claims by different firms on the same matter

2.48 In normal circumstances only one fixed fee may be claimed for each matter. It is therefore essential to register the claim at DSCC as soon as instructed directly.

2.49 Solicitors will also need to make particular checks, if asked to become involved after the start of a matter, to ensure that another firm has not already become entitled to the fixed fee. There are limitations on claiming if other solicitors have previously been involved (SCC Specification 9.670–9.73).

2.50 The contracts define circumstances when a new solicitor may not take over an existing case. The LAA expects reasonable enquiries to be made about whether there has been previous advice in the same matter in the last six months, and that these enquiries are recorded.[13] The contracts (SCC Specification 9.70) state that a second fixed fee should not be claimed where:
(a) the Client simply disagrees with the first advice and wants a second opinion;
(b) there is only a short time between the first and second occasions when the Police Station Advice and Assistance is sought and no material change of circumstances has occurred;
(c) the change requested is from a second to a third Provider (unless exceptionally it is reasonable for a further change); or
(d) there is no reasonable explanation for the Client seeking further Police Station Advice and Assistance from a new Provider.

2.51 However, they allow (SCC Specification 9.67) for a number of circumstances where more than one claim may be made:
(a) there is a gap in time and circumstances have changed materially between the first and second or subsequent occasions when the Police Station Advice and Assistance was sought;
(b) the Client has reasonable cause to transfer from the first Provider; or
(c) the first Provider has confirmed to you that he or she will make no claim for payment for the Police Station Advice and Assistance.

---

13 CBAM 5.11.15 confirms that: 'A Provider will, however, not be in breach of contract if they in good faith claim a Fixed Fee for the re-arrest where unknown to them a Fixed Fee has already been claimed in the Matter, provided they can show they made reasonable enquiries of the client as to whether he or she had received previous Police Station Advice and Assistance in the same Case in the previous six months and recorded this on file (9.68 of the SCC Specification). If in doubt, a Provider must assume that previous Advice and Assistance has been given and ensure that any work they carry out reflects the fact that some work may already have been done on the Matter to ensure that there is no element of repetition.'

2.52 These exceptions are significant. If a conflict is found to exist on attendance at the police station, only the new solicitor will be able to claim a fixed attendance fee for the conflicted suspect. If a client cannot identify the earlier solicitor (and the custody record does not assist), a reasonable attendance will generate a fixed fee. The same may apply when a client has entirely lost confidence, for good cause, in the original firm or wants a representative from a particular minority ethnic group, or the DSCC does not originally call the correct firm and the client will only work with the firm he actually named. Two solicitors instructed simultaneously may also claim if they attend.

2.53 All these explanations will need to be documented on the file.

2.54 A firm is expected to retain a matter until its conclusion (SCC Specification 9.51). However, a duty solicitor may return a case to DSCC (SCC Specification 9.51–9.53) when:

(a) A solicitor is unable to continue to act personally and there is no other suitable person in the organisation able to act and the firm is unable to instruct a suitable Agent;
(b) The Client removes or rescinds their instructions from the organisation;
(c) The organisation is unable to act because there are legitimate concerns about a breach of the professional code of conduct; or
(d) the original firm confirms that it will not claim a Police Station Advice and Assistance Fixed Fee or any other remuneration for the case.

2.55 Particular problems arise when a suspect is transferred from one police station to another at a considerable distance. The LAA considers[14] that an own solicitor should seek, within the fixed fee, to appoint a local agent, or attend himself. If neither is possible and there are substantial practical problems with both, the matter should be returned to the DSCC for allocation to the duty solicitor in the distant area. Each solicitor is then entitled to claim a fee.

Bails to return/RUI

2.56 Because the fixed fee covers all attendances, solicitors will wish to examine carefully the need to return. It is unlikely that an attendance can be justified until it is known that the client is present and the police have confirmed that there is to be an interview or identification procedure or a need to make a prepared statement or to make representations at charge.

14 CBAM 5.14.

2.57 Solicitors at the first attendance will consider having signed Form CRM14 and Form CRM15 in case there is a charge at a later stage, having obtained authority to complete the details of the charge once known, and the client's agreement to provide details of any financial change of circumstances. This is particularly important in areas with virtual courts.

Escape provisions

Value of claim[15]

2.58 If the value at prescribed rates of the work actually and reasonably done exceeds the relevant fee limit for the relevant scheme then you claim **the fixed fee + the amount by which the value exceeds the fee limit.**

2.59 Thus, if in an area the fixed fee is £310, and the escape limit is £930 and, if on assessment a claim is accepted at £1,400, the amount paid will be:

The fixed fee		£310
The excess of the claim over the fee limit (£1,400 – £930) =		£470
	Claim	£780

2.60 This removes any incentive to push towards the fee limit as in most cases it will lead to significant loss. This work will be subject to individual assessment by the LAA and should be claimed on Form CRM18. To ensure that CRM18 is processed without difficulty, it should be accompanied by:

- full file of papers (photocopies are acceptable);
- Form CRM11;
- completed Forms CRM1 and CRM2 if your claim includes any free standing advice or assistance.

2.61 The file should also contain:

- times of when the solicitor arrived and left the station;
- interview times;
- times the solicitor had to wait and the reasons for doing so;
- a copy of the full custody record.

---

15 See SCC Specification 9.95–9.97.

Calculating the value

2.62 Add together the value at the appropriate rate (including duty and enhanced duty rates) of:
- travel – note there are limits of 45 minutes on the time that may be spent in travelling to see a client (SCC Specification 9.102);
- waiting;
- advice and assistance (including letters and telephone calls) if there are valid Forms CRM1 and CRM2;
- attendances – this includes all attendances actually and reasonably undertaken and includes appropriate advice immediately after charge (SCC Specification 9.106); attendance on an ineffective bail to return will only be permitted if checks were first sought to be made (SNN Specification 9.2);
- a relevant telephone advice fee and/ or fee for call from Criminal Defence Direct (see above).

Compare the total with the fee limit.

Cases outside fixed fees

2.63 These are claims made under the following codes:
- INVE (warrant of further detention, etc);
- INVF (warrant of further detention (armed forces), etc).

2.64 The LAA has indicated that the same applies to:
- INVH (post-charge: breach of bail/warrant) – it must be emphasised that breach of police bail prior to charge is dealt with by fixed telephone or fixed attendance fee and not by hourly rates;
- INVI (post-charge: identification/recharge/referral back).

2.65 They are payable at the hourly rates specified above, including for travel and waiting. This appears to be necessary because the first claim is completed by charge; and yet there is no new allegation generating this additional post charge work.

2.66 Because the standard and particularly the litigators' graduated fee schemes provide for fixed fees, solicitors will normally wish to elect to claim this post-charge work as an additional police station claim (as is allowed by the decision of the LAA Costs Appeals Committee, CRIMLA 77).

Advocacy assistance[16]

On a warrant of further detention or at an armed forces custody hearing or on an application to vary pre-charge bail or oppose an extension of a bail time limit

2.67 These claims, at hourly rates, are payable in addition to the fixed or exceptional fees (SCC B9.141–9.187). Time spent on these matters should be separately recorded. One claim should be made for all the work undertaken in relation to each type of advocacy assistance. Upper limits (subject to CRM5 extensions) apply to all these claims (see appendix A). The sufficient benefit test applies but there is no financial eligibility test. All reasonable preparatory and follow-up work may be claimed.

2.68 The standard rate is claimed by own and duty solicitors. The enhanced rate is claimed by duty solicitors in unsocial hours.

On a warrant of further detention and at an Armed Forces custody

2.69 These rates apply to matters beginning on or after 1 April 2016.

Work type	National hourly rate	London hourly rate
Preparation		
Standard rate	£42.80	£45.35
Enhanced rate	£57.03	£60.50
Advocacy		
Standard rate	£53.84	£53.84
Enhanced rate	£71.77	£71.77
Travelling and waiting		
Standard rate	£24.00	£24.00
Enhanced rate	£31.98	£31.98
Routine letters written and telephone calls	per item	per item
Standard rate	£3.38	£3.51
Enhanced rate	£4.47	£4.65

Note: The enhanced rate applies to advocacy assistance provided by duty solicitors in unsocial hours only. The standard rate applies to advocacy assistance provided by duty solicitors outside unsocial hours and by own solicitors at any time.

16 CBAM 5.12.

On a warrant of further detention before the High Court or senior judge

2.70 This table applies to appropriate terrorist cases and to matters beginning on or after 1 April 2016.

Work type	National rate	London rate
Routine letter out	£6.84 per item	£6.84 per item
Routine telephone calls	£3.79 per item	£3.79 per item
All other preparation work including any work which was reasonably done arising out of or incidental to the proceedings, interviews with client, witnesses and other parties, obtaining evidence; preparation and consideration of, and dealing with, documents, negotiations and notices; dealing with letters written and received and telephone calls which are not routine	£68.44 per hour	£72.54 per hour
Attending counsel in conference or at the trial or hearing of any summons or application at court, or other appointment	£33.76 per hour	£33.76 per hour
Attending without counsel at the trial or hearing of any summons or application at court, or other appointment	£68.44 per hour	£68.44 per hour
Travelling and waiting	£30.34 per hour	£30.34 per hour

Note: No enhanced rates are payable for this unit of work.

In the magistrates' court in connection with an application to vary pre-charge police bail conditions or oppose an extension of bail time limits

2.71 Claims should include the time involved in giving any notice of appeal and any reasonable preparation and follow up work including reasonable preparation in the office, correspondence and telephone calls and advising the client of the consequences of the outcome. These rates apply to matters beginning on or after 1 April 2016.

Work type	National hourly rate	London hourly rate
Preparation		
Standard rate	£45.35	£47.95
Advocacy		
Standard rate	£56.89	£56.89
Travelling and waiting		
Standard rate	£24.00	£24.00
Routine letters written and telephone calls	per item	per item
Standard rate	£3.56	£3.70

Disbursements

2.72 All disbursements actually and reasonably incurred are payable. These may include items such as photographs, if required, but also hotel bills when the work cannot otherwise reasonably be done.

2.73 Travel costs are also met. The contract mileage rate is £0.45 per mile (SCC Specification 5.48; and see chapter 8). A bicycle rate of £0.20 per mile has been introduced Solicitors will wish to use the fastest method of transport, as the value of the travel time will seldom be recovered. Private transport or taxis will be essential for the safety of staff in the hours of darkness.

Method of claiming

2.74 The fixed fee and remaining hourly rate claims and claims for advocacy assistance are made separately in the normal way on Form CRM6. In cases reaching the escape figures, the additional claim (for the amount in excess of the fee limit) is made on Form CRM18 and sent to the appropriate assessment centre with all the relevant papers so that an assessment can take place.

CHAPTER 3

Magistrates' court proceedings[1]

3.2	**Court duty solicitor**
3.2	Attendance
3.4	Travel
3.5	Disbursements
3.6	Claim code
3.7	Exclusion
3.8	**Virtual courts**
3.12	**Costs without a representation order**
3.13	Pre-order costs
	Conditions • Claims
3.15	Early cover
	Conditions • Claims
3.17	Initial advice
	Conditions • Claims
3.18	**Costs with a representation order**
3.21	Claims
	Contempt
3.25	Payment
	Excluded cases • Non-excluded cases

continued

---

1 Provided for by Standard Crime Contract (SCC) Specification para 10; and Criminal Legal Aid (Remuneration) Regulations 2013 SI No 435 ('Remuneration Regulations 2013') reg 8 and Sch 4. See also Criminal Bills Assessment Manual (CBAM) 6.

3.39 Standard fee tables
Designated areas • Undesignated areas
3.40 Additional payments
Travel and waiting • Enhancement • Disbursements
3.45 Counsel
Assigned counsel • Attendance upon assigned counsel

Magistrates' court proceedings 37

3.1 A list of all magistrates' courts appears at appendix E. A summary of magistrates' court fees appears at appendix O.

Court duty solicitor[2]

Attendance

3.2 Attendance is paid by hourly rates for all time actually and reasonably spent at court, when not undertaking own client work. If a duty case concludes on the day, no claim may be made on a representation order for that work (Standard Crime Contract (SCC) Specification 10.14). A duty solicitor, may, if time allows, undertake own client work which may be remunerated separately.

3.3 It is reasonable to arrive in sufficient time to have cases ready for the court's normal start time, and to remain at court to complete all relevant paperwork or applications, including applications for a representation order. A claim cannot be made for a luncheon adjournment, until the time when prosecutors should attend to assist with issues ahead of an afternoon list.[3] It is appropriate to claim if the time is actually used on casework. Solicitors will seek to ensure that any waiting time is undertaken as duty solicitor. The rates below are *exclusive* of VAT and apply to all appearances on or after 1 April 2016.

Type of rate	National hourly rate	London hourly rate
Standard rate (attendance and waiting at a magistrates' court)	£49.14	£50.32
Enhanced rate (only payable in respect of work done on a day which is not a business day)	£61.41	£62.87
Travelling (only payable where the duty solicitor is called out (including being called to return) to the court from the office or attends on a day that is not a business day). Reasonable travel expenses may then also be claimed	£24.00	£24.00

2 SCC Specification10.1–10.20.
3 Decision of ICA 2.11.18.

Travel

3.4 Fees for travel time are payable (Remuneration Regulations 2013[4] Sch 4 para 4(1)):
- when there is no rota and a solicitor is called in; or
- when a rostered duty solicitor has left court and has to return; or
- on a Saturday and bank holiday (the travel may be claimed from a home address if that is further than the office).

In these circumstances and more generally, travel costs may also be recovered.

Disbursements

3.5 Travel and parking expenses may be claimed as disbursements whether or not travel time can be recovered.[5]

Claim code

3.6 'PROD' is used. No outcome code is required, nor are individual client details or case information, for billing purposes.

Exclusion

3.7 These provisions do not apply to the virtual court duty solicitor who claims for payment in accordance with the following section for clients introduced to them by the Defence Solicitor Call Centre (DSCC).

Virtual courts[6]

3.8 A claim for advocacy assistance for a virtual court appearance is the only claim that may be made if:
- a case concludes at a virtual court;
- the case is adjourned and a representation order is not granted;

---

4 Criminal Legal Aid (Remuneration) Regulations 2013 SI No 435 ('Remuneration Regulations 2013').
5 Decision of ICA 23.1.18.
6 SCC Specification 10.21–10.35; and CBAM 6.19. The Legal Aid Agency (LAA) provides a spreadsheet on which these claims should be made outside the normal reporting procedures.

- the solicitor declines to represent the client at the next hearing and there is no application for a representation order; or
- the solicitor advises the client not to take part in the virtual court and does not represent the client at any adjourned hearing.

3.9 No such claim may be made if:
- a representation order is granted to the solicitor at the virtual court, when the time involved becomes part of the core cost of the magistrates' court claim; or
- a representation order already exists, and this includes when there is an arrest for breach of bail.

3.10 The fees are as follows, exclusive of VAT:

Work type	London	National
Attendance in office hours	£182.50	£136.88
Attendance in unsocial hours	£219.00	£164.25

3.11 Claims for these fees are made not on Form CRM6 but on a virtual court solicitors' claim form.

Costs without a representation order[7]

3.12 There are three possible claims which may be used when a representation order is not granted, but only one of them may be made for any particular defendant.

Pre-order costs[8]

Conditions

3.13 Conditions for pre-order costs are:
1) An application for a representation order is made but refused on merits (whatever the means position).
2) The designated fee earner documented why they considered the merits test was met.
3) No claim is made for early cover.

---

7 CBAM 6.5.
8 SCC Specification 10.122–10.123, 10.115–10.121, 10.125–10.128.

Claims

Rates

3.14 These rates apply to cases where the work begins on or after 1 April 2016.

Work type	National	London
Routine letters and telephone calls: per item	£3.56	£3.70
Preparation: hourly rate	£45.35	£47.95
Advocacy: hourly rate	£56.89	£56.89
Travelling and waiting in undesignated areas: hourly rate	£24.00	–

- The total claim is *limited* to (inclusive of any disbursements):
  - London: £47.95 + VAT
  - National: £45.35 + VAT
- A separate claim may be made for each client. The claim code is PROP.

Early cover[9]

Conditions

3.15 Conditions for early cover are:
1) An application for a representation order is refused on means but granted on merits.
2) An application, properly completed, was received by the court by 9am on the sixth working day following the day of first instruction or earlier court hearing.
3) All reasonable steps were taken to complete and submit the form with supporting evidence.
4) No decision by the court was made before the first hearing.
5) You represent the client at the first hearing.
6) Progress is made at the first hearing or an adjournment is justified.

Claims

3.16 The rate is for cases on or after 1 April 2016.
- Disbursements cannot be claimed.
- A separate claim may be made for each client.

9 SCC Specification 10.122–10.123, 10.125–10.126, 10.129.

- The claim code is PROT.
- Fees: £68.44 + VAT.

Initial advice[10]

Conditions

3.17 Conditions for initial advice are:
1) No early cover.
2) Although CRM14 completed which would satisfy merits test (and solicitor should keep the form on the file).
3) Would fail means test.
4) Advice within ten working days of charge or process.
5) Not privately instructed.

Claims

The rate is for cases on or after 1 April 2016.
- Claim code: PROU.
- Fees: £22.81 + VAT.

Costs with a representation order

3.18 In the magistrates' courts the fees payable, as set out below, also apply to prescribed civil proceedings under Criminal Legal Aid (General) Regulations 2013[11] reg 9 (see codes CP20–24 and SCC B10.35). For Crown Court fees in prescribed proceedings reference should be made to chapter 10.

3.19 The calculation of fees includes magistrates court work and work advising on appeal and related bail proceedings at any level of court so that, for instance, time spent handling bail appeals to the Crown Court are included within the core costs of the a case (SCC Specification 10.73). It also includes any incidental and ancillary work (SCC Specification 10.95).

3.20 No claim may be made for the time involved in cases sent to the Crown Court for trial, unless part of the case remains in the magistrates' court or a case is remitted by the Crown Court (SCC Specification 10.76).

---

10 SCC Specification 10.124–10.126, 10.130.
11 SI No 9.

Claims

3.21 Payment for claims made for each case for which a representation order exists depends on the area in which the solicitor's office named in the representation order is situated and the court at which the work is carried out (rather, it is suggested, than the administrative centre for that court order (SCC Specification 10.77). Designated area fees apply if the office or that court is situated in the 'designated areas',[12] which include the criminal justice areas of:

- Greater Manchester;
- London;
- Merseyside;
- West Midlands;

as well as the local or unitary authority areas of:

- Brighton and Hove;
- Bristol;
- Cardiff;
- Derby and Erewash;
- Kingston-upon-Hull;
- Leeds and Bradford;
- Leicester;
- Nottingham;
- Portsmouth and Gosport;
- Newcastle and Sunderland (including Gateshead, North Tyneside, Blythe Valley and South Tyneside);
- Sheffield; and
- Southampton.

3.22 CBAM 6.6.2 p47 confirms that if a case starts in an undesignated area, and is transferred to a designated area, the fees for the undesignated area may be claimed.

3.23 Guidance on completing a claim on Form CRM6 is at appendix C. References in the guidance, at the date of publication, are at places substantially out of date.

Contempt

3.24 In the magistrates' court the normal rules apply to proceedings for contempt either because they are part of criminal proceedings (contempt in the face of the court) or because they are prescribed proceedings. For contempt in the face of the court, the court itself

[12] SCC Specification 1.1.

must unusually grant legal aid and without any means test (CBAM 6.13). Standard fees apply absent exceptional circumstances.

Payment

Figure 3.1 Costs with a representation order – summary

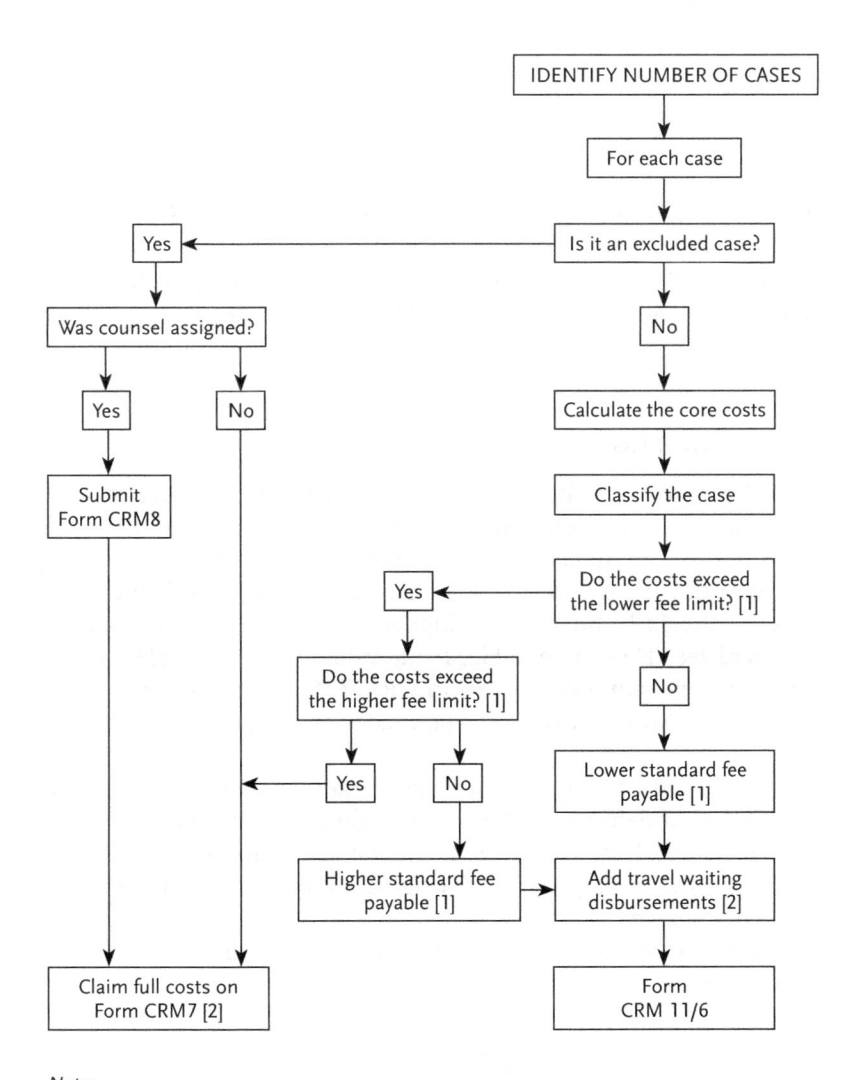

```
                                          IDENTIFY NUMBER OF CASES
                                                    │
                                                    ▼
                                              For each case
                                                    │
                                                    ▼
        Yes ◄──────────────────────────── Is it an excluded case?
         │                                          │
         ▼                                          ▼
  Was counsel assigned?                            No
         │                                          │
    ┌────┴────┐                                     ▼
   Yes        No                          Calculate the core costs
    │         │                                     │
    ▼         │                                     ▼
  Submit      │                              Classify the case
  Form CRM8   │                                     │
    │         │                                     ▼
    │         │                       Yes ◄── Do the costs exceed
    │         │                        │       the lower fee limit? [1]
    │         │                        │              │
    │         │                        ▼              ▼
    │         │              Do the costs exceed     No
    │         │              the higher fee limit? [1]│
    │         │                   │                   │
    │         │              ┌────┴────┐              ▼
    │         │             Yes       No     Lower standard fee
    │    ◄────┼──────────────┘        │       payable [1]
    │         │                       ▼              │
    │         │              Higher standard fee  Add travel waiting
    │         │              payable [1]          disbursements [2]
    │         │                       │              │
    ▼         ▼                       ▼              ▼
  Claim full costs on                          Form
  Form CRM7 [2]                                CRM 11/6
```

Notes
[1] Use appropriate fee table depending on location of solicitor and court.
[2] Travel and waiting cannot be claimed if the solicitor or court is in a designated area.

3.25 The number of cases must first be identified and any excluded case dealt with at hourly rates on Form CRM7.

Excluded cases

3.26 In all these cases, use Form CRM7 and claim the value of the full hourly rates. Cases fall outside standard fees:
- if any part of a claim is enhanced (SCC Specification 10.74);
- if an advocate is assigned (SCC Specification 10.75 and 10.78); the rates payable direct to assigned counsel appear at appendix P;
- if the proceedings are extradition proceedings;
- if the representation order is withdrawn before the case can be classified for standard fees.

Form CRM7 is also used when the fees exceed the higher fee limit. The codes to describe on form CRM7 the work undertaken appear at appendix C.

Non-excluded cases

3.27 All other cases must be categorised. For each case, the core costs of the case must be calculated and the figure compared with the fee limit in the relevant category. If the value does not exceed the lower fee limit (LFL) the lower standard fee (LSF) is payable. If the value exceeds the LFL, but not the higher fee limit (HFL), the higher standard fee (HSF) is payable. If the value exceeds the HFL a full claim may be submitted on Form CRM7 (SCC Specification 10.88 and 10.74). No claim can ever be made for the amount of the fee limit.

3.28 If a second claim falls to be made for a case then (except for the conclusion of deferred sentence proceedings), credit must be given for the value of the claim already made (SCC Specification 10.59, 10.66 and 10.97). In practice the original claim is withdrawn and the new claim lodged.

3.29 In order to calculate payment, the following must first be determined:
1) How many cases?
2) What is the correct category of the case?
3) What are the core costs of each case?

1) How many cases?[13]

3.30 Consider the following:

a) The number of defendants is irrelevant. There can only be one claim for all the defendants for whom you act in a single claim though this increases the core costs (SCC Specification 10.60 and 10.64).

b) The number of representation orders is irrelevant.

c) There is one case (SCC Standard terms A1.1; Specification 10.69 and 10.96) if:
   i) the charges were preferred at the same time;
   ii) the charges are founded on the same facts (warrants/re-arrest/ alternative charges/ withdrawal of order and late reinstated[14]); or
   iii) the charges are, or form part of, a series, ie where there is a sufficient nexus of fact or law. The indictment and joinder rules should be applied. Where SCC Specification 10.61 refers to a single claim for all cases joined, this means cases to which the joinder rules would apply and not cases that are merely being joined for sentence.

d) Cases do not form part of a series merely because they all involve dishonesty and/or all conclude on the same day (CRIMLA 40). Escape from lawful custody may be a separate case (CRIMLA 57).

e) Cases that are joined for trial are likely to be a series of offences; but the fact that cases are otherwise joined for sentence does not make them part of a series. Cases that would be heard on separate indictments at the Crown Court are more likely not to form part of a series (CRIMLA 50). Where there are a number of allegations of driving disqualified it is likely to be one case if they come together but every situation turns on its own facts (CRIMLA 63).

f) If a defendant is before a court for other reasons, no separate fee may be paid for breach proceedings, in respect of a community order, or other court order; similarly with an offence under Drugs Act 2005 s12 for failure to attend or stay at an initial drug assessment. This restriction applies to Bail Act offences as well as breach proceedings (SCC Specification 10.70–10.71).[15] The existence of such matters may affect the *category*, which must also be identified. In this context breach means breach of a sentence of

---

13 The LAA's view appears at CBAM 6.6.
14 CBAM 9.6.
15 For guidance see CCFG Appendix F.

the court. If the allegation amounts to a criminal offence, such as breach of a criminal behaviour order, the normal rules apply. An allegation of breach of post release supervision is not a community order nor is it a court order (rather arsing automatically from the imposition of the prison sentence), and a full claim can therefore be made for such case unless they amount to a series or are charged at the same time as other matters

g) Stand-alone Bail Act, breach proceedings or proceedings for failing to take part in a drugs assessment will represent a separate case.

h) Enforcement proceedings following the making of a confiscation order are separate proceedings that require a separate representation order (which will always be billed on form CRM 7).[16]

2) What is the correct category of the case?[17]

3.31 Consider the following categories:

Category 1B Summary only offences (save where shown)	Category 1A Either way offences	Category 2 Either way and summary only
1.1 Guilty pleas	1.1.1 Guilty pleas including guilty pleas in proceedings for low-value shoplifting as defined in Magistrates' Courts Act 1980 s22A(3) (low-value shoplifting)	2.1 Contested trials
1.2 Uncontested proceedings arising out of a breach of an order of a magistrates' court (including proceedings in a magistrates' court relating to a breach of a Crown Court community order or suspended sentence)	1.2.1 Proceedings which are dis continued or withdrawn or where the prosecution offer no evidence	2.2 Proceedings which were listed and fully prepared for trial in a magistrates' court but are disposed of by a guilty plea on the day of trial before the opening of the prosecution case

16 CCFG Appendix Q.
17 SCC Specification 10.90.

Magistrates' court proceedings 47

1.3 Proceedings which are discontinued or withdrawn or where the prosecution offers no evidence	1.3.1 Indictable only cases heard in the Youth Court	2.3 Proceedings which were listed and fully prepared for trial in a magistrates' court but are discontinued or withdrawn or where the prosecution offers no evidence or which result in a bind over on the day of trial before the opening of the prosecution case
1.4 Proceedings relating to summary offences which result in a bind over		2.4 Contested proceedings relating to a breach of an order of a magistrates' court (including proceedings relating to a breach of a Crown Court community order or suspended sentence)
1.5 Proceedings arising out of a deferment of sentence (including any subsequent sentence hearing) under Powers of Criminal Courts (Sentencing) Act 2000 s1		2.5 Proceedings where mixed pleas are entered
1.6 Proceedings prescribed under Criminal Legal Aid (General) Regulations 2013 reg 9, except where the case was listed and fully prepared for a contested hearing to decide whether an order should be made		2.6 Proceedings prescribed under Criminal Legal Aid (General) Regulations 2013 reg 9, where the case was listed and fully prepared for a contested hearing to decide whether an order should be made
1.7 Proceedings relating to either way offences which must be tried in a magistrates' court in accordance with Magistrates' Courts Act 1980 s22		

Notes on categories

1. A case which is committed for sentence is in category 1A. Newton hearings and hearings to show special reasons to avoid disqualification or endorsement are all guilty pleas and so in category 1A or 1B in the magistrates' court (CRIMLA 46 and 48).
2. A case is listed for trial when a not guilty plea is entered and the case is adjourned (CRIMLA 41).
3. Whether a case is fully prepared for trial will depend on the individual circumstances of the case. Only preparation proportionate to the specific charge is required. In cases with limited issues of fact, this will not be a significant amount of time. Regard will be had to evidence of appropriate consideration of the prosecution evidence; the existence of a proof, or sufficient instructions from the client; and evidence of consideration of issues relating to disclosure and relevant witnesses, whether or not they are warned to attend (CRIMLA 41).There is a two-part test. There must be preparation that is full in the circumstances and it must have been reasonable to prepare in that way. This will not apply, for instance, if the file indicated that the client would plead guilty should a complainant appear at trial. It is critical that there is evidence of all preparation on file. This might include a note for an advocate who might have to take over the case at short notice and/or draft lines of cross examination and draft closing speech. It is not essential that the client attend an appointment if there is evidence of preparation from consideration of the police station or other interviews and other documents available.
4. Discontinuance should only be claimed in category 1A or 1B if a better claim cannot properly be made in category 2. It is not necessary that notification be received on the day of trial if the case was fully prepared (CRIMLA 41).
5. Two claims are made when a sentence is deferred; the second is always in category 1B (SCC Specification 10.66). There are as many cases at the end of the deferred sentence as there were at the beginning (CRIMLA 70).
6. A mixed plea can be claimed whether or not there is any preparation.
7. Either way offences in the youth court which, if not grave crimes, can only be tried summarily should be claimed in category 1A as either way offences.

Special rules on categories

1. If a case would have been in category 2 but a warrant is issued for the defendant, that defendant's categorisation is changed to category 1A or 1B as appropriate (SCC Specification 10.94). This may be reversed on the arrest of the client with a supplementary bill (SCC Specification 10.67, although for the process involved see CBAM 9.5) giving credit for what has already been paid (SCC Specification 10.97).
2. If a case would have been in category 2 but there is a change of firm assigned, the former firm must claim in category 1A or 1B. If a solicitor merely moves from one firm to another, or the change is caused by matters such as a merger or because the old firm has lost its contract, only one claim, in the appropriate category, may be made (SCC Specification 10.92–10.93).
3. If part of a claim is in category 1A or 1B and part in category 2 (eg two defendants tried but one absconds), the solicitor will be paid in whichever category produces a larger fee (SCC B10.91).

3.32 *Indictable only and either way proceedings that are sent:* If a case is sent to the Crown Court, no claim may be made in the magistrates' court. The work will be claimed as part of the Crown Court bill (SCC Specification 10.36 and 10.76).

3.33 Though this is not the view of the LAA, this should *not* apply to any part of the case that is not sent, for which a claim may be made in the appropriate category. Nor does it apply to proceedings that are remitted to the magistrates' court under Crime and Disorder Act 1998 Sch 3 including ancillary bail applications, such as where a youth is remitted for sentence or the indictable only matter is withdrawn and the defendant is able to ask for summary trial on an either way matter.

3) What are the core costs of each case?

3.34 Reference should be made to chapter 1. The core costs include the value of the work actually and reasonably done by way of (SCC Specification 10.79):

- routine letters and telephone calls;
- advocacy;
- attending assigned advocate at court;
- preparation and attendances, including all post-charge work up to ten days before first hearing, if there are magistrates' court as opposed to sending proceedings, CRM forms are submitted within five days, and a representation order is granted to the firm making the claim (SCC 10.40). This can include a maximum of

- 30 minutes to assist in the completion of legal aid application forms (SCC 10.39);
- work done by an agent for the fee earner or by unassigned counsel.

3.35 *Unassigned counsel's preparation and advocacy:* Unassigned counsel are paid the fee agreed with the solicitor (SCC Specification 10.46–10.48, 10.50) but the fee payable to the solicitor cannot increase because unassigned counsel has been instructed (the maximum fee principle) (SCC Specification 10.49). For ex post facto claims the file should show that the same amount of time would have been spent preparing the case and for advocacy as if the advocacy was undertaken by an in-house advocate. Good preparation may reduce the time taken by the advocate.

3.36 At each stage the claim should include the work undertaken by agents (SCC Specification 10.79).

3.37 The value of the time involved in a bail appeal to the Crown Court during magistrates' court proceedings forms part of the core costs as does the value of time spent on advising on appeal.[18] Advocacy includes advocacy at bail applications made in the magistrates' court or an appeal during magistrates' court proceedings to the Crown Court (SCC Specification 10.36 and 10.73).

3.38 The work is valued at the following rates for cases beginning on or after 1 April 2016.

Work	Hourly rate
Preparation (including taking instructions, interviewing witnesses, ascertaining the prosecution case, advising on plea and mode of trial, preparing and perusing documents, dealing with letters and telephone calls which are not routine, preparing for advocacy, instructing counsel and expert witnesses, conference consultations, views and work done in connection with advice on appeal or case stated)	£45.35
Advocacy (including applications for bail and other applications to the court)	£56.89
Attendance at court where assigned (including conferences with advocate at court)	£31.03
Routine letters written and telephone calls – per item	£3.56
Travelling and waiting hourly rate (only claimable where the undesignated area fees apply)	£24.00

These rates are *exclusive* of VAT.

18 CBAM 6.9.

Standard fee tables

3.39 The standard fee tables for cases beginning on or after 1 April 2016 are set out below.

Designated areas

	LSF	LFL	HSF	HFL
Category 1A	£248.71	£272.34	£471.81	£471.85
Category 1B	£202.20	£272.34	£435.64	£471.85
Category 2	£345.34	£467.84	£723.35	£779.64

Undesignated areas

	LSF	LFL	HSF	HFL
Category 1A	£194.68	£272.34	£412.30	£471.85
Category 1B	£158.27	£272.34	£380.70	£471.85
Category 2	£279.45	£467.84	£640.94	£779.64

Notes:
1. All figures are *exclusive* of VAT.
2. A claim is made for a LSF or a HSF or on Form CRM7.
3. No claim may be made for a fee limit (LFL or HFL). These limits merely identify which fee is payable.
4. Form CRM7 is used if the core costs exceed the value of the higher fee limit in the relevant category. The codes to describe the work undertaken appear at appendix C.
5. The table for designated areas applies if the solicitors' office or the court in which the defendant appears is in such an area (see para 3.21 above).

Additional payments

Travel and waiting

3.40 When both court and firm are located outside the 'designated' areas, travel and waiting actually and reasonably undertaken are valued at £24.00 per hour exclusive of VAT. If a firm or the court is in a 'designated' area no travel and waiting may be claimed, even on a Form CRM7 claim (SCC Specification 10.80, 10.83, 10.85).

3.41 Even if no claim may be made for waiting time it must be recorded (SCC Specification 10.87).

Enhancement

3.42 Enhancement is available in the magistrates' court (SCC Specification 10.99–10.102) and the principles are set out in chapter 1.

3.43 If any single item in a bill enhances, the whole bill is excluded from standard fees, and this may be advantageous if a heavy loss would otherwise be made. Reasons must always be given for enhancement (SCC Specification 10.74(b)).

Disbursements

3.44 Disbursements (SCC Specification 10.83, 10.84) reasonably incurred and reasonable in amount are recoverable including travel costs. The payment of disbursements is considered in chapter 8.

Counsel

3.45 In most cases, counsel is unassigned and their preparation, attendance and advocacy time counts towards the calculation of the solicitor's core costs. Their travel time may be claimed by the solicitor in undesignated areas, provided that it is no greater than the claim from the solicitor's office. It is the solicitor's responsibility to agree and pay a specific fee for each piece of work undertaken which is the amount received by counsel. Thus, unassigned counsel's fee is always fixed but the solicitor's fee will vary depending on the core costs and hourly rate payable. The solicitor cannot recover more by using unassigned counsel than had the work been done in-house or by agents (the maximum fee principle). It is important that papers are prepared in such a way as to show that the same time would have been taken had a solicitor been undertaking the advocacy (SCC Specification 10.46–10.55).

Assigned counsel[19]

3.46 Counsel may, however, be assigned under Criminal Legal Aid (Determinations by a Court and Choice of Representative) Regulations 2013[20] reg 16. In that case, the LAA is responsible for payment of counsel's fees which should be submitted (on Form CRM8) by the solicitor with their own Form CRM7 (standard fees not being available when counsel is assigned).[21]

---

19 CBAM 6.8.13–6.8.20.
20 SI No 614.
21 SCC Specification 10.78.

3.47 The fees are prescribed by the Remuneration Regulations 2013 and SCC Specification 10.103–10.106. The fee table appears at appendix P.

3.48 Where hourly rates apply, they cannot fall below the minimum amount specified. In normal situations, the regulations prescribe a maximum rate, with pro rata allowances for parts of a day. The costs are assessed on the basis of the work reasonably done and the weight of the seriousness, importance and complexity of the case. However, there is no limitation the fee if:

> ... taking into account all the relevant circumstances ..., the exceptional circumstances of the case mean that the rates set out would not provide reasonable remuneration for some or all of the work allowed.

This exception is often deemed to apply by comparing the case with the generality of cases falling in the same category.

3.49 The normal rules for counsel apply to assigned counsel's travel time and expenses[22]

Attendance upon assigned counsel

3.50 When counsel is assigned, it may be reasonable to attend upon them both in conference and at court. The attendance must be reasonable and this is more likely to be the case when the case is serious or client has a disability, is young, or has limited English. The solicitor may also be paid for preparing instructions to counsel.[23]

---

22 CBAM 6.7.21–6.7.23.
23 CBAM 6.7.34–6.7.36.

CHAPTER 4

Prison law[1]

4.1	Introduction
4.3	**Fees available**
4.3	Advice and assistance: sentence cases
4.6	Advocacy assistance: disciplinary cases and parole board oral hearings
4.9	**Calculating core costs**
4.10	Advice and assistance
4.12	Disciplinary and parole hearings
4.13	**Additional payments**
4.13	Travel
4.15	Disbursements
4.18	**Number of cases**

---

1 Provided for by Standard Crime Contract (SCC) Specification 12 and by Criminal Legal Aid (Remuneration) Regulations 2013 SI No 435 ('Remuneration Regulations 2013') reg 8 and Sch 4. See also Criminal Bills Assessment Manual (CBAM) 13.

Introduction[2]

4.1 The provisions on prison law are contained in Standard Crime Contract (SCC) Specification 12. There must have been a successful application to undertake prison law work (SCC Specification 12.1). The sufficient benefit test applies (SCC Specification 12.5) and financial eligibility tests apply (SCC Specification 12.13–12.14). A fixed and standard fee regime applies in prison law cases (SCC Specification 12.2–12.3, 12.77–12.78). The standard fee arrangements bear a close resemblance to the magistrates' court scheme but with different technical rules. Prison codes appear at appendix F.

4.2 It is essential to identify:

a) the circumstances which engage the different fees;
b) the core costs of each case to see if the escape provisions or higher fees apply; and
c) the number of cases involved as the Legal Aid Agency (LAA) is anxious to avoid inappropriate case splitting (SCC Specification 12.23–12.31).

Fees available

Advice and assistance: sentence cases

4.3 No claim can be made for less than 48 minutes' work (SCC Specification 12.80).

4.4 A fixed fee of £200.75 then applies to all such cases beginning on or after 1 April 2016 unless the core costs exceed £602.25 when an hourly rates (see para 4.10 below) claim can be made (SCC Specification 12.78–12.79).

4.5 If it is clear that there is going to be an oral disciplinary or parole hearing the case must be charged as advocacy assistance as below. Advice and assistance may be given if it is not clear if there will be such an oral hearing. If an oral hearing is then listed a claim must be made at that point for advice and assistance and an advocacy assistance matter opened (SCC Specification 12.27–12.28).

---

2 See also CBAM 13.

Advocacy assistance: sentencing and disciplinary cases and parole board oral hearings

4.6 These are dealt with by standard fee regimes.

4.7 No claim may be made for less than 48 minutes' work (SCC Specification 12.87, 12.98). If the core costs (see para 4.9 below) do not exceed the lower fee limit (LFL) a lower standard fee (LSF) is payable; if the core costs exceed the LFL but not the higher fee limit (HFL), the higher standard fee (HSF) is payable. If the core costs exceed the HFL, a claim at hourly rates may then be made. No claim may be made for the amount of a fee limit (SCC Specification 12.65).

4.8 The fees for matters beginning on or after 1 April 2016 are as follows:

Scheme	LSF	LFL	HSF	HFL
Disciplinary cases	£203.93	£357.06	£564.16	£1,691.69
Parole cases	£437.21	£933.93	£1,454.44	£4,362.54

Calculating core costs

4.9 In identifying the core costs to reach the escape figure or next standard fee level, account is taken of work actually and reasonably undertaken (see chapter 1) at the following hourly rates. It should be noted that travel cannot contribute to core costs, but may be added to a limited extent if the claim is beyond the higher fee limit (SCC Specification 12.34). The amount of travel time is restricted by the contract (SCC Specification 12.35–12.37).

Advice and assistance

4.10 Rates are as follows:

Rates are for matters beginning on or after 1 April 2016	All areas
Routine letters written and telephone calls per item	£3.38
Preparation hourly rate	£42.80
Travel and waiting hourly rate*	£24.00

* Travel time cannot contribute to core costs.

4.11 A claim may include telephone advice given before the Forms CRM1/2 are signed if the client meets the means and merits test and subsequently signs the forms and is financially eligible (SCC Specification12.18–12.21).

Disciplinary and parole hearings

4.12   The figures are for matters beginning on or after 1 April 2016.

	All areas
Routine letters written and telephone calls per item	£3.70
Preparation hourly rate	£51.24
Advocacy hourly rate	£62.28
Travel and waiting hourly rate*	£24.00

* Travel time cannot contribute to core costs.

Additional payments

Travel

4.13   Travel time cannot be included in the calculation of core costs. However, if the case is exceptional because it reaches the escape figure as it is above the HFL, then the value of the travel time may be recovered subject to the following rules.

4.14   The normal limit is one hour per journey (two hours in all) but if after the case has become exceptional the client is moved between prisons, further from the solicitor's office, the limit is increased to three hours per journey (six hours in all) from the date of the move (if the move was after the escape threshold had been reached (SCC Specification 12.35–12.37)).

Disbursements

4.15   Reasonable disbursements including travel costs are allowed in addition to these fees. Prior authority is required for disbursements exceeding £500 (SCC Specification 12.38). No more than one expert may normally be instructed (SCC Specification 12.39).

4.16   Counsel's fees cannot normally be claimed as a disbursement and counsel are treated as would be unassigned counsel in magistrates' court cases. A fee must be agreed with the Bar payable from the standard or other fee (SCC Specification 12.41–12.42, 12.45). In advocacy assistance cases their time counts towards the core costs in those circumstances (SCC Specification 12.46).

4.17 An exception applies in advice and assistance cases that have reached the escape threshold. In these cases, counsel's fees may be claimed as a disbursement (SCC Specification 12.43) but subject to the maximum fee principle.

Number of cases

4.18 If advice and assistance has been given in a case, advice on appeal must be given as part of the same case (SCC Specification 12.60(b)).

4.19 Only one sentence case or one parole board case may be begun at any one time. A sentence case and a parole board case commenced concurrently are claimed as separate matters (SCC Specification 12.25). Where there are distinct disciplinary cases you may commence a concurrent matter (SCC B12.26). If there are a number of issues in a single matter, this will increase the core costs.

4.20 In cases where a client is subject to disciplinary or parole board proceedings, advice and assistance is available but if it is clear that there will be an oral hearing the claim must be for advocacy assistance only (SCC Specification 12.27). If it was not clear both may be claimed but the claim for advice and assistance falls due as soon as the matter is listed for an oral hearing (SCC B12.28).

4.21 If the prisoner has received advice from another solicitor, work cannot be started towards a new claim until six months has passed, unless there is a gap in time and circumstances have changed, the client has reasonable cause to transfer or the previous solicitor confirms they will not make a claim (SCC Specification 12.50).

4.22 If a matter has been completed, a new claim may only be made in relation to the same problem if:
a) a period of at least six months has elapsed; or
b) there has been a material development or change in instructions and a period of three months has elapsed since the claim was made following a failure to receive instructions; or
c) the advice initially provided formed only a minor part of the previous matter (SCC Specification 12.56).

CHAPTER 5

Crown Court work[1]

5.1	Overview
5.3	Principles applicable to litigators and advocates in cases sent to the Crown Court
5.4	Number of pages of prosecution evidence
	Summary of definition of PPE • Video and audio recordings, etc • Unused material • Ancillary applications • Electronic service of pictorial or documentary exhibits • Duplication and use of different formats • Formats
5.50	Categorisation of a case (see CCFG 2.1.6–2.1.33)
	Trial • Retrials • Cracked trial • Guilty plea
5.79	Number of days at trial
5.84	Number of cases
5.96	**Litigators' graduated fees**
5.97	Non-indictable jurisdiction and post trial work
	Representation in prescribed proceedings in the Crown Court
5.106	Indictable jurisdiction
	Defence elections for trial in either way case which do not result in a trial or discontinuance of all charges • Other cases on indictment • 1) The offence classification • 2) The number of PPE – PPE in excess of 10,000 pages • 3) Whether the case is a trial, cracked or guilty plea • 4) The length of a trial • 5) The number of defendants represented • 6) The proportion of the case on which the litigator represented the defendant and when there is more than one trial • Retrial fees • VHCC cases
5.154	Calculation of the litigator graduated fee
	Stage 1 • Stage 2 • Stage 3
5.161	Discontinuances and dismissals

continued

---

1 Provided for by the Criminal Legal Aid (Remuneration) Regulations 2013 SI No 435 ('Remuneration Regulations 2013').

5.165 Escape provisions: additional payments; special preparation and confiscation
Unused material in long cases • Special preparation (Sch 2 para 20), ie electronic evidence and PPE in excess of 10,000 and confiscation proceedings (Sch 2 para 26) • Enhanced fees in confiscation cases (Sch 2 para 2) • Hourly rates

5.184 Special circumstances
Warrant cases (Sch 2 para 23) • Retrials • Evidence provision fee • Disbursements (reg 17)

5.189 Advocacy in the Crown Court

5.191 Non-indictable crime
Normal fees • Contempt of court • Mark-ups • Escape provisions • Prescribed proceedings in the Crown Court

5.204 Indictable crime
Defence elections for trial in either way cases • Other cases on indictment • Preliminary hearings • Bail hearings • Graduated fees

5.233 Calculations
For trials • For guilty pleas • For cracked trials • Mark-ups • Defendants unfit to plead or stand trial • Retrials

5.251 Supplementary fees
Interim hearings • Sentencing hearings • Hearings paid by daily and half daily fees (when not part of main hearings) • Work paid by hourly rates • Special preparation • Wasted preparation

5.282 Special circumstances
Early discontinuance or dismissal • Confiscation proceedings • Retrials • Cross-examination of a witness • Mitigation only • Provision of written or oral advice • Warrants • Discharge of legal aid

5.301 Disbursements

5.303 Payment and distribution of the advocacy fee

Overview

5.1 The following general points should be noted:
- Litigators' fees are always separate from, and added to, advocacy fees.
- Fees for cases that are not sent for trial but are committed for sentence or for breach of a court order, or for appeals, are described at paras 5.97–5.105 and 5.191–5.202.
- Fees for prescribed proceedings such as appeals against a football banning order made in civil proceedings in the magistrates' court are described in chapter 10.
- Fees for cases sent for trial at the election of the defendant are fixed[2] unless:
  1) there is trial; or
  2) the Crown offers no evidence on *all* matters; or
  3) for advocates, the Crown:
     a) makes a substantive change to a count and the defendant pleads guilty; or
     b) offers no evidence on a count and the defendant subsequently pleads guilty.

  These are described at paras 5.106–5.110.
- In other indictable cases sent for trial, litigator and advocacy graduated fees are payable. Various proxies are used to identify the fee. The schemes are entirely mechanistic and the fees are calculated according to the rules whatever the justice of the outcome[3] whether advantageous[4] or disadvantageous.[5]
- Hourly rates are only payable in limited circumstances mainly around confiscation and special preparation.

5.2 When preparing a claim for Crown Court costs, it is always wise to:
- Check the Digital Case System to see if a better claim can be made. Both individual and joint files should be checked. For instance, an indictment may have been lodged putting the case in a better class for costs purposes. This will also show if there have been formal orders for joinder or severance, which affects the number of claims that can be made.

---

2 SI 2015 No 1369 for litigators and SI 2018 No 1323 for advocates.
3 *R v Kemp* (X15) 3633/99.
4 *R v Chubb* [2002] 2 Costs LR 333.
5 *R v Dhaliwal* [2004] 4 Costs LR 689.

- Check against the claim being made by litigator or advocate and the litigators and advocates for co-defendants to ensure consistency of outcome. This applies particularly to electronic evidence served. However, a claim can only be made for the counts relevant to the individual defendant(s) for whom the litigator or advocate holds a representation order.[6]
- Ensure you have kept copies of receipts for all papers or discs served by hand.

Principles applicable to litigators and advocates in cases sent to the Crown Court[7]

5.3 Certain concepts are common to both advocates' and litigators' graduated fee schemes. They are:

1) Numbers of pages of prosecution evidence (PPE). This proxy is less significant for advocates.
2) Whether the case is a trial, 'cracked trial' or 'guilty plea' (categorisation).
3) Number of days of trial.
4) Number of cases for which a fee may be claimed.

Number of pages of prosecution evidence[8]

5.4 This is a key factor for litigators, but is only relevant for advocates in relation to issues of:

- Banding (classification of the case) in bands 6.1 and 6.2 and 9.1–9.6 (see paras 5.214–5.218).
- Special preparation (see paras 5.269–5.278).
- Confiscation (see paras 5.285–5.290).

5.5 For advocates, page count applies when special preparation is claimed in the following cases:[9]

> ... the number of pages of prosecution evidence, as defined and determined in accordance with paragraph 1(2) to (5), exceeds–
> (i) in cases falling within bands 6.1 to 6.5 (dishonesty offences, including proceeds of crime and money laundering), 30,000;

---

6 *R v Sharif* SCCO 168/13.
7 Criminal Legal Aid (Remuneration) Regulations 2013 SI No 435 (Remuneration Regulations) Schs 1 and 2.
8 See also CCFG Appendix D.
9 Remuneration Regulations 2013 Sch 1 para 17, as amended by SI 2018 No 220 reg 19.

(ii) in cases falling within bands 9.1 to 9.7 (drugs offences), 15,000; or
(iii) in all other cases, 10,000,

and the appropriate officer considers it reasonable to make a payment in excess of the graduated fee payable under this Schedule . . .

5.6 The burden to show that PPE includes certain pages is on the claimant to the civil standard.[10] A page is counted however much or little appears on it. Images printed together on a single page only count as one page, however.[11] Title pages and separator pages should not be counted.[12]

5.7 The statutory definition appears in Remuneration Regulations 2013 Schs 1 and 2 para 1(2)–(5):

(2) For the purposes of this Schedule, the number of pages of prosecution evidence served on the court must be determined in accordance with sub-paragraphs (3) to (5).
(3) The number of pages of prosecution evidence includes all–
 (a) witness statements;
 (b) documentary and pictorial exhibits;
 (c) records of interviews with the assisted person; and
 (d) records of interviews with other defendants,
which form part of the served prosecution documents or which are included in any notice of additional evidence.
(4) Subject to sub-paragraph (5), a document served by the prosecution in electronic form is included in the number of pages of prosecution evidence.
(5) A documentary or pictorial exhibit which–
 (a) has been served by the prosecution in electronic form; and
 (b) has never existed in paper form,
is not included within the number of pages of prosecution evidence unless the appropriate officer decides that it would be appropriate to include it in the pages of prosecution evidence taking into account the nature of the document and any other relevant circumstances.

5.8 Thus the number of PPE *include* those served on the court falling within the definition of served prosecution documents, or included in any notice of additional evidence, or within the meaning given in *Secretary of State for Justice, the Lord Chancellor v SVS Solicitors* (below).[13]

10 *R v McCreadie* SCCO 350/12.
11 *R v Bowen* [2011] 4 Costs LR 693.
12 *R v El Treki* (X26).
13 [2017] EWHC 1045 (QB).

5.9 'Served prosecution papers' means papers served as the evidence in the case under Crime and Disorder Act 1998 s51 and relied upon as evidence by the Crown (*R v Matthews* SCCO 58/07; *Goodman and Farr v Secretary of State for Constitutional Affairs*[14]). It is otherwise where there is no evidence that the Crown intends to rely on the relevant pages.[15]

5.10 The meaning of a notice of additional evidence (NAE) may now be liberally interpreted. It was originally indicated that such a notice must be in writing.[16] However, the practice of the Crown of relying on additional evidence at trial without completing a formal notice has led to decisions such as *R v Qu*,[17] where it was held that served prosecution documents included prosecution documents which should have been accompanied by a NAE but were not, through no fault of the defence. As the documents were also served on the court, they counted towards PPE. Under the pressures of trial, a disc served by prosecution counsel on defence counsel was served prosecution evidence even though there was no notice of additional evidence.[18]

5.11 The issue of 'service' was fully considered in the authoritative decision in *Secretary of State for Justice, the Lord Chancellor v SVS Solicitors*.[19]

i) The starting point is that only served evidence and exhibits can be counted as PPE. Material which is only disclosed as unused material cannot be PPE.

ii) In this context, references to 'served' evidence and exhibits must mean 'served as part of the evidence and exhibits in the case'. The evidence on which the prosecution rely will of course be served; but evidence may be served even though the prosecution does not specifically rely on every part of it.

iii) Where evidence and exhibits are formally served as part of the material on the basis of which a defendant is sent for trial, or under a subsequent notice of additional evidence, and are recorded as such in the relevant notices, there is no difficulty in concluding that they are served. But paragraph 1(3) of Schedule 2 to the 2013 Regulations only says that the number of PPE 'includes' such material: it does not say that the number of PPE 'comprises only' such material.

---

14 [2006] EWHC 3669 (QB).
15 *R v Ward* [2012] 3 Costs LR 605.
16 *R v Sturdy* [1999] 1 Costs LR 1.
17 [2012] 3 Costs LR 599.
18 *Lord Chancellor v Edwards Hayes LLP* [2017] EWHC 138 (QB).
19 [2017] EWHC 1045 (QB).

iv) 'Service' may therefore be informal. Formal service is of course much to be preferred, both because it is required by the Criminal Procedure Rules and because it avoids subsequent arguments about the status of material. But it would be in nobody's interests to penalise informality if, in sensibly and cooperatively progressing a trial, the advocates dispensed with the need for service of a notice of additional evidence before further evidence could be adduced, and all parties subsequently overlooked the need for the prosecution to serve the requisite notice ex post facto.

v) The phrase 'served on the court' seems to me to do no more than identify a convenient form of evidence as to what has been served by the prosecution on the defendant. I do not think that 'service on the court' is a necessary precondition of evidence counting as part of the PPE. If 100 pages of further evidence and exhibits were served on a defendant under cover of a notice of additional evidence, it cannot be right that those 100 pages would be excluded from the count of PPE merely because the notice had for some reason not reached the court.

vi) In short, it is important to observe the formalities of service, and compliance with the formalities will provide clear evidence as to the status of particular material; but non-compliance with the formalities of service cannot of itself necessarily exclude material from the count of PPE.

5.12 In assisting a judge to make appropriate orders, it should be noted that Criminal Practice Direction I Part 3B provides that:

3B.2 A party who serves documentary evidence in the Crown Court should
  (a) paginate each page in any bundle of statements and exhibits sequentially;
  (b) provide an index to each bundle of statements . . .
  (c) provide an index to each bundle of documentary and pictorial exhibits . . .

3B.3 Where additional documentary evidence is served, a party should paginate . . . sequential[ly]. . . .

3B.4 The prosecution must ensure that the running total of the pages of prosecution evidence is easily identifiable on the most recent served bundle of prosecution evidence.

3B.5 For the purposes of these directions, the number of pages of prosecution evidence served on the court includes all
  (a) witness statements;
  (b) documentary and pictorial exhibits;
  (c) records of interview with the defendant; and
  (d) records of interviews with other defendants which form part of the . . . served prosecution documents or which are included in any notice of additional evidence, but does not include any document provided on CD-ROM or by other means of electronic communication.

The final provision follows the terms of the Remuneration Regulations 2013.

5.13 Service can include the inspection of pages at a police station where the crown is not prepared to release them for wider circulation.[20] Service was interpreted as meaning delivery or being brought to the attention of the defence

5.14 Defence lawyers have an obligation to check the validity of prosecution summaries. In a case where the evidence was central to the prosecution case, it was not sufficient to accept the prosecution view of what was relevant.[21]

Summary of definition of PPE[22]

5.15 The following table summarises the features of PPP.

Type of PPE	Type of service by prosecution	PPE or special preparation
Paper witness statements, interviews and documentary and pictorial exhibits	Paper	PPE
Paper witness statements, interviews and documentary and pictorial exhibits that are converted into digital format	Digital	PPE
Witness statements or interviews that have only ever existed in digital format	Digital	PPE
Documentary and pictorial exhibits in digital format (see CCFG paras 32–44 Appendix D for further detail)	Digital	The Appropriate Officer will take into account whether the document would have been printed by the prosecution and served in paper form prior to 1 April 2012. If so, then it will be counted as PPE.

---

20 *R v Parke* SCCO 67/16.
21 *LC v Edward Hayes LLP* 2017 EWHC 138(QB); *Secretary of State for Justice v SVS Solicitors* 2017 EWHC 1045 (QB).
22 Source: CCFG Appendix D.

		If the Appropriate Officer is unable to make that assessment, they will take into account 'any other relevant circumstances' such as the importance of the evidence to the case, the amount and the nature of the work that was required to be done and by whom, and the extent to which the electronic evidence featured in the case against the defendant.
A prosecution summary or transcript of an interview with a defendant	Paper or digital	PPE
ABE interviews	Paper or digital	Where the transcript is relied upon by the prosecution, it will be treated as PPE.
First Stage Streamlined Forensic Report (SFR1)	Paper or digital	The SFR1 is a short report that details the key forensic evidence the prosecution intends to rely on. The prosecution's aim is to achieve early agreement with the defence on forensic issues (or where this cannot be achieved, to identify the contested issues). Where an SFR1 does result in agreement of forensic issues, the SFR1 will be treated as PPE.
		Note, the SFR1 will be paid as PPE in circumstances where no SFR2 is served for whatever reason rather than solely because the SFR1 is agreed.

5.16 If a transcript has been expanded, the fullest transcript counts towards page count as well as the pages of the transcript in the served prosecution documents. Transcripts of video evidence asked for by the judge should be included in the page count.[23]

23 *R v Brazier* (X5).

70 *Criminal Costs: legal aid costs in the criminal courts / chapter 5*

5.17 Pages only count if they were produced by the prosecution (rather than merely referred to in general terms). Defence papers do not count.

5.18 NAEs are included in page count for graduated fees whatever their nature, eg transcript of first aborted trial.[24]

5.19 The Crown Court digital case system may assist in providing the best evidence of the pages served on the court, but this should always be checked, particularly as electronic evidence is frequently not recorded. Regard should be had to section G and H (Key documents), I, J, and K (evidence exhibits and transcripts). Written statements and exhibits (as well as transcripts) will count towards PPE (as long as not duplicated) whether it is lodged on the Crown Court system in sections G, H, I or J. It is service that matters.[25]

5.20 PPE include pages served for the trial of co-defendants after a guilty plea, but before sentence of the defendant for whom a solicitor acts, because a solicitor continues to act in the case until that time.[26]

5.21 The number of pages relevant to a pre-transfer claim is the number served on the court at the date of the transfer.[27]

5.22 In CCFG appendix D, the LAA summarises material that is, and is not, counted by them as PPE. The italicised notes do not form part of the LAA guidance:

> 3. The following material make up the PPE count:
> - The fullest committal bundle or set of served prosecution documents (*R v Brazier* (1998), *R v Sturdy* (1998), *R v Ward* (2012), and, if relevant, the total on the final Notice of Additional Evidence (NAE) should be used (*R v Powell* (2016)). As held in *R. v Rigelsford* (2005), where the prosecution only relies on a sample of evidence available, payment can only be paid for that which is formally admitted. This is also supported in other Senior Courts Costs Office decisions such as *R v Samoon and Baryali* (SCCO Ref: 24/16), *R v Motaung* (SCCO Ref 179/15) and *R v Powell* (SCCO Ref 7/16), where the CPS had extracted and served on the defence the relevant pages from a disc and clearly disclosed the balance of material on the disc as unused.
> - When a transcript has been expanded, either by the prosecution or the defence, because the one provided by the prosecution was deemed to be insufficient to go before the jury, the fullest transcript produced should be included in the page count (*R v Brazier* (1998)). [*Note the case does not fully support this statement and there is an argument that all transcripts should count.*]

---

24 *R v Taylor* [2005] 4 Costs LR 712.
25 *R v Andall* SCCO 06/17.
26 *R v Debenham* SCCO 10/12.
27 *R v Greenwood* [2010] 2 Costs LR 268.

Crown Court work 71

- Transcripts of video evidence that the judge requests. [*Note:* or it is suggested that if the crown chooses to produce a transcript that must also count.]
- A page of prosecution evidence is included in the count irrespective of the number of lines of content.

Pages or Types of Evidence Not Counted as PPE

4. The following aspects or types of evidence are not counted as PPE and are wrapped up in the graduated fee. The following is a non-exhaustive list of items excluded from the PPE proxy:
   - Unused Material.
   - Other digital exhibits (e.g. CCTV, video evidence (including video interviews), and audio evidence). [*Note:* but still images from the film will count – see para 5.23.]
   - Versions of a transcript that have been edited for the jury. [*Note:* but it is arguable that expanded versions may be additional to a more edited one.]
   - Title pages, index pages, exhibit labels, separator pages, fax covering sheets.
   - No allowances for small or large typefaces, or duplicated pages (including those that have minor differences (*R v El Treki* (2001)).
   - Evidence served after the litigator or advocate is no longer representing the client.
   - Defence generated evidence (including the product of any defence analysis of forensic computer images or copies of electronic storage media (eg hard drives)). *Note:* the circumstances in *R v Brazier* (1988) mentioned in para 3 is an exception.
   - Transcripts edited for the purpose of being put before the jury [*Note* this is subject to argument]
   - Recordings of interviews with victims, and transcripts of those interviews, do not fall within the PPE definition in regulations and are not considered PPE (*R v Gleeson* (2011)).
   - Pre-sentence and psychiatric reports.
   - Physical exhibits.
   - Software or databases.
   - Advance disclosure. [*Note:* unless there is no other page count to use particularly if a case is discontinued early in the proceedings.]
   - Defence generated printed material (*R v Ward* (2012)).
   - Applications for Special Measures.
   - Prosecution Opening.
   - Case Summary.
   - Indictment.
   - Application to adduce bad character or hearsay evidence.
   - Evidence served for confiscation proceedings.
   - Admissions.

Video and audio recordings, etc

5.23   Video and audio recordings, DVDs and CD-ROMs do not count towards PPE, nor is payment as special preparation available, because these records do not fall to be described as documentary or pictorial exhibits. A document is a still image, not moving footage not intended to be converted to still images or which cannot be so converted.[28]

5.24   Such records only count to the extent that they are reduced by the Crown to an exhibited transcript.[29]

5.25   Real evidence does not fall within PPE unless photographed, and as such included as an exhibit.[30]

Unused material

5.26   Unused material cannot count as PPE for graduated fees but the material will do so if served by formal NAE[31] – otherwise unused material cannot be taken into account. This means that no payment can be made for what may amount to many hours of surveillance material on which the Crown does not rely as evidence.

Ancillary applications

5.27   A notice of intention to adduce bad character evidence is not a NAE within the Funding Order. The wording followed the earlier Order when no such notices could be given. This interpretation is consistent with the ability of a co-defendant to serve such a notice which could not count as it is not prosecution material. The documents were not statements, exhibits or interviews.[32]

Electronic service of pictorial or documentary exhibits

5.28   The intention of the Remuneration Regulations 2013 is to ensure that, as the criminal justice system is moving towards digital working and the increased service of digital evidence, there is no difference in legal aid funding whether the evidence is served digitally or on paper.

---

28   *R v Uddin* [2010] 2 Costs LR 274; *Lord Chancellor v Michael J Reed Ltd* [2009] EWHC 2981 (QB); *R v Oseoteko* [2014] 1 Costs LR 190: *Maclaverty Cooper Atkins v Lord Chancellor* [2014] EWHC 1387 (QB).
29   *Lord Chancellor v McLarty & Co Solicitors* [2011] EWHC 3182 (QB).
30   *Goodman and Farr v Secretary of State for Constitutional Affairs* [2006] EWHC 3669 (QB).
31   *R v Sturdy* [1999] 1 Costs LR 1 (X9).
32   *R v McCall* [2011] 5 Costs LR 914 which involved a police disciplinary file.

The current Regulations seek to preserve the status quo in so far as remuneration is concerned, despite the changes in the manner of service. If evidence is relied upon that would previously have been served in paper form, it should be included in the PPE count.

5.29 All witness statements included in the bundles or under a notice of additional evidence will thus count as PPE whether the original statement was created in paper form or digital form. Similarly, if the prosecution create a summary or transcript of an interview with a defendant, this does not need to have existed in paper form to be paid as PPE.

5.30 There has been substantial litigation over the issue of whether electronically served pictorial and documentary exhibits count towards page count, which usually generates a higher fee than if the work is calculated as special preparation. A Crown Court judge has jurisdiction, during the course of the trial, to order the Crown to serve documents on paper as part of case management powers, where this is required to benefit the conduct of the trial and not for remuneration purposes.[33]

5.31 Where the Regulations refer to 'the nature of the document and any other relevant circumstances', relevant circumstances are not limited to whether the material would previously have been printed out.[34] Whether to make a payment for electronic material is a discretionary judgement and each case is decided on its own merits. The data may need detailed consideration to show the part played by a particular defendant, or the relationship between defendants or to separate a defendant from others In summary, it appears that the position can be summarised as follows:

1) Time should have been taken to consider the electronic material.
2) The material should be an important or integral part to the case (having evidential weight) against the defendant for whom the lawyer acts, or for instance show the relationship between defendants or separate a defendant from others. Electronic pages will count as PPE where it constitutes the evidential basis upon which the crown was able to prepare and put together telephone schedules used at trial, so that such schedules can be checked for accuracy.
3) The defence lawyers must show that the pages claimed are relevant to the defence or to an understanding of the prosecution case so as

---

33 *R v Furniss* [2015] 1 Costs LR 1521; and *Secretary of State for Justice, Lord Chancellor v SVS Solicitors* [2017] EWHC 1045 (QB); *R v AS*, Luton Crown Court, 22 June 2015.
34 *R v Napper* [2014] 5 Costs LR 947.

to assist the client.[35] If relevance or lack of duplication is not identified with precision the court may take a broad brush approach.[36]

4) It will be unusual for both litigator and advocate to be able to claim for page count where they are the same person.[37] There should not be duplication. In *R v Lennon*[38] the costs judge held that where a case goes to trial and there are separate persons within a firm acting as litigator and as advocate, there is no requirement to prove the number of hours that each worked but rather the graduated fee should be a based on the same page count including pages served electronically. Each has a separate professional duty and should be paid the full PPE. An in-house advocate cannot be distinguished from independent counsel. Cases may be distinguished when a guilty plea is entered.

5.32 The law in this area has been significantly clarified by the decision in *Secretary of State for Justice v SVS Solicitors*.[39] The following extracts are significant. The decision makes clear that the CPS clarification of documents as unused material will not be final for costs purposes:

> 42. In *Furniss*, Haddon-Cave J – who, as trial judge, was in the best position to assess all relevant circumstances – concluded that the electronic material was clearly –
>
> '... integral to the prosecution case and required the defence to review and examine it in detail for the purposes of properly preparing the defence cases. The crucial nature of this material to the trial was not in any dispute.'
>
> He emphasised forcefully that the defence advocates had had to check all of the telephone downloads with care if they were to agree to the schedule of calls and other details which the prosecution wished to put before the jury. He noted that it would have been open to the defence teams to refuse to agree the schedule until all relevant material had been properly served ...
>
> ...
>
> 43. Similarly, in the *Edward Hayes* case ([2017] EWHC 138 (QB)), Nicola Davies J noted that the prosecution relied on a schedule of text messages which were at the core of the Crown's case. She said, at paragraph 20 –

---

35 *R v Shoaib* SCCO 142/18.
36 *R v Sereika* SCCO 68/13.
37 *R v Napper* 2014 5 Costs LR 947.
38 SCCO 186/15.
39 [2017] EWHC 1045 (QB).

'Given the importance of the evidence it is unsurprising that the defence refused to agree to admission of the extracted data until it was able to examine all the data on the download. This was the defence application to the trial judge which he granted. The request was not only reasonable, it enabled the defendant's legal team to properly fulfil its duty to the defendant. It enabled the defendant's legal representatives to satisfy themselves of the veracity of the extracted date and to place the same in a context having examined and considered the surrounding and/or underlying data. It also enabled the defendant's legal team to extract any communications which they deemed to be relevant. Given the importance of the extracted material to the Crown's case and resultant duty upon the defendant's team to satisfy itself of the veracity and context of the same I am satisfied that this was additional evidence which should have been accompanied by a Notice in the prescribed form.'

44. I respectfully agree with those general observations as to the duties of the defence when asked to agree a schedule or some proposed agreed facts. The agreement of schedules and/or agreed facts, which reduce a mass of evidence and exhibits to a much more convenient and efficient form, is central to the proper progression of very many criminal trials. But it is important to bear in mind that the role of the defence lawyers is often not confined to checking the accuracy of the summaries of the material which the prosecution has chosen to include: it often extends also to checking the surrounding material to ensure that the schedule does not omit anything which should properly be included in order to present a fair summary of the totality of the evidence and exhibits which are being summarised. It may therefore often be necessary to review what has been omitted before being able to agree to the accuracy of that which has been included . . .

. . .

46. I make those general observations because it seems to me that difficulty has arisen in the present case because both the CPS and the Determining Officer assumed that only the evidence and exhibits on which the prosecution rely can ever be 'served', and that 'served' evidence is necessarily identical to the evidence and exhibits on which the prosecution rely. Sometimes that will be so; but it is in my judgment a mistake to think that it will always be so. It is frequently the case that the prosecution evidence and exhibits include material which cannot realistically be said to be "relied upon" by the prosecution, for example because it is an irrelevant part of a statement or exhibit which also contains relevant material, or because it is a part of the material which is inconsistent with the way the prosecution case is put but is necessarily included in order to be fair to the defence . . .

.... The key point, as it seems to me, is that if the prosecution do wish to rely on a sub-set of the data obtained from a particular source, it will often be necessary for all of the data from that source to be exhibited so that the parts on which the prosecution rely can fairly be seen in their proper context ...

...

50 ...

vii) Where the prosecution seek to rely on only part of the data recovered from a particular source, and therefore serve an exhibit which contains only some of the data, issues may arise as to whether all of the data should be exhibited. The resolution of such issues will depend on the circumstances of the particular case, and on whether the data which have been exhibited can only fairly be considered in the light of the totality of the data. It should almost always be possible for the parties to resolve such issues between themselves, and it is in the interests of all concerned that a clear decision is reached and any necessary notice of additional evidence served. If, exceptionally, the parties are unable to agree as to what should be served, the trial judge can be asked whether he or she is prepared to make a ruling in the exercise of his case management powers. In such circumstances, the trial judge (if willing to make a ruling) will have to consider all the circumstances of the case before deciding whether the prosecution should be directed either to exhibit the underlying material or to present their case without the extracted material on which they seek to rely.

viii) If – regrettably – the status of particular material has not been clearly resolved between the parties, or (exceptionally) by a ruling of the trial judge, then the Determining Officer (or, on appeal, the Costs Judge) will have to determine it in the light of all the information which is available. The view initially taken by the prosecution as to the status of the material will be a very important consideration, and will often be decisive, but is not necessarily so: if in reality the material was of central importance to the trial (and not merely helpful to the defence), the Determining Officer (or Costs Judge) would be entitled to conclude that it was in fact served, and that the absence of formal service should not affect its inclusion in the PPE. Again, this will be a case-specific decision. In making that decision, the Determining Officer (or Costs Judge) would be entitled to regard the failure of the parties to reach any agreement, or to seek a ruling from the trial judge, as a powerful indication that the prosecution's initial view as to the status of the material was correct. If the Determining Officer (or Costs Judge) is unable to conclude that material was in fact served, then it must be treated as unused material, even if it was important to the defence.

ix) If an exhibit is served, but in electronic form and in circumstances which come within paragraph 1(5) of Schedule 2 [to the

Remuneration Regulations], the Determining Officer (or, on appeal, the Costs Judge) will have a discretion as to whether he or she considers it appropriate to include it in the PPE. As I have indicated above, the LAA's Crown Court Fee Guidance explains the factors which should be considered. This is an important and valuable control mechanism which ensures that public funds are not expended inappropriately.

x) If an exhibit is served in electronic form but the Determining Officer or Costs Judge considers it inappropriate to include it in the count of PPE, a claim for special preparation may be made by the solicitors in the limited circumstances defined by Paragraph 20 of Schedule 2.

xi) If material which has been disclosed as unused material has not in fact been served (even informally) as evidence or exhibits, and the Determining Officer has not concluded that it should have been served (as indicated at (viii) above), then it cannot be included in the number of PPE. In such circumstances, the discretion under paragraph 1(5) does not apply.

5.33 Where it is ambiguous whether the papers contained on a disc sent by the Crown Prosecution Service (CPS) are unused or prosecution evidence, there is no requirement for a formal NAE. The court can find the material was 'served prosecution documents' if they played a material part in the prosecution's case requiring analysis by the defence. This was telephone data going to the part played by each defendant and their degree of involvement. It was the basis of the prosecution schedules. It was not unused or material of peripheral interest. Dinu was alone acquitted.[40]

5.34 The prosecution's view as to page count is not final, though very influential. There is no burden on the defence to show the material is not unused. The court must carry out its own review.[41]

5.35 While it is desirable for the LAA to receive the disc of electronic evidence, it cannot, in a case where the Crown has requested its return because of the sensitive nature of its contents, refuse to consider the issue. The LAA must consider all the relevant factors to decide on PPE.[42]

5.36 The development of the case-law can be examined, but must be read subject to the decisions in *SVS Solicitors* and *Edward Hayes* above. Only decisions of the High Court are binding on costs judges and determining officers. All other cases are illustrative only and decided

---

[40] *R v Dinu* SCCO 146/16.
[41] *R v Ali* [2017] 4 Costs LRO 533.
[42] *R v Walsh* SCCO 197/16.

on their own facts. The LAA is very free with quotation of such cases, which often have limited relevance to the issues in the particular case.

5.37 In *R v Lee*[43] the judge considered scheduled readings of tracker devices and handset reports relating to the use of mobile telephones. The evidence was vital to the prosecution case and substantially relied upon. PPE was allowed. Similarly in *R v Jalibaghodelehzi*[44] the material was downloads from mobile telephones which was crucial evidence and referred to in the prosecution opening. The solicitors had printed it out to work on it. It connected the defendant to the importation of drugs. The material required the same degree of consideration as evidence served in the case and was an important part of the prosecution case. The nature of the document and all the relevant circumstances must be considered. They will be PPE if they require a similar degree of consideration to evidence served on paper; solicitors using telephone data to show a lack of contact between their client and other defendants (on the 'drug phone' in this case) should be paid by PPE for the work involved (*R v Dodd*[45] following *Napper* (below) and *Jalibaghodelehzi*). In *Jalibaghodelehzi* the distinction made was between the need for an electronic search to identify if a particular defendant's telephone number appears (special preparation) and the material forming an important part of the prosecution's case (PPE).

5.38 In *R v Chilton*,[46] in a very brief judgment, the costs judge held that the pages did not have to be pivotal to the prosecution case; merely relevant. While the views of a trial judge as to whether material ought to be treated as PPE was not binding on the LAA, considerable weight should be given to that view.

5.39 In *R v Wortley*[47] the judge identified the significance to the prosecution case of the material in question. A critical schedule was dependent upon it and considerable reference was made to the electronic disc at trial and in trial preparation. If a judge orders that that the Crown may only rely on material, which was originally served digitally if it is served with a NAE and on paper, that order, which will be very unusual, may not be gainsaid by the LAA and the pages count as PPE (*R v Nutting*[48]).

43 SCCO 343/13.
44 [2014] 4 Costs LR 781 (SCCO).
45 [2014] 6 Costs LR 1131.
46 SCCO 400/14.
47 SCCO 06/14.
48 [2013] Costs LR 1037 (SCCO).

5.40 In *R v Gillett*[49] and also *R v Murray*[50] (as well as in *R v Napper*[51]) the costs judges confirmed that the fact that material never existed in paper form is not a decisive factor. However, in the former case there was no evidence that the time taken to consider the material by the litigator or advocate (both employed by the same firm) was significant. The costs judge also referred to the fact that the allegation was not of conspiracy but that factor must also be linked to the facts of the particular case.

5.41 Further decisions in *R v Fiaz*[52] and *R v Nicholson*,[53] emphasised that a primary factor is whether the electronic material was crucial to the prosecution's case, the latter adopting the reasoning in *R v Jalibaghodelehzi*, above.

5.42 In *R v Roberts*[54] the costs judge held that the nature of all material served electronically must be considered as only relevant material or potentially relevant material may count towards page count. If time is taken only to discover that the material is not relevant this should be charged a special preparation.

5.43 Whether digital pages count towards PPE is case-dependent – not every page served electronically will be PPE, but must meet the relevant importance test: *R v Sana*.[55] That before the current scheme the pages would have been served digitally is not relevant. The nature of the document and all the relevant circumstances must be considered. They will be PPE if they require a similar degree of consideration to evidence served on paper.

5.44 The LAA has adjusted its guidance, set out in Appendix D of the CCFG, to take some account of the case-law. Parts remain contentious.

> 14. Therefore, claims for electronic evidence will be assessed according to the following principles:
> - Whether the document would have been printed by the prosecution and served in paper form prior to 1 April 2012 is a relevant circumstance under paragraph 1(5) of Schedules 1 and 2 to the Regulations that the Appropriate Officer will take into account. If the Appropriate Officer can conclude that the material would have

---

49 SSCO 185/14.
50 SCCO 233/14.
51 [2014] 5 Costs LR 947 (SCCO).
52 SCCO 57/14.
53 SCCO 197/14.
54 SCCO 112/14.
55 [2014] Costs LR 1143 (SCCO).

been printed prior to 1 April 2012, it will be counted as PPE for both the litigator and advocate.
- If the Appropriate Officer is unable to make that assessment, the Appropriate Officer will take into account 'any other relevant circumstances' such as the importance of the evidence to the case, the amount and the nature of the work that was required to be done and by whom, and the extent to which the electronic evidence featured in the case against the defendant.

15. Some examples of documentary or pictorial exhibits that will ordinarily be counted as PPE are:
- Scene of crime photographs.
- Prosecution analysis carried out on phone data.
- Bank statements.
- Raw phone data where a detailed schedule has been created by the prosecution which is served and relied on and is relevant to the defendant's case.
- Raw phone data if it is served without a schedule having been created by the prosecution, but the evidence nevertheless remains important to the prosecution case and is relevant to the defendant's case e.g. it can be shown that a careful analysis had to be carried out on the data in order to dispute the extent of the defendant's involvement.
- Raw phone data where the case is a conspiracy and the electronic evidence relates to the defendant and co-conspirators with whom the defendant had direct contact.

16. The following additional information (relevant to the case in question) must be submitted for all claims where electronically served evidence is being claimed as PPE:
- The disc or discs/other electronic service media containing the material.
- The full prosecution list/s of all evidence served in the case.
- An explanation as to which of the electronically served exhibits are being claimed as PPE (i.e. for each exhibit listed, explain why you consider that the nature of this document and the relevant circumstances, specific to your client's case, mean that the Appropriate Officer should decide that it is appropriate to include this particular item of material within the PPE, and if so, how many additional pages are being claimed from the total page count within that exhibit).
- A Schedule in the following format should be considered in all cases and may be required in cases involving high electronic evidence counts/multiple discs:
    - Disc A, Folder B, Sub Folder C, Document D – 12 pages
    - Disc A, Folder E, Document F – 109 pages
    - Disc G, Folder H, Document J, Tab K (if a spreadsheet is claimed for) – 105 pages

17. Depending on the case, it may also assist the assessment of your claim if you provide some or all of the following additional justification:
- The prosecution case summary.
- The defence case statement.
- Any defence schedules prepared from the electronic evidence.
- Any skeleton arguments submitted relevant to the electronic evidence claimed as PPE.
- Litigator's attendance notes.
- Full, detailed work logs or file notes showing all work undertaken in relation to the material served electronically.

Assessment of Electronic Evidence

18. The basic position under the Regulations is that electronically served evidence is not included in the number of pages of prosecution evidence unless the Appropriate Officer concludes that it would be appropriate to include the material as PPE. (*R v Tunstall* SCCO Ref: 220/15) and *R v Sana* [2014] 6 Costs LR 1143).

19. If the Appropriate Officer is unable to conclude that the electronic evidence ought to be included within the pages of prosecution evidence it may be remunerated as special preparation (under the LGFS). (Paragraph 17(1)(C) Schedule 1 (advocates) and paragraph 20(1)(a) Schedule 2 (litigators)

20. Whether material is properly remunerated as PPE or special preparation will depend on the specific facts of the case. The following costs judge decisions provide some guidance on the distinction between material paid as PPE and material paid as special preparation:
- *R v Jalibahodelezhi* [2014] 4 Costs LR 781: material should be paid as PPE where it is pivotal to the case and requires same degree of consideration as paper evidence.
- *R v Sibanda* (SCCO Ref 227/14): where a defendant is charged with substantive offences telephone data relating to co-defendants is not sufficiently relevant to merit inclusion in the PPE. *R v Sana* [2014] 6 Costs LR 1143: The Costs Judge held that if some electronic evidence is relevant to the case and some is irrelevant to the case, the nature of the document and the circumstances mean that it is not reasonable to treat the irrelevant material as PPE. However, reasonable time spent considering the material could still be the subject of a claim under the special preparation rules.
- *R v T Mahmood and Z Mahmood* (SCCO Ref 149/16;155/16 and 185/16): In cases where a telephone report is served it may be appropriate to subdivide a report into its individual sections and allow only the relevant tabs or sections. In particular, there is a distinction between "social material" i.e. audio files, images, photographs, internet history, cookies, installed applications etc

that may properly be remunerated as special preparation and telecommunications data i.e. contacts, call history, SMS and other messages which is more likely to be paid as PPE.

- *R v Robertson* (SCCO Ref 22/17): Personal photographs or images contained on a defendant's telephone are unlikely to merit inclusion within the pages of prosecution evidence.
- *R v Yates* (SCCO Ref 66/17): In certain cases, it is appropriate to draw a distinction between material directly attributable to the defendant which is integral to the case and should be included in the PPE and material attributable to the co-defendant which is useful only as additional background and therefore payable as special preparation.
- *R v Daugnitis* (SCCO ref. 154/17, 155/17, 177/17): That duplicate material is served in multiple formats is a relevant consideration that the determining officer should take into account. Where it is clear that the duplicate documents would not have required separate consideration they should only be included in the page count once. There is a distinction between material in PDF which provides a dependable page count and is formatted in a way which permits the material to be read and printed in page format so that the printed page will reflect the page on screen and material in Excel format which does not provide a representative or predictable page count (as it is subject to the version of Excel used and the print settings of the user). Excel data is intended to be manipulated electronically using various search tools and filters, if printed the data would become distorted and incomprehensible and may include a number of blank pages. Depending on the circumstances of the case the appropriate method of remuneration for time spent considering or manipulating the Excel data may be special preparation which is based on actual time reasonably spent. [*Note:* but see paras 5.47–5.49 below.]

Duplication and use of different formats

5.45 If there is a doubt about whether material was served as PPE, this does not mean it cannot be treated as PPE. Rather the relevant authority must make a decision.

> The disallowance of any of the served material on the basis that it duplicates copies included in the crown's report runs contrary to the guidance given by Mrs Justice Nicola Davies DBE in *Lord Chancellor v Edward Hayes LLP*. It was incumbent upon the appellant to check the contents of the report against the data from which it was derived: that was not duplication but additional work.
>
> The disallowance of pages from the PPE count on the basis that the appellant, in undertaking that checking exercise, identified some of the material as irrelevant or on the basis, if such is the case, that it

otherwise incorporated an element of duplication also seems to me to be contrary to her findings, quoted above, on the importance of considering material in context.

Bearing in mind the guidance of both Nicola Davies J and Holroyd J, it seems to me that something more is needed to exclude served evidence from the PPE count than a broad finding to the effect that some of it proved to be irrelevant or duplicative.[56]

5.46 Consideration of duplicates should be avoided, unless for instance thumbnails in an extraction report are too small to be viewed and a full-sized image is not available quickly, for instance by a hyperlink.[57] Extraction reports, because they are produced digitally, are not hearsay and are admissible without the underlying data.[58]

Formats

5.47 Particular and separate problems arise over the use of both PDF and Excel formats in service. Each case will turn on its own facts, though in normal circumstances the PDF format will be used.[59] Claims cannot be made for both formats[60] even when the Excel format was used to obtain a translation.[61]

5.48 When relevant telephone records are central to the defence case and served in Excel format to reduce those documents to PDF format, hugely reducing the page count, would not represent a fair level of remuneration.[62]

5.49 This should be contrasted with a more normal case where the use of Excel was not the appropriate measurement of page count. The *same* material was sent in each format and duplication was a relevant consideration. Much of the Excel material was irrelevant, including blank pages, and contained technical detail even though Excel was easier to manipulate and analyse. A further claim to carry out relevant analysis could be made for special preparation. PDF was a better proxy in this matter for PPE.[63]

---

56 *R v McCarthy* SCCO 36/17.
57 *R v Shaoib* SCCO 142/18.
58 *R v MA* [2018] 2 Costs LR 419.
59 *R v Frempong* SCCO 84/18.
60 *R v Muiyoro* SCCO 70/18.
61 *R v Ludic* SCCO 73/17.
62 *R v O'Rourke* SCCO 10/17; 34/17; 47/17.
63 *R v Daugnitis; R v Cvetkovas; R v Liumas* SCCO 154/17; 155/17; 177/17.

Categorisation of a case (see CCFG 2.1.6–2.1.33)

5.50 There are three possible categories for each case. In order of desirability for maximising fees they are a trial; cracked trial; or a 'guilty' plea. If defendants represented by a litigator are dealt with differently, the litigator chooses the best categorisation and applies the mark-ups below.[64]

Trial

5.51 Decisions of the costs judges and the High Court have significantly changed the point at which a trial comes into being for the purposes of the Remuneration Regulations 2013.

5.52 A trial beginning only when a jury is sworn is at odds with modern practice, and more particularly the deciding of key evidential issues and the making of rulings before the jury is sworn. *R v Wembo*[65] held that a trial:

> ... should be taken to be the date upon which ... submissions are first made to the trial judge in a continuous process which results in the empanelling of a jury without break of time and in the leading of evidence and the returning of a verdict.

5.53 The matter was comprehensively considered by the High Court in *Lord Chancellor v Ian Henery Solicitors Ltd*.[66]

5.54 The principles are as follows:

1) Whether or not a jury had been sworn is not conclusive in determining whether a trial has begun.
2) A trial has begun if a jury has been sworn, the case opened and evidence has been called even if the trial comes to an early conclusion through change of attitude by one of the parties.
3) A trial will also have begun if the jury has been sworn and the case has been opened to any extent.
4) A trial will not have begun even if a jury has been sworn if there has been no trial in a meaningful sense, eg there is an acceptable plea before the opening begins.
5) A trial will have begun even if no jury has been sworn if submissions have been made in a continuous process resulting in the empanelment of the jury, the opening of the evidence and the calling of evidence.

---

64 See Remuneration Regulations 2013 Schs 1 and 2 Pt 6.
65 [2011] 5 Costs LR 926.
66 [2011] EWHC 3246 (QB). CCFG 2.1.12–2.1.13; 3.1.6–3.1.10.

6) In accordance with modern practice a trial may well have begun in a meaningful sense if a jury has been selected but not sworn and the court deals with substantial matters of case management.
7) A case will be determined by its own facts and a judge should be willing to express a view.

5.55 Individual decisions include *R v Budai*[67] where it was held on the facts that the swearing of an interpreter on the day listed for trial, a panel of 18 jurors being selected, and the indictment being amended did not mean that a trial had begun. In *R v Bullingham*[68] although no jury had been empanelled there was a *voir dire* to determine the admissibility of some evidence; the trial began at that point. Difficulties remain which will have to be handled on an individual basis. An application to stay for abuse may be a stand-alone hearing or the beginning of the trial if the matter would have proceeded straight to the empanelment of the jury. Similarly it seems likely that a guilty plea at the end of legal argument as to whether the offence is made out would be a trial if a trial would have been listed had the submission failed. A trial commenced when there were discussions of significant evidential import with the consent of the judge on the day of the listing for trial (which resulted in an unexpected offer of a guilty plea to a lesser offence). In *Coles* discussions around timeline documents, involving a ten-handed conspiracy, were particularly important. This was a significant matter of case management within the decision in *Henery* point 6.[69] Similarly, on the facts in *R v Sallah* SCCO 281/18, a meaningful trial had begun when detailed submissions were made on the admissibility of evidence and the Crown, after consideration, offered no evidence before a jury was sworn.

5.56 A trial begins at the start of a formal preparatory hearing[70] and this would appear to be the case even if a guilty plea is entered as a result of the legal findings made at that hearing (CCFG 2.1.10 does not appear to be correct). The days used for the preparatory hearing count as days of trial.[71]

5.57 A trial also includes a Newton hearing.[72] If the planned Newton hearing does not take place, even by the reading of a section 9 statement or the making of section 10 admissions, the case reverts to its original

67 [2011] 6 Costs LR 1073.
68 [2011] 6 Costs LR 1078.
69 *R v Coles* SCCO 51/16.
70 *R v Jones* X 2000.
71 CCFG 2.1.10; 3.1.2–3.1.5.
72 See *R v Newton* (1982) 4 Cr App R (S) 388; and Sch 1 para 2(8), Sch 2 para 2(4); CCFG 2.2.2–5.

classification.[73] A costs judge held that if no evidence is received at the listed Newton hearing, having been heard while the defendant gave evidence at the trial of a co-defendant, the sentencing hearing did not amount to a Newton hearing.[74] However, the same judge held it was otherwise where a defendant prepares for a Newton Hearing and appears at it, when the court hears evidence given on matters which concern the disputed facts at the Newton hearing of a co-defendant, and then relies upon the evidence to support the submissions of this defendant's advocate, there will be Newton hearing within the Remuneration Regulations 2013. The judge has heard evidence on which he can make findings of fact which are disputed between the crown and this defendant The fact that it was led and cross examined for another defendant does not change that analysis. The defence had waited to hear this evidence before deciding whether to call evidence of their own and the judge referred to his findings in sentencing.[75]

5.58 If a Newton trial is listed but does not proceed because of the absence of a prosecution witness, the defence version then being accepted, it is the supplementary fee for an ineffective trial that is for that day payable to the advocate.[76] See 'supplementary costs' at paras 5.262–5.263 below.

5.59 A case is a trial notwithstanding that a trial jury could not agree.[77] A trial which 'settled' at the close of the prosecution case by a guilty plea to an additional lesser charge was a trial.[78] Once a trial has begun, there cannot be a cracked trial.[79]

5.60 Where there is a video cross-examination ahead of the first hearing at which a plea is entered, in accordance with the provisions of Youth Justice and Criminal Evidence Act 1999 s28, a trial has begun and each day of cross examination counts as a day of the trial (even though there is later a crack).[80]

Retrials[81]

5.61 The costs judges initially held that there can be a retrial in three circumstances:

73 Criminal Justice Act 1967. *R v Riddell* (X3); *R v Hunter-Brown* (X29); *R v Ayres* (X32).
74 R v Hunt [2016] 2 Costs LR 429.
75 R v Morfitt SCCO 55/16.
76 *R v Ayres* [2002] 2 Costs LR 330.
77 *R v Finn* [2006] 3 Costs LR 525.
78 *R v Alays* [2007] 2 Costs LR 321.
79 *R v Maynard* (X19); *R v Karra* (X19A).
80 CCFG Appendix R.
81 See CCFG 2.1.15–17, 2.2.7–11; 3.1, 3.1.27 and appendix O. The calculations of fees for retrials are considered in Part 5.2 at page 86 and in Part 5.3 at page 115.

1) The jury cannot reach agreement and the judge orders a retrial.
2) There is a successful appeal against conviction and there is a retrial.
3) There is a successful prosecution application to set aside an ordered acquittal and there is a retrial.

5.62 The stopping of a case part heard, for any other reason, is not always enough and the days of the original trial and retrial are added together to reach the length of trial uplift.

5.63 Thus when a trial commences but is abandoned after three days and there is then a gap of over three months before a full trial of seven days, there is no retrial but rather a trial of ten days.[82] See also *R v Nettleton*[83] and *R v Howitt*[84] where there was a gap of five months but still a single trial for costs purposes.

5.64 However, a degree of flexibility has been introduced by *R v Nettleton and others*.[85] Each case is fact specific and the 'temporal and procedural matrix' of the individual case falls to be considered. The appointment of a new judge to hear the second 'trial' will mean that for costs law there is a retrial. The fact that more evidence has been served between trials is not of itself enough. Consideration should be given to the question whether the second trial can be said to have picked up where the first had left off.

5.65 A cracked trial can follow a trial when a retrial date is fixed.[86]

5.66 The detailed analysis required to identify the best fee is shown by *R v Khan and others (ex Liverpool Crown Court T20117540)*[87] where, on the facts, it was held that a trial and retrial existed rather than a single trial.

5.67 The first trial of four days existed because:

- the judge indicated that the trial had begun;
- a jury was sworn;
- the Crown sought that the trial (at a later date) should continue but the judge ordered otherwise; and
- the court file showed an order for a new trial.

---

82 *R v Cato* SCCO 115/11, applying *R v Forsyth* SCCO 155/10 and *R v Seivwright* [2011] 2 Costs LR 327.
83 [2013] 1 Costs LR 186.
84 SCCO 386/12.
85 SCCO 58/13.
86 *Lord Chancellor v Purnell* [2009] EWHC 3158(QB); *R v Hussain* SCCO 217/13; *R v Chowdhury* [2009] 3 Costs LR 514.
87 SCCO 316/13.

5.68   There was then a sufficient break in the procedural and temporal matrix to allow for a fee for a retrial to be paid for the remaining 52 days when:
- An original advocate had for professional reasons to withdraw ending the original trial with new advocates for the second trial.
- The Crown sought an adjournment for the second part of the proceedings to submit new forensic evidence and this was allowed whereas it had been refused for the first trial.
- The court log indicated that there was an adjournment for a new trial and the judge had, against representations by the Crown, discharged the first jury.

5.69   Similarly in *R v Geeling*,[88] acknowledging that a trial does not necessarily require a jury to be sworn, there was on the facts a trial and retrial. The matter was listed in September 2010 for abuse of process arguments. The case then came before a jury in September 2011. The judge held that a gap of over a year will likely prevent a trial being continuous The test (*Seivwright*[89]) is whether the 'trial' and 'retrial' are part of the same temporal and procedural matrix. Here there was no procedural connection where the 'trial' was an abuse of process argument and the 'retrial' proceeded on a different indictment with fewer defendants and different counsel and after the service of some hundreds of pages of NAE and 18,000 pages in all including unused material. The fact that the same judge heard the case was not of necessity but for convenience. The first 'trial' had run its course.

5.70   When a new advocate conducts a retrial, that advocate must submit the fees claim.

Cracked trial[90]

5.71   A cracked trial exists if there is no trial (either because of a guilty plea or because the Crown offer no evidence) but the case in relation to any count proceeded beyond the first hearing at which the defendant indicates a not guilty plea to one or more charges. If no plea is entered, there cannot be a cracked trial.

5.72   Where a not guilty plea is entered and the case adjourned for a mention, a cracked trial exists.[91] If at, or after, the hearing at which a

---

88   SCCO 40/14.
89   [2011] 2 Costs LR 327.
90   CCFG 2,1,18–32; 3.1.14–3.1.26.
91   *R v Dawson* [1999] 1 Costs LR 4.

not guilty plea is entered, counts are severed and following acquittal on the first indictment no evidence is offered on the second, that second is a cracked trial.[92]

5.73 A retrial is a cracked trial if it cracks notwithstanding that a jury could not agree at the first trial.[93] Where a jury acquit of murder but could not agree on manslaughter or violent disorder and a date for a retrial is fixed at which the case does not proceed to trial, there is a trial fee (for the original trial) and a cracked trial fee in respect of the later events.[94] It is not an extension of the earlier trial. The fixing of the date or of a warned list for the retrial is the key[95] so that there is a real possibility of a retrial.

5.74 If a jury is selected but not sworn before the defendant pleads guilty, there may be a trial or a cracked trial.[96] Where a prosecution is stayed, the case is a cracked trial whether or not the advocate was present on the occasion of the stay.[97]

5.75 The severance of an indictment results in an additional case and if one case is ordered to remain on the file, that is a cracked trial.[98]

Guilty plea[99]

5.76 All other cases, including the Crown discontinuing or offering no evidence at or before the first hearing at which the defendant enters a not guilty plea, are classified as guilty pleas. A case where a trial date had been fixed before a not guilty plea is entered and an indication of guilty plea is then given, is classified as a guilty plea.[100] The fixing of a provisional trial date under early guilty plea procedures is not enough to create a trial for graduated fee purposes when the case concluded before a not guilty plea is entered – it was a guilty plea.[101]

5.77 Where a guilty plea is entered, a guilty plea fee is payable even though the full value of the offence is not known and there are to be

---

92 *R v Chubb* [2002] 2 Costs LR 333.
93 *R v Frampton* [2005] 3 Costs LR 527.
94 *Lord Chancellor v Purnell* [2009] EWHC 3158 (QB).
95 *R v Hussain* SCCO 217/13; *R v Chowdhury* [2009] 3 Costs LR 514 distinguishing *R v Pelepenko* SCCO 186/2001 where there was no expectation of a retrial. CCFG 3.1.24 is not a full description of the law.
96 *R v Coles* SCCO 51/16 cf *R v Sanghera* [2008] 5 Costs LR 823.
97 *R v Carty* [2009] 3 Costs LR 500.
98 *R v McCarthy* SCCO 36/17.
99 CCFG 2.1.18–32.
100 *Lord Chancellor v Frieze* [2007] EWHC 1490 (QB).
101 *Lord Chancellor v Woodhall* [2013] EWHC 764 (QB).

confiscation proceedings.[102] It will be otherwise if there is a Newton hearing which is always a trial for graduated fee purposes.

5.78 Special rules apply where a case, sent to the Crown Court, is dismissed by the judge before jury is empanelled.[103] See paras 5.161–5.164 and 5.282–5.284.

Number of days at trial

5.79 These may be days of trial or retrial and some ancillary hearings. The total is the number of days or part of a day that a trial (including a Newton hearing) lasts. In the case of a Newton hearing, the first day of trial is the day on which the plea is entered.[104] All days or part of a day spent considering ancillary matters during the course of the trial are included. Non-sitting days do not count.[105]

5.80 If an advocate is ordered to attend on a day when the jury does not sit and the court is not called upon to adjudicate on any issue, this day does not count towards the number of days of trial.[106]

5.81 A day on which sentence is imposed counts towards the length of trial if it takes place on the last day of the trial. However, if sentencing is adjourned the sentencing day does not count towards the length of trial uplift.

5.82 The number of days during which a cross examination by video is carried out under Youth Justice and Criminal Evidence Act 1999 s28 are all days of trial, even if there is later a guilty plea.

5.83 Special rules apply to determine the number of days of a trial if a hearing is held to determine whether the defendant is unfit to plead or stand trial:[107]

(a) if the trial continues, it is categorised as a trial adding the length of the fitness hearing to the trial length;
(b) if the trial does not continue, the litigator may elect for the most profitable of:
   (i) a trial fee, the length of trial being the combined length of hearings to determine fitness and under Criminal Procedure (Insanity) Act 1964 s4A as to whether the act was done or omission made;

---

102 *R v Harris* [2009] 3 Costs LR 507.
103 Sch 1 para 22, Sch 2 paras 21 and 22.
104 Sch 1 para 2(8), Sch 2 para 2(4); *R v Gemeskel* (X2).
105 *R v Nassir* (X13).
106 *R v Budai* [2011] 6 Costs LR 1073.
107 Remuneration Regulations 2013 Sch 1 para 31 and Sch 2 para 25.

(ii) a cracked trial fee; or
(iii) (available as an alternative if there is a guilty plea) a guilty plea fee.

Number of cases

5.84 A case means Crown Court proceedings against a single defendant, arising from a single indictment or notice of appeal or committal for sentence or breach of a Crown Court order.[108]

5.85 If an indictment is quashed and a new indictment for a different offence is preferred that will amount to a second case unless it is purely a tidying up exercise.[109]

5.86 Draft indictments become, on service by filing on the Digital Case System, an indictment and so count as a case.[110]

5.87 Severance creates a separate case and if one case is ordered to remain on the file, that is a cracked trial.[111]

5.88 The rules on the number of cases are applied mechanically to each individual set of circumstances. Fundamentally the issue is to identify the number of indictments involving each defendant. However, different iterations of the same indictment will be a single case.[112]

5.89 If there is more than one indictment, there will be as many cases as there are indictments if there has been no formal order for joinder[113] or if there has been a misjoinder.[114] The fact that the cases are listed together for directions and adjourned together[115] or listed together for sentence or indeed are sentenced together,[116] is not enough to make them a single case.

5.90 A voluntary bill creates an additional case if it is not formally joined.[117] Formal joinder would appear to reduce the number of indictments.[118]

---

108 Remuneration Regulations 2013 Sch 1 para 1 and Sch 2 para 1.
109 *R v Sharif* SCCO 168/13.
110 *Lord Chancellor v McCarthy* [2012] EWHC 2325 (QB). See also (in relation to terminating rulings) *R v PW* [2016] EWCA Crim 745. *R v T; R v Burton* [2018] EWCA Crim 2485.
111 *R v McCarthy* SCCO 36/17; CCFG 2.1.2–2.1.5, 3.1.2–3.1.5.
112 *Lord Chancellor v McCarthy* [2012] EWHC 2325 (QB).
113 *R v Hussain* [2011] 4 Costs LR 689.
114 *R v Bowen* [2011] 4 Costs LR 693.
115 *R v Forrester* [2012] 4 Costs LR 811.
116 *R v Ototo* SCCO 8/11.
117 *R v Bowen* [2011] 4 Costs LR 693.
118 *Lord Chancellor v Eddowes, Perry and Osbourne* [2011] EWHC 420 (QB).

5.91 A breach of the terms of a sentence imposed at the Crown Court must be treated as a separate case from the proceedings in which the order was made. A breach amounting to a criminal offence in its own right, which will be dealt with by an indictment or a committal for sentence, is also a separate case.

5.92 Once the number of cases has been calculated, different rules apply for litigators from those applicable to advocates.

5.93 This is significant for advocates, as a fee is payable for each advocate properly attending. Cases tried concurrently earn for the advocate the fee for the main hearing with a mark-up for each other case. The meaning of concurrent hearings is considered under the paragraph on mark-ups at para 5.244–5.247.[119] For litigators a full fee is paid for each separate indictment.

5.94 The summary hearing of a Bail Act allegation ahead of the main trial is treated as a standard appearance (see para 5.257). When a defendant is tried and acquitted on the third day on the first indictment and a second indictment is then cracked on that day the cases are not concurrent and two fees are payable.[120] For two cases to be heard concurrently, the main hearing in each case must have been heard at the same time.[121] If an indictment is severed these are separate cases.

5.95 It should be noted that once the number of cases has been identified, consideration must again be given to the page count. Only the papers relevant to each particular case may be counted[122] although there will be cases where all the pages are relevant to all the cases.

Litigators' graduated fees[123]

5.96 Great efficiency is required, as the fixed and graduated fees allow no room for unnecessary or repeated work.

---

119 *R v Fury* [2011] 5 Costs LR 919.
120 *R v Tooth* [2007] 2 Costs LR 302.
121 *R v Fletcher* (X6); *R v Fairhurst* (X6A).
122 *R v Brindle* SCCO 91/11.
123 Remuneration Regulations 2013 Sch 2. Claims are normally made on Form LF1.

Figure 5.1 Summary of calculation of litigator's fee

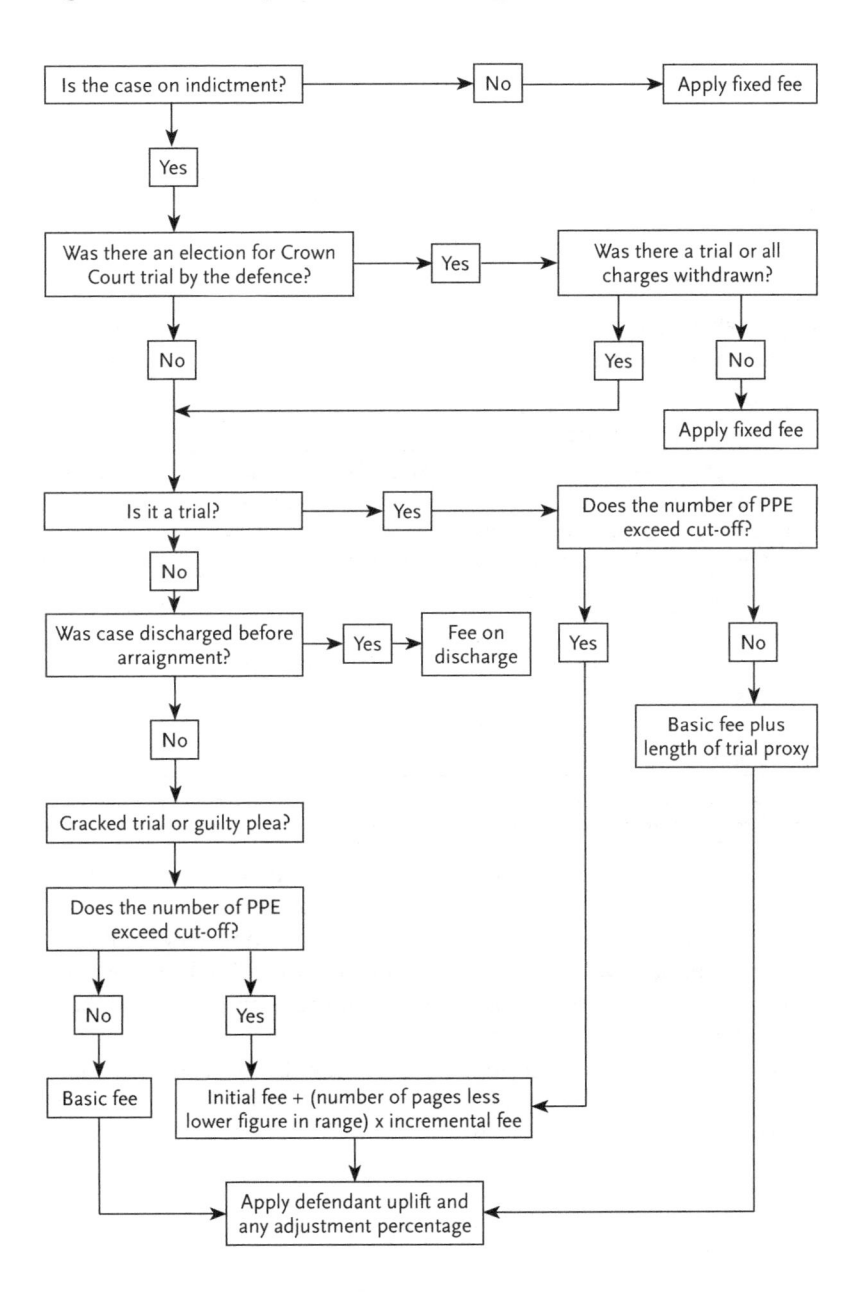

Non-indictable jurisdiction and post trial work

5.97 This jurisdiction is normally dealt with by fixed fees to which there are no additions, though the exceptional provisions on confiscation below may apply (and hourly rates apply to 'prescribed' proceedings: see chapter 10). The fee includes any attendance upon an advocate at the Crown Court and such attendances, unless required by professional duties, are unlikely to be made. The fees are given in the table (see below) and are exclusive of VAT.[124] These fees relate to cases beginning on or after 1 April 2016.

Attendance type	Fee
Appeal against sentence	£155.32
Appeal against conviction	£349.47
Committal for sentence	£232.98
Contempt proceedings[125] – involving a non-defendant (for defendants the work is covered by the normal fee). These proceedings should be distinguished from contempt in civil proceedings which are prescribed proceedings (see chapter 10)	£116.49
Breach of Crown Court order	£77.66
Hearing subsequent to sentence: Crime and Disorder Act 1998 s1CA (variation and discharge of orders under s1C)	£155.32
Powers of Criminal Courts (Sentencing) Act 2000 s155 (alteration of Crown Court sentence)	£155.32
Serious Organised Crime and Police Act 2005 s74 (assistance by defendant; review of sentence)	£155.32

5.98 There are no mark-ups for acting for additional defendants[126] but a separate fixed fee is paid for each appeal or committal.

5.99 The fact that cases are sentenced together is not relevant if they commenced as two cases. If the cases are committed on separate dates but listed together separate fixed fees remain payable as there were two sets of proceedings.[127]

5.100 Even if cases are committed on the same day for sentence there are separate proceedings and so separate cases when they were charged separately and there were:

---

124 Criminal Legal Aid (Remuneration) Regulations 2013 SI No 435 (Remuneration Regulations 2013) Sch 2 para 19.
125 Remuneration Regulations 2013 Sch 2 para 17.
126 *R v Sturmer and Lewis* SCCO 277/08, [2009] 2 Costs LR 364.
127 *R v Griffiths* SCCO 277/10.

a) two prosecution files;
b) two applications for a representation order;
c) two magistrates' court numbers;
d) two S numbers in the Crown Court;
e) two memoranda of conviction.[128]

5.101 Fixed fees for a committal for sentence or breach will be payable in addition to any litigator's graduate fee for a case that is sent for trial at the same time.

5.102 Solicitors will, prior to appeal or committal, need to consider with a client whether they can provide a professional service at such fees and advise clients appropriately where there are alternative ways to proceed. Thus, for example, if there are disputed facts on a guilty plea it will be necessary to consider with a client whether the fact that a trial fee is payable for a Newton hearing in the Crown Court may enable the case to be better prepared.

5.103 The fees for breach in this table are limited to breach of a Crown Court sentencing order.[129] Where the breach is itself a criminal offence, full graduated fees are available. Guidance is given in CCFG Appendix F. If a person commits two breaches of an order separately alleged, two fees will be payable.[130]

5.104 The fee for contempt proceedings is limited to contempt arising during the course of the criminal proceedings and not those that are identified as prescribed proceedings.

Representation in prescribed proceedings in the Crown Court

5.105 These are described in chapter 10 and may arise on an application to vary or discharge an order[131] and the Remuneration Regulations 2013 provide that hourly rates apply as if the work was carried out in the magistrates' court. Care should be taken not to exceed the fee limit of £1,368.75 without obtaining authority to do so on Form CRM5.

Indictable jurisdiction

Defence elections for trial in either way case which do not result in a trial or discontinuance of all charges

5.106 The normal rules, for cases where the magistrates' court declines jurisdiction, are set out below. Those rules also apply if a trial takes

128 *R v Schilling* SCCO 22/11.
129 CCFG Appendix I.
130 CCFG 3.18.
131 SCC B10.133–10.144.

96 Criminal Costs: legal aid costs in the criminal courts / chapter 5

place following a defence election, or if following such an election the Crown offers no evidence in relation to *all* matters.

5.107 However, a very rigid fixed fee scheme applies if, the particular defendant elects for trial, and there is no trial either because there is an acceptable plea by the defence to one or more matters. The fixed fee applies even if the Crown substitutes a different charge to which the defendant would have pleaded guilty in the magistrates' court.

5.108 The fixed fee is £330.33 per set of proceedings for all cases where the representation order is dated on or after 1 April 2016.[132]

5.109 The fixed fee for advocacy is paid in addition.

5.110 If there are confiscation proceedings, the normal rules (at paras 5.165–5.183) apply in addition to the fixed fee.

Other cases on indictment

5.111 The following rules apply in:
- indictable only cases;
- either way cases where the magistrates' court declines jurisdiction;
- either way cases categorised as a trial notwithstanding a defence election;
- an either way defence election case when the Crown offers no evidence on all charges.

5.112 To calculate the appropriate fee, six pieces of information are required. Each is considered in this chapter:
A   What class is the case in
B   How many pages of prosecution evidence are there
C   What category is the case in (guilty plea/cracked trial/trial)
D   How long is any trial
E   How many defendants were represented
F   For what proportion of the case was the defendant represented.

5.113 Subject to very limited exceptions (see paras 5.165–5.179) there are no additional payments and no payment is made for attendance upon an advocate. When the proceedings are sent to the Crown Court under Crime and Disorder Act 1998 s51 there is no fee for that part of the magistrates' court case other than as part of the litigator's fee.

132 Remuneration Regulations 2013 Sch 2 para 11.

Crown Court work 97

1) The offence classification[133]

5.114 For litigators' fees there are 11 classes of work. They are summarised as follows and the full schedule appears in appendix G.

A Homicide and related grave offences (and Mental Health Act 1983 s41)
B Serious violence or damage and serious drugs offences
C Lesser offences in same groups as B
D Sexual offences and offences against children (and unfit to plead (on election)) but also see J below)
E Burglary
F Other offences of dishonesty (but see G and K)
G Other offences of dishonesty if exceeding £30,000 (and see also K below)

The fees payable for Classes F and G are now the same but the distinction remains important in confiscation proceedings as enhancement of fees is available for confiscation work in Class G.

H Miscellaneous (and residuary)
I Offences against public justice
J Serious sexual offences
K High value offences of dishonesty (exceeding £100,000)

5.115 The fee is based on the charges faced by the particular defendant represented.[134]

5.116 Inchoate offences fall within the same class as the completed offence.[135]

5.117 If a case involves allegations in more than one class, the lawyer may choose whichever is more profitable.[136] This includes reliance placed upon an allegation contained in a draft indictment even though that charge was not put at the plea and trial preparation hearing (PTPH)[137] (previously a plea and case management hearing).

5.118 Class A may be used if the case concludes with a restriction order under Mental Health Act 1983 s41.[138] If a defendant is unfit to plead or stand trial, the lawyer may, if he or she chooses, select Class D.[139]

---

133 CCFG 3.3.
134 *R v Mira* (X54); *R v Martini*; CCFG 2.3.4 and Appendix J.
135 Remuneration Regulations 2013 Schs 1 and 2 para 3(1)(b).
136 Remuneration Regulations 2013 Sch 1 para 27; Sch 2 para 24.
137 *Lord Chancellor v McCarthy* [2012] EWHC 2325 (QB).
138 Remuneration Regulations 2013 Schs 1 and 2 para 3(1)(g).
139 Remuneration Regulations 2013 Schs 1 and 2 para 3(1)(f).

5.119 A robbery (Class C) is an armed robbery (Class B) if either the defendant was armed with a firearm or an imitation, or the victim so believed, or the defendant was in possession of an offensive weapon: *R v Stables*.[140] The analysis in *R v Stables* has been placed in guidance issued by the LAA (CCFG 2.3.7–2.3.14), which confirms that there will be an armed robbery where:

> (a) ... a defendant or co-defendant to the offence was armed with a firearm or imitation firearm, or the victim thought that they were so armed, eg the Defendant purported to be armed with a gun and the victim believed him to be so armed although it subsequently turned out that he was not ...
>
> (b) where the defendant or co-defendant to the offence was in possession of an offensive weapon, namely a weapon that had been made or adapted for use for causing injury to or incapacitating a person, or intended by the person having it with him for such use. However, where the defendant, or co-defendant, only intimate that they are so armed, the case should not be classified as an armed robbery. ...

5.120 There are three categories of offensive weapon covered by the offence:

i) *Articles made for causing injury to the person.* Articles falling within this category are considered to be offensive weapons per se, and there is no need to go on to consider the intention or purpose of the person carrying them. An important criterion in determining whether or not a particular weapon comes within this category appears to be that the article in question has no other reasonable use. The LAA has produced a list in guidance (CCFG Appendix P) of weapons which have been classified as offensive weapons under legislation. This guidance was confirmed in *R v Tai*[141] when a robbery whilst in possession of a knuckle duster (a weapon made or adapted to cause injury to a person) was held to be in Class B as an armed robbery. Because of amendments by the Criminal Justice Act 1988 (Offensive Weapons) (Amendment) Order 2016[142] this classification will also cover zombie knives, zombie killer knives and zombie slayer knives.

ii) *Articles that have been adapted for use for causing injury to the person*, such as sharpened screwdrivers, deliberately broken bottles and so on. Many household and industrial items are capable of being modified in this way, so inclusion in or exclusion from this

---

140 *R v Stables* (X12), 1999.
141 SCCO 4/16.
142 SI No 803.

category is once again largely a matter of fact to be determined on a case-by-case basis.

iii) *Articles that are not specifically made or adapted for the purpose of causing injury, but which may be considered offensive if court or jury a decides that the defendant intended them to be used for the purpose of causing injury to the person.* Examples might include a sledgehammer or axe. The determining officer has a discretion to allow a claim to be paid as an armed robbery or robbery where the Defendant has an article that is not made or adapted for the purpose of causing injury. A case is more likely to be paid as an armed robbery where the article is similar in nature to an offensive weapon listed in CCFG Appendix P. Whether the item is capable of causing serious and long term injury will be the determining factor, taking into account all of the facts of the case.

5.121 The snatch of a telephone from a moped would be in Class C but the use of the moped as a weapon will make B the correct classification[143] as an offensive weapon will have been used. Those are not limited to those listed in the Criminal Justice Act 1988 (Offensive Weapons) Order 1988 SI No 2019. A motorcycle helmet used as a weapon in a robbery was an offensive weapon in *R v Day* SCCO 173/18 and a wooden chair in *R v St Martin* SCCO 141/15. A shod foot was also used but no decision was announced on whether that could be an offensive weapon.

5.122 When a defendant is charged with attempting to cause or inflict GBH, without any reference to Offences against the Person Act 1861 s18 or s20, a claim should be made in Class B.[144]

5.123 Allegations of dishonesty may fall into one of three classes depending on the amount alleged to be involved. In undertaking this calculation, the value of alternative charges cannot be used more than once. The value of offences taken into consideration (TICs) may not be used.[145] However, the values are otherwise aggregated.[146] If the full value does not appear on the face of the indictment, it is necessary to produce other evidence to satisfy this requirement, such as the prosecution case opening or summary; prosecution statements;[147] or a letter from the prosecution or court. The burden of

---

143 *R v Jedran* SCCO 54/18.
144 CCFG 3.3.10; *R v Davis* as intent is required for an attempt.
145 *R v Knight* (X35).
146 Remuneration Regulations 2013 Sch 2 para 3(1)(d).
147 *R v Nelson* SCCO 417/09.

proof is on the defence lawyer to the civil standard and a common sense view should be taken of the values involved in the case.[148]

5.124 An allegation of conspiracy to burgle may include an aggravated burglary and so allow a claim in Class B.[149] This remained the case even though the indictment referred to basic burglary if, on the facts, the allegation against an individual defendant involved allegations of aggravated burglary. Reclassification is not based purely on the offence alleged but on a detailed analysis of the basis on which the Crown brings its case.

5.125 All offences under section 170(1) (but not section 170(2)) of the Customs and Excise Management Act 1979 can fall in to the dishonesty categories and thus a choice can be made between those classes and the classes appropriate for drugs, whichever results in a higher payment.[150]

5.126 Sexual offences fall into Class D or Class J, depending on the specific offence charged.

5.127 If a case involves offences which do not appear in the schedules, the claim is in Class H. Where there is dissatisfaction with the Class H classification, an application can be made to the appropriate officer to reclassify the offence to one that is more appropriate in all the circumstances of the particular case.[151] This must imply opportunities to argue that, although the offence does not appear in the table of offences, a different classification should apply. This is certainly true of offences created since the table was last reviewed. This group will include offences under Prison Act 1952 s40B (inserted by the Offender Management Act 2007) of taking drugs into a prison which should be classified as Class B. Cases involving the mentally ill that fall in Class H may be more appropriately classified as Class D (which is used where there is unfitness to plead).

5.128 In *Environment Agency v Flanagan*[152] the work undertaken was akin to that undertaken in a fraud trial and the Crown alleged dishonesty, even though that was not an ingredient of the offence charged. That offence had fallen in Class H and so could be reclassified.

5.129 The most appropriate category for keeping a brothel is D.[153]

5.130 Trade mark offences have been classed as F, G or K if they could alternatively have been charged as offences of dishonesty. Bigamy

---

148 *R v Garness* SCCO 132/13.
149 *R v Nutting* SCCO 215/13, [2013] Costs LR 1037.
150 *Lord Chancellor v Ahmed* [2014] 1 Costs LR 21.
151 Remuneration Regulations 2013 Schs 1 and 2 para 3(2) and (3).
152 SCCO 215/13.
153 *R v Somers* SCCO 162/11.

(Offences against the Person Act 1861 s57) would appear to be better placed in Class C.

5.131 Outside Class H the classification is rigid. Thus a conspiracy to commit an offence in a specific class (in this case B) is also in the same class even if it might have involved dishonesty otherwise placing it in Class K.[154]

5.132 A hearing whether contested or otherwise relating to breach of bail, failure to surrender to bail or on the execution of a bench warrant is classified not as an offence at all but as a 'standard appearance'.

5.133 A claim for costs should include a copy of the indictment. The content of a representation order is not acceptable to the LAA.

2) The number of PPE – PPE in excess of 10,000 pages[155]

5.134 See paras 5.4–5.49 for the identification of PPE.

5.135 If a case, which is not a very high cost case (VHCC), has more than 10,000 pages, it is treated as having 10,000 pages for the calculation of the graduated fee. The 10,000 page cut-off is lawful (see para 5.170 below).

5.136 Special preparation may then be claimed for the number of pages by which the PPE exceeds 10,000. The fee is calculated on the number of hours it reasonably takes to read the excess, by a fee earner of the grade actually and reasonably used.

5.137 Special preparation can also be claimed where a case is heard on indictment and any of the relevant prosecution material is served in electronic form only, does not count towards PPE, and it is reasonable to make an additional payment based on the number of hours considered reasonable to view the material at the hourly rates appearing below. Electronic evidence is any document provided on CD-ROM or by other means of electronic communication. It does not include audio or video cassettes. To claim the time reasonably spent considering a CD-ROM, it must contain evidence (and not unused material) which falls within the definition of Remuneration Regulations 2013 Sch 2 para 1(2), as amended (see para 5.7).

5.138 If the electronic evidence includes prosecution evidence or exhibits it is often financially advantageous to claim the PPE mark-up described at paras 5.4–5.49 when this is possible.

5.139 More information on special preparation appears at paras 5.168–5.179.

---

154 *R v O'Donnell and Fawley* [2012] 2 Costs LR 431.
155 An attempt to reduce the maximum page count for PPE to 6,000 pages was set aside in *R (Law Society) v Lord Chancellor* [2018] EWHC 2094 (Admin).

3) Whether the case is a trial, cracked or guilty plea

5.140 A case is a trial if the rules at paras 5.51–5.60 apply or there is a Newton hearing. A case is a cracked trial if it is not resolved by a guilty plea or an acquittal at the first hearing at which a plea is indicated. A case is a guilty plea if it is resolved by an acquittal or conviction at or before the first hearing at which a plea is indicated.

5.141 Special rules apply when there has been a Crime and Disorder Act 1998 s51 sending and the case is discontinued before any evidence is served or an application is made to dismiss (see paras 5.161–5.164).

4) The length of a trial

5.142 See paras 5.79–5.83.

5.143 If a case which is not a VHCC lasts more than 200 days, it is treated as if it lasted 200 days.[156]

5) The number of defendants represented

5.144 The multipliers applicable also appear at appendix H and are set out below:

Total number represented	Percentage uplift
2–4	20%
5 +	30%

6) The proportion of the case on which the litigator represented the defendant and when there is more than one trial[157]

5.145 If a firm does not represent a defendant throughout a case, or the case goes to retrial (as to which see paras 6.61–6.70 above), only a percentage of the calculated fee will apply in accordance with the complex provisions of Remuneration Regulations 2013 Sch 2 para 13. The details appear at appendix H and are set out below.

5.146 In cases which have been sent for trial at the election of the defendant, the initial fee payable on a transfer is £330.33 (from 1 April 2016). However, if a trial does in fact result the original litigator is entitled to claim the balance of the fee due under the table that follows, but giving credit for the amount already received.

---

156 Remuneration Regulations 2013 Sch 2 para 2(6).
157 CCFG 3.13.

Scenario	Percentage of the total fee	Case type used to determine total fee	Timing of claim
Cracked trial before retrial where there is no change of litigator	25%	Cracked trial	–
Retrial, where there is no change of litigator	25%	Trial	–
Transfer at or before the first hearing at which the assisted person enters a plea (original litigator)	25%	Cracked trial	–
Transfer at or before the first hearing at which the assisted person enters a plea – guilty plea (new litigator)	100%	Guilty plea	–
Transfer at or before the first hearing at which the assisted person enters a plea – cracked trial (new litigator)	100%	Cracked trial	–
Transfer at or before the first hearing at which the assisted person enters a plea – trial (new litigator)	100%	Trial	–
Before trial transfer (original litigator)	75%	Cracked trial	–
Before trial transfer – cracked trial (new litigator)	100%	Cracked trial	–
Before trial transfer – trial (new litigator)	100%	Trial	–
During trial transfer (original litigator)	100%	Trial	Claim up to and including the day before the transfer

Scenario	Percentage of the total fee	Case type used to determine total fee	Timing of claim
During trial transfer (new litigator)	50%	Trial	Claim for the full trial length
Transfer after trial or guilty plea and before sentencing hearing (original litigator)	100%	Trial, cracked trial or guilty plea as appropriate	Claim for the full trial length excluding the length of the sentencing hearing
Transfer after trial or guilty plea and before sentencing hearing (new litigator)	10%	Trial	Claim for one day or for the length of the sentencing hearing if longer than one day
Transfer before retrial (original litigator)	25%	Cracked trial	–
Transfer before cracked retrial (new litigator)	50%	Cracked trial	–
Transfer before retrial (new litigator)	50%	Trial	Claim for the full retrial length
Transfer during retrial (original litigator)	25%	Trial	Claim up to and including the day before the transfer
Transfer during retrial (new litigator)	50%	Trial	Claim for the full retrial length
Transfer after retrial or cracked retrial and before sentencing hearing (original litigator)	25%	Trial or cracked trial as appropriate	Claim for the full retrial length, excluding the length of the sentencing hearing
Transfer after retrial or cracked retrial and before sentencing hearing (new litigator)	10%	Trial	Claim for one day or for the length of the sentencing hearing if longer than one day

The proportions shown are of the total fee so that the original page count is included.

A litigator may not be treated as both the original and a new litigator in the same case. A transfer occurs if the defendant had previously represented himself or been privately represented by the same firm. A case is not treated as transferred where:

a) a firm of solicitors is named as litigator in the representation order and the solicitor or other appropriately qualified person with responsibility for the case moves to another firm;

b) a firm of solicitors is named as litigator in the representation order and the firm changes (whether by merger or acquisition or in some other way), but so that the new firm remains closely related to the firm named in the order; or

c) a solicitor or other appropriately qualified person is named as litigator in the representation order, and responsibility for the case is transferred to another solicitor or appropriately qualified person in the same firm or a closely related firm.

5.147 Where a case is transferred to a new litigator and then transferred again, that litigator is treated as follows:

Scenario	Litigator treatment
Transfer before trial or retrial	Original litigator
Transfer during trial or retrial	New litigator
Transfer after trial or retrial but before the sentencing hearing	No payment to be made

5.148 Because of the need for certainty in a graduated fee scheme, there must be defined point of time, which can be objectively ascertained, at which a transfer takes place. This is the signing of an amendment to the representation order being seen and accepted by the solicitor whose acceptance is subject to carrying out proper conflict checks. As a result courts should, before amending an order, ensure that the solicitor has seen a full list of witnesses and a case summary.[158]

5.149 The page count for PPE is that at the date of transfer away. The trial length is also determined at that point.[159]

5.150 Where a representation order is withdrawn this is treated as a transfer away from the litigator at the date of withdrawal.

---

158 *Tuckers Solicitors v Lord Chancellor* [2013] EWHC 3817 (QB).
159 CCFG 3.13.4.

5.151 Where a defendant has self-represented or paid privately and a representation order is then granted, this is treated as a transfer to a new litigator.[160]

Retrial fees

5.152 Remuneration Regulations 2013 Sch 2 para 13 identifies how fees for retrials are calculated and this emphasises the need to identify whether the particular case is a trial and retrial, a longer trial, or more than one trial Page count does not increase if there is a retrial.

> 13 (1) Where following a trial an order is made for a retrial and the same litigator acts for the assisted person at both trials the fee payable to that litigator is–
> (a) in respect of the first trial, a fee calculated in accordance with the provisions of this Schedule; and
> (b) in respect of the retrial, 25% of the fee, as appropriate to the circumstances of the retrial, in accordance with the provisions of this Schedule.

VHCC cases

5.153 Special rules apply in VHCC cases. When a case is transferred to a new litigator[161] because it is a VHCC, the outgoing solicitor is paid by the Complex Crime Unit (CCU) at VHCC rates for the work actually and reasonably done by them. The payment is under the individual VHCC contracts unless the representation order is withdrawn when the table above applies.[162]

Calculation of the litigator graduated fee

5.154 The calculation is best done on the LAA litigator fee calculator available at: www.justice.gov.uk. However, as with all computer systems, care is needed in their operation to ensure that the correct claims are made.

5.155 In managing a case, solicitors will wish to calculate in advance the likely fee. The following stages apply.

Stage 1

5.156 Identify whether the number of PPE exceeds the relevant cut-off identified for cracked trials, guilty pleas and trial.

---

160 CCFG 3.13.6.
161 Remuneration Regulations 2013 Sch 2 para 13(8).
162 Remuneration Regulations 2013 Sch 2 para 13(9).

Crown Court work 107

Stage 2

5.157 If the number does *not* exceed the cut-off, the payments below are due.

Number of pages not exceeding cut-off for cracked trials and guilty pleas

a) A basic fee.
b) A defendant uplift on the basic fee for the number represented by the firm.
c) An adjustment of the basic fee if the firm did not act throughout the case.

Number of pages not exceeding cut-off for trials

a) A basic fee.
b) A length of trial uplift/depending on the number of days of trial.
c) A defendant uplift on (a) and (b) for the number represented by the firm.
d) An adjustment of the total of (a) and (b) if the firm did not act throughout the case.

Stage 3

5.158 If the number of PPE *exceeds* the 'cut off', the payments below are due.

Number of pages exceeding cut-off for cracked trials and guilty pleas

A 'final' fee as defined below.
A final fee (F) is represented by:

$I + (D \times i)$

where:
- I is the initial fee as appropriate for the class of case;
- D is the number of pages minus the lower figure and of the relevant PPE range; and
- i is the incremental fee per page set out;

and a defendant uplift on the final fee for the number represented by the firm (and an adjustment on the final fee if the firm did not act throughout the case).

Number of pages exceeding cut-off for trials

A 'final' fee as defined below.
A final fee (F) is represented by:

$I + (D \times i)$

where:
- I is the initial fee as appropriate for the class of case;
- D is the number of pages of relevant prosecution material *minus* the lower figure of the relevant PPE range; and
- i is the incremental fee per page;

and a defendant uplift on the final fee for the number represented by the firm (and an adjustment to the final fee if the firm did not act throughout the case).

5.159 The uplifts for the number of defendants represented by a firm are set out in appendix H.

5.160 The adjustment for firms that do not act throughout apply when this is a transfer of legal aid or a representation order is withdrawn or a VHCC is agreed, or there is a retrial. These appear above and at appendix H.

Discontinuances and dismissals[163]

5.161 Special rules apply where the proceedings have been sent or transferred.[164]

5.162 When those proceedings are discontinued or dismissed fees are payable as follows:

Scenario	Fee
If proceedings discontinued prior to service of the evidence	50% of the appropriate basic guilty plea fee
If proceedings discontinued or dismissed on a defence application (with any surviving allegations remitted to the magistrates' court)	The full fee appropriate for a guilty plea

5.163 Defendant uplifts apply to these figures.[165]

5.164 An application to dismiss which does not succeed adds no value to the litigator's fee.

Escape provisions: additional payments; special preparation[166] and confiscation

5.165 These are very limited. The graduated fees include any attendance upon an advocate at court and such attendances, unless required by professional duties, are unlikely to be provided.

---

163 For worked examples, see CCFG Appendix G; CCFG 3.21.
164 Crime and Disorder Act 1998 s51; Remuneration Regulations 2013 Sch 2 para 21.
165 Remuneration Regulations 2013 Sch 2 para 22.
166 In relation to confiscation, reference should be made to CCFG Appendix Q.

5.166　　No additional fee is normally payable for any work done in connection with a sentencing or deferred sentencing hearing.

Unused material in long cases

5.167　　Significant risks of injustice arise in cases with significant amounts of unused material as no additional provision is made for the situation. A firm's only remedy, in a case that may exceed 25 days at trial, is to seek a VHCC contract if the firm is on the VHCC panel or can reach a suitable agency agreement with such a firm.

Special preparation (Sch 2 para 20), ie (i) electronic evidence and PPE in excess of 10,000 and (ii) confiscation proceedings (Sch 2 para 26) [167]

5.168　　Hourly rates are available for special preparation –

(a) where a documentary or pictorial exhibit is served by the prosecution in electronic form and–
   (i) the exhibit has never existed in paper form; and
   (ii) the appropriate officer does not consider it appropriate to include the exhibit in the pages of prosecution evidence; or
(b) in respect of pages of prosecution evidence which exceed 10,000.

5.169　　Because the rules for payment of special preparation by litigators and by advocates are different, careful consideration may be given to how the work on a case is to be divided between them. Unused material may often advantageously be considered by the advocate.

5.170　　The 10,000 page limit is lawful.[168] The Remuneration Regulations 2013 provides that:

> 20(3)　The amount of the special preparation fee must be calculated from the number of hours which the appropriate officer considers reasonable–
>
> (a) where sub-paragraph (1)(a) applies, to view the prosecution evidence; and
> (b) where sub-paragraph (1)(b) applies, to *read* the excess pages.

5.171　　In *R v Starynskyj*[169] this was given a very restrictive meaning as excluding the administrative task of scheduling (following *R v Nazir*[170]) whilst acknowledging that this may lead to additional reading time. It

---

167　Use Form LF1 special preparation to validate the claim. See CCFG 3.20.
168　*R v Jagelo* 2015 SCCO 96/15.
169　SCCO 9/16.
170　SCCO 135/13.

is suggested that making notes including, if this is easiest, making notes in a schedule, *while* reading, the provision should allow for reasonable remuneration. Careful attendance records should be kept.

5.172 If the work is actually and reasonably undertaken, these extra payments will be paid by the appropriate hourly rate for the work in connection with such material. This will only apply to material that would qualify as PPE if that material were in paper form.[171] An audio record, even though served as evidence or an exhibit, cannot count towards page count or (for that reason) as special preparation, save to the extent that they are reduced by the Crown to a transcript.[172]

5.173 The work is remunerated depending on the grade of fee earner engaged in the following areas:[173]

a) for preparation, including taking instructions, interviewing witnesses, ascertaining the prosecution case, preparing and perusing documents, dealing with letters and telephone calls, instructing an advocate and expert witnesses, conferences, consultations and work done in connection with advice on appeal;
b) for attending at court where an advocate is instructed including conferences with the advocate at court; attendances are often made in such cases;
c) for travelling and waiting; and
d) for writing routine letters and dealing with routine telephone calls.

Chapter 1 sets out the relevant considerations.

5.174 Fee earners are at three grades. These are defined by Remuneration Regulations 2013 reg 2.

5.175 Senior solicitor (Grade A) means a solicitor who in the judgment of the appropriate officer has the skill knowledge and experience to deal with the most difficult and complex cases.

5.176 Solicitor, legal executive or fee earner of equivalent experience (Grade B) means a solicitor, Fellow of the Institute of Legal Executives or equivalent senior fee earner who in the judgment of the appropriate officer has good knowledge and experience of the conduct of criminal cases.

5.177 Trainee solicitor or fee earner of equivalent experience (Grade C) means a trainee solicitor or other fee earner who is not a Fellow of the Institute of Legal Executives who in the judgment of the appropriate officer carries out routine work on a case.

5.178 Grade A is a senior solicitor and so must be qualified. Grade B is a solicitor, legal executive or fee earner of equivalent experience.

---

171 *Lord Chancellor v Michael J Reed Ltd* [2009] EWHC 2981 (QB).
172 *Lord Chancellor v McLarty & Co Solicitors* [2011] EWHC 3182 (QB).
173 Sch 2 para 27: sub paras (b)–(d) only apply to confiscation proceedings.

Grade C is for trainees and those of equivalent experience. It must be reasonable to use the fee earner of the relevant grade.

5.179 In making that decision, not only is the complexity of the case relevant,[174] but the nature of the defendant.[175] TONG suggests that Grade A fee earners will deal with cases in classes 1 and 2[176] and the unusually serious or complex cases in other classes but subject in both cases to appropriate delegation. Complexity is of particular relevance in confiscation proceedings.[177] There is a rule of thumb that about seven years' experience of criminal work is required but with specialist firms the experience can be gained more quickly.[178] An unqualified but experienced member of staff may qualify as a Grade B fee earner and attention can be given to the person's total experience of criminal law.[179] The definitions in the Remuneration Regulations 2013 suggest that if the work conducted is more than routine Grade B at least should be claimed. Those attending court in confiscation proceedings will often need to read themselves in to a case if they are not the fee earner handling the matter.

Enhanced fees in confiscation cases (Sch 2 para 2)

5.180 Additional payments are also available in connection with confiscation proceedings and this should be separately recorded. For this reason, a confiscation file should be opened at the first opportunity as the fees are additional to the graduated fees. The work relates to all confiscation cases including those committed under Proceeds of Crime Act 2002 s70.

5.181 For work in connection with confiscation proceedings only, enhancement remains available on the terms that follow. A fee earner of a lower grade undertaking work beyond the skills normally expected at that level may justify enhancement (principles are set out in chapter 1):

1) Enhancement is available for preparation, attendance at court where more than one representative is instructed, routine letters

---

174 *R v Green* TMC S13.
175 *R v Bury Magistrates' Court ex p Cornthwaite* CO 296/95.
176 As defined, in the original guidance by the Consolidated Criminal Practice Direction: Classification of Crown Court Business and Allocation to Crown Court Centres. This appears now to accord with Classes 1 and 2 of the Criminal Practice Directions XIII Part B1, Classification.
177 See also *R v Halcrow* TMC S14.
178 *R v Badham* SCTO 621/93.
179 *R v Ali* TMC S12.

written and routine telephone calls in respect of offences in Classes A, B, C, D, G, I, J or K in the table of offences.
2) Enhanced fees are payable if taking into account all the relevant circumstances of the case:
   a) the work was done with exceptional competence, skill or expertise;
   b) the work was done with exceptional despatch; or
   c) the case involved exceptional complexity or other exceptional circumstances.
   Exceptional means unusual or out of the ordinary compared with the generality of criminal proceedings.
3) Enhancement is paid by a percentage uplift dependent on:
   a) the degree of responsibility accepted by the fee earner;
   b) the care, speed and economy with which the case was prepared; and
   c) the novelty, weight and complexity of the case;
   but because of the decision in *Backhouse* will not be less than 100 per cent which is also the maximum;[180] see chapter 1 above on enhancement generally).

5.182 Enhancement is not available for the special preparation in considering pages over 10,000 or electronic material.[181]

Hourly rates[182]

5.183 These rates are exclusive of VAT and apply to cases with a representation order dated on or after 1 April 2016.

Class of work	Grade of fee earner	Rate	Variations
Preparation	Senior solicitor	£48.36 per hour	£50.87 per hour for a litigator whose office is situated within the City of London or a London borough
	Solicitor, legal executive or fee earner of equivalent experience	£41,06 per hour	£43.12 per hour for a litigator whose office is situated within the City of London or a London borough

---

180 *R v Backhouse* TMC S3.
181 *Lord Chancellor v McLarty & Co Solicitors* [2011] EWHC 3182 (QB); *R v Brandon* [2012] 2 Costs LR 424.
182 Remuneration Regulations 2013 Sch 2 para 27.

Attendance at court where more than one representative instructed	Trainee or fee earner of equivalent experience	£27.15 per hour	£31.03 per hour for a litigator whose office is situated within the City of London or a London borough
	Senior solicitor	£38.55 per hour	–
	Solicitor, legal executive or fee earner of equivalent experience	£31.03 per hour	–
	Trainee or fee earner of equivalent experience	£18.71 per hour	–
Travelling and waiting	Senior solicitor	£22.58 per hour	–
	Solicitor, legal executive or fee earner of equivalent experience	£22.58 per hour	–
	Trainee or fee earner of equivalent experience	£11.41 per hour	–
Writing routine letters and dealing with routine telephone calls		£3.15 per item	£3.29 per item for a litigator whose office is situated within the City of London or a London borough

Special circumstances

Warrant cases (Sch 2 para 23)[183]

5.184 Where a defendant fails to appear and a warrant is issued and not executed for three months, special rules apply.

183 See CCFG 3.23.

Indictable cases

1) If the warrant is issued at or before the first hearing at which a plea is entered, a guilty plea fee is payable.
2) If the warrant is issued after the first hearing at which a plea is entered but before trial, a cracked trial fee is payable.
3) If the warrant is issued during trial and the trial aborts, a trial fee is payable as if the trial ended on that day.

Fixed fee cases

1) The appropriate fee is paid.
2) If the warrant is then executed within 15 months and the matter proceeds, credit has to be given for the amount already paid. After 15 months a further full fee would be paid.

Retrials

5.185 If there is a retrial, as now defined (see paras 5.61–5.70), two bills are delivered; one for the original and one for the retrial. The second bill abates in accordance with the table in appendix H.

Evidence provision fee[184]

5.186 As part of the implementation of Crown Court means testing an evidence provision fee was introduced where solicitors assist a client to provide documents in support of an application. This fee is only payable if the case is on indictment and evidence is required and provided above what is needed for the magistrates' court.

5.187 The fee is set at two levels:

£45	Where 1–4 items of such a kind are provided.
£90	Where 5 or more items of such a kind are provided; or where a case involves a self-employed applicant and is referred to the National Courts Team.

Disbursements (reg 17)

5.188 Disbursements including travel expenses connected to preparation or court attendance are payable in addition to the litigator's graduated fee. Vouchers for disbursements over £20 should be sent to the LAA; vouchers for those over £10 should be kept on file. Disbursements are considered in more detail in chapter 8.

---

184 See CCFG Appendix K.

Advocacy in the Crown Court[185]

5.189 Fees are as follows.

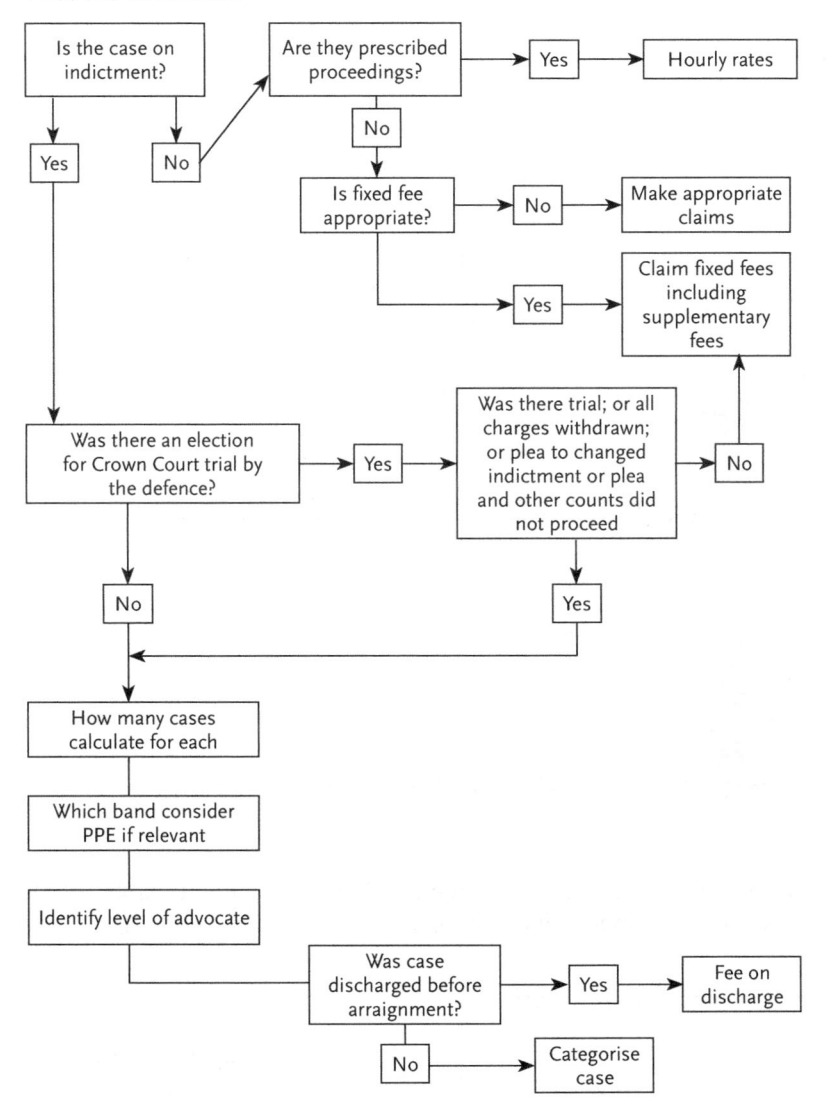

```
[Is the case on indictment?]
  │
  ├── Yes ──────────────────────────┐
  │                                  │
  └── No ──> [Are they prescribed proceedings?]
                │
                ├── Yes ──> Hourly rates
                │
                └── No ──> [Is fixed fee appropriate?]
                              │
                              ├── No ──> Make appropriate claims
                              │
                              └── Yes ──> Claim fixed fees including supplementary fees
                                              ▲
                                              │
   [Was there an election for Crown Court     │
    trial by the defence?]                    │
        │                                     │
        ├── Yes ──> [Was there trial; or all charges withdrawn; or plea to changed indictment or plea and other counts did not proceed]
        │                │                    │
        │                ├── No ──────────────┘
        │                │
        │                └── Yes ──┐
        │                          │
        └── No ───────────────────>┤
                                   ▼
                    [How many cases calculate for each]
                                   │
                    [Which band consider PPE if relevant]
                                   │
                    [Identify level of advocate]
                                   │
                    [Was case discharged before arraignment?]
                              │
                              ├── Yes ──> Fee on discharge
                              │
                              └── No ──> Categorise case
```

---

185 Remuneration Regulations 2013 Sch 1. Claims are normally made on Form AF1.

```
                Trial          Cracked trial        G PLEA
                  │                 │                  │
           ┌──────┴─────┐    ┌──────┴──────┐     ┌─────┴─────┐
           │How many days│   │ When cracked│──┬──│ 1st       │
           └──────┬─────┘    └──────┬──────┘  │  │ 2nd       │──▶
                  │             3rd Third     │  │ Third     │
                  │                 │         │  └─────┬─────┘
                 FEE               FEE                FEE
```

Indictable crime
ADD IN EACH CASE

Mark up for number of Defendants

Supplementary fees

If more than one case were they heard concurrently

```
           ┌──────┴──────┐
          No             Yes
           │              │
      Full fee       Add 20% to
      for each       best fee
```

Consider nature of a re-trial

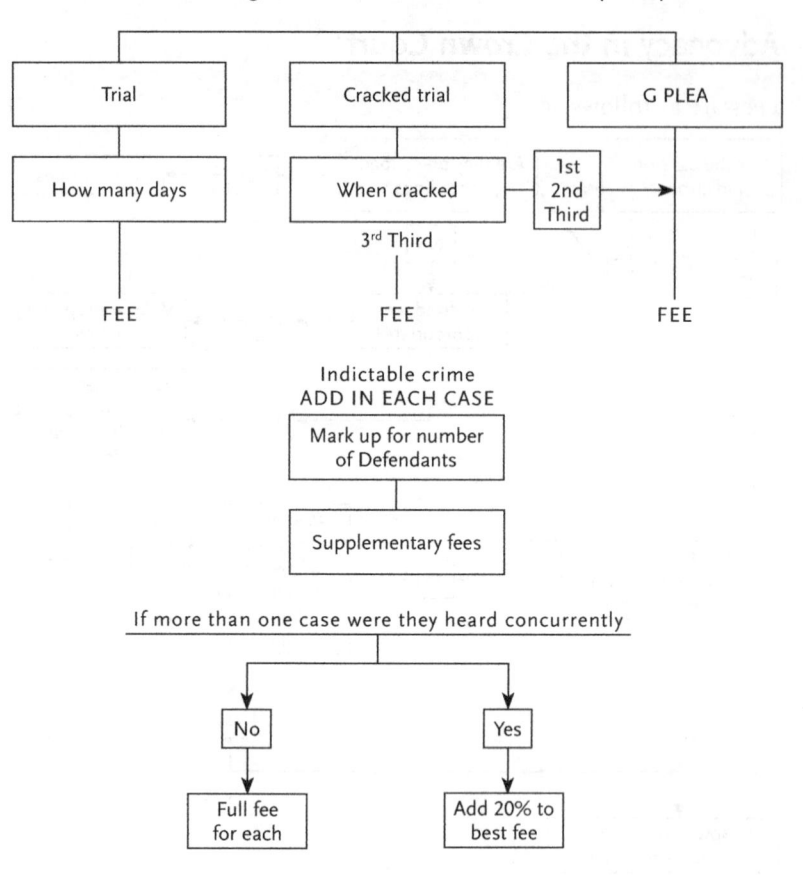

5.190 These fees are always additional to a litigator's fee. Full tables of all advocacy fees appear at appendix I.

Non-indictable crime

5.191 This includes committals for sentence, appeals against conviction and sentence, and committals for breach of Crown Court orders, Civil (prescribed) proceedings are dealt with in chapter 10.

Normal fees

5.192 The following fees are prescribed for the main hearing, ie the hearing at which sentence is imposed or the appeal against conviction is heard in routine cases. The order also allows fees for a QC and leading juniors but such cases would always fall into the exceptional group described below.

5.193 The fee is payable for each day of the main hearing.[186]

5.194 All figures in these tables are exclusive of VAT and are for cases with representation orders dated on or after 1 April 2018 and on or after 31 December 2018.

Hearing type	Para no (SI 2013 No 435 Sch 1) as amended	Rate 1.4.18 to 30.12.18	Rate from 31.12.18
Appeals to the Crown Court against conviction	20(1)	£250 per day	£330 per day
Appeals to the Crown Court against sentence	20(1)	£150 per day	£250 per day
Proceedings relating to breach of an order of the Crown Court	20(1)	£108 per day	£109 per day
Committal for sentence	20(1)	£150 per day	£152 per day

5.195 The order also allows for subsidiary fees (see table below).

Hearing type	Para no (SI 2013 No 435 Sch 1) as amended	Rate 1.4.18 to 30.12.18	Rate from 31.12.18
Non effective appeals, committals for sentence and breach hearings, eg failure of the assisted person or a witness to attend, the unavailability of a pre-sentence report or other good reason	20(2)	£87 per day	£88 per day
Bail application mentions and other applications in appeals, committals for sentence breach hearings	20(3)	£87 per day	£88 per day

186 *R v Hines* (X24).

Contempt of court[187]

5.196 Fixed fees are provided for advocacy for contempt in the face of the court. The fee for contempt proceedings is limited to contempt arising during the course of the criminal proceedings and not those that are identified as prescribed proceedings. These are dealt with in chapter 10. These fees are for cases started on or after 1 April 2016 and on or after 31 December 2018.

	Where there is no litigator		Where there is a litigator	
	1.4.18 to 30.12.18	from 30.12.18	1.4.18 to 30.12.18	from 31.12.18
QC	£300	£303	£175	£177
Leading junior	£225	£227	£125	£126
Led junior or junior alone	£150	£152	£100	£101

Mark-ups

5.197 Where two or more cases involving the same advocate are heard concurrently, the advocate is paid an additional 20 per cent of the fixed fee for each additional case, whether that involves separate allegations or separate defendants.[188]

5.198 This rule is different from that applicable to litigators.

Escape provisions

5.199 Remuneration Regulations 2013 Sch 1 para 20(4) allows for fees greater than these fixed fees:

> Where it appears to the appropriate officer that the fixed fee allowed under sub-paragraph (1) would be inappropriate taking into account all of the relevant circumstances of the case the appropriate officer may instead allow fees of such amounts as appear to the appropriate officer to be reasonable remuneration for the relevant work in accordance with sub-paragraph (5).

5.200 There is no requirement for exceptional circumstances. At a time when that was a requirement, National Taxing Team (NTT) guidance indicated that a reasonable fee beyond the fixed fee could be paid if

---

187 Remuneration Regulations 2013 Sch 1 para 21.
188 Remuneration Regulations 2013 Sch 1 para 27(2).

work was carried out substantially in excess of that required in an average case of the same type when:

- a magistrates' court would have declined jurisdiction;
- an appeal committal or breach lasted more than a day;
- a Newton hearing took place.

The current Regulations set a lower standard than this guidance required.

5.201 The method of calculation is provided for by Sch 1 para 20(5). It allows:

(a) a fee for preparation including, where appropriate, the first day of the hearing including, where they took place on that day –
   (i) short conferences;
   (ii) consultations;
   (iii) applications and appearances (including bail applications);
   (iv) views at the scene of the alleged offence; and
   (v) any other preparation.
(b) a refresher fee for any day or part of a day for which a hearing continued, including, where they took place on that day–
   (i) short conferences;
   (ii) consultations;
   (iii) applications and appearances (including bail applications);
   (iv) views at the scene of the alleged offence; and
   (v) any other preparation; and
(c) subsidiary fees for –
   (i) attendance at conferences, consultations and views at the scene of the alleged offence not covered by paragraph (a) or (b);
   (ii) written advice on evidence, plea, appeal, case stated or other written work; and
   (iii) attendance at applications and appearances (including bail applications and adjournments for sentence) not covered by paragraph (a) or (b).

5.202 The fee to charge is a judgment dependent on the facts of the case, but a good indication is given by calculating the appropriate graduated fee for the offence(s) in question.

Prescribed proceedings in the Crown Court

5.203 Appeals in relation to football banning and similar orders referred to in Criminal Legal Aid (General) Regulations 2013[189] reg 9 are payable at hourly rates in accordance with the SCC, set out in chapter 10. Advocacy fees must fall within the total fees limit of £1,368.75 and

---

189 SI No 9.

consideration must be given in appropriate cases to obtaining an authority on Form CRM5 to exceed that limit.

Indictable crime

Defence elections for trial in either way cases

5.204 The normal rules, for cases where the magistrates' court declines jurisdiction, are set out below. Those rules also apply if
- there is a trial; or
- the trial is a cracked trial because:
  a) the prosecution offer no evidence on all counts against the defendant and the judge directs that a not guilty verdict be entered; or
  b) after the election by the defendant
     i) there is a substantive change to a count on the indictment and the defendant pleads guilty; or
     ii) the defendant pleads guilty to one or more counts on the indictment and the prosecution offer no evidence on a remaining count or otherwise do not proceed to trial on a remaining count.[190]

5.205 However, a very rigid fixed fee scheme applies if the particular defendant elects for trial, and those exceptions do not apply.

5.206 The fixed fee is £365[191] per set of proceedings for cases with a representation order dated on or after 31 December 2018.[192] That fixed fee applies however many hearings there may be and for whatever reason. It includes also the value of all travel time including to conferences.

5.207 If there are confiscation proceedings the normal rules (at paras 5.285–5.290) apply and an additional sum is paid in addition to the fixed fee.

Other cases on indictment

5.208 These rules apply whenever there are:
- indictable only offences; or
- where the magistrates decline jurisdiction; or

---

190 Between 1 April 2018 and 30 December 2018, the wording of para (b)(ii) was the prosecution offer no evidence on a count against the defendant and the defendant subsequently pleads guilty.
191 The fee was £194 for orders dated between 1 April 2018 and 30 December 2018.
192 Criminal Legal Aid (Remuneration) Regulations 2013 Sch 1 para 10.

- when there is a trial following a defence election; or
- following a defence election;
- the trial is a cracked trial because:
  a) the prosecution offer no evidence on all counts against the defendant and the judge directs that a not guilty verdict be entered; or
  b) after the election by the defendant:
     i) there is a substantive change to a count on the indictment and the defendant pleads guilty; or
     ii) the defendant pleads guilty to one or more counts on the indictment and the prosecution offer no evidence on a remaining count or otherwise do not proceed to trial on a remaining count.[193]

Preliminary hearings

5.209 These are defined by the Remuneration Regulations 2013 as a 'standard appearance'.

5.210 If a preliminary hearing becomes a hearing at which a guilty plea is entered, the hearing becomes the main hearing and generates the basic guilty plea fee with such additional payment as may be due (see paras 5.235–5.536).

Bail hearings

5.211 If a defendant is arrested for breach of Crown Court bail conditions and produced before a magistrates' court the hearing is Crown Court proceedings and will receive a standard appearance fee.[194]

5.212 All bail hearings in the Crown Court, including contested proceedings, are treated as a 'standard appearance'.

Graduated fees

5.213 To calculate the correct graduated fee it is necessary to collect a quantity of basic data about the relevant case. Good work logs are essential if hourly rates or special preparation are to be claimed.

---

193 Between 1 April 2018 and 30 December 2018, the wording of para (b)(ii) was the prosecution offer no evidence on a count against the defendant and the defendant subsequently pleads guilty.
194 *R v Richardson* [2008] 2 Costs LR 320; *R v Bailey* (X16).

The offence 'banding'[195]

5.214 To identify the relevant band, it is necessary to refer to two documents. The basic document is Table A (see appendix I) which sets out 17 bands. However there are a number of sub-classifications within those bands which appear in Table B in the AGFS Banding Document, published by the Ministry of Justice.[196] The band within which an offence described in Table B in the Banding Document falls may depend on the facts of the case. Where it is necessary to establish the value of a fraud or property damage, the weight of drugs and the seriousness of the offence, the LAA indicate that the indictment and then the prosecution case summary or witness statements will be the best sources. See generally CCFG Appendix M.

5.215 Specific bands take account of mental health issues. Cases in which a restriction order is made under Mental Health Act 1983 s41 falls in band 1.3. A case in which the defendant is unfit to plead may be placed in band 5.3.

5.216 Cases in band 17.1 are referred to as standard cases and are excluded from other bands. A case not listed in any band also falls in band 17.1. If the case would fall within band 17.1, the LAA (and a

---

195 Criminal Legal Aid (Remuneration) (Amendment) Regulations 2018 SI No 220; and CCFG 2.3.
196 Between 1 April 2018 and 30 December 2018 Version 1.1 applied. From 31 December 2018 Version 1.2 applies. The banding documents are at: www.gov.uk/government/publications/banding-of-offences-in-the advocates-graduated-fee-scheme. The following changes have been made in Version 1.2 when compared with Version 1.1:
Table A
- Offences Against the Person Act s20 offence has been re-banded from 3.5 to 3.4. The descriptions for both 3.4 and 3.5 have also been amended.
- 'Indictable only' has been removed from the description of burglary at 11.2. All burglary cases will now fall under 11.2, including either way burglaries, which were previously banded at 17.1.
Table B
- Offence number 92 has been re-banded from 3.5 to 3.4.
- Offence numbers 556, 557, 574, 783, 784, 785, 827 and 842 have been re-banded from 17.1 to 3.4.
- Offence numbers 540, 541, 542, 543, 555 and 767 have been re-banded from 17.1 to 3.5.
- Offence numbers 834, 835, 836, 837 and 838 have been re-banded from 17.1 to 5.3.
- Offence numbers 504, 549, 550, 563, 565, 568, 573, 674, 675, 676, 679 and 769 have been re-banded from 17.1 to 8.1.
- Offence numbers 449, 450, 516, 517, 518, 519, 521, 522, 523, 524 and 525 have been re-banded from 17.1 to 16.3.

Crown Court work 123

costs judge) may be invited to apply a more appropriate band.[197] A specific application must be made.

5.217 A claim may only be made in relation to charges faced by the particular defendant(s) represented.[198]

5.218 CCFG 2.3 gives guidance on banding but it is in places, outdated. Reference should be made to the case-law on case classification for litigators in paras 5.114–5.133. This applies particularly to issues around what is an armed robbery and when an aggravated burglary may arise. The decision in *R v Nutting*[199] is more recent than the case of *Crabb* quoted by the LAA. This case looked behind the indictment and that will assist in other cases also.

The number of PPE

5.219 This is a key factor for litigators, but is only relevant for advocates in relation to issues of:

- Banding (classification of the case) in bands 6.1 and 6.2 and 9.1 through 9.6 (see paras 5.214–5.217).
- Special preparation (see paras 5.269–5.278).
- Confiscation (see paras 5.285–5.290).

5.220 For advocates, page count applies when special preparation is claimed in the following cases:[200]

> ... the number of pages of prosecution evidence, as defined and determined in accordance with paragraph 1(2) to (5), exceeds–
> (i) in cases falling within bands 6.1 to 6.5 (dishonesty offences, including proceeds of crime and money laundering), 30,000;
> (ii) in cases falling within bands 9.1 to 9.7 (drugs offences), 15,000; or
> (iii) in all other cases, 10,000,
>
> and the appropriate officer considers it reasonable to make a payment in excess of the graduated fee payable under this Schedule.

5.221 See paras 5.269–5.271; 5.285–5.290 and appendix I.

Whether the case is a trial, cracked trial or guilty plea – categorisation

5.222 See paras 5.50–5.77.

---

197 Criminal Legal Aid (Remuneration) Regulations 2013 reg 28(7), as amended.
198 *R v Mira* (X54); CCFG 2.3.4.
199 [2013] 6 Costs LR 1037.
200 Criminal Legal Aid (Remuneration) Regulations 2013 Sch 1 para 17(1)(b), as amended by SI 2018 No 220 reg 19.

The length of a trial

5.223 See paras 5.79–5.83.

5.224 A daily refresher is paid after the first day. The length of trial uplifts depends on the total length of the trial undergone by the particular defendant represented, whatever the length of the overall trial.[201]

The category of advocate

5.225 Categories are:
1) QC.
2) Leading junior.
3) Led junior.
4) Other advocate.

The main hearing: the basic fee

5.226 It is then necessary to identify, for each case, the main hearing, as it is for the hearing that the primary fee is payable.

5.227 For example:
- trial: it is the trial;
- guilty plea: the hearing at which the plea is taken, or if there is more than one, the last of them;
- cracked trial: the hearing at which the case became a cracked trial or at which a formal verdict of not guilty was entered if the Crown offered no evidence, whether or not the parties attended the hearing. Where an indictment has two counts and one guilty plea is entered and the case adjourned for sentence when the other not guilty plea is accepted, the case 'cracked' at the first hearing.[202]

5.228 A basic fee, varying in amount, is always payable. The fee is payable for a single trial advocate representing one assisted person on one indictment in a trial.

5.229 Mark-ups are payable where there is more than one assisted person and/or more than one indictment.

5.230 There being advocates for each defendant in a case will result in higher total payments.

5.231 Included within the basic fee is preparation by the advocate, including:
a) reading the papers in the case;
b) contact with prosecutors;
c) written or oral advice on plea;

---

201 *Secretary of State for Constitutional Affairs v Stork* [2006] 1 Costs LR 69.
202 *R v Johnson* [2007] 2 Costs LR 316.

Crown Court work

d) researching the law, preparation for examination of witnesses, and preparation of oral submissions;
e) viewing exhibits or undisclosed material at police stations;
f) written advice on evidence;
g) preparation of written submissions, notices or other documents for use at the trial; and
h) attendance at views at the scene of the alleged offence.

This is limited to preparation done before the trial, except in proceedings in which a preparatory hearing has been ordered under Criminal Justice Act 1987 s8 (commencement of trial and arraignment), in which case it is limited to preparation done before the date on which the jury is sworn (or on which it became certain, by reason of pleas of guilty or otherwise, that the matter would not proceed to trial).

5.232 The basic fee includes:
- the first day of trial, any work carried out in the magistrates' court;
- any work on audio or video recording and unused material and the first three conferences.

Calculations

For trials

5.233 Where the main hearing is a trial, the appropriate basic fee is selected for the offence(s) in question, depending on the advocate making the claim, from the tables in the Remuneration Regulations 2013 (appendix I).

5.234 To this basic fee ADD each of the following:
- length of trial uplift for each day or part thereof; and
- supplementary payments as set out below.

For guilty pleas

5.235 Where the main hearing is a guilty plea, select the appropriate basic fee (see appendix I) for the offence(s) in question depending on the advocate making the claim.

5.236 To the basic fee ADD:
- supplementary payments as set out below.

For cracked trials

5.237 It is necessary to know at which point the case cracked: whether in the first third, second third or final third.

5.238 This is determined by calculating the number of days from the date on which the case is first put in a warned list, or given a fixed date of hearing to the start of that warned list or the date of that fixture.

5.239 The number of days is divided in three equal parts and any days remaining are added to the last third.

5.240 A case that does not begin on the fixed date or in the period of the first warned list is treated as cracking in the last third. Retrials fall in the last third if they crack.

5.241 The Remuneration Regulations 2013 specify the fee, depending on when the case cracks.

5.242 If the case cracks in the first or second third, a guilty plea fee is paid.

5.243 If the case cracks in the final third select the appropriate cracked trail fee (see appendix I). To the basic fee ADD supplementary payments as set out below.

Mark-ups[203]

5.244 A trial under Bail Act 1976 s6 does not attract a separate fee but is paid as if it were a bail hearing.

5.245 Under Remuneration Regulations 2013 Sch 1 para 27(2) where two or more cases (whether on indictment or not) involving the same advocate are heard concurrently, the advocate must select the principal case and at the main hearing for each of the concurrent cases there is paid an additional 20 per cent of the appropriate basic or fixed fee for the principal case.

5.246 If the main hearings are on separate days. they are not heard concurrently.[204] In *R v Fury*[205] there was a plea bargain and following a guilty plea, no evidence was offered on a second case. Such hearings were held not to be concurrent but rather to take place consecutively so that two full fees were payable:

> ... hearings are concurrent only if they are combined or conjoined or somehow interlinked ... This will be so in the more common situation where ... the defendant either pleads guilty or is to be sentenced in all of the cases. ... The cases will not be considered independently of each other. For example, there would be one speech in mitigation covering all of the cases ... Where, however, the defendant pleads guilty in one case and the other case is dismissed the cases will have

---

203 CCFG 2.27.
204 CCFG 2.27.2.
205 [2011] 5 Costs LR 919.

no bearing on each other. . . . The same would apply where both cases are dismissed.

5.247 Mark-ups of 20 per cent of the fee are payable for additional defendants at the main hearing and are also payable for supplementary fees for hearings dealing with:
- standard appearances and PTPH and FCMH;
- hearings for abuse of process, disclosure, admissibility, or withdrawal of plea hearings;
- confiscation;
- sentencing;
- ineffective trials.[206]

Defendants unfit to plead or stand trial

5.248 Where a hearing is held to decide whether a defendant is fit to plead or stand trial (the fitness hearing), the following apply under Remuneration Regulations 2013 Sch 1 para 31:
1) If the trial continues, the length of the fitness hearings is added to the length of the trial.
2) In other circumstances the fee is whichever of the following the advocate elects:
   (a) a trial fee adding the length of the fitness hearing to that of any hearing under Criminal Procedure (Insanity) Act 1964 s4A; or
   (b) a cracked trial fee.
3) If there is a guilty plea, the fee is whichever of the following the advocate elects:
   (a) a trial fee based on the length of the fitness hearing; or
   (b) a guilty plea fee.

Retrials

5.249 Remuneration Regulations 2013 Sch 1 para 2(2)–(7) make special arrangements for the payment of fees for advocates in relation to retrials depending whether the same advocate appeared on both occasions. A fixed fee is paid if there was a defence election and at the retrial there is a cracked trial or guilty plea. In other cases, if a new advocate appears a full fee is paid. If the same advocate appears the advocate will have the fee for retrial (or if they elect for the trial) reduced by a percentage:

---

206 Criminal Legal Aid (Remuneration) Regulations 2013 Sch 1 para 27; CCFG 2.27.5.

a) 30 per cent, where the new trial started within one month of the conclusion of the first trial;
b) 20 per cent, where the new trial did not start within one month of the conclusion of the first trial;
c) 40 per cent, where the new trial becomes a cracked trial or guilty plea within one month of the conclusion of the first trial; or
d) 25 per cent where the new trial becomes a cracked trial or guilty plea more than one month after the conclusion of the first trial.

5.250 An advocate may elect to submit a trial bill notwithstanding that a retrial was to take place and submit the election later. The LAA could use its recoupment powers if there was as a result an overpayment.[207] Any election may later be varied.[208]

Supplementary fees

5.251 It is then necessary to add to these figures any relevant supplementary fees. Advocates seek particularly to classify hearings as one of those for which daily or half daily rates or hourly fees are payable, as these will generate additional fees. As any issue as to admissibility of evidence or disclosure falls into such payments, this will not uncommonly be possible.

5.252 These supplementary fees are considered as follows:
1) Interim hearings.
2) Sentencing hearings.
3) Hearings paid by daily and half daily fees.
4) Work paid by hourly rates.
5) Special circumstances including:
   a) early discontinuance or dismissal;
   b) confiscation
   c) retrial;
   d) cross-examination of a witness
   e) mitigation only
   f) advice cases
   h) warrant cases.

5.253 The value of any time spent on audio or video recordings and up to three conferences are included within the basic fee .

---

207 *R v Connors* [2014] 5 Costs LR 942.
208 *R v Luck* SCCO 135/16; CCFG 2.2.7 requires amendment to take account of this decision.

5.254　All first fees quoted are for cases with representation orders dated on or after 31 December 2018. The figures in brackets below are the fees for orders dated between 1 April 2018 and 30 December 2018.

Interim hearings

5.255　Rates for interim hearings are as follows.

Hearing type	Para no (Sch 1)	QC rate	Leading junior rate	Other advocate rate
Standard appearance not included within basic fee	12(2)	£182 (180) per day	£136 (135) per day	£91 (90) per day
Plea and trial preparation hearings	19A	£253 (250) per day	£192 (190) per day	£126 (125) per day
Further case management hearing	19A	£202 (200) per day	£152 (150) per day	£101 (100) per day

5.256　If a guilty plea is entered at the PTPH, a guilty plea fee is payable, appropriate to the band and advocate concerned.[209]

5.257　Standard appearances mean (Sch 1 para 1(1)):

> An appearance ... in any of the following hearings unless it is an 'excluded hearing'
>
> ...
>
> (b) a pre-trial review;
>
> ...
>
> (bb) a case management hearing;
> (c) the hearing of a case listed for plea which is adjourned for trial;
> (d) any hearing (except a trial, a plea and case management hearing, a pre-trial review or a hearing referred to in paragraph 2(1)(b)) which is listed but cannot proceed because of the failure of the assisted person or a witness to attend, the unavailability of a pre-sentence report or other good reason;
> (e) custody time limit applications;
> (f) bail and other applications (except where any such applications take place in the course of a hearing referred to in paragraph 2(1)(b));
> (g) the hearing of the case listed for mention only, including applications relating to the date of the trial (except where an application takes place in the course of a hearing referred to in paragraph 2(1)(b)) ... [which relates to fixed fees];

---

209 Criminal Legal Aid (Remuneration) Regulations 2013 Sch 1 para 19A(2).

(i) a preliminary hearing; or
(j) a hearing, whether contested or not, relating to breach of bail, failure to surrender to bail or execution of a bench warrant . . .

An 'excluded hearing' means
(a) the first hearing at which the assisted person enters a plea
(b) any hearing which forms part of the main hearing
(c) any hearing for which a fee is payable under a provision of this Schedule other than those listed at (b)–(j) above.

Sentencing hearings

5.258 Fees for sentencing hearings are as follows.

Hearing type	Para no (Sch 1)	QC rate	Leading junior rate	Other advocate rate
Sentencing hearing	15	£253 (250) per day	£192 (190) per day	£126 (125) per day
Deferred sentencing hearing	15(2)	£324 per day	£238 per day	£173 per day

5.259 Where a CBO is sought at the sentencing stage in criminal proceedings, it is to be paid as a standard appearance (applying *R v Brinkworth*[210]).

5.260 If sentencing takes place at the same time as a confiscation hearing, two fees are payable.[211]

Hearings paid by daily and half daily fees (when not part of main hearings)

5.261 Note that a half day ends before lunch or begins after lunch. Mark-ups for additional defendants are payable for the first four groups.

Scenario	Para no (Sch 1)	QC rate	Leading junior rate	Other advocate rate
Abuse of process. In these cases an additional 20% is paid for each additional defendant	13(1)(a) and (3)	£263 (260) per half day	£197 (195) per half day	£131 (130) per half day

---

210 [2006] 3 Costs LR 512.
211 Criminal Legal Aid (Remuneration) Regulations 2013 Appendix 1 para 14(2).

Crown Court work

		£502 (497) per full day	£349 (346) per full day	£240 (238) per full day
Hearings as to disclosure or witness summonses. In these cases an additional 20% is paid for each additional defendant. A hearing relating to a failure to disclose is likely to be classified as a standard appearance (*R v Russell* (X31))	13(1)(b), (c) and (3)	The same	The same	The same
Hearing as to admissibility of evidence. In these cases an additional 20% is paid for each additional defendant	13(1)(d) and (3)	The same	The same	The same
Ground Rules hearing	13(1)(da) and (3)	The same	The same	The same
Hearings on withdrawal of guilty pleas made by a different advocate from that present when plea entered. Hearing of an unsuccessful application to withdraw a guilty plea made by a different advocate from that present when the plea was entered. In these cases an additional 20% is paid for each additional defendant	13(1)(e) and (3)	The same	The same	The same
Confiscation hearings Where the number of pages relevant to confiscation is 50 pages or less	14	The same	The same	The same

Scenario	Para no (Sch 1)	QC rate	Leading junior rate	Other advocate rate
Second and subsequent days of an application to dismiss which does not succeed	22(6)	The same	The same	The same
Ineffective trial	16	£300 per day	£300 per day	£300 per day
Noting brief	23	£108 per day	£108 per day	£108 per day
Contempt in the face of the court other than by a defendant (advocate alone)	21	£303 (300) per day	£227 (225) per day	£152 (150) per day
Contempt, etc when there is advocate and litigator appointed	21	£177 (175) per day	£126 (125) per day	£101 (100) per day

5.262 If a Newton trial is listed but does not proceed due to the absence of a prosecution witness, the defence version then being accepted, it is the fee under Sch 1 para 16 that is payable (see *R v Ayres*[213]).

5.263 CCFG 2.16 states:

> 2. The appropriate officer will use their discretion when assessing whether an ineffective trial fee or a daily attendance fee is payable for a listed trial day. A daily attendance fee will be payable where:
> - The Advocate reasonably attended court for the 'parts of a day' referred to at paragraph 4 of Schedule 1 of the 2013 Regulations, and the case was called on but for whatever reason was unable to progress, or
> - The parties attended and no other activity is shown, but a linked case describes case progression activity.
>
> 3. An ineffective trial fee is likely to be payable where:
> - Advance notice is given that the court would not sit on a day previously or originally listed for trial.
> - The Judge stated that the trial would not sit on the day listed but would remain listed for conference purposes.
>
> 4. These principles for assessing the fee payable is supported by the decision of *R v Sarfraz* (SCCO 122 – 2016).

212 This fee applies to juniors alone and to led juniors.
213 [2002] 2 Costs LR 330 (X32).

Work paid by hourly rates

Conferences and views

5.264 Hourly rates for conferences and views are as follows.

Scenario	Para no (Sch 1)	QC rate	Leading junior rate	Other advocate rate
Conferences and views	19	£80.80 (80) per hour	£60.60 (60) per hour	£40.40 (40) per hour

5.265 The basic fee includes the first three reasonable pre-trial conferences or views per advocate. Beyond that number, and subject to conditions, hourly rates are paid for:

- attendances at pre-trial conferences with prospective or actual expert witnesses other than at court;
- attendance at the scene of the alleged offence;
- attendances at pre-trial conferences with the assisted person not held at court.

5.266 In addition, the hourly rates will be paid for reasonable travelling time to attend the view of the scene or for a pre-trial conference where it is reasonably held away from chambers or office.

5.267 The conditions for reasonable hourly rates to be paid are:

- for trials (or the anticipated length of a trial that cracks) lasting not less than 21 days and up to 25 days: one further pre-trial conference of up to two hours;
- for trials (or cracked trials) lasting not less than 26 days and up to 35: two further pre-trial conferences of up to two hours;
- for trials (or cracked trials) lasting not less than 36 days and up to 40 days: three further pre-trial conferences of up to two hours.

5.268 Conferences cannot be claimed in fixed fee cases including either way case where the defence elect unless an exception applies (see para 5.204).

Special preparation

5.269 Hourly rates for special preparation are as follows.

Scenario	Para no (Sch 1)	QC rate	Leading junior rate	Other advocate rate
Special preparation*	17	£74.74 (74) per hour	£56.56 (56) per hour	£39.39 (39) per hour

* See CCFG 2.17.

5.270 This fee is payable where:

17(1) (a) it has been necessary for an advocate to do work by way of preparation substantially in excess of the amount normally done for cases of the same type because the case involves a [very unusual or][214] novel point of law [or factual issue];[215] or

(b) the number of pages of prosecution evidence, as defined and determined in accordance with paragraph 1(2) to (5), exceeds–
  (i) in cases falling within bands 6.1 to 6.5 (dishonesty offences, including proceeds of crime and money laundering), 30,000;
  (ii) in cases falling within bands 9.1 to 9.7 (drugs offences), 15,000; or
  (iii) in all other cases, 10,000,

and the appropriate officer considers it reasonable to make a payment in excess of the graduated fee payable under this Schedule

5.271 A page limit has been held to be lawful;[216] advocates must justify why a case falls within the Remuneration Regulation 2013, and detailed work logs should be supplied.

5.272 Under a previous version of Sch 1 para 17(1)(a) above it was held that there is a three-part test:

1) The work must be necessary. The volume of unused material cannot alone justify a claim.[217]
2) That work must be substantially in excess of the amount normally done for cases of the same type. Type is not to be given too narrow a meaning, ie manslaughter, not manslaughter by drugs, sexual assault and rape, not historic sexual assault and rape.[218] An attempt should be made to identify the work that would normally be required.
3) A point of law or factual issue must be novel.

---

214 The words in square brackets did not apply between 1 April 2018 and 30 December 2018.
215 The words in square brackets did not apply between 1 April 2018 and 30 December 2018.
216 *R v Jagelo* SCCO 96/15.
217 *Johnson* (X2003).
218 *R v Teret* [2016] 3 Costs LRO 393.

5.273 In relation to (a) there must be a novel part of law or factual issue whatever the quality of the preparation may have been.[219]

5.274 For a further description of relevant case-law in relation to (a), see also *R v Marandola*[220] and the overview in *R v Ranjit*,[221] but the cases are inevitably fact specific and relate to a different version of this provision.

5.275 The hourly rate is payable for the number of hours appropriate for the excess work or which are reasonable to view the prosecution evidence. Where the criterion is met by reason of a novel point of law, only those hours spent on that point may be remunerated. It does not allow for a general hourly rate to be paid for work 'above the norm'.[222] However, where the unusual or novel or factual issue added 600 pages to the unused material, the time spent researching the complainant's alleged unusual medical condition could be claimed as special preparation given its exceptional nature.[223]

5.276 Because the rules for payment of special preparation by litigators and by advocates are different, careful consideration may be given to how the work on a case is to be divided between them.

5.277 The same hourly rate is also paid, as special preparation, to an advocate whose only role is to give written or oral advice. It is also paid for the length of reasonable preparation time spent by an advocate solely appointed to mitigate a sentence.

5.278 Special preparation is not available in relation to confiscation proceedings.[224]

Wasted preparation

5.279 Hourly rates for wasted preparations are as follows.

Scenario	Para no (Sch 1)	QC rate	Leading junior rate	Other advocate rate
Wasted preparation	18	£74.74 (74) per hour	£56.56 (56) per hour	£39.39 (39) per hour

---

219 See *Meeke and Taylor v Secretary of State for Constitutional Affairs* [2006] 1 Costs LR 1.
220 [2006] 1 Costs LR 184.
221 [2006] 3 Costs LR 541.
222 *R v Kholi* [2010] 6 Costs LR 982.
223 *R v Bishop* (2008) 5 Costs LR 808.
224 See CCFG 2.17.13.

5.280 These fees are payable provided:
- there are at least eight hours' preparation and there is a trial of at least five days; or a cracked trial with more than 150 PPE;
- a trial advocate is prevented from representing the assisted person in the main hearing in any of the following circumstances:
  (a) the trial advocate is instructed to appear in other proceedings at the same time as the main hearing in the case and has been unable to secure a change of date for either the main hearing or the other proceedings;
  (b) the date fixed for the main hearing is changed by the court despite the trial advocate's objection;
  (c) the trial advocate has withdrawn from the case with the leave of the court because of his or her professional code of conduct or to avoid embarrassment in the exercise of his or her profession;
  (d) the trial advocate has been dismissed by the assisted person or the litigator; or
  (e) the trial advocate is obliged to attend at any place by reason of a judicial office held by him or her or other public duty.

5.281 A wasted preparation fee is payable when objection is taken to a new trial date because of a pre-booked holiday. It does not require to be because of professional commitments.[225]

Special circumstances

Early discontinuance or dismissal[226]

5.282 Under Crime and Disorder Act 1998 s51 if proceedings are sent and the Crown discontinues, or such proceedings are dismissed:

(a) *before the evidence is served* the advocate's fee is one half of the basic fee payable to such an advocate for such an offence on a guilty plea;

(b) *after the service of evidence* the appropriate guilty plea fee applies (including page mark-up) – even if other charges are remitted to the magistrates' court.

5.283 Where there is a failed application to dismiss, daily and half daily fees are payable as follows:

---

225 *R v Ghaffar* [2009] 6 Costs LR 980.
226 Remuneration Regulations 2013 Sch 1 para 22; CCFG Appendix G gives worked examples.

QC

£502 (£497) per full day
£263 (£260) per half day

Leading junior

£349 (£346) per full day
£197 (£195) per half day

Other advocate

£240 (£238) per full day
£131 (£130) per half day.

5.284 A 20 per cent uplift of the guilty plea *basic* fee is paid for each additional defendant beyond the first.

Confiscation proceedings[227]

5.285 For confiscation hearings, including those following a committal under Proceeds of Crime Act 2002 s70, a special scheme applies where the number of pages involved in the confiscation proceedings exceeds 50. Under that figure the advocate is just paid the daily or half daily fees.

5.286 A confiscation hearing must take place but there is no requirement for evidence to be called or an order to be made.[228]

5.287 Pages for this purpose include:

- the Proceeds of Crime Act 2002 section 16 statement served and relied upon by the prosecution for the purpose of the confiscation hearing together with any annexes or exhibits attached thereto;
- documents served as part of the main trial bundle, where such documents are specifically relied upon and referred to in the section 16 statement but are not served again; and
- any defence expert report and the documents and exhibits attached, provided that the report had been obtained with the prior approval of the LAA or is allowed on taxation, excluding any documents annexed to the report which have already been counted under either of the two points above or which consist of financial records or similar data.

5.288 Where the relevant page count is between 51 and 1,000, there will be a payment as set out in the PPE table below for preparation and the

227 Sch 1 para 14; and see CCFG 2.14 and Appendix Q.
228 CCFG 2.14.6.

first day of the confiscation hearing. Thereafter, the daily and half daily supplemental fee for confiscation hearings is payable.

5.289 Where the relevant page count exceeds 1,000, then in addition to the rates set out above for a page count between 751 and 1,000 there will be paid a reasonable fee for the time spent considering the pages in excess of 1,000 at the hourly rate below.

5.290 If sentencing takes place at the same time as a confiscation hearing, two fees are payable.[229]

Fees for confiscation hearings

	Fees for QC	Fee for leading junior	Fee for junior alone	Fee for led junior
1. Daily and half daily rates				
Half daily rate	£263 (260)	£197 (195)	£131 (130)	£131 (130)
Daily rate	£502 (497)	£349 (346)	£240 (238)	£240 (238)
2. Pages of evidence				
51–250	£655 (649)	£546 (541)	£437 (433)	£327 (324)
251–500	£983 (973)	£819 (811)	£655 (649)	£491 (486)
501–750	£1311 (1,298)	£1092 (1,081)	£874 (865)	£655 (649)
751–1,000	£1965 (1,946)	£1638 (1,622)	£1311 (1,298)	£983 (973)
3. Preparation				
Hourly rates	£74.74 (74)	£56.56 (56)	£39.39 (39)	£39.39 (39)

5.291 **Retrials**[230]

If a case is properly defined as a retrial (see paras 5.61–5.70) and if the same advocate (but not otherwise) appears at original and retrials and:

(a) the defendant is assisted at both trials; or
(b) the defendant is involved only in the retrial; or
(c) the new trial is a guilty plea or cracked trial (in which situation the case is always in the final third);

the advocate must, at their election, reduce the main graduated fee (but not the supplemental fees such as for sentence or confiscation) for one of the two trials by the percentage applicable below.

---

229 Criminal Legal Aid (Remuneration) Regulations 2013 Appendix 1 para 14(2).
230 Remuneration Regulations 2013 Sch 1 para 2(3).

Crown Court work 139

Scenario	Percentage
If retrial start within one month of conclusion of first trial	30%
If retrial starts later than that	20%
If retrial becomes guilty plea or cracked trial within one month of the conclusion of the first trial	40%
If retrial becomes guilty plea or cracked trial later than that	25%

Cross-examination of a witness[231]

5.292 An advocate appointed solely to cross-examine a witness under Youth Justice and Criminal Evidence Act 1999 s38 is paid a trial graduated fee with a daily fee calculated by reference to the number of days actually attended by the advocate.

Mitigation only[232]

5.293 An advocate appointed solely to mitigate is paid the supplementary fee for a sentencing hearing but in addition a special preparation fee. These fees are also payable where a QC is appointed at this late stage to mitigate.[233]

Scenario	Para no (Sch 1)	QC rate	Leading junior rate	Other advocate rate
Hearing for mitigation of sentence (when not otherwise instructed)	34	£263 (260) per day	£175 (173) per day	£109 (108) per day

The special preparation fee is calculated for the reasonable number of hours of preparation for that appearance using the hourly rate set out above for special preparation.

Provision of written or oral advice[234]

5.294 Where an advocate is instructed solely to advise, a special preparation fee will be payable for the reasonable number of hours of preparation for that advice using the hourly rates set out above for special preparation.

231 Sch 1 para 32.
232 Sch 1 para 34.
233 *R v Gravette* (2016) (LAA Guidance).
234 Sch 1 para 33.

Warrants[235]

5.295 Schedule 1 para 24A deals with the situations which arise when a person fails to attend a hearing, a Bail Act warrant is issued and the case does not proceed in the absence of the defendant.

5.296 For cases on indictment when a warrant is not executed for three months, a guilty plea fee is payable.

5.297 For other cases, the full relevant fee is payable.

5.298 The paragraph makes provision for the adjustment of fees if the warrant is executed within 15 months and the case then proceeds. This may result in an additional or reduced fee.

5.299 If the delay exceeds 15 months and there is later a trial, the earlier fee may be retained as well as the trial fee paid.[236]

Discharge of legal aid

5.300 The fee payable would appear to depend on the state of the case at the moment of discharge. Standard appearance fees are payable if there is no main hearing before legal aid is withdrawn.[237]

Disbursements

5.301 Travel expenses are payable to advocates for all reasonable attendances at conferences[238] and views permitted for the relevant proceedings.

5.302 Travel and other expenses incidental to court appearances may also be paid if the advocate appears at a court not within 40 kilometres of their office or chambers, provided that they cannot exceed those payable to any local Bar or nearest advocate's office unless previously authorised or justified in all the circumstances.[239]

Payment and distribution of the advocacy fee[240]

5.303 Only one fee will be paid for advocacy in each case to junior counsel; and one to leading counsel if any. Payment is made to the

---

235 CCFG 2.24A
236 The legislation giving effect to the decision in *Mehmood and Horvathova* SCCO 76/16 and 194/16 save that only a guilty plea fee would now be payable three months after the warrants for failure to appear were issued.
237 *R v Muoka* [2013] 3 Costs LR 523.
238 *R v Carlyle* [2002] 1 Costs LR 192.
239 For amounts allowable, see CCFG 2.29.
240 Remuneration Regulations 2013 Sch 1 para 26.

'trial advocate' – that is, the advocate who appeared at the main hearing.

5.304 Where there is more than a single advocate, the leading 'trial advocate' pays for work of that level and the junior pays for work at the level undertaken by other advocates.

5.305 Where there is more than one defendant, the court must be notified in writing of the name of the additional trial advocate as soon as he or she is appointed to ensure each is paid a full fee. This is particularly significant if a single advocate appeared at the first hearing at which a plea is entered.

5.306 The trial advocate has to account for VAT but, where the advocate is a solicitor, accounts should be rendered by the firm. Moneys held for the Bar should be paid into client account or if none exists into office account as long as it can be paid out within 14 days.

5.307 All appeal actions must be taken by the trial advocate, as must the provision of information for supplementary fees.

CHAPTER 6

Costs in relation to appeals and reviews[1]

6.1	**Part 1: Costs under the Standard Crime Contract**
6.2	Matter type claim codes
6.3	Extent
6.6	Fees
	Advice and assistance on appeal against conviction and sentence by a newly instructed representative; and on an application to the CCRC • Representation on an appeal by way of case stated
6.10	**Part 2: Claims in the Court of Appeal and Divisional Court**
6.10	Representation orders: making the claim
6.12	Remuneration
6.14	**Part 3: Costs in the Supreme Court**

---

1 Provided for by Standard Crime Contract (SCC) Specification para 11 and Criminal Legal Aid (Remuneration) Regulations 2013 SI No 435 ('Remuneration Regulations 2013') reg 8 and Sch 4. See also Criminal Bills Assessment Manual (CBAM) 11. Costs in the Court of Appeal and Divisional Court are provided for by the Remuneration Regulations 2013 reg 6 and Sch 3.

Part 1: Costs under the Standard Crime Contract

6.1 The Standard Crime Contract (SCC)[2] provides for appeals and reviews in the following cases:
- Advice and assistance on appeals against conviction or sentence (where a newly instructed representative is not covered by an existing determination) or applications to the Criminal Cases Review Commission (CCRC) provided under Legal Aid, Sentencing and Punishment of Offenders Act (LASPO) 2012 s15(2)(c).
- Representation on an appeal by way of case stated provided under section 16 of the Act.
- Representation in the Crown Court under a Representation Order in Prescribed Proceedings on appeal from the magistrates' court provided under section 16 of the Act.[3]

Matter type claim codes

6.2 Matter type claim codes are as follows.

Code	Matter type
APP A	Advice and assistance in relation to an appeal (except CCRC)
APP B	Advice and assistance in relation to a CCRC application
APP C	Representation on an appeal by way of case stated

Extent

6.3 Work in this class (SCC Specification 11) covers appeals and reviews against conviction and sentence, where a newly instructed representative is not covered by an existing representation order, and representation on appeals by way of case stated. It is paid at hourly rates. The principles applicable are those set out in chapter 1. In relation to appeals against conviction and sentence by a new representative there are extendable costs limits of £456.25 in CCRC cases and £273.75 otherwise. There is no limit for appeals by way of case stated. There is a financial eligibility test.

---

2 SCC Standard terms 1.1 and Specification para 11.
3 These proceedings are civil proceedings supported by criminal legal aid and are dealt with in chapter 10.

6.4 Representation in the Crown Court in prescribed proceedings on appeal from the magistrates' court is covered in chapter 10. In appeals in prescribed proceedings, the extendable limit is £1,368.75. There are limitations if advice has already been given and other strict contractual requirements.

6.5 All figures below refer to matters started on or after 1 April 2016.

Fees

6.6 The rates payable matters on or after 1 April 2016 are as follows.

Advice and assistance on appeal against conviction and sentence by a newly instructed representative; and on an application to the CCRC

6.7

	London	National
Routine letters written and routine telephone calls per item	£3.51	£3.38
Preparation hourly rate	£45.35	£42.80
Travel and waiting hourly rates	£24.00	£24.00

Representation on an appeal by way of case stated

6.8

	High Court
Routine letters out per item	£6.84
Routine telephone calls per item	£3.79
All other preparation work hourly rate	£68.74
	(£72.54 for London)
Attending counsel hourly rate	£33.76
Attending without counsel at trial or hearing hourly rate	£68.44
Travelling and waiting hourly rate	£30.34

6.9 As advocates are not party to the SCC, no provision for their fees appears. Reference should be made to appendix J as the fees set out below are as appropriate to the Administrative Court (as a Divisional Court) as they are to the Court of Appeal.[4]

Part 2: Claims in the Court of Appeal and Divisional Court

Representation orders: making the claim

6.10 In relation to the Court of Appeal, the Remuneration Regulations 2013 provide for payments to litigators in the rare cases when a representation order is granted in appeal proceedings; and for advocates. The rates appear in Schedule 3 (see appendix J). Regulation 6 provides for litigators; enhancement is available under paragraph 8 of Schedule 3 except for cases in Classes F, G and H. Paragraph 9 provides power to increase the rates payable to advocates in exceptional circumstances.

> ... Any claim must–
> (a) summarise the items of work done by a fee earner in respect of which fees are claimed according to the classes of work available;
> (b) state, where appropriate, the dates on which the items of work were done, the time taken, the sums claimed and whether the work was done for more than one assisted person;
> (c) specify, where appropriate, the level of fee earner who undertook each of the items of work claimed;
> (d) give particulars of any work done in relation to more than one indictment or a retrial; and
> (e) specify any disbursements claimed, the circumstances in which they were incurred and the amounts claimed in respect of them.
> (4) Where the litigator claims enhancement in relation to an item of work, the litigator must give full particulars in support of the claim.
> (5) The litigator must specify any special circumstances which the litigator considers should be drawn to the attention of the appropriate officer.

6.11 Representation orders in the Court of Appeal may be retrospective in their effect.[5]

---

4 Criminal Legal Aid (Remuneration) Regulations 2013 SI No 435 ('Remuneration Regulations 2013') reg 3(9).
5 Criminal Legal Aid (Determinations by a Court and Choice of Representative) Regulations 2013 SI No 614 reg 8(2).

Remuneration

6.12 In determining fees in accordance with Schedule 3 (appendix J) the Registrar of Criminal Appeals must, subject to the provisions of the Schedule:
    (a) take into account all the relevant circumstances of the case including the nature, importance, complexity or difficulty of the work and the time involved; and
    (b) allow a reasonable amount in respect of all work actually and reasonably done by a fee earner of appropriate seniority.

6.13 Reference should be made to chapter 1 for a discussion of the relevant issues. Disbursements will also be allowed with controls on travel costs and the costs of transcripts. These issues are discussed at chapter 8.

Part 3: Costs in the Supreme Court

6.14 Costs in the Supreme Court fall outside the Remuneration Regulations 2013 (see reg 7) and are dealt with by order of the Supreme Court. The court has issued a series of practice directions to assist those appearing before it and reference should particularly be made to Practice Direction 12.

CHAPTER 7

Very high cost criminal cases[1]

7.1	Definition
7.4	Notification
7.7	Appointment
7.8	Individual case contracts
7.9	Remuneration
7.14	Cases ceasing to be very high costs cases

1 The LAA publishes a VHCC Contract Guide available at: www.gov.uk.

Definition

7.1 Remuneration Regulations 2013[2] reg 2 identifies, and the Standard Crime Contract (SCC) requires, the notification in writing as soon as possible of any case likely to fall within the definition of a very high cost case (VHCC) – essentially a case that may last for no fewer than 25 days. However, the Legal Aid Agency (LAA) presently only requires notification if the case may last no fewer than 40 days.[3]

7.2 The full definition in the Remuneration Regulations 2013 reg 2(1) is:

> ... a case in which a section 16 determination has been made and which the Director classifies as a Very High Cost Case on the grounds that –
> (a) in relation to fees claimed by litigators –
>   (i) if the case were to proceed to trial, the trial would in the opinion of the Director be likely to last for more than 40 days and the Director considers that there are no exceptional circumstances which make it unsuitable to be dealt with under an individual case contract for Very High Cost Cases made by the Lord Chancellor under section 2(1) of the Act [Legal Aid, Sentencing and Punishment of Offenders Act 2012]; or
>   (ii) if the case were to proceed to trial, the trial would in the opinion of the Director be likely to last no fewer than 25 and no more than 40 days and the Director considers that there are circumstances which make it suitable to be dealt with under an individual case contract for Very High Cost Cases made by the Lord Chancellor under section 2(1) of the Act;
> (b) in relation to fees claimed by advocates, if the case were to proceed to trial, the trial would in the opinion of the Director be likely to last for more than 60 days and the Director considers that there are no exceptional circumstances which make it unsuitable to be dealt with under an individual case contract for Very High Cost Cases made by the Lord Chancellor under section 2(1) of the Act.

7.3 VHCCs do not fall within the SCC,[4] and no further claim can be made under the contract[5] once a case has been classified by the LAA as a VHCC.[6]

---

2 Criminal Legal Aid (Remuneration) Regulations ('Remuneration Regulations 2013') 2013 SI No 435.
3 Crown Court Fee Guidance (CCFG) 1.12.
4 SCC Specification 7.1; CCFG 1.3.2; *Lord Chancellor v Alexander Johnson* [2011] EWHC 2113 (QB).
5 SCC Specification 7.5.
6 SCC Specification 7.2.

Notification

7.4 The Very High Cost (Crime) Cases Arrangements 2013 and SCC Specification 7.3 set out the notification rules and identify the features which will, for costs purposes, classify the case. In Part B the Arrangements identify the eligibility criteria for litigators or advocates to undertake cases of over 60 days. Part C contains the eligibility criteria for shorter VHCC cases.

7.5 Notification is required of any case likely to last 25 days or more as soon as it appears that the case is likely to be a VHCC and in any event within five working days of the earliest hearing at which the court sets a length of trial estimate or the defence team has identified that the case will be or is likely to be a VHCC.

7.6 A failure to notify without good reason enables the LAA to refuse to pay the firm in question costs to the value of any loss resulting.[7]

Appointment

7.7 If the LAA decides to treat the case as a VHCC, the representation order must be in favour of a firm on the VHCC panel. Each such firm then enters into an individual contract as to the basis on which it will undertake the work. If a firm is instructed to pass a case to another provider, a claim by them can only be made to that date.[8]

Individual case contracts

7.8 The contract contains its own definition of A, B and C grade fee earners. It sets out the criteria which determine, for costs purposes, the category into which a particular case falls. There are detailed provisions to prevent work shifting between litigators and advocates. It is critical to agree a case plan and then individual stage plans before any work is carried out, as payment will otherwise be refused.

Remuneration

7.9 Graduated fees will be paid to litigators in case lasting less than 60 days. Otherwise the rates are set out in the Remuneration Regulations 2013 reg 12A and Sch 6 and appear in appendix K.

7 Remuneration Regulations 2013 reg 12(2).
8 SCC Specification 7.6.

7.10 When a firm, not on the panel, is instructed to give up a case, a claim may be made for the costs due until the case is transferred at the rates set out in the individual case contract of the new litigator.[9]

7.11 Firms entering into the VHCC contract and continuing to act will be paid for all their work, including that prior to the contract, at individual contract rates.[10]

7.12 The fees suggested by the LAA as payable to counsel are susceptible to judicial review and the LAA must be open and transparent in its discussions about fees, disclosing all relevant policies guidance and protocols.[11]

7.13 If a representation order is withdrawn when graduated fees are payable (on the declassification from VHCC), those graduated fees will be paid at the percentages set out in the table for transfer cases in appendix H.[12]

Cases ceasing to be very high costs cases

7.14 There is a presumption that, once a case is accepted as a VHCC case, that classification will be maintained. However, if a case is declassified, all the work will again be undertaken under the relevant graduated fee scheme.

7.15 Where a case ceases to be a VHCC and the fee reverts to the normal methods of payment to a litigator or an advocate, the litigator or advocate must repay any money paid under the VHCC contract. However, if they were a case manager there will, in addition, be payable an administration fee for the administrative work associated with the VHCC contract. The fee is calculated as a fee for three hours' work for each stage or part stage except for pre-contract work (stage 0) or part of a stage up to the date of declassification.

---

9 Remuneration Regulations 2013 Sch 2 para 13(8).
10 Remuneration Regulations 2013 Sch 2 para 13(8).
11 *R (Ames) v Lord Chancellor* [2018] EWHC 2250 (Admin).
12 Remuneration Regulations 2013 Sch 2 para 13(9).

CHAPTER 8

Disbursements[1]

8.1	Definition
8.2	Prior authorities
8.8	Payments on account of disbursements
8.11	Travel costs and parking
8.23	Transcripts
8.24	Livenote
8.26	Copying
8.28	Experts
8.35	Interpreters and translators
8.37	Intermediaries
8.38	Forensic science laboratory charges
8.40	Other expenses (including witness expenses)

---

1 See generally Criminal Bills Assessment Manual (CBAM) 7 and Criminal Legal Aid (Remuneration) Regulations ('Remuneration Regulations') 2013 SI No 435 regs 13–17. For prison law cases, see SCC Specification 12. For crime higher, see Crown Court Fees Guidance (CCFG) 1.17.

Definition

8.1 Disbursements actually and reasonably incurred in the best interests of the client[2] and reasonable in amount may be recovered in addition to profit costs. Disbursements are out of pocket expenses properly incurred and which but for the provision of legal aid would be chargeable to a client for undertaking criminal law work.[3] Reasonableness takes into account all the circumstances of the case.[4] In making judgements, hindsight must be avoided. The test is reasonableness, not necessity.[5]

Prior authorities

8.2 Prior authority for disbursements (and for performing an act which is either unusual in its nature or involves unusually large expenditure)[6] may be obtained electronically on Form CRM4. No question may then be raised about the propriety of any step taken or disbursement incurred unless the litigator knew or ought to have known that the purpose for which the authority had been given had failed or become irrelevant or unnecessary before the liability was incurred.[7]

8.3 A claim can still be made even if no authority was obtained and a claim is not limited to the amount of the authority if the larger sum was reasonable.[8]

8.4 In giving a quotation, an expert must explain why the work is needed but the Legal Aid Agency (LAA) must give reasons for refusing or limiting an authority.[9] Experts should include within their quotation, any estimate for travel time required, so that it is included within the prior authority. They should quote hourly rates and not an overall fee unless a fixed fee is payable under the Remuneration Regulations 2013.

---

2 SCC Specification 5.38 and 5.40.
3 SCC Specification 1.2.
4 SCC Specification 5.45
5 *R v Shields* TMC S20.
6 SCC Specification 5.27; Criminal Legal Aid (Remuneration) Regulations 2013 SI No 435 (Remuneration Regulations 2013) reg 13.
7 SCC Specification 5.29; Remuneration Regulations 2013 reg 17(3).
8 SCC Specification 5.32; Remuneration Regulations 2013 reg 17(5); and *R v Matthews* TMC S26.
9 *R (T) v Legal Aid Agency* [2013] EWHC 960 (Admin).

8.5 An authority may also be sought to have travel and accommodation expenses in order to attend the main hearing at the Crown Court.[10] Advocates and litigators seeking advance authority for travel and accommodation costs should refer to CCFG 1.13.4. Guidance on rates appears at CCFG 1.17.12.

8.6 Private client fees may be incurred if a prior authority has been refused and the expenditure is expressly authorised by the client.[11]

8.7 The circumstances in which prior authority can be obtained for High Court proceedings appear at CBAM 7.1.8. The Registrar of Criminal Appeals handles applications for that court.

Payments on account of disbursements

8.8 In the magistrates' court payments may be added to the standard monthly payment (SMP) if there is a prior authority, the expenditure is incurred in pursuance of that authority and the amount involved for the single disbursement is likely to exceed the value of the SMP inclusive of VAT.[12]

8.9 For smaller amounts, such payments are not made. It is, as a result, common to insert a contractual term that disbursements will not be paid until the relevant payment is received from the LAA.

8.10 In the Crown Court payments on account may be obtained on production to the LAA of the authority to incur the expenditure of £100 or more and the invoice involved.[13] If individual accounts, for instance for an interpreter, would not reach £100, but more than one attendance its necessary, it is good practice to obtain an authority for the total likely to be involved.[14]

Travel costs and parking[15]

8.11 A mileage rate for contract work of £0.45 per mile is prescribed in the Standard Crime Contract (SCC) Specification at 5.48. The bicycle mileage rate is £0.20 per mile. In relation to the higher, including

10 Remuneration Regulations 2013 reg 13(3). For details as to how to make an application, see CBAM 7.1.5.
11 SCC Specification para 8.43.
12 SCC Specification 10.107–10.111.
13 Remuneration Regulations 2013 reg 14.
14 See CCFG 1.14.
15 See CCFG 1.17.12; and additionally CBAM 3.30–3.37.

Crown, courts, guidance is given in the Guide to Allowances under Part V of the Costs in Criminal Cases (General) Regulations 1986[16] identifying the two possible rates paid for the distance actually and reasonably travelled. These are a public transport rate and a standard rate. The guidance[17] states:

> 8.6 *24(5)* – *Private Motor Vehicles*. A witness may choose to travel to court using a private motor vehicle. Where a private motor vehicle is used the expense incurred may be reimbursed by payment of a mileage rate. There are two categories of mileage rate – public transport rate and standard rate.
>
> 8.7 The standard rate of mileage may *only* be paid where the use of a private motor vehicle was necessary (for example, because no public transport was available), or where a considerable saving of time is made (for example, where the witness would have been required to stay overnight, or leave and return at unreasonable hours, if public transport was used), or the use of a private motor vehicle was otherwise reasonable (for example, in the case of elderly or disabled witnesses, or witnesses carrying exhibits).
>
> 8.8 In all other cases, public transport rates apply. The public transport rate is a rate per mile calculated to be equivalent to the average cost of public transport. Thus, where the court at which a witness is required to attend is reasonably accessible by public transport, though the witness may choose to use a private motor vehicle, reimbursement is limited to the public transport cost.
>
> Regulation 24: Travelling allowances[18]
>
> | (a) Public Transport Rate – |
> |---|
> | Motor cars 0.25p |
> | (b) Standard Rate – |
> | Motor cars 0.45p |

8.12 These principles are confirmed by CCFG 1.17.13. In the Crown Court, Remuneration Regulations 2013 reg 17(2) provides that if the costs are abnormally large by reason of distance, they may be reduced to what otherwise would be reasonable. Reasons must be given to justify such travel, for example particular expertise or the perception by the client of too close a local contact with official bodies or the police.[19]

---

16 SI No 1335.
17 The last version of this guide is dated June 2007 and available at: http://webarchive.nationalarchives.gov.uk/. See also CCFG 1.17.12.
18 CCFG 1.17.12.
19 See *Truscott v Truscott; Wraith v Sheffield Forgemasters* [1997] 2 Costs LR 74.

Disbursements 157

8.13 If private transport can reasonably be justified, the mileage rate payable is £0.45 in all cases, whether inside or outside the designated areas. Reasonable parking costs will then also be met. However, if public transport could reasonably have been used, the mileage rate reduces to £0.25 and parking costs will be disallowed. It is therefore important to justify each journey.

8.14 There are many justifications for using private transport, eg:
- the need for confidentiality;
- the weight of the papers;
- the impossibility of reaching the court or prison on time, or returning at a reasonable hour, without private transport;
- the absence of public transport;
- disability needs;
- the need to travel on to another appointment; and
- very often the fact that it is cheaper than public transport.[20]

In this calculation the cost to the litigator of the travel time (at legal aid rates) may be included even though this may be lost in standard or graduated fees.

8.15 Any reduction must make allowance for such notional travel time.[21] This was confirmed in *R v Lawlor*.[22] The balancing exercise between travel time and travel costs is required whether the cost of time added using a slower means of transport is borne by the solicitor or the LAA. If a saving in direct travel cost will be outweighed by the additional cost of the time wasted in travelling by less efficient means, then the less efficient means of transport will not be a reasonable choice by the solicitor.

8.16 Mileage should in normal circumstances (during the week) be calculated from the solicitor's office unless the solicitor's home is nearer, but Google is not a reliable substitute for local knowledge of typical traffic conditions and public transport difficulties at particular times of day.

8.17 The cost of tolls and charges can be recovered if required by the needs of the client.[23]

8.18 The LAA will allow VAT on travel costs when added by practitioners who are registered.

---

20 See CBAM 3.9.18–3.9.20.
21 *R v Slessor* TMC S23.
22 SCCO 444/15.
23 CBAM 3.13.33–3.13.35.

8.19 Advocates cannot normally recover travel costs if there is a local Bar, unless prior authority is obtained. Travel costs will then normally be paid as if from the nearest bar unless the advocate's office or chambers is nearer.

8.20 The LAA sets out the rates that will normally be allowed for travel and accommodation costs in the Crown Court Fee Guidance.[24]

8.21 Receipts for all disbursements should when available be kept on file and all disbursements of over £20 (exclusive of VAT) must be vouched with the relevant bill.

8.22 Disbursements incurred in the magistrates' court may be claimed on the Crown Court bill when there is no lower court bill on which the claim can be made.[25]

Transcripts[26]

8.23 If a trial is to take place, a transcript of any police interview should normally be obtained unless one has been provided, in full, by the Crown, or it is clear that it will play no part in the proceedings. Little reliance should be placed on prosecution summaries. As long as the transcript is prepared outside the office and not by a fee earner, its reasonable cost will be a recoverable disbursement. The checking and consideration of a transcript is fee earner work and so part of profit costs.

Livenote[27]

8.24 Livenote is a real-time court transcription service used in long and complex cases. The cost is divided equally among the court, prosecution and defence. To get funding for the defence share of the cost, the defence team must send a Livenote application form (in an email) to the Complex Crime Unit (CCU).

8.25 Any costs of the electronic presentation of evidence may also be recovered.[28]

---

24 CCFG 2.29.
25 Remuneration Regulations 2013 reg 5(2).
26 CBAM 7.10.
27 CBAM 7.12.
28 CBAM 7.13.

Copying[29]

8.26 Routine photocopying during the course of a case is an office overhead and cannot be recovered. However, larger quantities of photocopying do not fall within this description and as a result of judicial decisions, the LAA had issued guidance which was approved by the costs judge in *R v Brown*:[30]

> In-house photocopying charges for routine copying are not recoverable since these constitute general office overheads. Solicitors may claim as a disbursement an outside agency's charges for bulk photocopying, ie in excess of 500 pages (which is a cumulative figure per case) provided the assessor considers such a course of action reasonable, ie where the copies are so exceptionally bulky that it would not be reasonable to expect the solicitor's normal office facilities to cope. An exception to this rule applies in cases where the Crown does not provide a second set of prosecution papers to the defence or where counsel is assigned in the Magistrates' court in which case the 500 page limit does not apply.

8.27 In those circumstances, both external and in-house copying charges can be recovered.[31] It is wise to obtain a CRM4 authority for volumes costing £100 or more. Copying fees for copying unused material may be met.[32] The collation of photocopying is part of profit costs.

Experts[33]

8.28 The reasonable costs of experts (whether in the magistrates' court or the Crown Court) can be recovered, but these costs are subject to the limitations set out in Remuneration Regulations 2013 reg 16 and Sch 5 (see appendix L). An expert's costs of attending at court are met by the court from central funds, and letters of instruction should ensure that no other liability falls upon the solicitor.

8.29 It is good practice to obtain a prior authority on Form CRM4. This enables a payment on account to be made and the expert's fee to be paid without delay. The LAA will wish to establish that it is

---

29 CBAM 7.14; CCFG 1.17.6.
30 SCCO 215/10.
31 See *Landau and Cohen v Lord Chancellor's Department (R v Abraham)* [1999] 2 Costs LR 5.
32 CBAM 7.17.2.
33 CBAM 7.2.

reasonable to instruct an expert and whether the proposed expert has the necessary experience and skills.[34]

8.30 Schedule 5 (see appendix L) covers a wide range of experts, from medical and forensic to interpreters and translators. Where an expertise is not referred to, the LAA will use the figures set out in the Schedule as a guide to the appropriate rate to be allowed.[35]

8.31 Regulation 16(2) provides that the fixed fee or hourly rates may be increased if the LAA considers it is reasonable to do so in exceptional circumstances as defined by regulation 16(3). This requires that the expert evidence is key to the client's case and either:

(a) the complexity of the material is such that an expert with a high level of seniority is required; or
(b) the material is of such a specialised and unusual nature that only very few experts are available to provide the necessary evidence.

8.32 Where Schedule 5 (see appendix L) refers to London rates, it is the address of the expert which will determine which rates are payable.

8.33 Reasonable medical evidence can be obtained and this may be preferable to a court ordered report to which privilege will not attach. CBAM 7.2.9, quoting CRIMLA 3 as amended, confirms that reports may be commissioned to assist in decision-making and in mitigation, and questions will only be raised when the stage has been reached that court might order a report to support a Mental Health Act disposal.

8.34 The SCC limits the remuneration rate for travel by experts in relation to work conducted under the contract. The rate may not exceed £40 per hour or a mileage rate of £0.45.[36]

Interpreters and translators

8.35 Interpreters are essential for those who cannot fluently speak English. If a defendant cannot read English, translations – though not required of every document – must be provided of the key documents and statements, and are a reasonable disbursement.[37] This right is also provided by EU Directive 2012/13/EU guaranteeing a right to information in criminal proceedings including rights to interpretation and translation.

---

34 CBAM 7.2.4–7.2.5.
35 Remuneration Regulations 2013 reg 17(6), (7).
36 SCC Specification 5.49.
37 CBAM 7.9.

8.36 Experts and interpreters[38] required during the preparation of a case are a charge on the legal aid fund but at court experts and interpreters for the defendant are paid from central funds.[39]

Intermediaries

8.37 The costs of the initial conference will be met from the legal aid fund, but Her Majesty's Courts and Tribunals Service (HMCTS) will meet later expenditure. The rates are:
- Preparation: £36.80 per hour.
- Travel: £16.60 per hour.[40]

Forensic science laboratory charges

8.38 In guidance, the LAA confirms that where appropriate, charges levied upon the defence by prosecution forensic science laboratories for provision of documentation to the defence expert and for allowing the expert access to their premises, equipment and staff may be payable by the LAA. It states that the LAA will only authorise payment where it considers the charge to be reasonably incurred and reasonable in value, and has granted prior authority to incur the cost. While it is good practice to obtain such an authority, it is not required as a matter of law.

8.39 The LAA states that it will not pay for charges levied for the following activities:[41]

a) forensic work undertaken by the prosecution at the request of the police in relation to evidence obtained by the police up to and including the preparation of reports and statements for use in the criminal justice system;

b) the preparation of statements and exhibits for service on the defence as part of the prosecution case;

c) the provision of unused material which the prosecutor deems meets the tests for disclosure as unused material set out in the Criminal Procedure and Investigations Act 1996, both at the primary and secondary disclosure stages;

d) completion of further forensic work *requested by the police/prosecutor* to rebut a defence put forward by the defendant, which may or may

---

38 CBAM 7.8.
39 Costs in Criminal Cases (General) Regulations 1986 SI No 1335 regs 16–20.
40 CBAM 7.6.
41 Guidance on Forensic Science Laboratory Charges in Criminal Matters, Legal Aid Agency, August 2014, available: at www.gov.uk.

not be highlighted in a Defence expert's report or Defence Statement.

Other expenses (including witness expenses)

8.40 Any reasonable expenses can be recovered. Costs of overnight stays and incidental costs, if reasonable, are at prescribed rates.[42] Couriers will only be allowed in an emergency not caused by the solicitor's delay.

8.41 The cost of enquiry agents[43] may be recoverable as disbursements if the agent is undertaking work identifiable as enquiry agent work such as locating a witness – whose proof may then be taken. If fee earner work alone is undertaken, then the expense is part of profit costs.[44]

8.42 The LAA will not pay for investment in technology, but will pay expenses which relate to particular cases. This includes the expense of computer-assisted transcripts and electronic presentation of evidence (CBAM 7.13).[45]

8.43 A witness's out-of-pocket expenses for attending court are normally a charge on central funds, but if refused may be recovered from the legal aid fund.[46] Witnesses in custody will be produced at public expense.[47] The costs of a witness giving evidence by video link will be met.[48]

8.44 Unless exceptional circumstances apply,[49] the travel and other expenses of the defendant cannot normally be recovered.[50]

8.45 The LAA will meet the cost of a second post mortem[51] including consequential costs. It will also met the cost of Data Protection Searches.[52]

---

42 See CBAM 3.31–3.32; and CCFG 1.17.12–1.17.16.
43 CBAM 7.7.
44 *Smith Graham (Solicitors) v Lord Chancellor* [1999] All ER (D) 957.
45 See generally on this issue *R v Great Western Trains* [2004] 2 Costs LR 331.
46 CBAM 7.4; SCC Specification 5.47.
47 CBAM 7.4.
48 CBAM 7.5.
49 *R v Legal Aid Board ex p Eccleston* (1998) CBAM 7.3.2, 7.3.3.
50 *R v Arney* TMC S24. On acquittal they can be recovered from central funds: CBAM 7.3.4.
51 CBAM 7.15.
52 CBAM 7.16.

CHAPTER 9

Administrative issues

9.1 **Appeals**
9.1 Crime lower
9.3 Crown Court cases
9.7 Court of Appeal

9.8 **Time limits, extensions and late claims**
9.8   Crime lower
9.10 Crown Court cases
9.11 When time begins to run
Confiscation cases • Cases where an appeal is lodged • Retrials • Extensions

9.25 **Interim staged and hardship payments on account**
9.26 Interim payments of disbursements
9.30 Interim payments to crown court advocates in case awaiting determination
9.31 Interim payments to crown court litigators
9.38 Staged payments for advocates
9.39 Hardship payments

9.41 **Overpayments**

163

Appeals

Crime lower[1]

9.1 An appeal from an initial assessment lies to an Independent Costs Assessor, in writing within 28 days of notification of the assessment decision. An extension of 14 days may be granted if sought within 21 days of that notification if there are reasonable grounds.[2]

9.2 If the Legal Aid Agency (LAA) makes representations to the Assessor, a reply should be sent within 14 days.[3] Assessors normally consider the papers in writing but there can be oral representations in limited circumstances.[4] It should be remembered that the review may result in a decrease as well as an increase in the amount payable.[5]

Crown Court cases[6]

9.3 If a practitioner is dissatisfied with the decision of the determining officer, an application should be made within 21 days of receipt of the decision for a redetermination.[7] If the result remains unsatisfactory, an application should be made within 21 days of the receipt of the redetermination for written reasons for the decision. It is important that all relevant issues are raised in the application as only the matters set out can be pursued further.[8]

9.4 An appeal then lies[9] to the Senior Courts Costs Office (SCCO), within 21 days from the receipt of the written reasons. The appeal follows the procedure set out in Part 45 of the Criminal Procedure Rules. A form (appellant's notice (criminal costs appeal to a costs judge)) is prescribed.[10]

---

1 Criminal Bills Assessment Manual (CBAM) 4; Standard Crime Contract (SCC) Specification 8.19–8.38.
2 SCC Specification 8.20.
3 SCC Specification 8.22.
4 SCC Specification 8.23.
5 SCC Specification 8.28.
6 Criminal Legal Aid (Remuneration) Regulations ('Remuneration Regulations') 2013 SI No 435 regs 28–30. See Crown Court Fees Guidance (CCFG) 1.28–1.30.
7 Remuneration Regulations 2013 reg 28.
8 Remuneration Regulations 2013 regs 28(3)(b) and 29(5).
9 Remuneration Regulations 2013 reg 29.
10 A copy of the appeal to the SCCO, in graduated fee cases, should be sent to the LAA Central Legal Team 7th Floor Zone C (7.39) LAA, 102 Petty France, London, SW1H 9AJ.

9.5 There is a final appeal to the High Court.[11] This requires a certificate that a point of principle of general importance is involved. Applications should be made to the SCCO within 21 days of the receipt of the decision of the costs judge; and the appeal must then be lodged within 21 days of the receipt of the certificate.

9.6 Proceedings in the SCCO and the High Court are civil and costs follow the event. Private client rates apply. Only in the most significant cases is the LAA represented before the costs judge.

Court of Appeal

9.7 Remuneration Regulations 2013 Sch 3 contains provisions in para 11 in relation to costs appeals. There is a process of redetermination and appeal to the costs judge as in Crown Court cases.

Time limits, extensions and late claims

Crime lower[12]

9.8 All claims should be submitted within three months of the end of the matter, case or duty session. Where a warrant for an arrest is issued, the three-month time limit runs from six weeks after the date of issue. Where a client withdraws instructions, the time will run from the withdrawal or transfer of the representation order.[13] The original submission date will be maintained if a claim is initially rejected.[14]

9.9 However, under the contract there is no specific sanction for a failure to comply with this requirement. CBAM 9.3.6 does not appear to be justified by the terms of the Standard Crime Contract (SCC). Other paragraphs of the specification provide for the rejection of a claim, but this does not appear in SCC Specification 8.3. However, SCC Standard Terms 14.5, 24 and 25 contain provisions to deal with persistent breaches.

---

11 Remuneration Regulations 2013 reg 30.
12 SCC Specification 8.3; CBAM 9.3.
13 CRIMLA 75.
14 CBAM 9.3.4.

Crown Court cases[15]

9.10 Claims must be submitted within three months of the conclusion of the proceedings.[16] Once a claim has been submitted within the time limit, an amended bill may be delivered without limit of time. This is consistent with the power of the LAA to recoup over-payments for an unlimited time (see para 9.41).

When time begins to run

Confiscation cases

9.11 The LAA seeks[17] to draw a distinction between litigators and advocates, although the wording of the relevant paragraphs is identical and the courts have pointed out that a representation order covers all the proceedings to which it relates.[18] The LAA regards the time for litigators in the main case as beginning to run on acquittal or sentence, while for advocates time runs from the end of confiscation proceedings. Their justification is practical, in that the advocate's fee varies if there are confiscation proceedings, while the litigator's graduated fee is fixed and the confiscation account is paid separately by hourly rates. The distinction seems unjustified, although for cash-flow reasons litigators should lodge the trial bill as early as possible.

Cases where an appeal is lodged

9.12 There are differing decisions on whether time runs from the sentencing of a defendant, or from the time that advice on appeal is given. Surprisingly in *R v Dumbaya*[19] the costs judge held that, even if the advice was out of time, it was the delivery of that document that started the three-month time limit.

9.13 To the opposite effect is the decision in *R v Fletcher*,[20] that it was the acquittal or sentence that started the time running. This seems sounder in principle. Otherwise the calculation of the contribution payable by a client could be extensively delayed and there is no need

---

15 Remuneration Regulations 2013. The issue is considered at CCFG Appendix A.
16 Remuneration Regulations 2013 regs 4(3) and 5(3).
17 See CCFG Appendix A.
18 *R v Taylor* [2013] 2 Costs LR 374 disapproving of the earlier decision in *R v Turnbull* SCCO 86/12.
19 [2012] 5 Costs LR 976.
20 SCCO 85/12.

for costs purposes to delay lodging the bill. If there is positive advice, and an appeal is lodged, the work may be claimed from the Registrar of Criminal Appeals; in other circumstances no additional fee is due.

Retrials

9.14 Time runs from the end of a retrial.[21]

9.15 For litigators it may be wise to delay the initial bill until it is clear if there is a trial and a retrial or a single longer trial which can have very different effects on the remuneration payable.

Extensions

9.16 It is good practice to seek an extension of time before the time limit expires, but this is not essential.[22]

9.17 Under Remuneration Regulations 2013 reg 31, any time limit may be extended, for 'good reason', and the bill will then be paid in full. This is a term of art and requires that there is no fault on the part of the practitioner. Bad management cannot justify the use of this provision.

9.18 The requirement for a time extension will often arise out of the needs of the client so that the file has to be retained to deal with an urgent appeal or with co-defendants whose cases continue or because there are related proceedings in another (often civil) jurisdiction. The reason for delay must normally be outside the control of the practitioner. In *R v Grigoropolou and others*[23] the judge indicated that bereavement, burglary, flood, serious illness, may be sufficient. The incorrect insertion of the concluding date of the case met the requirement in the leading case. Problems in obtaining responses from the CPS on page count were thought no longer to qualify.[24] It is suggested that the highest proper page count should be inserted and appeal procedures be used as necessary.

9.19 Under Remuneration Regulations 2013 reg 31(2) if there is no 'good reason', the time limit may in 'exceptional circumstances' be extended, when a percentage reduction may be made in the amount billed. Because of the mechanical nature of the graduated fee schemes exceptional circumstances will be difficult to identify. When to disallow the entire claim would be a disproportionate sanction,

21 *R v Hart-Badger* [2013] 1 Costs LR 181.
22 *R v North Kent Justices ex p McGoldrick & Co* (1996) 160 JP 30 on identical wording in the Costs in Criminal Cases (General) Regulations 1986 SI No 1335.
23 [2012] 5 Costs LR 982.
24 And see *R v Fletcher* SCCO 85/12; CCFG Appendix A para 2.4.

9.20 exceptional circumstances may be found and a percentage reduction in the fees payable may be made.

Each case will have to be considered on its own merits (*Grigoropolou* (above) developing the decision in *R v Lafayette*[25]). See also *R v Fletcher*[26] and *R v Turnbull*[27] where a deduction of ten per cent was in each case thought to be proportionate.

9.21 Sickness can amount to good reason for late submission if supported by suitable evidence. Otherwise it may be an exceptional circumstance.[28]

9.22 An unintentional but careless delay of six to seven months in submitting a bill should not deprive a solicitor of disbursements to the value of £2,000 (in a total bill of £3,000). This amounted to exceptional circumstances.[29]

9.23 An appeal on these issues lies to the costs judge. The SCCO has indicated that the time limits will, because of the need to calculate the value of a client's contribution order, be more rigorously enforced than in the past.

9.24 There is no power to reverse an extension of time once granted.[30]

Interim staged and hardship payments on account

9.25 The Remuneration Regulations 2013 allow for various types of interim staged or hardship payments.

Interim payments of disbursements[31]

9.26 Disbursements under the SCC are paid as part of the standard monthly payment and the prior authority sought electronically on Form CRM4 provides security against the sum being reduced or refused on audit. There is a payment on account only in wholly exceptional case where the disbursement exceeds the standard monthly payment.[32]

---

25 [2010] 4 Costs LR 650.
26 SCCO 85/12.
27 SCCO 86/12.
28 *R v Aldridge* SCCO 221/13.
29 *R v Cox* SCCO 299/12.
30 *R v Aldridge* SCCO 221/13.
31 See CCFG 1.14. Use Form LF1 interim.
32 SCC Specification 10.107–10.110.

9.27 However, in the higher courts Remuneration Regulations 2013[33] payments will be made where the firm has incurred a liability of £100 or more for a disbursement and a claim is made electronically on Form CRM4.

9.28 Once prior authority has been given an application for a payment on account may be made by submitting the authority and the invoice concerned. This significantly reduces the cash flow difficulties of having to meet liabilities for disbursements before the end of a case.

9.29 If there are likely to be a series of bills individually below £100 (such as for interpreters) it is best to identify the total costs likely to be involved over a period of time so that an authority can be obtained and a payment on account made.

Interim payments to crown court advocates in case awaiting determination[34]

9.30 This entitlement arises when the graduated fee is £4,000 or more and there is a delay of six months since the conclusion of the proceedings against the person represented; three months must also have elapsed since the claim was lodged or all proceedings concluded. This will assist where there are continuing proceedings against co-defendants or protracted confiscation proceedings. Forty per cent of the fees due is paid.[35]

Interim payments to crown court litigators[36]

9.31 In each case the interim payment is made on the basis of the pages of prosecution evidence (PPE) at the relevant date and any defendant uplift appropriate.

9.32 A first interim payment is due in cases where there has been an effective hearing at which a not guilty plea has been entered, *except* in cases where the defendant elected for trial.

9.33 The value of the claim is 75 per cent of the cracked trial rate for the particular case (see paras 5.129–5.133).

9.34 A second interim payment is due where a trial has commenced and the estimated length is at least ten days.

33 Remuneration Regulations 2013 reg 14.
34 Remuneration Regulations 2013 reg 18. See CCFG 1.18–1.19.
35 Remuneration Regulations 2013 reg 19.
36 Remuneration Regulations 2013 reg 17A; see CCFG 1.17A. Claims are made on Form LF3 to the LAA's Nottingham office. The claim at the end of the case is then made on Form LF3A.

9.35　The value of the claim is the fee for a one-day trial for the particular case. The value of the first interim payment (if claimed) will be deducted.

9.36　The third set of interim payments is made in relation to cases that go to retrial. When a *different* litigator is instructed the first interim claim can be made when the date of the retrial date is set and the representation order transferred. The value is 50 per cent of the cracked trial fee. The second interim payment is available once the trial had commenced and is estimated to last for at least ten days. The fee is that for a one-day trial les any first interim payment made.

9.37　Claims are made on Form LF3 with the final claim on Form LF3A.

Staged payments for advocates[37]

9.38　This entitlement arises for each occasion when there has been preparation of 100 hours or more if the Crown Court case is likely to have in excess of 12 months between the sending (or later grant of legal aid) and the conclusion of the case.

Hardship payments[38]

9.39　These applications can be made when:
- the firm or advocate has acted in relation to Crown Court proceedings for at least six months; and final payment is unlikely for three months; and
- the delay is likely to cause financial hardship; and
- the amount due is at least £5,000.

9.40　The LAA also has extra-statutory arrangements in place where significant bills in excess of £10,000 are delayed in payment.

Overpayments

9.41　Even where the mistake is their own,[39] the LAA has a general power under Remuneration Regulations 2013 reg 25 to recover overpayments identified later by them. All payments made as interim payments are deducted from the final claim.[40]

37　Remuneration Regulations 2013 reg 20. See CCFG 1.20.
38　Remuneration Regulations 2013 reg 21. See CCFG 1.21.
39　*The Lord Chancellor v Eddowes Perry and Osbourne Ltd* [2011] EWHC 420 (QB), applied in *R v Geeling* SCCO 40/14.
40　See also SCC Specification 8.53–8.54.

CHAPTER 10
Relevant civil proceedings

10.3	Part 1: Prescribed proceedings
10.7	Magistrates' court proceedings
10.8	Crown Court proceedings
10.15	Part 2: Civil proceedings related to criminal cases
10.19	Part 3: Civil proceedings in the youth court and other courts: injunctions and breach of injunctions
10.19	Injunctions
10.22	Provision for the Independent Bar
10.23	Breach of a civil injunction
10.25	Other civil proceedings where criminal law solicitors may act

172 Criminal Costs: legal aid costs in the criminal courts / chapter 10

10.1 Three groups of case are considered in this chapter:
- Part 1 Prescribed proceedings under Criminal Legal Aid (General) Regulations 2013 reg 9, as amended, both in the magistrates' courts and the Crown Court.[1]
- Part 2 Civil proceedings related to criminal cases.[2]
- Part 3 Civil injunction proceedings.[3]

10.2 Contempt of court: Contempt in the face of the court is provided for by Legal Aid, Sentencing and Punishment of Offenders Act (LASPO) 2012 s14 and forms part of the normal criminal costing regime. Other contempts of court are prescribed proceedings as set below, whether in the county court (*Brown v Haringey LBC*[4]) or the High Court[5] or Court of Appeal (*Devon CC v Teresa Kirk*[6]), and whether the proceedings are criminal, civil or family.[7]

Part 1: Prescribed proceedings[8]

10.3 These are civil proceedings but are conducted under criminal legal aid. This is authorised by LASPO 2012 s14(h). Paragraph 10.131 of the Standard Crime Contract (SCC) 2017 extends these provisions to stand-alone applications for one of these orders. A summary of the remuneration rates appears at appendix M.

10.4 The civil proceedings involved are listed in Criminal Legal Aid (General) Regulations 2013[9] reg 9. They include civil applications for domestic violence protection orders,[10] closure orders if a criminal behaviour is involved,[11] football banning orders, restraining orders on acquittal; and sexual risk orders, among many others. CBAM Annex A lists relevant proceedings and the representation orders

1 SI No 9. Criminal Bills Assessment Manual (CBAM) 6.18 (domestic violence protection orders); 6.129 (closure orders); and generally CBAM Schedule B.
2 CBAM 13.1 and 13.2.
3 CBAM 13.3.
4 [2015] EWCA Civ 483.
5 *King's Lynn and West Norfolk Council v Bunning* [2013] EWHC 3390 (QB).
6 [2016] EWCA Civ 1221.
7 Criminal Legal Aid (General) Regulations 2013 reg 9(v).
8 Criminal Legal Aid (General) Regulations 2013 SI No 9 reg 9 (as amended). For guidance, see CCFG Appendix N (and appendix I).
9 Criminal Legal Aid (Remuneration) Regulations 2013 SI No 435 ('Remuneration Regulations 2013').
10 CBAM 6.17.
11 CBAM 6.18.

required. A contempt other than in the face of the court is covered by these provisions.[12]

10.5 Variations of Crown Court orders of this type may be sought under these provisions. CCFG Appendix N lists a number of the relevant proceedings.

10.6 These prescribed proceedings are subject to a costs limitation (which can be extended on form CRM5) of £1,368.75.

Magistrates' court proceedings

10.7 In the magistrates' courts, the remuneration arrangements are the same as those for criminal cases and reference should be made to chapter 3.

Crown Court proceedings

10.8 Special provision is made for proceedings in the Crown Court.[13]

10.9 Guidance is offered at Crown Court Fees Guidance (CCFG) Appendix O, although the statutory references need in some cases to be updated.

10.10 Where the case originates by way of appeal, the hourly rates in para 10.13 apply.[14]

10.11 In relation to proceedings other than on appeal from the Magistrates' court), these rules apply if there is no other provision for payment in the Remuneration Regulations 2013.[15] An extendable upper fee limit of £1,368.75 applies to this work. In such proceedings, counsel is always treated as unassigned and cannot charge more than the relevant hourly rates. The same hourly rates apply to proceedings originating in the Crown Court on appeal.[16]

10.12 While claims for Crown Court prescribed proceedings are made as part of the normal monthly return, the amounts involved are paid separately from the standard monthly payment.

---

12 LASPO 2012 s14(g) makes specific provision for a representation order for a contempt in the face of the court which are therefore criminal proceedings subject to normal costs rules with a specific fixed fee in the Crown Court.
13 SCC Specification 10.134.
14 Remuneration Regulations 2013 Sch 4 para 10.
15 Remuneration Regulations 2013; Standard Crime Contract (SCC) Specification 10.131–10.142.
16 Remuneration Regulations 2013 Sch 4 para 7.

174   *Criminal Costs: legal aid costs in the criminal courts* / *chapter 10*

10.13   It should be noted that London rates are still available under these provisions. The figures are for cases beginning on or after 1 April 2016.

	London	National
Routine letters written and telephone calls per item	£3.70	£3.56
Preparation hourly rate	£47.95	£45.35
Advocacy hourly rate	£56.89	£56.89
Travelling and waiting hourly rate	£24.00	£24.00

10.14   Where prescribed proceedings take place in the High Court or a county court, the rates are as follows, again subject to the extendable costs limitation of £1,368.75. The figures are for cases beginning on or after 1 April 2016.

Item	London	National
Routine letters out per item	£6.84	£6.02
Routine telephone calls per item	£3.79	£3.33
All other preparation work hourly rate	£68.44 (£72.54 where the provider's office is in London)	£60.23 (£63.88 where the provider's office is in London)
Attending counsel in conference or at the trial or hearing of any summons or application at court or other appointment – hourly rate	£33.76	£29.66
Attending without counsel at the trial or hearing of any cause or the hearing of any summons or other application at court or other appointment – hourly rate	£68.44	£60.23
Travelling and waiting hourly rate	£30.34	£26.65

Part 2: Civil proceedings related to criminal cases

10.15   The Crime Contract makes special provision for related work in the High Court, family and county court.[17] This will cover, for instance,

17   SCC Specification 10.151–10.162.

proceedings for leave to see a family law file in connection with an abuse allegation, and to oppose the grant of a voluntary bill. Bail applications, appeals by way of case stated and work in the 'associated civil work' class are excluded from this provision.[18]

10.16 There is no financial eligibility test.[19]

10.17 Prior authority always has to be obtained from the LAA.[20] Criminal payment rates apply[21] which are the same as those for Legal Representation under the civil specification.[22]

10.18 The provisions on associated civil legal aid work also allow those with criminal contracts to undertake judicial review and habeas corpus applications and a limited range of work (following restrictions introduced by LASPO 2012[23]), under the Proceeds of Crime Act 2002.[24] Claims are made in accordance with the civil scheme.

Part 3: Civil proceedings in the youth court and other courts: injunctions and breach of injunctions[25]

Injunctions

10.19 The youth court has jurisdiction to deal with civil and gang injunctions affecting those under 18. However, these require either legal help or the grant of civil legal aid.[26] The rates are set out in Civil Legal Aid (Remuneration) Regulations 2013 Sch 1.

10.20 The first stage is the giving of advice. This is dealt with as controlled work-legal help. The rates are as follows: a standard fee of £157 unless the escape threshold is reached.[27] These figures apply to all cases started on or after 23 March 2015.

---

18 SCC Specification 10.151.
19 SCC Specification 10.154.
20 SCC Specification 10.151.
21 SCC Specification 10.156.
22 SCC Specification 10.157.
23 LASPO 2012 Sch 1 para 40.
24 SCC Specification 13.
25 For breach proceedings see SCC Specification 10.168–10.178.
26 CBAM 14.3.
27 Civil Legal Aid (Remuneration) Regulations 2013 SI No 422 Sch 1 and Pts 1 and 2.

Remuneration for legal aid services: applications for and appeals against Part 1 injunctions

CONTROLLED WORK: LEGAL HELP Standard fee £157 but:			
Escape threshold	Applicable rate where escape threshold reached		
£471	Preparation, attendance and advocacy	£46.53 (London rate)	£43.88 per hour (non-London rate)
	Travel and waiting time	£24.62 per hour	£24.62 per hour
	Routine letters out and telephone calls	£3.60 per item	£3.47 per item

10.21 Thereafter for the proceedings, the matter is dealt with by licensed work – legal representation, for which the rates are as follows:[28]

LICENSED WORK: LEGAL REPRESENTATION		
Activity	Higher courts	County courts and magistrates' courts
Routine letters out	£6.75 per item	£5.94 per item
Routine telephone calls	£3.74 per item	£3.29 per item
Preparation and attendance	£71.55 per hour (London rate) £67.50 per hour (non-London rate)	£63.00 per hour (London rate) £59.40 per hour (non-London rate)
Attendance at court or conference with counsel	£33.30	£29.25
Advocacy	£67.50 per hour	£59.40 per hour
Travelling and waiting time	£29.93 per hour	£26.28 per hour

Provision for the Independent Bar[29]

10.22 Special provision has been made for the Bar in these proceedings if they are *assigned* to deal with the case when the following rates apply. Proceedings in the youth court are handled at the county court rates.

---

28 Civil Legal Aid (Remuneration) Regulations 2013 Sch 1 Pt 3.
29 Civil Legal Aid (Remuneration) Regulations 2013 SI No 422 Sch 2.

Proceedings on appeal to the Crown Court are handled at the High Court rates.

REMUNERATION OF BARRISTERS IN INDEPENDENT PRACTICE IN RELATION TO WORK THAT IS NOT CONTROLLED WORK, ADVOCACY SERVICES IN FAMILY PROCEEDINGS OR OTHER LEGAL SERVICES IN RELATION TO INQUESTS	
Category	Hourly rate
Preparation and attendance in the High Court or Upper Tribunal	£71.55 (London rate) £67.50 (non-London rate)
Preparation and attendance in the county court	£63.00 (London rate) £59.40 (non-London rate)
Attendance at court or conference in the High Court or Upper Tribunal	£33.30
Attendance at court or conference in the county court	£29.25
Advocacy in the High Court or Upper Tribunal	£67.50
Advocacy in the county court	£59.40
Travel and waiting time in the High Court or Upper Tribunal	£29.93
Travel and waiting in the county court	£26.28

Breach of a civil injunction[30]

10.23 Breach is dealt with as a contempt of court and so falls within Criminal Legal Aid (General) Regulations 2013 reg 9(v). It should be distinguished from breach of a criminal behaviour order which is dealt with as a criminal offence in the normal way.

10.24 Remuneration for breach of a civil injunction is by a standard fee scheme which mirrors that at chapter 3. Core costs should be calculated in accordance with the escape threshold rates below and the total value compared with fee limits. Travel and waiting are then added and it should be noted that for these hearings payments *are* made in all courts for travel and waiting.[31] These figures relate to

---

30 Anti-Social Behaviour, Crime and Policing Act 2014 Part 1; CBAM 6.14–6.15; SCC Specification 10.168–10.178; Matter Type ASAS should be used.
31 SCC Specification 10.174; Remuneration Regulations 2013 Sch 4 para 5A.

cases with a representation order dated on or after 1 April 2016. If counsel is assigned, which is automatic in the High or County court, a claim can be made at £70 per hour.[32]

Remuneration for legal aid services: breach of a Part 1 injunction STANDARD FEES				
	Lower standard fee	Lower standard fee limit	Higher standard fee	Higher standard fee limit
Category 1B	£158.27	£272.34	£380.70	£471.85
Category 2	£279.45	£467.84	£640.94	£779.64

Escape Threshold Rates	
All areas	
Routine letters written and telephone calls per item	£3.56
Preparation hourly rate	£45.35
Advocacy hourly rate (including applications for bail and other applications to the court)	£56.89
Hourly rate for attendance at court where counsel is assigned (including conferences with counsel at court)	£31.03
Travelling and waiting hourly rate	£24.00

Other civil proceedings where criminal law solicitors may act

10.25 Where an adult is concerned in civil injunction proceedings, the hearing will take place in the High Court or County Court. The remuneration rates are those set out at paras 10.20 and 10.21 above.

10.26 Where breach of a civil injunction by an adult is alleged, this too will be dealt with in the county court (under Criminal Legal Aid (General) Regulations 2013 reg 9) and the standard fee scheme above at para 10.24 applies together with payment for travel and waiting.

---

32 CBAM 6.15.2.

APPENDICES

A Claims summary for Crime Lower   179

B Criminal matter type code descriptions for magistrates' court work   183

C Guidance for reporting Crime Lower Work   195

D Police station scheme codes   209

E Magistrates' court codes   279

F Prison ID codes   293

G Crown Court litigators' offence classes   297

H Mark-ups for litigators   313

I Advocates' rate bands and graduated fee tables   315

J Crown Court hourly rates and Court of Appeal fees   339

K Very high cost cases (VHCC) payment rates   343

L Experts' fees and rates   345

M Prescribed proceedings fees   349

N Crime Lower Rates   351

O Magistrates' court fees and Crown Court fees for non-indictable offences   361

P Payments for assigned counsel   363

APPENDIX A

Claims summary for Crime Lower

The availability of advice and assistance, advocacy assistance and representation is summarised in the following table.

See Contract Specifications for

- Criminal investigations   SCC Specification 9
- Criminal proceedings   SCC Specification 10
- Appeals and reviews   SCC Specification 11
- Prison law   SCC Specification 12
- Associated civil work   SCC Specification 13

Guidance on applying for extensions to the limits on form CRM5e is at CBAM8. The figures below relate to matters or cases commencing on or after 1 April 2016.

Advice and assistance claims	Merits	Means	Authority	Limits
Criminal law (excluding criminal proceedings)	Sufficient benefit test	Regs [2]Pt 2	Devolved power [1]	£273.75 but 2 hours if no evidence of means Zero until seek such evidence
Police station telephone advice*	Sufficient benefit test	None	Devolved power	Fixed fee
Police station attendance*	Sufficient benefit test	None	Devolved power	None [6]
Prison law	Sufficient benefit test	Regs [2]Pt 2	Devolved power	None [6]
Appeal: CCRC	Sufficient benefit test	Regs [2]Pt 2	Devolved power	£456.25
Appeal: others	Sufficient benefit test	Regs [2]Pt 2	Devolved power	£273.75
Associated civil legal aid	Funding Code	Regs [9]	Devolved power	Civil [7]

Advocacy assistance claims	Merits	Means	Authority	Limits [8]
Warrant for further detention/bail hearings/armed forces custody hearing	None	None	Devolved power	£1,368.75
Duty solicitor session* [3]	None (unless non imp and not in custody)	None	Devolved power	None
Prison law	Sufficient benefit test	Regs [2]Pt 2	Devolved power	None [6]
Pre-order costs	Interests of justice, submission and refusal of Forms CRM 14/15 SCC 10.115	None	Devolved power	1 hour + VAT (limit)
Early cover	SCC 10.122	None	Devolved power	£68.44 + VAT
Initial advice	SCC 10.124	None	Devolved power	£22,81 + VAT

Representation claims	Merits	Means	Authority	Limits
Magistrates' court/ Crown Court	Interests of justice [5]	Regs[2] Pt 3	LAA	None [6]
Prescribed proceedings other than on appeal	Interests of justice	Regs[2] Pt 3	LAA	£1,368.75
High Court/county court proceedings	Interests of justice	None	High Court/LAA	None. Bill to High Court
High Court representation on appeal by way of case stated	Interests of justice	Regs [2]	High Court	None: (subject to RDCO) bill to High Court
Associated civil legal aid investigative help and legal representation	Funding Code (proceeds of crime: interests of justice)	Civil regs	LAA	Civil [8]

* No application form needed.

[1] Power to grant or refuse is solicitor's.

[2] Criminal Legal Aid (Financial Resources) Regulations 2013 SI No 471.

[3] If a case concluded by duty solicitor, no application for a representation order may be made.

[4] Merits test in Contract Specification 12.
[5] Legal Aid, Sentencing and Punishment of Offenders Act 2012 s17. See *R (David Sonn) v West London MC* When considering the risk of loss of liberty the test is real and practical not theoretical risk. However, for a man with a long history of identical shoplifting offences, often resulting in custody, it was unreasonable to refuse legal aid; *R (Punatar & Co) v Horseferry Road Magistrates Court* [2002] EWHC 1196 (Admin), the LA must consider the application on the basis of the charge known to the solicitor at the time of the application for which they attend court even if that charge was withdrawn at the first hearing *Highgate Justices ex p Lewis* [1977] Crim LR 611). In assessing whether the accused is likely to lose his liberty, regard must be had to the facts alleged by the prosecution, rather than the maximum penalty that could theoretically be imposed (So it is not enough that the offence carries a custodial sentence: the court must consider whether a custodial sentence might be imposed in the particular case. *Liverpool City Magistrates ex p McGhee* [1993] Crim LR 609, An unpaid work requirement could not be regarded as a sentence which deprives the accused of liberty. However, the list of criteria in LASPO 2012 s17) is not exhaustive, and so the possibility of a community order with a relevant requirement) may be a factor in deciding whether or not to make a representation order. *Liverpool City Magistrates ex p McGhee*. The factor which includes expert cross-examination of witnesses (see s17(2)(d) means expert cross-examination of witnesses, not cross-examination of expert witnesses); *Scunthorpe Justices ex p S* (1998) *The Times*, 5 March 1998, refusal of legal aid to an accused aged 16 who sought to challenge whether a police officer had acted in the execution of his duty was irrational. The expertise needed to cross-examine police witnesses, and to find, select and proof defence witnesses, was beyond an accused aged 16. *R (GKR Law Solicitors) v Liverpool Magistrates' Court* [2008] EWHC 2974 (Admin) it is appropriate to grant representation to a defendant in relation to a special reasons hearing, where a witness in the case was the defendant's 12-year-old son. The child was a witness entitled to and requiring special measures and consideration would need to be given to video-interviewing the young witness in order to ensure best evidence is given; such measures would be outside the competence and resources of the defendant. *R (Matara) v Brent Magistrates' Court* (2005) 169 JP 576, an interpreter would be provided at court without legal aid but that did not meet the point that it was the claimant's case that he was unable to understand what was being said at the time of his arrest, a point which lay at the heart of his defence. It went to his ability to state his own case and the overall fairness of the trial *Chester Magistrates' Court ex p Ball* (1999) 163 JP 813 Any defendant of previous good character pleading not guilty to a charge equal to, or more significant than Public Order Act 1986 s5 in terms of nature and seriousness might be granted legal aid regardless of his social or professional standing, because there might be damage to the defendant's reputation. *Gravesend Magistrates' Court ex p Baker* (1977) 161 JP 765 the defendant was charged with driving with excess alcohol and put forward special reasons based on spiked drinks. The applicant should be granted legal aid because a scientific expert would be required and the assistance of a solicitor would be necessary to identify witnesses, take proper proofs and extract the defence from the defendant in the witness box.
[6] Subject to standard and graduated fee schemes which may limit the total bill.
[7] Civil Legal Aid (Merits Criteria) Regulations 2013 SI No 104.
[8] Limitations may be extended on application to the LAA Guidance on obtaining extensions is given at CBAM8.
[9] Civil Legal Aid (Financial Resources and Payment for Services) Regulations 2013 SI No 480.

APPENDIX B

Criminal matter type code descriptions for magistrates' court work[1]

1 Offences against the person
- Assault (common) (Criminal Justice Act 1988 s39)
- Battery (common) (Criminal Justice Act 1988 s39)
- Assault occasioning actual bodily harm (Offences against the Person Act 1861 s47)
- Wounding or inflicting grievous bodily harm (Offences against the Person Act 1861 s20)
- Wounding or causing grievous bodily harm with intent (Offences against the Person Act 1861 s18)
- Making threats to kill (Offences against the Person Act 1861 s16)
- Racially aggravated assaults (Crime and Disorder Act 1998 s29(1))
- Assault on constable in execution of duty (Police Act 1996 s89)
- Resisting or wilfully obstructing constable (Police Act 1996 s89)
- Assault with intention to resist arrest (Offences against the Person Act 1861 s38)
- Attempting to choke, suffocate, strangle, etc (Offences against the Person Act 1861 s21)
- Endangering the safety of railway passengers (Offences against the Person Act 1861 ss32, 33, 34)
- Causing bodily injury by explosives (Offences against the Person Act 1861 s28)
- Using gunpowder to explode, or sending to any person an explosive substance, or throwing corrosive fluid on a person, with intent to grievous bodily harm (Offences against the Person Act 1861 s29)
- Placing explosives, etc with intent to do bodily injury to any person (Offences against the Person Act 1861 s30)
- Making or having gunpowder, etc with intent to commit or enable any person to commit a felony (Offences against the Person Act 1861 s64)
- Causing miscarriage by poison, instrument (Offences against the Person Act 1861 s58)
- Supplying instrument, etc to cause miscarriage (Offences against the Person Act 1861 s59)

---

1 Annex D to *Guidance for Reporting Crime Lower Work*, Legal Aid Agency, June 2018.

- Concealment of birth (Offences against the Person Act 1861 s60)
- Administering chloroform, laudanum, etc (Offences against the Person Act 1861 s22)
- Administering poison, etc so as to endanger life (Offences against the Person 1861 s23)
- Administering poison with intent to injure, etc (Offences against the Person Act 1961 s24)
- Circumcision of females (Prohibition of Female Circumcision Act 1985 s1)
- Kidnapping (common law)
- Hostage taking (Taking of Hostages Act 1982 s1)
- False imprisonment (common law)
- Torture (Criminal Justice Act 1988 s134)

2 Homicide and related grave offences
- Murder (common law)
- Manslaughter (common law)
- Causing death by dangerous driving (Road Traffic Act 1991 sl)
- Causing death by careless driving while under the influence of drink or drugs (Road Traffic Act 1988 s3A)
- Aggravated vehicle taking resulting in death (Theft Act 1968 s12A)
- Killing in pursuance of suicide pact (Homicide Act 1957 s4)
- Complicity to suicide (Suicide Act 1961 s2)
- Soliciting to murder (Offences against the Person Act 1861 s4)
- Child destruction (Infant Life (Preservation) Act 1929 s1(1))
- Infanticide (Infanticide Act 1938 s1(1))
- Abortion (Offences against the Person Act 1861 s58)
- Supplying or procuring means for abortion (Offences against the Person Act 1861 s59)
- Concealment of birth (Offences against the Person Act 1861 s60)

Firearms offences
- Possession of firearm without certificate (Firearms Act 1968 s1)
- Possession or acquisition of shotgun without certificate (Firearms Act 1968 s2)
- Dealing in firearms (Firearms Act 1968 s3)
- Shortening of shotgun or possession of shortened shotgun (Firearms Act 1968 s4)
- Possession or acquisition of certain prohibited weapons, etc (Firearms Act 1968 s5)
- Possession of firearm with intent to injure/endanger life (Firearms Act 1968 s16)
- Possession of firearm or imitation firearm with intent to cause fear of violence (Firearms Act 1968 s16A)
- Use of firearm to resist arrest (Firearms Act 1968 s17)
- Possession of firearm with criminal intent (Firearms Act 1968 s18)
- Carrying loaded firearm in public place (Firearms Act 1968 s19)
- Possession of firearm without certificate (Firearms Act 1968 s19)
- Trespassing with a firearm (Firearms Act 1968 s20)

Criminal matter type code descriptions for magistrates' court work

- Possession of firearms by person convicted of crime (Firearms Act 1968 s21(4))
- Acquisition by or supply of firearms to person denied them (Firearms Act 1968 s21 (5))
- Failure to comply with certificate when transferring firearm (Firearms Act 1968 s42)
- Shortening of smooth bore gun (Firearms Amendment Act 1988 s6(1))

Prison offences
- Permitting an escape (common law)
- Rescue (common law)
- Escape (common law)
- Escaping from lawful custody without force (common law)
- Breach of prison (common law)
- Prison mutiny (Prison Security Act 1992 s1)
- Assaulting prison officer whilst possessing firearm, etc (Criminal Justice Act 1991 s90)
- Harbouring escaped prisoners (Criminal Justice Act 1961 s22)
- Assisting prisoners to escape (Prison Act 1952 s39)
- Offences under the Terrorism Act 2000
- Offences against international protection of nuclear material (Nuclear Material (Offences) Act 1983 s2)
- Offences under the Northern Ireland (Emergency Provisions) Act 1991

3 Sexual offences and offences against children
- Offences under the Sexual Offences Act 2003
- Child abduction by connected person (Child Abduction Act 1984 s 1)
- Child abduction by other person (Child Abduction Act 1984 s2)
- Keeping brothel and related offences (Sexual Offences Act ss33, 34, 35, and 36)
- Keeping a disorderly house (common law: Disorderly Houses Act 1751 s8)
- Soliciting (Street Offences Act 1959 s1)
- Taking, having, etc indecent photographs of children (Protection of Children Act 1978 s1)
- Sexual intercourse with patients (Mental Health Act 1959 s128)
- Ill treatment of persons of unsound mind (Mental Health Act 1983 s127)
- Bigamy (Offences against the Person Act 1861 s57)
- Abuse of position of trust (Sexual Offences (Amendment) Act 2000 s3)
- Abandonment of children under two (Offences against the Person Act 1861 s27)
- Cruelty to persons under 16 (Children and Young Persons Act 1933 s1)

4 Robbery
- Robbery (Theft Act 1968 s8(1))
- Armed robbery (Theft Act 1968 s8(1))
- Assault with weapon with intent to rob (Theft Act 1968 s8(2))

5 Burglary
- Burglary (domestic) (Theft Act 1968 s9(3)(a))

- Going equipped to steal (Theft Act 1968 s25)
- Burglary (non-domestic) (Theft Act 1968 s9(3)(b))
- Aggravated burglary (Theft Act 1968 s10)

6 Criminal damage and arson
- Criminal damage (Criminal Damage Act 1971 s1(1))
- Destroying or damaging property with the intention or recklessness as to endanger life (Criminal Damage Act 1971 s1(2))
- Aggravated criminal damage (Criminal Damage Act 1971 s1(2))
- Threats to destroy or damage property (Criminal Damage Act 1971 s2)
- Racially aggravated criminal damage (Crime and Disorder Act 1998 s30)
- Possessing anything with intent to destroy or damage property (Criminal Damage Act 1971 s3)
- Possessing bladed article/instrument (Criminal Justice Act 1988 s139)
- Prohibition of the carrying of offensive weapons without lawful authority or reasonable excuse (Prevention of Crime Act 1953 s1)
- Arson (Criminal Damage Act 1971 s1(3))
- Aggravated arson (Criminal Damage Act 1971 s1(2), (3))
- Racially aggravated arson (Crime and Disorder Act 1998 s30)

7 Theft (including taking vehicle without consent)
- Theft (Theft Act 1968 s1)
- Taking conveyance without authority (Theft Act 1968 s12)
- Taking or riding a pedal cycle without authority (Theft Act 1968 s 12(5) and s12(6))
- Aggravated vehicle taking (Theft Act 1968 s12A)
- Handling stolen goods (Theft Act 1968 s22)
- Receiving property by another's mistake (Theft Act 1968 s5(4))
- Removal of articles from places open to the public (Theft Act 1968 s11)
- Abstraction of electricity (Theft Act 1968 s13)
- Making off without payment (Theft Act 1978 s3)

8 Fraud, forgery and other offences of dishonesty
- Fraud (common law)
- Forgery (Forgery and Counterfeiting Act 1981 s1)
- Copying a false instrument (Forgery and Counterfeiting Act 1981 s2)
- Using a false statement (Forgery and Counterfeiting Act 1981 s3)
- Using a copy of a false instrument (Forgery and Counterfeiting Act 1981 s4)
- Custody or control of false instruments, etc (Forgery and Counterfeiting Act 1981 s5)
- Offences relating to money orders, share certificates, passports, etc (Forgery and Counterfeiting Act 1981 s5)
- Counterfeiting notes and coins (Forgery and Counterfeiting Act 1981 s14)
- Passing, etc counterfeiting notes and coins (Forgery and Counterfeiting Act 1981 s15)
- Offences involving the custody/control of counterfeit notes and coins (Forgery and Counterfeiting Act 1981 s16)

Criminal matter type code descriptions for magistrates' court work 189

- Making, custody or control of counterfeiting materials, etc (Forgery and Counterfeiting Act 1981 s175)
- Illegal importation: Counterfeit notes or coins (Customs and Excise Management Act 1979 s50)
- Offences involving the making/custody/control of counterfeiting materials and implements (Forgery and Counterfeiting Act 1981 s17)
- Reproducing British currency (Forgery and Counterfeiting Act 1981 s18)
- Offences in making, etc imitation of British coins (Forgery and Counterfeiting Act 1981 s19)
- Prohibition of importation of counterfeit notes and coins (Forgery and Counterfeiting Act 1981 s20)
- Prohibition of exportation of counterfeit notes and coins (Forgery and Counterfeiting Act 1981 s21)
- Destruction of registers of births, etc (Forgery Act 1861 s36)
- Making false entries in copies of registers sent to registrar (Forgery Act 1861 s37)
- Fraudulent evasion: counterfeit notes or coins (Customs and Excise Management Act 1979 s170(2)(b), (c))
- Obtaining services by deception (Theft Act 1978 s1)
- Evasion of liability by deception (Theft Act 1978 s2)
- Obtaining property by deception (Theft Act 1968 s15)
- Obtaining a money transfer by deception (Theft Act 1968 s15A)
- Obtaining pecuniary advantage by deception (Theft Act 1968 s16)
- False accounting (Theft Act 1968 s17)
- Liability of company officers for offences of deception committed by the company (Theft Act 1968 s18)
- False statements by company directors (Theft Act 1968 s19)
- Suppression, etc of documents (Theft Act 1968 s20)
- Procuring execution of a valuable security by deception (Theft Act 1968 s20)
- Advertising rewards for return of goods stolen or lost (Theft Act 1968 s23)
- Dishonestly retaining a wrongful credit (Theft Act 1968 s24A)
- Fraudulent use of telecommunication system (Telecommunications Act 1984 s42)
- Possession or supply of anything for fraudulent purpose in connection with use of telecommunication system (Telecommunications Act 1984 s42A)
- Offences under the Companies Act 1985
- Insider dealing (Criminal Justice Act 1993 s52)
- False declarations of insolvency in voluntary liquidations (Insolvency Act 1986 s89)
- Concealment of property and failure to account for losses (Insolvency Act 1986 s354)
- Concealment or falsification of books and papers (Insolvency Act 1986 s355)
- False statements (Insolvency Act 1986 s356)
- Fraudulent disposal of property (Insolvency Act 1986 s357)
- Absconding with property (Insolvency Act 1986 s358)

- Fraudulent dealing with property obtained on credit (Insolvency Act 1986 s359)
- Undischarged bankrupt concerned in a company (Insolvency Act 1986 s360)
- Failure to keep proper business accounts (Insolvency Act 1986 s361)
- Misleading statements and practices (Financial Services Act 1986 s47)
- Fraudulent inducement to make a deposit (Banking Act 1987 s35(1))
- Counterfeiting customs documents (Customs and Excise Management Act 1979 s168)
- Offences in relation to dies or stamps (Stamp Duties Management Act 1891 s13)
- Counterfeiting of dies or marks (Hallmarking Act 1973 s6)
- Fraudulent application of trademark (Trade Marks Act 1938 s58A)
- False application or use of trademarks (Trade Marks Act 1994 s92)
- Forgery of driving documents (Road Traffic Act 1960 s233)
- Forgery and misuse of driving documents (Public Passenger Vehicles Act 1981 s65)
- Forgery, etc of licences and other documents (Road Traffic Act 1988 s173)
- Mishandling or falsifying parking documents (Road Traffic Regulations Act 1984 s115)
- Forgery, alteration, etc of documents, etc (Goods Vehicles (Licensing of Operators) Act 1995 s38)
- False records or entries relating to driver's hours (Transport Act 1968 s99)
- Forgery, alteration, fraud of licences, etc (Vehicle (Excise) Act 1971 s26)
- Forgery, alteration, etc of licences, marks, trade plates, etc (Vehicle Excise and Registration Act 1994 ss44 and 45)
- Forgery of documents, etc: Motor vehicles (EC Type approval) Regulations 1992 reg 11(1) and Motor cycles, etc (EC Type approval) Regulations 1999 reg 20(1)
- Fraudulent evasion of agricultural levy (Customs and Excise Management Act 1979 s68A(1) and (2))
- Evasion of duty (Customs and Excise Management Act 1979 s170)
- Trade description offences (9 offences) (Trade Descriptions Act 1968 ss1, 8, 9, 12, 13, 14, 18)
- VAT offences (VAT Act 1994)

9 Public order offences

- Breach of any order made by a court
- Causing explosion likely to endanger life or property (Explosive Substances Act 1883 s2)
- Attempt to cause explosion, making or keeping explosive, etc (Explosive Substances Act 1883 s3)
- Making or possession of explosive under suspicious circumstances (Explosive Substances Act 1883 s4)
- Bomb hoaxes (Criminal Law Act 1977 s51)
- Contamination of goods with intent (Public Order Act 1986 s38)
- Placing wood, etc on railway (Malicious Damage Act 1861 s35)
- Exhibiting false signals, etc (Malicious Damage Act 1861 s47)
- Perjuries (7 offences) (Perjury Act 1911 s1–7(2))

Criminal matter type code descriptions for magistrates' court work 191

- Offences akin to perjury: False testimony of unsworn child witnesses in criminal proceedings (Children and Young Persons Act 1933 s38)
- Perverting the course of public justice (common law)
- Public nuisance (common law)
- Contempt of court (common law)
- Blackmail (Theft Act 1968 s21)
- Corrupt transactions with agents (Prevention of Corruption Act 1906 s1)
- Corruption (common law)
- Corruption in public office (Public Bodies Corrupt Practices Act 1889 s1)
- Embracery (common law)
- Fabrication of evidence with intent to mislead a tribunal (common law)
- Personation of jurors (common law)
- Concealing an arrestable offence (Criminal Law Act 1967 s5)
- Assisting offenders (Criminal Law Act 1967 s4(1))
- False evidence before European Court (European Communities Act 1972 s11)
- Intimidating a witness, juror, etc (Criminal Justice and Public Order Act 1994 s51(1))
- Harming, threatening to harm a witness, juror, etc (Criminal Justice and Public Order Act 1994 s51(2))
- Ticket touts (Criminal Justice and Public Order Act 1994 s166)
- Prejudicing a drug trafficking investigation (Drug Trafficking Act 1994 s58(1))
- Giving false statements to procure cremation (Cremation Act 1902 s8(2))
- False statement tendered under section 9 of the Criminal Justice Act 1967 (Criminal Justice Act 1967 s89)
- False statement tendered under section 102 of the Magistrates' Courts Act 1980 (Magistrates' Courts Act 1980 s106)
- Making a false statement to obtain or resist interim possession order (Criminal Justice and Public Order Act 1994 s75)
- Making false statement to authorised officer (Trade Descriptions Act 1968 s29(2))
- Riot (Public Order Act 1986 s1)
- Violent disorder (Public Order Act 1986 s2)
- Affray (Public Order Act 1986 s3)
- Fear or provocation of violence (Public Order Act 1986 s4)
- Intentional harassment, alarm, or distress (Public Order Act 1986 s4A)
- Harassment, alarm or distress (Public Order Act 1986 s5)
- Harassment of debtors (Administration of Justice Act 1970 s40)
- Offence of harassment (Protection from Harassment Act 1997 ss1 and 2)
- Putting people in fear of violence (Protection from Harassment Act 1997 s4)
- Breach of restraining order/injunction (Protection from Harassment Act 1997 ss3 and 5)
- Racially aggravated public order offences (Crime and Disorder Act 1998 s31)
- Racially aggravated harassment, etc (Crime and Disorder Act 1998 s32)
- Using words or behaviour or displaying written material stirring up racial hatred (Public Order Act 1986 s18)

- Publishing or distributing written material stirring up racial hatred (Public Order Act 1986 s19)
- Public performance of play stirring up racial hatred (Public Order Act 1986 s20)
- Distributing, showing or playing a recording stirring up racial hatred (Public Order Act 1986 s21)
- Broadcasting programme stirring up racial hatred (Public Order Act 1986 s22)
- Possession of written material or recording stirring up racial hatred (Public Order Act 1986 s23)
- Possession of offensive weapon (Prevention of Crime Act 1953 s1)
- Possession of bladed article (Criminal Justice Act 1988 s139)
- Criminal libel (common law)
- Blasphemy and blasphemous libel (common law)
- Sedition
- Indecent display (Indecent Displays (Control) Act 1981 s1)
- Presentation of obscene performance (Theatres Act 1968 s2)
- Obstructing railway or carriage on railway (Malicious Damage Act 1861 s36)
- Obscene articles intended for publication for gain (Obscene Publications Act 1964 s1)
- Offences of publication of obscene matter (Obscene Publications Act 1959 s2)
- Agreeing to indemnify sureties (Bail Act 1976 s9(1))
- Absconding by person released on bail (Bail Act 1976 s6(1), (2))
- Personating for purposes of bail, etc (Forgery Act 1861 s34)
- Sending prohibited articles by post (Post Office Act 1953 s11)
- Impersonating Customs officer (Customs and Excise Management Act 1979 s3)
- Obstructing Customs officer (Customs and Excise Management Act 1979 s16)
- Penalty on keepers of refreshment houses permitting drunkenness, disorderly conduct, or gaming, etc therein (Metropolitan Police Act 1839 s44)
- Penalty on persons found drunk (Licensing Act 1872 s12)
- Drunkenness in a public place (Criminal Justice Act 1967 s91)
- Drunk in a late night refreshment house (Late Night Refreshment Houses Act 1969 s9(4)) [this provision was repealed by Licensing Act 2003]
- Drunk while in charge of a child (Licensing Act 1902 s2(1))
- Drunk on an aircraft (Air Navigation Order 2000 and Civil Aviation Act SI No 1562 art 65(1))
- Intimidation or annoyance by violence or otherwise (Trade Union and Labour Relations (Consolidation) Act 1992 s241)
- Offences under the Official Secrets Acts 1911, 1920 and 1989
- Unlawful interception of communications by public and private systems (Regulation of Investigatory Powers Act 2000 s1)
- Disclosure of telecommunication messages (Telecommunications Act 1984 s45)
- Incitement to disaffection (Incitement to Disaffection Act 1934 ss1 and 2)

Criminal matter type code descriptions for magistrates' court work 193

10 Drug offences
- Restriction of importation and exportation of controlled drugs (Misuse of Drugs Act s3)
- Producing or supplying a Class A, B or C drug (Misuse of Drugs Act 1971 s4)
- Possession of controlled drugs (Misuse of Drugs Act 1971 s5(2))
- Possession of a Class A, B or C drug with intent to supply (Misuse of Drugs Act 1971 s5(3))
- Cultivation of cannabis plant (Misuse of Drugs Act 1971 s6)
- Occupier knowingly permitting drugs offences, etc (Misuse of Drugs Act 1971 s8)
- Activities relating to opium (Misuse of Drugs Act 1971 s9)
- Prohibition of supply, etc of articles for administering or preparing controlled drugs (Misuse of Drugs Act 1971 s9A)
- Offences relating to the safe custody of controlled drugs (Misuse of Drugs Act 1971 s11)
- Practitioner contravening drug supply regulations (Misuse of Drugs Act 1971 ss12 and 13)
- Incitement (Misuse of Drugs Act 1971 s19)
- Assisting in or inducing commission outside United Kingdom of offence punishable under a corresponding law (Misuse of Drugs Act 1971 s20)
- Powers of entry, search and seizure (Misuse of Drugs Act 1971 s23)
- Illegal importation of Class A, B or C drugs (Customs and Excise Management Act 1979 s50)
- Fraudulent evasion of controls on Class A, B or C drugs (Customs and Excise Management Act 1979 s170(2)(b)(c))
- Failure to disclose knowledge or suspicion of money laundering (Drug Trafficking Offences Act 1986 s26B)
- Tipping-off in relation to money laundering investigations (Drug Trafficking Offences Act 1986 s26C)
- Offences in relation to proceeds of drug trafficking (Drug Trafficking Act 1994 ss49, 50 and 51)
- Offences in relation to money laundering investigations (Drug Trafficking Act 1994 ss52 and 53)
- Manufacture and supply of scheduled substances (Criminal Justice (International Co-operation) Act 1990 s12)
- Drug trafficking offences at sea (Criminal Justice (International Co-operation) Act 1990 s18)
- Ships used for illicit traffic (Criminal Justice (International Co-operation) Act 1990 s19)
- Making and preserving records of production and supply of certain scheduled substances (Controlled Drugs (Substances Useful for Manufacture) Regulations 1991)
- Supply of intoxicating substance (Intoxicating Substances (Supply) Act 1985 s1)

11 Driving and motor vehicle offences (other than those covered by codes 1, 6 & 7)
- Dangerous driving (Road Traffic Act 1988 s2)

- Careless, and inconsiderate driving (Road Traffic Act 1988 s3)
- Driving, or being in charge, when under the influence of drink or drugs (Road Traffic Act 1988 s4)
- Driving or being in charge of a motor vehicle with excess alcohol (Road Traffic Act 1988 s5)
- Breath tests (Road Traffic Act 1988 s6)
- Provision of specimens for analysis (Road Traffic Act 1988 s7)
- Motor racing on highways (Road Traffic Act 1988 s12)
- Leaving vehicle in dangerous position (Road Traffic Act 1988 s22)
- Causing danger to road users (Road Traffic Act 1988 s22A)
- Restriction of carriage of persons on motor cycles (Road Traffic Act 1988 s23)
- Failing to stop at school gate (Road Traffic Act 1988 s28)
- Failure to comply with indication given by traffic sign (Road Traffic Act 1988 s36)
- Directions to pedestrians (Road Traffic Act 1988 s37)
- Using vehicles in dangerous condition (Road Traffic Act 1988 s40A)
- Contravention of construction and use regulations (Road Traffic Act 1988 s41A)
- Using, etc motor vehicle without test certificate (Road Traffic Act 1988 s47)
- Driving otherwise than in accordance with a licence (Road Traffic Act 1988 s87)
- Driving after refusal or revocation of licence (Road Traffic Act 1988 s94A)
- False declaration as to physical fitness (Road Traffic Act 1988 s92)
- Failure to notify disability (Road Traffic Act 1988 s94)
- Driving with uncorrected defective eyesight (Road Traffic Act 1988 s96)
- Driving while disqualified (Road Traffic Act 1988 s103)
- Using, etc motor vehicle without insurance (Road Traffic Act 1988 s143)
- Failure to produce driving licence, insurance, etc (Road Traffic Offenders Act 1988 s27)
- Failure to give, or giving false, name and address in case of dangerous or careless or inconsiderate driving or cycling (Road Traffic Act 1988 s168)
- Pedestrian contravening constable's direction to stop to give name and address (Road Traffic Act 1988 s169)
- Failing to stop and failing to report accident (Road Traffic Act 1988 s170)
- Duty of owner of motor vehicle to give information for verifying compliance with requirement of compulsory insurance or security (Road Traffic Act 1988 s171)
- Duty to give information as to identity of driver, etc in certain circumstances (Road Traffic Act 1988 s172)
- Pedestrian crossing regulations (Road Traffic Regulation Act 1984 s25)
- Street playgrounds (Road Traffic Regulation Act 1984 s29)
- Speeding (Road Traffic Regulation Act 1984 s89)
- Wanton or furious driving (Offences against the Person Act 1861 s35)
- Interference with vehicles (Criminal Attempts Act 1981 s9)
- Other road traffic offences (including policing, etc)

12 Other

- Proceedings for the making of anti-social behaviour orders, sex offender orders, etc

Criminal matter type code descriptions for magistrates' court work 195

- Failing to keep dogs under proper control resulting in injury and other dog offences (Dangerous Dogs Act 1991 s3)
- Hijacking of aircraft (Aviation Security Act 1982 s1)
- Destroying, damaging or endangering safety of aircraft (Aviation Security Act 1982 s2)
- Other acts endangering or likely to endanger safety of aircraft (Aviation Security Act 1982 s3)
- Offences in relation to certain dangerous articles (Aviation Security Act 1982 s4)
- Endangering safety at aerodromes (Aviation and Maritime Security Act 1990 s1)
- Hijacking of ships (Aviation and Maritime Security Act 1990 s9)
- Other offences under the Aviation and Maritime Security Act 1990 (Aviation and Maritime Security Act 1990 ss10, 11, 12, and 13)
- Piracy (Piracy Act 1837 s2)
- Offences under the Football Spectators Act 1989
- Throwing of missiles (Football (Offences) Act 1991 s2)
- Indecent or racialist chanting (Football (Offences) Act 1991 s3)
- Going onto the playing area (Football (Offences) Act 1991 s4)
- Offences in connection with alcohol on coaches and trains (Sporting Events (Control of Alcohol, etc) Act 1985 s1)
- Offences in connection with alcohol, containers, etc at sports grounds (Sporting Events (Control of Alcohol, etc) Act 1985 s2)
- Offences of cruelty (Protection of Animals Act 1911 s1)
- Penalties for abandonment of animals (Abandonment of Animals Act 1960 s1)
- Offences (Wild Mammals (Protection) Act 1996 s1)
- Raves (Criminal Justice and Public Order Act 1994 s63)
- Offences affecting enjoyment of premises
- Unlawful eviction and harassment of occupier (Protection of Eviction Act 1977 s1)
- Use or threat of violence for purpose of securing entry to premises (Criminal Law Act 1977 s6(1))
- Adverse occupation of residential premises (Criminal Law Act 1977 s7)
- Trespassing during the currency of an interim possession order (Criminal Justice and Public Order Act 1994 s76)
- Interim possession orders: false or misleading statements (Criminal Justice and Public Order Act 1994 s75)
- Aggravated trespass (Criminal Justice and Public Order Act 1994 s68)
- Failure to leave or re-entry to land after police direction to leave (Criminal Justice and Public Order Act 1994 s61)
- Unauthorised campers (Criminal Justice and Public Order Act 1994 s77)

APPENDIX C

Guidance for reporting Crime Lower Work

Extracted from LAA Guidance published in June 2018

7 Code guidance

7.1 This guidance covers the description and use of the Criminal Matter Types, Claim/Stage Reached and Outcome Codes.

7.2 Police station, Court and Prison ID codes are annexed to this document.

Criminal Matter Type code guidance

7.3 Criminal Matter Types are recorded for the Criminal Investigations Class of Work, those Matters and Cases in the Criminal Proceedings Class of Work where a Representation Order was issued, and for Prison Law Matters.

7.4 You must not record a Criminal Matter Type when making a Court Duty Solicitor claim or for any claim made in relation to the Appeals and Reviews or Associated Civil work Classes of Work.

7.5 A Criminal Matter Type is not required for a claim made under Claim/Stage Reached Codes INVH & INVI.

Recording Criminal Matter Type for criminal investigations

7.6 Where your client has been charged or warned, you should determine which heading the principal offence or charge that your client faces is listed under. A list of offences falling under a matter type can be found [at the end of this document].

7.7 Where you cannot locate the appropriate charge, you should select Code 12. Where your client has been released without charge, you must record the heading that covers the Criminal Matter Type that he or she was interviewed in relation to (if an interview took place).

7.8 Where you have given freestanding Advice and Assistance (INVA) only, you must record the heading that covers the Criminal Matter Type that advice was given in relation to.

7.9 Where you have only given Police Station Telephone Advice (INVB), you must record the heading that covers the Criminal Matter Type that advice was given in relation to. If you do not know what the nature of the matter was, you must record the Code 12.

Recording Criminal Matter Types for criminal proceedings

7.10 If you advise a witness or any other person who is not subject to an investigation or proceedings then record Code 12.

7.11 Where your client has been charged or summonsed, you must record the final charge that your client faces. Where your client is facing multiple charges, you should identify the most serious charge.

7.12 You should only record the original charge laid by the police if this has not altered during the course of the proceedings. In cases where the charge does alter it is the final charge that must be recorded.

Recording Criminal Matter Types for prison law

7.13 You should select the code that in your judgment best reflects the work undertaken on the case. Where there is more than one issue (and so code that could apply) you should identify the main issue in the case and select the appropriate code. Please also refer to Annex F for Criminal Matter Type Code descriptions.

7.14 Codes relating to treatment cases should only be used where you are reporting a Prison Law Treatment case which you have been granted prior approval to undertake. This will only be possible where you have made an application for criminal legal aid in a treatment matter prior to 2 December 2013.

Criminal Matter Type code table

Code	Description
Criminal investigations and proceedings codes	
1	Offences against the person
2	Homicide and related grave offences
3	Sexual offences and associated offences against children
4	Robbery
5	Burglary
6	Criminal damage
7	Theft (including taking vehicle without consent)
8	Fraud and forgery and other offences of dishonesty
9	Public order offences
10	Drug offences
11	Driving and motor vehicle offences (other than those covered by codes 1, 6 & 7)
12	Other offences
13	Terrorism
14	Anti-social behaviour orders
15	Sexual offender orders
16	Other prescribed proceedings
Prison Law Codes [codes for applications made pre 2 December 2013 are omitted]	
Prison Law Codes for applications made post 2 December 2013	

Guidance for reporting Crime Lower Work

Code	Description
18	Sentence calculations
33	Written representations – Parole Board
34	Written representations – Disciplinary
35	Oral representations
36	Breach of Part 1 injunction under Anti-social Behaviour, Crime and Policing Act 2014

Prison law codes for applications made post 21 February 2018

Code	Description
18	Sentence calculations
19	Category A (note these include cases involving Restricted Status prisoners/Inmates)
21	Close Supervision Centre referrals and assessments
23	Minimum Term Review applications
33	Written representations – Parole Board
34	Written representations – Disciplinary
35	Oral representations
37	Separation Centre
38	Pre-Tariff Reviews

. . . .

Table of claim/stage reached codes

Code	Description
Criminal investigation	
INVA	Advice and assistance (not at the police station)
INVB	Police station: telephone advice only
INVC	Police station: attendance
INVD	Police station: attendance (armed forces)
INVE	Warrant of further detention (including Terrorism Act 2000, advice and assistance and other police station advice where given)
INVF	Warrant of further detention (armed forces) (including Terrorism Act 2000, advice and assistance and other police station advice where given)
INVG	Duty solicitor hotel disbursements – requires prior authority
INVH	Police Station: Post-charge attendance – breach of bail/arrest on warrant
INVI	Police Station: Post-charge attendance – Post-charge identification procedure/recharge/referral back for caution, reprimand, warning
INVJ	Immigration matter

Code	Description
INVK	Extension to Pre Charge Bail
INVL	Varying pre Charge Bail
Criminal proceedings	
PROC	Magistrates' court advocacy assistance
PROD	Court duty solicitor session
PROE	Representation order – lower standard fee
PROF	Representation order – higher standard fee
PROG	Representation order – non-standard fee (claimed on CRM7)
PROH	Crown Court advocacy assistance
PROI	High court representation
PROJ	Second claim for deferred sentence
PROK	Revised Standard Fee (designated areas): Lower Standard Fee
PROL	Revised Standard Fee (designated areas): Higher Standard Fee
PROM	Revised Standard Fee (designated areas): Non-Standard Fee (claimed on CRM7)
PROP	Pre-order cover
PROT	Early cover
PROU	Refused means test – form completion fee
PROV	Fee for breach of Part 1 injunctions under Anti-social Behaviour, Crime and Policing Act 2014
Appeals and reviews	
APPA	Advice and assistance in relation to an appeal (except CCRC)
APPB	Advice and assistance in relation to CCRC application
APPC	Representation on an appeal by way of case stated
Prison law	
PRIA	Free standing advice and assistance
PRIB	Advocacy assistance at prison discipline hearings
PRIC	Advocacy assistance at parole board hearings
PRID	Advocacy Assistance at Sentence Reviews
Associated civil work	
ASMS	Legal Help and Associated Civil Work – miscellaneous
ASMS	Legal Help and associated Civil Work- Miscellaneous
ASPL	Legal Help and Associated Civil Work – public law
ASAS	Part 1 injunction under Anti-social Behaviour, Crime and Policing Act 2014

Claim/stage reached code guidance

7.18 The claim code/stage reached is made up of four characters. The first characters record the Class of Work that is being claimed for: Criminal Investigation (INV-), Criminal Proceedings (PRO-), Appeals and Reviews (APP-), Prison Law (PRI-) and Associated Civil work (AS-). The remaining characters record the unit of work within the Class of Work.

7.19 [Guidance on code INVG applying only to claims for work prior to the SCC 2017].

7.20 The code PROJ should be used to claim a second magistrates' court standard fee in cases where there is a deferred sentence. You must claim a category 1 standard fee for this work. When claiming designated area standard fees under code PROJ you should not include travel and waiting costs.

Table of Outcome Codes

Code	Description
Criminal investigation	
CN01	No further instructions
CN02	Change of solicitor
CN03	Client not a suspect
CN04	No further action
CN05	Simple caution, reprimand, warning
CN06	Charge, summons or reported for summons
CN07	Conditional caution
CN08	Fixed penalty notice
CN09	Released No Bail
CN10	Bail Varied/Extended
CN11	Bail Not Varied/Extended
Criminal proceedings	
CP01	Arrest warrant issued/adjourned indefinitely
CP02	Change of solicitor
CP03	Representation order withdrawn
CP04	Trial: acquitted
CP05	Trial: mixed verdicts
CP06	Trial: convicted
CP07	Discontinued (before any pleas entered)
CP08	Discontinued (after pleas entered)
CP09	Guilty plea to all charges put – not listed for trial
CP10	Guilty plea to all charges put after case listed for trial

Code	Description
CP11	Guilty plea to substitute charges put – after case listed for trial
CP12	Mix of guilty plea(s) and discontinuance – not listed for trial
CP13	Mix of guilty plea(s) and discontinuance – listed for trial
CP16	[sending] [committal]: discharged
CP17	Extradition
CP18	Case remitted from Crown to magistrates' court for sentencing
CP19	Deferred sentence
CP20	Granted [civil injunction]/sexual harm prevention order/other order
CP21	Part-granted [civil injunction]/sexual harm prevention order/other order
CP22	Refuse [civil injunction]/sexual harm prevention order/other order
CP23	Varied [civil injunction]/sexual offences order/other order
CP24	Discharged [civil injunction]/sexual offences order/other order
CP25	[Redundant]
CP26	[Redundant]
Prison law	
PL01	Discontinued
PL02	Change of solicitor
PL03	Written representations successful
PL04	Written representations refused
PL05	Adjudication guilty plea
PL06	Adjudication guilty after hearing
PL07	Adjudication not guilty after hearing
PL08	Adjudication cracked hearing
PL09	Parole paper hearing
PL10	Parole oral hearing successful
PL11	Parole oral hearing not successful
PL12	Proceeded to judicial review
PL13	No further action
PL14	Minimum Term Reviewed at the High Court

Outcome Code guidance

Purpose

7.21 The Outcome Code indicates the furthest point to which the Case or Matter progressed and the outcome achieved.

7.22 The appropriate Outcome Code can only be determined once the Case or Matter has reached the end of the relevant Class of Work (thereby triggering a claim) or has been disposed of finally.

7.23 Outcome Codes apply to Matters and Cases in the Criminal Investigations Class of Work (INVA to INVF and INVJ), magistrates' court representation under a Representation Order in the Criminal Proceedings Class of Work (PROE, PROF, PROK, PROL, PROV), and Matters and Cases in the Prison Law Class of Work (PRIA, PRIB, PRIC).

7.24 Outcome Codes are not required for Claim Code/Stage Reached, INVG, INVH, INVI, PROC & PROD, (Court Duty Solicitor session), PROH, PROI, PROJ, PROP to PROU or for Appeals and Reviews, and Associated civil work.

Format

7.25 The code consists of 4 characters. The first two letters indicate the specific class of work and the following two digits determine the individual outcome within the Class of Work.

7.26 The letter key is as follows:

7.27 CN = Criminal Investigations CP = Criminal Proceedings PL = Prison Law

7.28 It is important to note that the Outcome Codes are not interchangeable between Classes of Work, eg CP cannot be used for a Criminal Investigations claim and CN cannot be used for a Criminal Proceedings claim.

Application of specific codes

Criminal investigations

CN01 No further instructions

7.29 This code must be used when you are claiming because your client has not made any further contact with you even though the Matter has not concluded and you are not aware that their instructions have been transferred.

7.30 The SCC stipulates that two months must pass since the last contact with the client before any claim can be made [(Part A, para 4.57(i)).]

7.31 This code can only be used when claiming [in accordance with 4.57(h), ie] where you have had no contact from your client for two months. It must not be used in relation to a claim where it is known that no further work will be undertaken for the client in the same matter, [(Part A, para 4.57(h)).]

CN02 Change of solicitor

7.32 This code must be used when you have been advised by your client(s) that they no longer wish to instruct you and the Matter has not been disposed of.

CN03 Client not a suspect

7.33 This code must only be used when free standing Advice and Assistance or Police Station Advice and Assistance has been given to a client who is not directly the subject of a criminal investigation but qualifies for Advice and Assistance eg a witness at risk of self incrimination.

CN04 No further action

7.34 This code should only be used when the client(s) has been released without a reprimand, warning, summons or charge.

CN05 Simple [ ] caution
7.35 This code should only be used when the client(s) has been released following a simple caution [ ]. Any level of assistance can have been given, namely Advice and Assistance, Police Station Telephone Advice, Police Station Attendance, Warrants of Further Detention and armed forces custody hearings.

CN06 Charge, summons or reported for summons
7.36 This code should only be used when the client(s) has been charged with or summoned for a criminal offence. Any level of assistance can have been given.

CN07 Conditional caution
7.37 This code should only be used when the client(s) has received a conditional caution.

CN08 Fixed penalty notice
7.38 This code should only be used when the client(s) has received a fixed penalty notice.

CN09 Released no Bail
7.39 This code should only be used when the client(s) is released without bail.

CN10 Bail Varies/Extended
7.40 This code should only be used when providing Advocacy Assistance and the client(s) bail is varied or extended

CN11 Bail Not Varied/Extended
7.41 This code should only be used when providing Advocacy Assistance and the client(s)bail is not varied or extend ed

Criminal proceedings
General guidance
7.42 Matters that are **sent to the Crown Court for sentence** or end with a **Newton Hearing** should be given the Outcome Code that represents the actual outcome of the Matter in the magistrates' court. For instance, a client who was convicted of some Matters but acquitted of others, before a committal for sentence or Newton Hearing, should have the Outcome Code CP05 – Trial: mixed matters

7.43 Matters that are remitted back from the Crown Court should be given the Outcome Code that represents the final outcome of the Matter in the magistrates' court.

7.44 When deciding whether or not a case has been listed for trial, (Outcome Codes CP07 to CP13), the definition used for standard fee purposes should be used. CRIMLA 41 provides that a case is to be treated as listed for trial whenever it is adjourned following a not guilty plea, irrespective of whether the court actually lists the trial date at that point or simply adjourns to a pre-trial review date.

Additional guidance in relation to committal for trial [sending] hearings
7.45 For matters with representation orders dated on or after 6 April 2010, payment for such cases is made at the conclusion of the Crown Court

case for which the client was sent, rather than at the conclusion of the magistrates' court element of the case. This means that for all such matters, bills should be submitted as part of the Litigator Graduated Fee Scheme claim using the LF1 at the conclusion of the Crown Court element of the case.

7.46 [refers only to orders prior to 28 May 2013].

7.47–50 [redundant].

CP01 Arrest warrant issued/adjourned indefinitely

7.51 This code must be used when you are claiming because an arrest warrant has been issued or the court has adjourned the Matter, without a decision, indefinitely.

7.52 This code can only be used when claiming in accordance with the Standard Crime Contract [para 4.57(i)]. It must not be used in relation to a claim where it is known that no further work will be undertaken for the client in the same matter or case; [para 4.57(h).]

CP02 Change of solicitor

7.53 This code must be used when you have been advised by your client(s) that they no longer wish to instruct you and the representation order is transferred to another provider.

CP03 Representation order withdrawn

7.54 This code must be used when the representation order has been withdrawn or revoked before a conclusion to the case is reached.

CP04 Trial: acquitted

7.55 This code must be used when the client is acquitted at trial of all contested Matters (whether or not there are other guilty pleas). This code also includes contested breach proceedings.

CP05 Trial: mixed verdict

7.56 This code must be used when the client is convicted at trial of some contested Matters but is acquitted of other contested Matters (whether or not there are other guilty pleas). This code also includes contested breach proceedings where the client is convicted of some breaches and acquitted of others in a separate information or charge.

CP06 Trial: convicted

7.57 This code must be used when the client is convicted at trial of all contested Matters (whether or not there are other guilty pleas). This code also includes contested breach proceedings. It should not be used for any other outcome.

CP07 discontinued (before any pleas entered)

7.58 This code must be used when the proceedings have been discontinued and the Matter has not been listed for trial. This code also includes breach proceedings.

CP08 Discontinued (after pleas entered)

7.59 This code must be used when the proceedings have been discontinued after the Matter has been listed for trial. This code also includes breach proceedings.

CP09 Guilty plea to all charges put – not listed for trial
7.60 This code must be used when guilty pleas have been entered to all Matters put where the Matter has not been listed for trial. This code also includes breach proceedings.

CP10 Guilty plea to all charges put after case listed for trial
7.61 This code must be used when guilty pleas have been entered to all Matters put where the Matter has been listed for trial. This code also includes breach proceedings.

CP11 Guilty plea to substitute charges put – after case listed for trial
7.62 This code must be used when guilty pleas are entered to substitute charges where the matter has been listed for trial. This code includes breach proceedings.

CP12 Mix of guilty plea(s) and discontinuance – not listed for trial
7.63 This code must be used when a guilty plea has been entered to one or more Matters, one or more other Matters have been discontinued, or the Crown accepted a not guilty plea and formally offered no evidence, and the Matter has not been listed for trial. This code also includes breach proceedings.

CP13 Mix of guilty plea(s) and discontinuance – listed for trial
7.64 This code must be used when a guilty plea has been entered to one or more Matters, one or more other Matters have been discontinued, or the Crown accepted a not guilty plea and formally offered no evidence, and the Matter has been listed for trial. This code also includes breach proceedings.

CP16 [redundant]

CP17 Extradition
7.66 This code must be used for extradition hearings.

CP18 Case remitted from crown court to magistrates' court for sentencing
7.67 This code must be used when the matter has been passed back to the magistrates' court for sentencing.

CP19 Deferred sentence
7.68 This code must be used where a sentence has been deferred.

CP20 Granted antisocial behavior order/sexual offences order/other order
7.69 This code must be used where an application for an application for an antisocial behaviour (representation order dated prior to 23 March 2015) or other order has been contested and the conditions proposed by the applicant agency are granted in full.

CP21 Part granted antisocial behaviour/sexual offences order/other order
7.70 This code must be used where an application for an antisocial behaviour (representation order dated prior to 23 March 2015) or other order has been contested and the conditions proposed by the applicant agency are only granted in part.

CP22 Refused antisocial behaviour/sexual offences /other order
7.71 This code must be used where an application for an antisocial behaviour (representation order dated prior to 23 March 2015) or other order has been contested and the application is refused in full.

CP23 Varied antisocial behaviour/sexual offences/other order

7.72 This code must be used where an application has been made to vary an antisocial behaviour or other order whether the application was granted or not.

CP24 Discharged antisocial behaviour/sexual offences/other order

7.73 This code must be used where an application has been made to discharge an antisocial behaviour(representation order dated prior to 23 March 2015) or other order whether the application was granted or not.

CP25 [redundant]

CP26 [redundant]

Breach of antisocial behaviour/sexual offences order/other order

7.76 If the matter type is a breach of an antisocial behaviour (representation order dated prior to 23 March 2015) or other order then the matter type will be 14, 15 or 16 (see Matter code Type table below), but the Outcome Code will be one most suitable from the Outcome Code Table above, eg CP04, CP06, (but not CP20 to CP24).

Issue of [antisocial behaviour order] order/sexual offences order/other order following a criminal matter

7.77 If an antisocial behaviour order (representation order dated prior to 23 March 2015) is issued following a criminal matter then the Matter Type will be the substantive charge from the Matter Code table below (but not 14, 15, or 16), and the Outcome Code will be the most appropriate from CP01 to CP19 in the Outcome Code Table above.

Prison law

PL01 Discontinued

7.78 This code must be used when if disciplinary proceedings have been discontinued, or an application to the Parole Board has been abandoned.

PL02 Change of solicitor

7.79 This code must be used when you have been advised by your client(s) that they no longer wish to instruct you and the Matter has not been disposed of.

PL03 Written representations successful

7.80 This code must be used in circumstances where written representations have resulted in a successful outcome, [ ]in, Disciplinary Cases and Parole Board Cases.

PL04 Written representations refused

7.81 This code must be used in circumstances where written representations have not resulted in a successful outcome in Sentence, Disciplinary Cases and Parole Board Cases.

PL05 Adjudication guilty plea

7.82 This code must be used in Disciplinary Cases if your client admits the charge or charges against him or her.

PL06 Adjudication guilty after hearing
7.83 This code must be used in Disciplinary Cases if you client contests the charge and is found guilty.

PL07 Adjudication not guilty after hearing
7.84 This code must be used in Disciplinary Cases if your client successfully contests the charge and is found not guilty.

PL08 Adjudication cracked hearing
7.85 This code must be used in circumstances where the case is listed for a full hearing and the prisoner pleads guilty on the day of the hearing.

PL09 Parole paper hearing
7.86 This code must be used where written representations have been submitted to the Parole Board and there was no oral hearing.

PL10 Oral hearing successful
7.87 This code must be used in Parole Board Cases where the outcome was successful.

PL11 Oral hearing unsuccessful
7.88 This code must be used in Parole Board Cases where the outcome was unsuccessful.

PL12 Proceeded to judicial review
7.89 This code must be used if you send a letter in accordance with the Judicial Review Pre-Action Protocol, having exhausted internal remedies.

PL13 No further action
7.90 This code must be used when you are claiming because your client has not made any further contact with you even though the Matter has not concluded and you are not aware that their instructions have been transferred.
7.91 This code can only be used when claiming [in accordance with 4.57(i), i.e.] where you have had no contact from your client for two months. It must not be used in relation to a claim where it is known that no further work will be undertaken for the client in the same matter [paragraph 4.57(h).]

PL14 Minimum Term Reviewed at the High Court
7.92 This code can only be used when claiming in accordance of (sic) 12.77 of the Specification i.e. when the High Court has directed there to be an oral hearing in relation to a client's minimum term review. This is claimed in conjunction with the High Court court code.

Reporting work on the CRM7 form
7.93 CRM7 forms can be completed online through the LAA's e-forms system, or submitted in hard copy to the relevant processing centre. The CRM7 form must be used when reporting non-standard fee cases under the magistrates' court standard fee scheme, under claim codes PROG and PROM.
7.94 When reporting work on the CRM7 the following codes are used.

Guidance for reporting Crime Lower Work

Attendance codes for use on CRM 7

7.95 These codes are for the schedule of time on the CRM7 to indicate the nature of a person attended on.

Code	Type of person
C	Client
E	Expert Witness
P	Prosecutor/Police
S	Surety
D	Other defence Solicitor PR Probation
W	Witness
O	Other

Hearing codes for use on CRM 7

7.96 These codes are for the schedule of time on the CRM7 to indicate the nature of a hearing.

Code	Hearing type
DB	Defence bail application
CB	Crown Court bail application
HB	High Court bail application
VB	Vary bail conditions
PB	Prosecution bail application (including Judge-in-Chambers)
FR	Formal Remand
AD	Adjournment (client on bail)
MT	Mode of trial
NO	New offence
PL	Plea
PTR	Pre-trial Review
CMH	Case Management Hearing
CT	Cracked trial
ST	Summary trial
SE	Sentence

8 Equal opportunities monitoring

8.1 Completion of the ethnic origin and disability fields is voluntary. However, where the client is willing to provide this information it is compulsory to report this and the information will greatly assist us in monitoring and researching access to LAA funded services in line with our duties under the Equality Act 2010). This information will be treated in the strictest confidence and will be used purely for statistical monitoring and research.

Field	Use	Format
Gender	Gender of client	Single letter: F – Female M – Male U – Unknown
Ethnicity	Ethnicity of client	00 Other 01 White British 02 White Irish 03 Black or Black British African 04 Black or Black British Caribbean 05 Black or Black British Other 06 Asian or Asian British Indian 07 Asian or Asian British Pakistani 08 Asian or Asian British Bangladeshi 09 Chinese 10 Mixed White & Black Caribbean 11 Mixed White & Black African 12 Mixed White & Asian 13 Mixed Other 14 White Other 15 Asian or Asian British Other 99 Unknown
Disability	If a client considers himself or herself to have a disability use the most appropriate code. If the client has multiple disabilities please use the code that reflects the predominant disability. If the client does not consider himself or herself disabled then use code NCD. Where a client does not wish to provide this information use code UKN.	NCD – Not Considered Disabled PHY – Physical Impairment SEN – Sensory Impairment MHC – Mental Health Condition LDD – Learning Disability/Difficulty COG – Cognitive Impairment ILL – Long-Standing Illness Or Health Condition OTH – Other UKN – Unknown

APPENDIX D

Police station scheme codes

Editor's note:
1. Military cases outside England and Wales fall outside this scheme.
2. For each claim it is the fee for the first police station actually attended that is used. All fees are displayed exclusive of VAT.

PS scheme name	PS scheme code	Police station name	Police station ID
Abingdon, Didcot & Witney (South Oxfordshire)	1131	ABINGDON	RD003
		ABINGDON, DIDCOT & WITNEY (SOUTH OXFORDSHIRE) NON-POLICE STATION	RD900
		DIDCOT	RD004
		RAF BRIZE NORTON	RD001
		WANTAGE	RD005
		WITNEY	RD002
Aldershot/Petersfield (North East Hampshire)	1140	160 PROVST CO ALDERSHOT	RD041
		ALDERSHOT	RD046
		ALDERSHOT / PETERSFIELD (NORTH EAST HAMPSHIRE) NON-POLICE STATION	RD909
		ALTON (PETERSFIELD)	RD047
		FARNBOROUGH	RD045
		FLEET	RD044
		PETERSFIELD (ALTON)	RD048
		RAF ODIHAM	RD042
		RMP 160 PROVOST CO, BORDON	RD051
		RMP 31 SECTION SIB, ALDERSHOT	RD050
		WHITEHILL	RD049
		YATELEY	RD043

212 *Criminal Costs: legal aid costs in the criminal courts / Appendix D*

PS scheme name	PS scheme code	Police station name	Police station ID
Amman Valley	4001	AMMAN VALLEY NON-POLICE STATION	WA900
		AMMANFORD	WA002
		LLANDOVERY	WA001
Andover/ Basingstoke/ Winchester (NW Hants)	1141	ANDOVER	RD057
		ANDOVER / BASINGSTOKE / WINCHESTER (N W HANTS) NONPOLICE STATION	RD914
		BASING	RD054
		BASINGSTOKE	RD053
		BISHOPS WALTHAM	RD059
		DROXFORD	RD060
		STOCKBRIDGE	RD056
		TADLEY	RD052
		WHITCHURCH, HAMPSHIRE	RD055
		WINCHESTER	RD058
Ashbourne/Matlock/ High Peak (Buxton)	8002	ASHBOURNE	NT014
		ASHBOURNE / MATLOCK / HIGH PEAK (BUXTON) NON-POLICE STATION	NT901
		BAKEWELL	NT013
		BUXTON	NT011
		CHAPEL-EN-LE-FRITH	NT010
		GLOSSOP	NT015
		MATLOCK	NT012
		NEW MILLS	NT009
Ashby & Coalville/ Loughborough/ Melton Mowbray	8005	ASHBY & COALVILLE / LOUGHBOROUGH / MELTON MOWBRAY NON-POLICE STATION	NT904
		ASHBY-DE-LA ZOUCH	NT034
		COALVILLE	NT033
		EAST MIDLANDS AIRPORT	NT035
		LOUGHBOROUGH	NT036
		MELTON MOWBRAY [DESIGNATED]	NT038
		RAF COTTESMORE	NT037

PS scheme name	PS scheme code	Police station name	Police station ID
Ashford & Tenterden/ Dover/Folkestone	7002	ASHFORD	BG010
		ASHFORD & TENTERDEN/DOVER/ FOLKESTONE NON-POLICE STATION	BG900
		DEAL	BG004
		DOVER	BG003
		FOLKESTONE	BG008
		HM CUSTOMS FOLKESTONE	BG007
		HM CUSTOMS DOVER, PRIORY COURT	BG005
		HM CUSTOMS DOVER, ST JOHN'S ROAD	BG011
		HMC EASTERN DOCKS, DOVER	BG002
		LONGPORT	BG012
		LYDD	BG006
		SANDWICH	BG001
		TENTERDEN	BG009
Avon North & Thornbury	2001	AVON NORTH & THORNBURY NON-POLICE STATION	BR900
		CHIPPING SODBURY	BR005
		CRIBBS CAUSEWAY (BRISTOL)	BR006
		FILTON	BR004
		KINGSWOOD	BR003
		STAPLE HILL	BR002
		THORNBURY	BR001
Aylesbury	1132	AYLESBURY	RD009
		AYLESBURY NON-POLICE STATION	RD901
		RAF HALTON	RD008
		THAME	RD007
		WENDOVER	RD006
Bangor & Caernarfon	4011	BANGOR	WA051
		BANGOR & CAERNARFON NON-POLICE STATION	WA910
		CAERNARFON	WA049

PS scheme name	PS scheme code	Police station name	Police station ID
		LLANBERIS	WA050
		PENYGROES	WA048
Barking	1301	BARKING	LN001
		BARKING NON-POLICE STATION	LN900
		DAGENHAM	LN002
Barnsley	1212	BARNSLEY	LS056
		BARNSLEY NON-POLICE STATION	LS911
		CUDWORTH	LS055
		DODWORTH	LS054
		GOLDTHORPE	LS053
		GRIMETHORPE	LS052
		PENISTONE	LS051
		WOMBWELL	LS050
		WORSBOROUGH	LS049
Barnstaple	2017	BARNSTAPLE	BR115
		BARNSTAPLE NON-POLICE STATION	BR916
		BIDEFORD	BR109
		BRAUNTON	BR114
		CHULMLEIGH	BR116
		CLOVELLY	BR117
		COMBE MARTIN	BR113
		GREAT TORRINGTON	BR118
		HOLSWORTH	BR119
		ILFRACOMBE	BR112
		LYNTON	BR111
		SOUTH MOLTON	BR108
		WOOLACOMBE	BR110
Barrow In Furness	6004	ASKAM	MA037
		BARROW IN FURNESS	MA041
		BARROW IN FURNESS NON-POLICE STATION	MA903
		BOOTLE	MA036

Police station scheme codes 215

PS scheme name	PS scheme code	Police station name	Police station ID
		DALTON	MA040
		MILLOM	MA039
		RAVENGLASS	MA034
		SILECROFT	MA035
		ULVERSTON	MA038
Basildon	9008	BASILDON	EA026
		BASILDON NON-POLICE STATION	EA907
		BILLERICAY	EA027
		WICKFORD	EA025
Bath	2002	BATH	BR009
		BATH NON-POLICE STATION	BR902
		KEYNSHAM	BR008
		RADSTOCK	BR007
Bedford	9001	AMPTHILL	EA002
		BEDFORD	EA001
		BEDFORD NON-POLICE STATION	EA900
		BIGGLESWADE	EA143
		SANDY	EA144
Berwick & Alnwick	1014	ALNWICK	NE054
		AMBLE	NE053
		BERWICK	NE055
		BERWICK & ALNWICK NON-POLICE STATION	NE912
		RAF BOULMER	NE056
		SEAHOUSES	NE052
Beverley/Bridlington	1204	BEVERLEY	LS021
		BEVERLEY / BRIDLINGTON NON-POLICE STATION	LS903
		BRIDLINGTON	LS019
		BROUGH	LS016
		DRIFFIELD	LS018
		HORNSEA	LS017
		MARKET WEIGHTON	LS023

PS scheme name	PS scheme code	Police station name	Police station ID
		POCKLINGTON	LS020
Bexley	1302	BELVEDERE	LN003
		BEXLEY NON-POLICE STATION	LN901
		BEXLEYHEATH	LN004
		ERITH	LN005
		SIDCUP	LN006
		WELLING	LN007
Bicester/North Oxon (Banbury)	1135	BANBURY	RD022
		BICESTER	RD021
		BICESTER/NORTH OXON (BANBURY) NON-POLICE STATION	RD904
		CHIPPING NORTON	RD023
		RMP 160 PROVOST, BICESTER	RD024
		WOODSTOCK	RD020
Birmingham	3014	ACOCKS GREEN	BM195
		ASTON, QUEENS ROAD	BM194
		BELGRAVE ROAD	BM193
		BILLESLEY, YARDLEY WOOD ROAD	BM192
		BIRMINGHAM HQ (LLOYDS HOUSE)	BM197
		BIRMINGHAM NON-POLICE STATION	BM913
		BORDESLEY GREEN	BM191
		BOURNEVILLE LANE	BM190
		BRADFORD STREET	BM189
		BRIDGE STREET WEST	BM188
		BROMFORD LANE	BM211
		BTP BIRMINGHAM NEW STREET STATION	BM161
		CANTERBURY ROAD	BM187
		COVENTRY ROAD, SMALL HEATH	BM186
		DIGBETH	BM185
		DUDLEY ROAD	BM184

Police station scheme codes 217

PS scheme name	PS scheme code	Police station name	Police station ID
		DUKE STREET (TRAFFIC)	BM214
		EDWARD ROAD	BM183
		ERDINGTON, WITTON ROAD	BM182
		HARBORNE ROSE ROAD	BM168
		HARBOURNE HIGH STREET	BM181
		HM CUSTOMS ALPHA TOWER B'HAM	BM160
		HM CUSTOMS CONTAINERBASE BIRMINGHAM	BM215
		HM CUSTOMS ST JAMES HOUSE	BM216
		HM CUSTOMS SUTTON COLDFIELD	BM217
		HM CUSTOMS TWO BROADWAY	BM218
		HOLYHEAD ROAD	BM180
		KINGS HEATH HIGH STREET	BM179
		KINGS NORTON, WHARF ROAD	BM178
		KINGSTANDING ROAD	BM177
		LADYWOOD	BM176
		LONGBRIDGE	BM175
		MOSELEY, WOODBRIDGE ROAD	BM219
		NECHELLS GREEN, FOWLER STREET	BM174
		QUINTON ROAD WEST	BM173
		SHARD END, PACKINGTON AVENUE	BM220
		SHELDON	BM172
		SPARKHILL, STRATFORD ROAD	BM171
		STECHFORD, STATION ROAD	BM170
		STEELHOUSE LANE	BM169
		SUTTON COLDFIELD	BM167
		THORNBRIDGE AVENUE (MOTORWAY)	BM166
		THORNHILL ROAD	BM165
		VYSE STREET	BM164

218 *Criminal Costs: legal aid costs in the criminal courts / Appendix D*

PS scheme name	PS scheme code	Police station name	Police station ID
		WALSALL ROAD	BM163
		WOODBRIDGE ROAD	BM162
Bishop's Stortford/ East Hertfordshire	9018	BISHOP'S STORTFORD	EA072
		BISHOP'S STORTFORD/EAST HERTFORDSHIRE NON-POLICE STATION	EA917
		BUNTINGFORD	EA070
		CHESHUNT (EDMONTON)	EA073
		HERTFORD	EA069
		HODDESDON	EA068
		SAWBRIDGEWORTH	EA071
Bishopsgate	1303	BISHOPSGATE	LN008
		BISHOPSGATE NON-POLICE STATION	LN902
		BTP LIVERPOOL STREET STATION	LN009
		HM CUSTOMS FETTER LANE	LN010
		HM CUSTOMS LOWER THAMES STREET	LN011
		SNOWHILL	LN012
		WOOD STREET	LN013
Blackburn/Accrington/ Ribble Valley	6019	ACCRINGTON	MA194
		BLACKBURN	MA191
		BLACKBURN / ACCRINGTON / RIBBLE VALLEY NON-POLICE STATION	MA918
		CHURCH	MA193
		CLITHEROE	MA197
		DARWEN	MA190
		GISBURN	MA195
		GREAT HARWOOD	MA192
		GREENBANK, BLACKBURN	MA198
		LONGRIDGE	MA196
Blackpool	6020	BISPHAM	MA201
		BLACKPOOL CENTRAL	MA200

Police station scheme codes 219

PS scheme name	PS scheme code	Police station name	Police station ID
		BLACKPOOL NON-POLICE STATION	MA919
		BLACKPOOL SOUTH	MA199
		KIRKHAM	MA204
		LYTHAM	MA203
		ST ANNES	MA202
Bolton	6012	BOLTON (ASTLEY BRIDGE)	MA149
		BOLTON (ST HELENS ROAD)	MA148
		BOLTON CENTRAL	MA147
		BOLTON NON-POLICE STATION	MA911
		BREIGHTMET	MA146
		FARNWORTH	MA145
		HORWICH	MA144
		WESTHOUGHTON	MA143
Bootle & Crosby	5001	BOOTLE & CROSBY NON-POLICE STATION	LV900
		COPY LANE (BOOTLE)	LV005
		CROSBY (ALEXANDER ROAD)	LV004
		FORMBY	LV003
		GLADSTONE DOCK (NOT FOUND)	LV001
		MARSH LANE (BOOTLE)	LV002
		PORT OF LIVERPOOL	LV006
Boston/Bourne/ Stamford	8008	BOSTON	NT065
		BOSTON / BOURNE / STAMFORD NON-POLICE STATION	NT907
		BOURNE	NT055
		COLSTERWORTH	NT054
		HOLBEACH	NT062
		KIRTON	NT061
		SIBSEY	NT060
		SPALDING	NT064
		STAMFORD	NT056

220   Criminal Costs: legal aid costs in the criminal courts / Appendix D

PS scheme name	PS scheme code	Police station name	Police station ID
		SWINESHEAD	NT059
		WHAPLODE	NT058
		WRANGLE	NT057
Bournemouth & Christchurch	2008	BOSCOMBE	BR055
		BOURNEMOUTH	BR054
		BOURNEMOUTH & CHRISTCHURCH NON-POLICE STATION	BR907
		CHRISTCHURCH	BR057
		HIGHCLIFFE	BR056
		KINSON	BR053
		WINTON	BR052
Bradford	1219	BRADFORD EXCHANGE	LS101
		BRADFORD NON-POLICE STATION	LS918
		BRADFORD NORTH/TOLLER LANE	LS096
		BRADFORD SOUTH	LS100
		DUDLEY HILL	LS099
		ECCLESHILL	LS094
		MANNINGHAM	LS098
		ODSAL	LS097
		SHIPLEY	LS095
Braintree	9010	BRAINTREE	EA032
		BRAINTREE NON-POLICE STATION	EA909
		HALSTEAD	EA031
		HEDINGHAM	EA030
		WETHERSFIELD MOD POLICE	EA034
Brecon & Radnor	4004	BRECON	WA013
		BRECON & RADNOR NON-POLICE STATION	WA903
		BUILTH WELLS	WA012
		CRICKHOWELL	WA011
		HAY-ON-WYE	WA010
		LLANDRINDOD WELLS	WA009

Police station scheme codes 221

PS scheme name	PS scheme code	Police station name	Police station ID
Brent	1304	BRENT NON-POLICE STATION	LN903
		BTP WEMBLEY PARK	LN014
		CAREY WAY (WEMBLEY)	LN015
		HARLESDEN	LN016
		KILBURN	LN017
		WEMBLEY	LN018
		WEMBLEY (STADIUM)	LN019
		WILLESDEN GREEN	LN020
Brentford	1305	BRENTFORD	LN021
		BRENTFORD NON-POLICE STATION	LN904
		CHISWICK	LN022
		FELTHAM	LN023
		HOUNSLOW	LN024
		RMP HOUNSLOW CAVALRY	LN025
Brentwood	9009	BRENTWOOD	EA028
		BRENTWOOD NON-POLICE STATION	EA908
Bridport West Dorset	2010	BRIDPORT WEST DORSET NON-POLICE STATION	BR909
		BLANDFORD	BR049
		BRIDPORT	BR065
		DORCHESTER	BR066
		LYME REGIS	BR064
		WEYMOUTH	BR067
Brighton & Hove & Lewes	7013	BRIGHTON	BG064
		BRIGHTON & HOVE & LEWES NON-POLICE STATION	BG913
		BTP BRIGHTON	BG063
		HM CUSTOMS NEWHAVEN	BG069
		HOVE	BG062
		LEWES, UCKFIELD	BG068
		NEWHAVEN	BG067

PS scheme name	PS scheme code	Police station name	Police station ID
		NEWHAVEN HARBOUR, BT POLICE (NOT FOUND)	BG066
		SEAFORD	BG065
Bristol	2004	AVONMOUTH	BR032
		BISHOPSWORTH	BR028
		BRISLINGTON	BR033
		BRISTOL CENTRAL (BRIDEWELL)	BR027
		BRISTOL NON-POLICE STATION	BR903
		BROADBURY ROAD	BR026
		CLEVEDON	BR020
		HM CUSTOMS BRISTOL AIRPORT	BR031
		LOCKLEAZE	BR021
		NAILSEA	BR030
		PORTISHEAD	BR029
		REDLAND	BR025
		SOUTHMEAD	BR024
		ST GEORGE	BR023
		TRINITY ROAD	BR022
Bromley	1306	BECKENHAM	LN026
		BIGGIN HILL	LN027
		BROMLEY	LN028
		BROMLEY NON-POLICE STATION	LN905
		CHISLEHURST	LN029
		ORPINGTON	LN030
		PENGE	LN031
		RAF BIGGIN HILL	LN032
		WEST WICKHAM	LN033
Burnley/Rossendale	6018	BACUP	MA184
		BARNOLDSWICK	MA188
		BURNLEY	MA189
		BURNLEY / ROSSENDALE NON-POLICE STATION	MA917

Police station scheme codes 223

PS scheme name	PS scheme code	Police station name	Police station ID
		COLNE	MA186
		HASLINGDEN	MA183
		NELSON	MA185
		PADIHAM	MA187
		RAWTENSTALL	MA182
Bury	6013	BURY	MA154
		BURY NON-POLICE STATION	MA912
		PRESTWICH	MA152
		RADCLIFFE	MA151
		RAMSBOTTOM	MA150
		WHITEFIELD	MA153
Camberwell Green	1307	BRIXTON	LN034
		BTP STOCKWELL STATION (LONDON)	LN035
		CAMBERWELL GREEN NON-POLICE STATION	LN906
		CARTER ST (CLOSED 1/12/93)	LN036
		CLAPHAM	LN037
		EAST DULWICH	LN038
		GYPSY HILL	LN039
		HERNEHILL (FAVERSHAM)	LN040
		SOUTHWARK	LN041
		STREATHAM	LN042
		VAUXHALL	LN067
Cambridge	9003	CAMBRIDGE	EA010
		CAMBRIDGE NON-POLICE STATION	EA902
		SAWSTON	EA011
Canterbury/Thanet	7006	BROADSTAIRS	BG014
		CANTERBURY	BG017
		CANTERBURY / THANET NONPOLICE STATION	BG901
		HM CUSTOMS CANTERBURY	BG018
		MARGATE	BG016

PS scheme name	PS scheme code	Police station name	Police station ID
		RAF MANSTON KENT	BG013
		RAMSGATE	BG015
Cardiff	4019	CANTON	WA095
		CARDIFF CENTRAL	WA094
		CARDIFF NON-POLICE STATION	WA918
		CATHAYS	WA093
		DOCKS (BUTE TOWN)	WA085
		ELY, S WALES	WA092
		FAIRWATER	WA083
		LLANEDEYRN	WA091
		LLANISHEN	WA090
		RAILWAY STATION (CENTRAL)	WA084
		ROATH	WA089
		RUMNEY	WA088
		TROWBRIDGE	WA087
		WHITCHURCH, SOUTH WALES	WA086
Carmarthen East Dyfed	4002	CARMARTHEN	WA004
		CARMARTHEN EAST DYFED NON-POLICE STATION	WA901
		NEWCASTLE EMLYN	WA003
Carrick/Kerrier (Camborne)/Penwith	2021	CAMBORNE	BR175
		CARRICK / KERRIER (CAMBORNE) / PENWITH NON-POLICE STATION	BR920
		FALMOUTH	BR169
		HAYLE (PENZANCE)	BR165
		HELSTON	BR167
		ISLES OF SCILLY (PENZANCE)	BR164
		PENRYN	BR168
		PENZANCE	BR166
		PERRANPORTH	BR178
		RAF ST MAWGAN	BR173
		REDRUTH (CAMBORNE)	BR174

Police station scheme codes 225

PS scheme name	PS scheme code	Police station name	Police station ID
		ST AGNES (NEWQUAY)	BR172
		ST COLUMB (NEWQUAY)	BR171
		ST IVES (PENZANCE)	BR163
		ST MAWES (CAMBORNE)	BR176
		TRURO	BR177
Central Dorset	2007	CENTRAL DORSET NON-POLICE STATION	BR906
Central London	1308	BELGRAVIA	LN043
		BTP BAKER STREET	LN044
		BTP PADDINGTON	LN045
		BTP TOTTENHAM COURT ROAD	LN046
		BTP VICTORIA STATION	LN047
		BTP WATERLOO STATION	LN048
		BTP WHITFIELD STREET	LN075
		CENTRAL LONDON NON-POLICE STATION	LN907
		CHARING CROSS (EX BOW ST)	LN049
		CHELSEA	LN050
		EBURY BRIDGE, BTP (LONDON SOUTH HQ)	LN051
		GERALD ROAD	LN052
		HARROW ROAD	LN053
		HM CUSTOMS WATERLOO STATION	LN054
		HORSEFERRY ROAD	LN055
		HYDE PARK	LN056
		KENNINGTON	LN057
		KENSINGTON	LN058
		MARYLEBONE	LN059
		NOTTING DALE	LN060
		NOTTING HILL	LN061
		PADDINGTON GREEN	LN062
		PALACE OF WESTMINSTER	LN063

PS scheme name	PS scheme code	Police station name	Police station ID
		RMP ROCHESTER ROW, LONDON	LN064
		ST JOHNS WOOD	LN065
		TOTTENHAM COURT ROAD	LN066
		VINE STREET	LN068
		WEST END CENTRAL	LN069
		WHITEHALL	LN070
Chelmsford/Witham	9016	CHELMSFORD	EA062
		CHELMSFORD / WITHAM NON-POLICE STATION	EA915
		MALDON (CHELMSFORD)	EA063
		SOUTH WOODHAM FERRERS	EA064
		SOUTHMINSTER	EA065
		WITHAM	EA033
Cheltenham	2014	CHELTENHAM	BR099
		CHELTENHAM NON-POLICE STATION	BR913
		STOW ON THE WOLD [DESIGNATED]	BR097
		TEWKESBURY	BR098
		WHITTINGTON	BR096
Chester/Vale Royal (Northwich)	6003	BLACON	MA028
		CHESTER/VALE ROYAL (NORTHWICH) NON-POLICE STATION	MA902
		CHESTER, NUNNS ROAD	MA027
		ELLESMERE	MA229
		ELLESMERE PORT (CLOSED)	MA030
		FRODSHAM	MA025
		HOLMES CHAPEL	MA021
		MALPAS	MA031
		NESTON	MA029
		NORTHWICH	MA024
		TARPORLEY	MA023

Police station scheme codes 227

PS scheme name	PS scheme code	Police station name	Police station ID
		WESTERN AREA (BLACON)	MA033
		WHITCHURCH, CHESHIRE	MA026
		WINSFORD	MA022
Chesterfield	8003	BOLSOVER	NT022
		CHESTERFIELD	NT021
		CHESTERFIELD NON-POLICE STATION	NT902
		CLAY CROSS	NT020
		DRONFIELD	NT017
		KILAMARSH	NT016
		SHIREBROOK	NT019
		STAVELEY	NT018
Chichester & District	7014	BOGNOR REGIS	BG073
		CHICHESTER	BG072
		CHICHESTER & DISTRICT NON-POLICE STATION	BG914
		MIDHURST	BG071
		PETWORTH	BG070
Chippenham/ Trowbridge	2012	BRADFORD ON AVON	BR084
		CALNE	BR078
		CHIPPENHAM	BR077
		CHIPPENHAM / TROWBRIDGE NON-POLICE STATION	BR911
		CORSHAM	BR076
		DEVIZES	BR083
		LUDGERSHALL	BR086
		MALMESBURY	BR075
		MELKSHAM	BR082
		PEWSEY	BR085
		RMP UPAVON	BR079
		TIDWORTH	BR074
		TROWBRIDGE (WILTSHIRE)	BR087
		WARMINSTER	BR081
		WESTBURY	BR080

PS scheme name	PS scheme code	Police station name	Police station ID
Chorley/Ormskirk/ South Ribble & Leyland	6023	ADLINGTON	MA215
		AUGHTON	MA220
		BAMBERBRIDGE	MA222
		BURSCOUGH	MA219
		CHORLEY	MA216
		CHORLEY / ORMSKIRK / SOUTH RIBBLE & LEYLAND NON-POLICE STATION	MA922
		COPPULL	MA214
		LEYLAND	MA223
		ORMSKIRK	MA218
		PENWORTHAM	MA221
		SKELMERSDALE	MA217
		WHEELTON	MA213
Clacton & Harwich/ Colchester	9011	BRIGHTLINGSEA	EA146
		CLACTON	EA037
		CLACTON & HARWICH / COLCHESTER NON-POLICE STATION	EA910
		COLCHESTER	EA036
		COPFORD	EA042
		HARWICH	EA039
		PARKESTON QUAY	EA038
		RMP COLCHESTER GARRISON	EA035
		WALTON	EA041
		WEST MERSEA	EA040
Clerkenwell/ Hampstead	1309	ALBANY STREET	LN071
		BTP EUSTON	LN072
		BTP KINGS CROSS	LN073
		BTP ST PANCRAS	LN074
		CLERKENWELL / HAMPSTEAD NON-POLICE STATION	LN908
		HAMPSTEAD	LN076
		HM CUSTOMS WOBURN PLACE	LN077

Police station scheme codes 229

PS scheme name	PS scheme code	Police station name	Police station ID
		HOLBORN	LN078
		KENTISH TOWN	LN079
		TAVISTOCK PLACE BTP (NOT FOUND)	LN080
		WEST HAMPSTEAD	LN081
Colwyn Bay	4012	ABERGELE	WA056
		COLWYN BAY	WA055
		COLWYN BAY NON-POLICE STATION	WA911
		CONWY	WA054
		LLANDUDNO	WA053
		LLANWRST	WA052
Corby (Kettering)/ Wellingborough	8016	CORBY	NT112
		CORBY (KETTERING) / WELLINGBOROUGH NON-POLICE STATION	NT915
		KETTERING	NT113
		RUSHDEN, KETTERING	NT114
		WELLINGBOROUGH	NT115
Coventry	3016	CHACE AVENUE	BM205
		COVENTRY BTP	BM207
		COVENTRY NON-POLICE STATION	BM915
		FLETCHAMSTEAD HIGHWAY	BM208
		HM CUSTOMS COVENTRY	BM206
		LITTLE PARK STREET	BM210
		STONEY STANTON ROAD	BM209
Crawley/Horsham	7015	BTP GATWICK AIRPORT	BG078
		BURGESS HILL	BG080
		CRAWLEY	BG075
		CRAWLEY/HORSHAM NON-POLICE STATION	BG915
		EAST GRINSTEAD	BG081
		GATWICK	BG074

PS scheme name	PS scheme code	Police station name	Police station ID
		HM CUSTOMS GATWICK AIRPORT	BG077
		HAYWARDS HEATH	BG079
		HORSHAM	BG076
Crewe & Nantwich/ Sandbach & Congleton/ Macclesfield	6001	ALSAGER	MA007
		CONGLETON	MA010
		CONGLETON, MACCLESFIELD	MA006
		CREWE	MA009
		CREWE & NANTWICH / SANDBACH & CONGLETON / MACCLESFIELD NON-POLICE STATION	MA900
		EASTERN AREA (MIDDLEWICH)	MA032
		KNUTSFORD	MA005
		M6 MOTORWAY POST (KNUTSFORD)	MA004
		MACCLESFIELD	MA003
		MIDDLEWICH	MA020
		NANTWICH	MA008
		POYNTON	MA001
		DONNINGTON	MA012
		SANDBACH	MA011
		WILMSLOW	MA002
Cromer & North Walsham	9022	AYLSHAM	EA106
		AYLSHAM PIC	EA931
		CROMER	EA089
		CROMER & NORTH WALSHAM NON-POLICE STATION	EA921
		HOLT	EA088
		NORTH WALSHAM	EA091
		RAF COLTISHALL	EA092
		SHERINGHAM	EA087
		STALHAM	EA090
Croydon	1310	ADDINGTON	LN082

PS scheme name	PS scheme code	Police station name	Police station ID
		CROYDON	LN083
		CROYDON NON-POLICE STATION	LN909
		KENLEY	LN084
		NORBURY	LN085
		SOUTH NORWOOD	LN086
Cynon Valley	4021	ABERCYNON	WA105
		ABERDARE	WA104
		CWMBACH	WA103
		CYNON VALLEY NON-POLICE STATION	WA920
		MOUNTAIN ASH	WA102
		TRECYNON	WA101
Dacorum (Hemel Hempstead)	9017	BERKHAMSTED	EA067
		DACORUM (HEMEL HEMPSTEAD NON-POLICE STATION	EA916
		HEMEL HEMPSTEAD	EA066
		TRING	EA149
Darlington	1003	DARLINGTON	NE010
		DARLINGTON NON-POLICE STATION	NE902
		DARLINGTON RAIL STATION, BTP	NE011
		TEESIDE AIRPORT	NE012
Dartford & Gravesend	7001	BLUEWATER SHOPPING CENTRE	BG019
		DARTFORD	BG023
		DARTFORD & GRAVESEND NON-POLICE STATION	BG902
		GRAVESEND	BG022
		HM CUSTOMS GRAVESEND	BG020
		NORTH KENT	BG919
		SWANLEY	BG021
Denbighshire	4013	DENBIGH	WA060
		DENBIGHSHIRE NON-POLICE STATION	WA912

PS scheme name	PS scheme code	Police station name	Police station ID
		RHYL	WA059
		RUTHIN	WA058
		ST ASAPH	WA057
		ST ASAPH CUSTODY SUITE	WA061
Derby/Swadlincote	8004	CHADDESDEN	NT025
		COTTON LANE	NT028
		DERBY / SWADLINCOTE NONPOLICE STATION	NT903
		DERBY CENTRAL (NOT FOUND)	NT027
		FULL STREET (STATION CLOSED)	NT026
		LITTLEOVER	NT030
		PEARTREE	NT024
		ST MARY'S WHARF (DERBY)	NT029
		ST MARY'S GATE	NT023
		SWADLINCOTE	NT032
Dereham	9027	ATTLEBOROUGH	EA105
		DEREHAM	EA115
		DEREHAM NON-POLICE STATION	EA926
		WYMONDHAM	EA114
Derwentside	1006	CONSETT	NE021
		DERWENTSIDE NON-POLICE STATION	NE905
		STANLEY	NE020
Dewsbury	1218	BATLEY	LS093
		DEWSBURY	LS092
		DEWSBURY NON-POLICE STATION	LS917
		HECKMONDWIKE	LS091
Diss/Thetford	9026	DISS	EA113
		DISS/THETFORD NON-POLICE STATION	EA925
		EYE	EA132
		HARLESTON	EA112
		THETFORD	EA111

Police station scheme codes 233

PS scheme name	PS scheme code	Police station name	Police station ID
Dolgellau	4014	DOLGELLAU	WA062
		DOLGELLAU NON-POLICE STATION	WA913
Doncaster	1213	ADWICK	LS062
		ARMTHORPE	LS066
		ASKERN	LS061
		CONISBOROUGH	LS060
		DONCASTER	LS065
		DONCASTER NON-POLICE STATION	LS912
		EDLINGTON	LS057
		MEXBOROUGH	LS064
		ROSSINGTON	LS059
		STAINFORTH	LS058
		THORNE	LS063
Dudley & Halesowen	3012	BRIERLEY HILL	BM153
		DUDLEY	BM152
		DUDLEY & HALESOWEN NON-POLICE STATION	BM911
		HALESOWEN	BM149
		HM CUSTOMS DUDLEY	BM225
		KINGSWINFORD	BM151
		SEDGELEY	BM150
		STOURBRIDGE	BM148
Durham	1005	CHESTER LE STREET	NE019
		DURHAM	NE018
		DURHAM NON-POLICE STATION	NE904
Ealing	1311	ACTON	LN087
		EALING	LN088
		EALING NON-POLICE STATION	LN910
		SOUTHALL	LN089
Easington	1007	EASINGTON	NE024

PS scheme name	PS scheme code	Police station name	Police station ID
		EASINGTON NON-POLICE STATION	NE906
		PETERLEE	NE023
		SEAHAM	NE022
East Cornwall	2020	BODMIN	BR160
		BUDE	BR154
		CALLINGTON	BR153
		CAMELFORD	BR156
		EAST CORNWALL NON-POLICE STATION	BR919
		FOWEY	BR150
		GUNNISLAKE	BR152
		HMS RALEIGH	BR161
		KINGSAND	BR147
		LAUNCESTON	BR159
		LISKEARD	BR158
		LOOE	BR148
		LOSTWITHIEL	BR151
		MEVAGISSEY	BR149
		NEWQUAY	BR170
		SALTASH	BR162
		ST AUSTELL	BR157
		TORPOINT	BR146
		WADEBRIDGE	BR155
East Derbyshire (Ripley)/Ilkeston	8001	ALFRETON	NT005
		ALFRETON – HALL STREET	NT008
		BELPER	NT007
		BUTTERLEY	NT006
		EAST DERBYSHIRE (RIPLEY)/ILKESTON NON-POLICE STATION	NT900
		HEANOR	NT004
		ILKESTON	NT002

PS scheme name	PS scheme code	Police station name	Police station ID
		LONG EATON	NT001
		RIPLEY – DIVISIONAL HQ	NT003
East Gwent	4008	ABERGAVENNY	WA033
		CALDICOT	WA032
		CHEPSTOW	WA031
		CWMBRAN	WA030
		EAST GWENT NON-POLICE STATION	WA907
		MONMOUTH	WA029
		PONTYPOOL	WA028
Eastbourne	7018	CROWBOROUGH	BG082
		EASTBOURNE	BG084
		EASTBOURNE NON-POLICE STATION	BG916
		HAILSHAM	BG083
		UCKFIELD	BG085
Ely	9004	ELY NON-POLICE STATION	EA903
		ELY, CAMBS	EA012
Enfield	1312	EDMONTON	LN090
		ENFIELD	LN091
		ENFIELD NON-POLICE STATION	LN911
		PONDERS END	LN092
		SOUTHGATE	LN093
		WINCHMORE HILL	LN094
Epsom	7011	EPSOM	BG042
		EPSOM NON-POLICE STATION	BG908
		WALTON ON THAMES	BG043
Exeter	2018	AXMINSTER	BR130
		BEER (EXETER)	BR121
		COLYTON (EXMOUTH)	BR120
		CREDITON	BR129
		CULLOMPTON	BR128
		EXETER	BR127

PS scheme name	PS scheme code	Police station name	Police station ID
		EXETER NON-POLICE STATION	BR917
		EXMOUTH	BR126
		HONITON	BR125
		ROYAL MARINE POLICE, LYMPSTONE	BR131
		SEATON	BR124
		SIDMOUTH	BR123
		TIVERTON	BR122
Felixstowe/Ipswich & District/Woodbridge	9029	CAPEL ST MARY	EA127
		FELIXSTOWE	EA126
		FELIXSTOWE/IPSWICH & DISTRICT/WOODBRIDGE NON-POLICE STATION	EA928
		HM CUSTOMS FELIXSTOWE	EA125
		IPSWICH	EA124
		WOODBRIDGE	EA123
Fleetwood	6021	CLEVELEYS	MA208
		FLEETWOOD	MA207
		FLEETWOOD NON-POLICE STATION	MA920
		POULTON-LE-FYLDE	MA206
		THORNTON	MA205
Gateshead	1010	FELLING	NE040
		GATESHEAD	NE039
		GATESHEAD NON-POLICE STATION	NE909
		WHICKHAM	NE038
Gloucester	2015	CINDERFORD	BR102
		COLEFORD	BR101
		GLOUCESTER CENTRAL	BR100
		GLOUCESTER NON-POLICE STATION	BR914
Goole	1205	GOOLE	LS024
Goole	1205	GOOLE NON-POLICE STATION	LS904

Police station scheme codes 237

PS scheme name	PS scheme code	Police station name	Police station ID
Gosport & Fareham	1144	FAREHAM	RD101
		GOSPORT	RD100
		GOSPORT & FAREHAM NON-POLICE STATION	RD913
		HMS SULTAN	RD098
		PARKGATE	RD099
Grantham & Sleaford	8011	GRANTHAM	NT080
		GRANTHAM & SLEAFORD NON-POLICE STATION	NT910
		HECKINGTON	NT078
		LONG BENNINGTON	NT079
		RAF CRANWELL	NT082
		SLEAFORD	NT077
Grays	9012	CORRINGHAM	EA046
		GRAYS NON-POLICE STATION	EA911
		GRAYS THURROCK	EA045
		SOUTH OCKENDON	EA044
		TILBURY	EA043
Great Yarmouth	9023	ACLE	EA097
		CAISTER ON SEA	EA096
		GORLESTON ON SEA	EA095
		GREAT YARMOUTH	EA094
		GREAT YARMOUTH NON-POLICE STATION	EA922
		HM CUSTOMS GREAT YARMOUTH	EA093
Greenwich/Woolwich	1313	BROCKLEY	LN095
		CATFORD	LN096
		DEPTFORD	LN097
		ELTHAM	LN098
		GREENWICH	LN099
		GREENWICH / WOOLWICH NON-POLICE STATION	LN912
		LEE ROAD	LN100

PS scheme name	PS scheme code	Police station name	Police station ID
		LEWISHAM	LN 101
		PLUMSTEAD	LN 102
		SHOOTERS HILL	LN 103
		SYDENHAM	LN 104
		THAMESMEAD	LN 105
		WESTCOMBE PARK	LN 106
		WOOLWICH	LN 107
Grimsby & Cleethorpes	1201	CLEETHORPES	LS 003
		GRIMSBY	LS 002
		GRIMSBY & CLEETHORPES NON-POLICE STATION	LS 900
		IMMINGHAM	LS 001
Guildford & Farnham	7008	FARNHAM	BG 045
		GODALMING	BG 048
		GUILDFORD	BG 047
		GUILDFORD & FARNHAM NON-POLICE STATION	BG 909
		GUILDFORD BTP	BG 046
		HASLEMERE	BG 044
Halifax	1216	BRIGHOUSE	LS 088
		HALIFAX	LS 087
		HALIFAX NON-POLICE STATION	LS 915
		HEBDEN BRIDGE	LS 086
		SOWERBY BRIDGE	LS 085
		TODMORDEN	LS 084
Haringey	1314	HARINGEY NON-POLICE STATION	LN 913
		HIGHGATE	LN 108
		HORNSEY	LN 109
		MUSWELL HILL	LN 110
		ST ANN'S ROAD	LN 111
		TOTTENHAM	LN 112

PS scheme name	PS scheme code	Police station name	Police station ID
		WOOD GREEN	LN113
Harlow & Loughton	9013	CHIGWELL	EA051
		EPPING	EA048
		HARLOW	EA047
		HARLOW & LOUGHTON NON-POLICE STATION	EA912
		LOUGHTON	EA050
		ONGAR	EA049
Harrogate & Ripon	1207	BOROUGHBRIDGE	LS035
		HARROGATE	LS037
		HARROGATE & RIPON NON-POLICE STATION	LS906
		KNARESBOROUGH	LS036
		PATELEY BRIDGE	LS034
		RIPON	LS033
Harrow	1315	EDGWARE	LN114
		HARROW	LN115
		HARROW NON-POLICE STATION	LN914
		PINNER	LN116
Hartlepool	1001	HARTLEPOOL	NE001
		HARTLEPOOL NON-POLICE STATION	NE900
Hastings	7016	BEXHILL	BG087
		HASTINGS	BG086
		HASTINGS NON-POLICE STATION	BG917
Havering	1316	COLLIER ROW	LN117
		HAROLD HILL	LN118
		HAVERING NON-POLICE STATION	LN915
		HORNCHURCH	LN119
		RAINHAM	LN120
		RAINHAM ID SUITE	LN121
		ROMFORD	LN122

PS scheme name	PS scheme code	Police station name	Police station ID
Heathrow	1317	BTP HEATHROW	LN204
		HEATHROW NON-POLICE STATION	LN931
		HM CUSTOMS HEATHROW TERMS 1–4	LN206
Hendon/Barnet	1318	BARNET	LN123
		COLINDALE	LN124
		FINCHLEY	LN125
		GOLDERS GREEN	LN126
		HENDON	LN127
		HENDON/BARNET NON-POLICE STATION	LN916
		MILL HILL	LN128
		WEST HENDON	LN129
		WHETSTONE (BARNET)	LN130
Hereford/Leominster	3005	BREDWARDINE	BM228
		BROMYARD	BM067
		CHURCH STRETTON	BM063
		CHURCH STRETTON (LEOMINSTER)	BM069
		CLEOBURY MORTIMER	BM076
		CRAVEN ARMS (LEOMINSTER)	BM068
		DORE	BM226
		HEREFORD	BM074
		HEREFORD / LEOMINSTER NONPOLICE STATION	BM904
		HM CUSTOMS HEREFORD	BM073
		KINGSTONE	BM072
		KINGTON	BM071
		LEDBURY	BM130
		LEOMINSTER	BM066
		MADLEY	BM227
		PETERCHURCH	BM070
		ROSS ON WYE	BM075

Police station scheme codes 241

PS scheme name	PS scheme code	Police station name	Police station ID
		ST WEONARDS	BM077
		TENBURY WELLS	BM065
High Wycombe & Amersham	1133	AMERSHAM	RD012
		CHESHAM	RD011
		GERRARDS CROSS	RD010
		HIGH WYCOMBE	RD015
		HIGH WYCOMBE & AMERSHAM NON-POLICE STATION	RD902
		MARLOW	RD014
		RAF WALTERS ASH STRIKE CMAND	RD013
Highbury Corner	1319	BTP FINSBURY PARK	LN131
		CALEDONIAN ROAD	LN132
		HIGHBURY CORNER NON-POLICE STATION	LN917
		HIGHBURY VALE	LN133
		HOLLOWAY	LN134
		ISLINGTON (TOLPUDDLE STREET)	LN135
Hinckley/Market Harborough	8007	HINCKLEY	NT052
		HINCKLEY/MARKET HARBOROUGH NON-POLICE STATION	NT906
		LUTTERWORTH	NT051
		MARKET BOSWORTH	NT050
		MARKET HARBOROUGH	NT053
Huddersfield	1217	HOLMFIRTH	LS090
		HUDDERSFIELD	LS089
		HUDDERSFIELD NON-POLICE STATION	LS916
Hull	1203	BRANSHOLME	LS015
		BTP HULL RAILWAY STATION	LS008
		HESSLE	LS013
		HM CUSTOMS KING GEORGE DOCKS	LS014
		HULL CENTRAL	LS012

PS scheme name	PS scheme code	Police station name	Police station ID
		HULL NON-POLICE STATION	LS902
		KINGSTON-UPON-HULL	LS011
		PRIORY ROAD	LS022
		TOWER GRANGE	LS010
		WITHERNSEA	LS009
Huntingdon	9005	HUNTINGDON	EA017
		HUNTINGDON NON-POLICE STATION	EA904
		RAF WYTON	EA016
		RAMSEY	EA015
		ST IVES	EA014
		ST NEOTS	EA013
Isle of Wight	1142	COWES	RD069
		ISLE OF WIGHT NON-POLICE STATION	RD910
		NEWPORT	RD068
		RYDE	RD067
		VENTNOR	RD070
		YARMOUTH	RD066
Keighley & Bingley	1220	BINGLEY	LS105
		ILKLEY	LS104
		KEIGHLEY	LS103
		KEIGHLEY & BINGLEY NON-POLICE STATION	LS919
		PPOTTINGLEY (NOT FOUND)	LS106
Kendal & Windermere	6005	AMBLESIDE	MA051
		BURNSIDE	MA047
		BURTON IN KENDAL	MA046
		CARTMEL	MA045
		KENDAL	MA050
		KENDAL & WINDERMERE NON-POLICE STATION	MA904
		LINDALE	MA044

Police station scheme codes 243

PS scheme name	PS scheme code	Police station name	Police station ID
		MILNTHORPE	MA049
		SEDBERGH	MA043
		TEBAY	MA042
		WINDERMERE	MA048
Kidderminster/ Redditch	3006	ALVECHURCH	BM083
		ASTLEY	BM102
		ASTWOOD BANK	BM266
		BARNT GREEN	BM267
		BEWDLEY	BM091
		BROMSGROVE	BM087
		BURLISH	BM232
		CHADDESLEY	BM234
		CLIFTON-ON-TEME	BM236
		CORBETT	BM235
		CRABBS CROSS	BM094
		FRANKLEY	BM196
		GREAT WITLEY	BM093
		HAGLEY	BM088
		HARTLEBURY	BM237
		HEADLESS CROSS	BM095
		HOPWOOD	BM082
		INKBERROW	BM081
		KIDDERMINSTER	BM090
		KIDDERMINSTER / REDDITCH NON-POLICE STATION	BM905
		MARTLEY	BM231
		REDDITCH	BM080
		ROCK	BM230
		ROMSLEY	BM086
		RUBERY	BM085
		STOKE WORKS	BM084
		STOURPORT ON SEVERN	BM089

PS scheme name	PS scheme code	Police station name	Police station ID
		WINYATES	BM096
		WOLVERLY	BM233
		WYTHALL	BM079
Kings Lynn & West Norfolk	9024	DERSINGHAM	EA154
		DOWNHAM MARKET	EA104
		FAKENHAM	EA103
		HUNTSTANTON	EA102
		KINGS LYNN	EA101
		KINGS LYNN & WEST NORFOLK NON-POLICE STATION	EA923
		RAF MARHAM	EA100
		SWAFFHAM	EA098
		WELLS NEXT THE SEA, NORFOLK	EA099
Kingston-Upon-Thames	1320	COBHAM	LN136
		EAST MOLESEY	LN137
		ESHER	LN138
		KINGSTON	LN139
		KINGSTON-UPON-THAMES NON-POLICE STATION	LN918
		NEW MALDEN	LN140
		SURBITON	LN141
Knowsley	5005	HALEWOOD	LV010
		HUYTON	LV009
		KIRKBY	LV008
		KNOWSLEY NON-POLICE STATION	LV901
		PRESCOT	LV007
Lancaster	6022	HEYSHAM	MA209
		LANCASTER	MA211
		LANCASTER NON-POLICE STATION	MA921
		MORECAMBE	MA210

Police station scheme codes   245

PS scheme name	PS scheme code	Police station name	Police station ID
Leamington/ Nuneaton/Rugby	3004	ALCESTER (CLOSED)	BM059
		ALDERMINSTER	BM251
		ATHERSTONE	BM051
		BAGINTON	BM044
		BARFORD	BM245
		BEDWORTH	BM042
		BIDFORD-ON-AVON	BM254
		BISHOPS ITCHINGTON	BM045
		BRAILES	BM253
		CLAVERDON	BM238
		COLESHILL	BM060
		ETTINGTON	BM250
		GAYDON	BM244
		GREAT ALNE	BM053
		HARBURY	BM243
		HATTON	BM242
		HENLEY IN ARDEN	BM058
		HM CUSTOMS COVENTRY AIRPORT	BM043
		ILMINGTON	BM054
		KENILWORTH	BM050
		KINETON	BM047
		LEAMINGTON / NUNEATON / RUGBY NON-POLICE STATION	BM903
		LEAMINGTON SPA	BM049
		LONG COMPTON	BM052
		LONG ITCHINGTON	BM241
		LONG MARSTON	BM249
		MIDDLE TYSOE	BM255
		NUNEATON	BM041
		RAF FARNBOROUGH (CLOSED)	BM061
		RUGBY	BM040
		SHIPSTON ON STOUR	BM057

246 Criminal Costs: legal aid costs in the criminal courts / Appendix D

PS scheme name	PS scheme code	Police station name	Police station ID
		SNITTERFIELD	BM055
		SOUTHAM	BM039
		STOCKINGFORD	BM062
		STOCKTON	BM037
		STONELEIGH	BM240
		STRATFORD-UPON-AVON	BM056
		STUDLEY	BM248
		TANWORTH IN ARDEN	BM252
		TREDINGTON	BM247
		WARWICK	BM048
		WELLESBOURNE	BM239
		WESTON UNDER WETHERLEY	BM046
		WOLSTON	BM038
		WOTTON WAWEN	BM246
Leeds	1221	BTP LEEDS RAILWAY STATION	LS113
		CENTRAL BRIDEWELL, LEEDS	LS120
		CHAPELTOWN	LS119
		HM CUSTOMS LEEDS	LS117
		HOLBECK	LS115
		HORSFORTH	LS114
		KILLINGBECK (GIPTON)	LS118
		LEEDS NON-POLICE STATION	LS920
		MILLGARTH	LS112
		MORLEY	LS111
		OTLEY	LS110
		PUDSEY	LS109
		ROTHWELL	LS116
		WEETWOOD	LS108
		WETHERBY	LS107
Leicester	8006	BEAUMONT LEYES	NT039
		BRAUNSTONE	NT040
		CHARLES STREET	NT043

PS scheme name	PS scheme code	Police station name	Police station ID
		EUSTON STREET (LEICESTER)	NT049
		HAMILTON	NT041
		LEICESTER NON-POLICE STATION	NT905
		MANSFIELD HOUSE	NT047
		OAKHAM (SYSTON)	NT044
		SPINNEY HILL	NT048
		SYSTON	NT045
		WELFORD ROAD (LEICESTER)	NT046
		WIGSTON	NT042
Lichfield & Tamworth/Burton Upon Trent/Uttoxeter	3003	ALREWAS	BM033
		BARTON-UNDER-NEEDWOOD	BM031
		BURTON-UPON-TRENT	BM030
		CHASETOWN	BM034
		LICHFIELD	BM036
		LICHFIELD & TAMWORTH / BURTON-UPON-TRENT / UTTOXETER NON-POLICE STATION	BM902
		SHENSTONE	BM221
		TAMWORTH	BM035
		UTTOXETER	BM032
Lincoln/ Gainsborough	8010	CAISTOR	NT075
		GAINSBOROUGH	NT074
		LINCOLN	NT072
		LINCOLN / GAINSBOROUGH NON-POLICE STATION	NT909
		MARKET RASEN	NT073
		RAF DIGBY	NT122
		RAF SCAMPTON	NT076
		RAF WADDINGTON	NT081
Liverpool	5003	ADMIRAL STREET	LV026
		ALLERTON	LV025
		BELLE VALE	LV024

248 *Criminal Costs: legal aid costs in the criminal courts / Appendix D*

PS scheme name	PS scheme code	Police station name	Police station ID
		BTP LIME STREET RAIL STATION (LIVER)	LV012
		COPPERAS HILL	LV023
		EATON ROAD	LV022
		FARNWORTH ST (EATON ROAD)	LV027
		GARSTON	LV021
		HM CUSTOMS SANDON HOUSE (LIVER)	LV011
		LIVERPOOL NON-POLICE STATION	LV902
		LOWER LANE	LV020
		MAIN BRIDEWELL	LV019
		SPEKE	LV018
		ST ANNE STREET	LV017
		STANLEY ROAD	LV016
		TUEBROOK	LV015
		WALTON LANE	LV014
		WAVERTREE ROAD	LV013
Llanelli	4003	BURRYPORT	WA008
		CROSSHANDS	WA007
		KIDWELLY	WA006
		LLANELLI	WA005
		LLANELLI NON-POLICE STATION	WA902
Lower Rhymney Valley/North Bedwellty/South Bedwellty	4010	ABERTILLERY	WA047
		BARGOED	WA044
		BEDWAS	WA043
		BLACKWOOD	WA039
		BLACKWOOD, SOUTH BEDWELLTY (NOT FOUND)	WA046
		BRYNMAWR	WA038
		CAERPHILLY	WA042
		EBBW VALE	WA037

PS scheme name	PS scheme code	Police station name	Police station ID
		LOWER RHYMNEY VALLEY/ NORTH BEDWELLTY/SOUTH BEDWELLTY NON-POLICE STATION	WA909
		RHYMNEY	WA041
		RISCA	WA045
		TREDEGAR	WA036
		YSTRAD MYNACH	WA040
Lowestoft/Beccles & Halesworth/ Aldeburgh	9028	BECCLES	EA119
		BUNGAY	EA118
		HALESWORTH	EA117
		LEISTON	EA121
		LOWESTOFT	EA120
		LOWESTOFT / BECCLES & HALESWORTH / ALDEBURGH NON-POLICE STATION	EA927
		SAXMUNDHAM	EA122
		SOUTHWOLD	EA116
Luton	9002	DUNSTABLE	EA009
		HM CUSTOMS, LUTON (NOT FOUND)	EA007
		HM CUSTOMS LUTON AIRPORT	EA008
		LEIGHTON BUZZARD (DUNSTABLE)	EA003
		LUTON	EA006
		LUTON AIRPORT	EA005
		LUTON NON-POLICE STATION	EA901
		RAF STANBRIDGE	EA004
Maidstone & West Malling	7005	BOUGHTON	BG026
		MAIDSTONE	BG025
		MAIDSTONE & WEST MALLING NON-POLICE STATION	BG903
		WEST MALLING	BG024
Malton & Rydale	1210	HELMSLEY	LS045
		MALTON	LS044

PS scheme name	PS scheme code	Police station name	Police station ID
		MALTON & RYDALE NON-POLICE STATION	LS909
		PICKERING	LS043
Manchester	6008	BOOTLE ST	MA118
		BTP PICADILLY STATION, MANCHESTER	MA106
		CHEETHAM HILL	MA117
		CHORLTON	MA105
		COLLYHURST	MA116
		DIDSBURY	MA115
		ELIZABETH SLINGER	MA120
		GARTSIDE STREET	MA121
		GORTON	MA114
		GREENHEYS	MA113
		GREYMARE LANE	MA112
		HALL LANE	MA111
		HARPURHEY	MA104
		HM CUSTOMS MANCHESTER AIRPORT	MA107
		LEVENSHULME	MA110
		LONGSIGHT	MA109
		MANCHESTER NON-POLICE STATION	MA907
		NEWTON HEATH/ANCOATS	MA108
		NEWTON ST	MA103
		PENDLETON	MA142
		PLANT HILL RD	MA102
		WYTHENSHAWE	MA119
Mansfield	8012	MANSFIELD	NT086
		MANSFIELD NON-POLICE STATION	NT911
		RAVENSHEAD	NT083
		SELSTON	NT084
		SUTTON-IN-ASHFIELD	NT085

Police station scheme codes 251

PS scheme name	PS scheme code	Police station name	Police station ID
March & Wisbech	9006	MARCH	EA019
		CHATTERIS	EA145
		MARCH & WISBECH NON-POLICE STATION	EA905
		WHITTLESEY	EA018
		WISBECH	EA020
Medway	7003	BTP CHATHAM RAILWAY STATION	BG029
		CHATHAM	BG030
		GILLINGHAM, KENT	BG028
		MEDWAY NON-POLICE STATION	BG904
		ROCHESTER	BG027
Mendip & South Somerset	2003	CHARD	BR017
		CREWKERNE	BR016
		FROME	BR012
		ILMINSTER	BR015
		MENDIP & SOUTH SOMERSET NON-POLICE STATION	BR922
		RNAS YEOVILTON	BR018
		SHEPTON MALLET	BR011
		SOMERTON	BR014
		WELLS, AVON & SOMERSET	BR010
		WINCANTON	BR013
		YEOVIL	BR019
Merthyr Tydfil	4023	DOWLAIS	WA117
		MERTHYR TYDFIL	WA116
		MERTHYR TYDFIL NON-POLICE STATION	WA922
		TREHARRIS	WA115
Mid Glamorgan & Miskin	4022	FERNDALE	WA114
		LLANTRISANT	WA113
		MID GLAMORGAN NON-POLICE STATION	WA921
		PONTYPRIDD	WA112

PS scheme name	PS scheme code	Police station name	Police station ID
		PORTH	WA111
		TAFFS WELL	WA110
		TALBOT GREEN	WA106
		TON PENTRE	WA109
		TONYPANDY	WA108
		TONYREFAIL	WA107
Mid Wales	4005	LLANIDLOES (NEWTOWN)	WA014
		MID WALES NON-POLICE STATION	WA904
		NEWTOWN	WA016
		WELSHPOOL	WA015
Milton Keynes	1134	BLETCHLEY	RD016
		BUCKINGHAM	RD019
		CENTRAL MILTON KEYNES	RD018
		MILTON KEYNES NON-POLICE STATION	RD903
		NEWPORT PAGNELL	RD017
Mold & Hawarden	4015	BUCKLEY	WA065
		CAERGWRLE	WA064
		DEESIDE	WA070
		FLINT	WA069
		HAWARDEN	WA066
		HOLYWELL	WA068
		MOLD	WA067
		MOLD & HAWARDEN NON-POLICE STATION	WA914
		SALTNEY	WA063
Neath	4026	NEATH	WA128
		NEATH NON-POLICE STATION	WA925
		SEVEN SISTERS	WA127
		SKEWEN	WA126
		YSTRAD GYNLAIS	WA125
Newark	8013	CAYTHORPE	NT087

Police station scheme codes 253

PS scheme name	PS scheme code	Police station name	Police station ID
		NEWARK	NT088
		NEWARK NON-POLICE STATION	NT912
Newcastle & Ogmore	4025	ABERKENFIG	WA124
		BRIDGEND	WA123
		MAESTEG	WA122
		NEWCASTLE & OGMORE NON-POLICE STATION	WA924
		OGMORE VALE	WA121
		PORTHCAWL	WA120
Newcastle Upon Tyne	1009	BTP NEVILLE ST NEWCASTLE	NE031
		NEWBURN (CLOSED)	NE035
		NEWCASTLE AIRPORT/HM CUSTOMS	NE037
		NEWCASTLE CENTRAL	NE034
		NEWCASTLE EAST	NE033
		NEWCASTLE NORTH, ETAL LANE (GOSFORTH)	NE036
		NEWCASTLE WEST (WESTGATE ROAD)	NE032
		NEWCASTLE-UPON-TYNE NON-POLICE STATION	NE908
Newham	1321	EAST HAM	LN142
		FOREST GATE	LN143
		NEWHAM NON-POLICE STATION	LN919
		NORTH WOOLWICH	LN144
		PLAISTOW	LN145
		STRATFORD POLICE STATION (WEST HAM)	LN147
		THE CITY AIRPORT	LN146
Newport	4009	MAINDEE	WA035
		NEWPORT CENTRAL	WA034
		NEWPORT NON-POLICE STATION	WA908
North Anglesey	4016	ALMWCH	WA073
		HOLYHEAD	WA072

PS scheme name	PS scheme code	Police station name	Police station ID
		LLANGEFNI	WA071
		NORTH ANGLESEY NON-POLICE STATION	WA915
North Ceredigion/ South Ceredigion	4006	ABERAERON	WA019
		ABERYSTWYTH	WA018
		CARDIGAN	WA020
		MACHYNLLETH	WA017
		NORTH CEREDIGION / SOUTH CEREDIGION NON-POLICE STATION	WA905
North Tyneside	1011	FOREST HALL	NE044
		NORTH SHIELDS	NE043
		NORTH TYNESIDE NON-POLICE STATION	NE910
		WALLSEND	NE042
		WHITLEY BAY	NE041
North West Surrey (Woking)	7009	ADDLESTONE	BG050
		CAMBERLEY	BG049
		EGHAM	BG052
		NORTH WEST SURREY (WOKING) NON-POLICE STATION	BG910
		WOKING	BG051
Northallerton & Richmond	1206	CATTERICK	LS027
		CATTERICK GARRISON	LS026
		LEYBURN	LS029
		NORTHALLERTON	LS030
		NORTHALLERTON & RICHMOND NON-POLICE STATION	LS905
		RAF LEEMING	LS032
		RICHMOND (N. YORKS)	LS031
		STOKESLEY	LS025
		THIRSK	LS028
Northampton	8017	BRACKLEY	NT118
		DAVENTRY	NT120

PS scheme name	PS scheme code	Police station name	Police station ID
		HM CUSTOMS, NORTHAMPTON	NT121
		NORTHAMPTON (CAMPBELL SQUARE)	NT117
		NORTHAMPTON NON-POLICE STATION	NT916
		TOWCESTER	NT119
		WESTON FAVELL	NT116
Norwich & District	9025	HM CUSTOMS NORWICH AIRPORT	EA110
		LODDON	EA108
		LONG STRATTON	EA107
		NORWICH	EA109
		NORWICH & DISTRICT NON-POLICE STATION	EA924
		REEPHAM	EA155
		WYMONDHAM PIC	EA930
Nottingham	8014	ARNOLD (HIGH STREET)	NT106
		BEESTON	NT105
		BESTWOOD PARK	NT104
		BINGHAM	NT107
		BRIDEWELL	NT090
		BROXTOWE	NT103
		BULWELL	NT102
		CANNING CIRCUS	NT101
		CARLTON	NT031
		CLIFTON	NT100
		EASTWOOD	NT099
		HUCKNALL	NT098
		KIMBERLEY	NT097
		NOTTINGHAM CENTRAL	NT096
		NOTTINGHAM NON-POLICE STATION	NT913
		OXCLOSE LANE	NT089
		RADFORD ROAD	NT095

PS scheme name	PS scheme code	Police station name	Police station ID
		SHERWOOD LODGE	NT094
		ST ANNS	NT093
		STATION STREET	NT092
		WEST BRIDGFORD	NT091
Old Street	1322	DALSTON, LONDON	LN148
		HACKNEY	LN149
		OLD STREET NON-POLICE STATION	LN920
		SHOREDITCH (CITY ROAD)	LN150
		STOKE NEWINGTON	LN151
Oldham	6017	CHADDERTON	MA181
		FAILSWORTH	MA180
		OLDHAM	MA179
		OLDHAM NON-POLICE STATION	MA916
		ROYTON	MA178
		SHAW	MA177
		UPPERMILL	MA176
Oxford	1136	COWLEY	RD025
		OXFORD NON-POLICE STATION	RD905
		ST ALDATES (OXFORD CENTRAL)	RD026
Pembrokeshire	4007	FISHGUARD	WA027
		HAVERFORD WEST	WA024
		NARBERTH	WA026
		NEYLAND	WA021
		PEMBROKE DOCK	WA023
		PEMBROKESHIRE NON-POLICE STATION	WA906
		SAUNDERSFOOT	WA025
		TENBY	WA022
Penrith/Carlisle	6006	ALSTON	MA074
		APPLEBY	MA073

PS scheme name	PS scheme code	Police station name	Police station ID
		BRAMPTON	MA065
		BURGH BY SANDS	MA064
		CALDBECK	MA071
		CARLISLE	MA067
		CORBY HILL	MA063
		COTE HILL	MA062
		DALSTON, CUMBRIA	MA061
		DURDAR	MA060
		IREBY	MA059
		IRTHINGTON	MA058
		KIRKBRIDE	MA057
		KIRKOSWALD	MA070
		LONGTOWN	MA056
		LOW HESKET	MA055
		MELMERBY	MA069
		PENRITH	MA072
		PENRITH/CARLISLE NON-POLICE STATION	MA905
		ROAD HEAD	MA054
		ROCKCLIFFE	MA053
		SKELTON	MA068
		SMITHFIELD	MA052
		WIGTON	MA066
Peterborough	9007	BTP PETERBOROUGH	EA024
		PETERBOROUGH	EA023
		PETERBOROUGH NON-POLICE STATION	EA906
		RAF WITTERING	EA022
		THORPEWOOD (PETERBOROUGH)	EA021
Plymouth	2019	DARTMOOR PRISON	BR145
		HMS DRAKE	BR135
		IVYBRIDGE (CHARLES CROSS)	BR133

258 *Criminal Costs: legal aid costs in the criminal courts / Appendix D*

PS scheme name	PS scheme code	Police station name	Police station ID
		MOD ALBERT GATE (PLYMOUTH)	BR 142
		MOD NAVAL BASE, DEVONPORT	BR 144
		OKEHAMPTON	BR 141
		PLYMOUTH CHARLES CROSS	BR 140
		PLYMOUTH CROWNHILL	BR 139
		PLYMOUTH DEVENPORT	BR 138
		PLYMOUTH NON-POLICE STATION	BR 918
		PLYMPTON	BR 137
		PLYMSTOCK	BR 136
		PRINCETOWN (USE DARTMOOR PRISON)	BR 132
		ROYAL MARINES, STONE HOUSE PLYMOUTH	BR 143
		TAVISTOCK	BR 134
Pontefract & Castleford	1222	CASTLEFORD	LS 123
		HEMSWORTH	LS 125
		KNOTTINGLEY	LS 124
		PONTEFRACT	LS 122
		PONTEFRACT & CASTLEFORD NON-POLICE STATION	LS 921
		SOUTH KIRKBY	LS 121
Poole East Dorset	2009	FERNDOWN	BR 061
		GRAVEL HILL	BR 059
		POOLE	BR 058
		POOLE EAST DORSET NON-POLICE STATION	BR 908
		RMP BOVINGTON CAMP	BR 051
		ROYAL SIGNALS, BLANDFORD	BR 050
		SHAFTESBURY	BR 048
		SHERBORNE	BR 047
		STURMINSTER NEWTON	BR 046
		SWANAGE	BR 045

PS scheme name	PS scheme code	Police station name	Police station ID
		VERWOOD	BR063
		WAREHAM	BR044
		WIMBORNE	BR060
		WIMBOURNE	BR062
Port Talbot	4024	CYMMER	WA119
		PORT TALBOT	WA118
		PORT TALBOT NON-POLICE STATION	WA923
Portsmouth/ Waterlooville (South East Hampshire)	1143	ALSFORD	RD093
		COSHAM, HAVANT	RD092
		FRATTON	RD091
		HM CUSTOMS PORTSMOUTH	RD088
		HAVANT	RD087
		HAYLING ISLAND	RD086
		MOD RN PORTSMOUTH	RD096
		PORTSMOUTH / WATERLOOVILLE (SOUTH EAST HAMPSHIRE) NON-POLICE STATION	RD912
		PORTSMOUTH CENTRAL	RD090
		PORTSMOUTH ID CENTRE	RD094
		RN PORTSMOUTH (OLD NAVY ACAD)	RD097
		SOUTHSEA	RD089
		WATERLOOVILLE	RD095
Preston	6024	BTP PRESTON STATION	MA228
		FULWOOD	MA226
		LEA	MA225
		PRESTON	MA224
		PRESTON NON-POLICE STATION	MA923
		RMP FULWOOD BARRACKS, PRESTON	MA227
Pwllheli	4017	BLAENAU FFESTINIOG	WA074
		PORTHMADOG	WA076

PS scheme name	PS scheme code	Police station name	Police station ID
		PWLLHELI	WA075
		PWLLHELI NON-POLICE STATION	WA916
Rayleigh/Southend On Sea	9015	BENFLEET	EA029
		BTP SOUTHEND	EA061
		CANVEY ISLAND	EA059
		HM CUSTOMS SOUTHEND AIRPORT	EA056
		LEIGH, ESSEX	EA055
		RAYLEIGH	EA060
		RAYLEIGH / SOUTHEND ON SEA NON-POLICE STATION	EA914
		ROCHFORD	EA058
		SHOREBURYNESS	EA147
		SOUTHEND	EA057
		WESTCLIFF	EA148
Reading	1137	HENLEY	RD038
		LODDEN VALLEY	RD039
		READING	RD037
		READING NON-POLICE STATION	RD907
		WOODLEY	RD036
Redbridge	1323	BARKINGSIDE	LN152
		CHADWELL HEATH	LN153
		ILFORD	LN154
		REDBRIDGE NON-POLICE STATION	LN921
		WANSTEAD	LN155
		WOODFORD	LN156
Richmond-Upon-Thames	1324	BARNES	LN157
		HAM	LN158
		HAMPTON	LN159
		RICHMOND	LN160
		RICHMOND-UPON-THAMES NON-POLICE STATION	LN922

Police station scheme codes 261

PS scheme name	PS scheme code	Police station name	Police station ID
		TEDDINGTON	LN161
		TWICKENHAM	LN162
Rochdale/Middleton	6015	BIRCH SERVICE AREA	MA170
		HEYWOOD	MA169
		LITTLEBOROUGH	MA167
		MIDDLETON	MA168
		MILNROW	MA166
		MOSSLEY	MA171
		ROCHDALE	MA165
		ROCHDALE/MIDDLETON NON-POLICE STATION	MA914
Rotherham	1214	DINNINGTON (MALTBY)	LS068
		KIVETON PARK (MALTBY)	LS067
		MALTBY	LS073
		RAWMARSH	LS072
		ROTHERHAM	LS071
		ROTHERHAM MAIN STREET	LS070
		ROTHERHAM NON-POLICE STATION	LS913
		WATH-UPON-DEARNE	LS069
Salford	6011	ECCLES	MA140
		HIGHER BROUGHTON (PARK LANE)	MA139
		HM CUSTOMS ALDINE HOUSE, SALFORD	MA141
		IRLAM	MA134
		LITTLE HULTON	MA135
		SALFORD NON-POLICE STATION	MA910
		SWINTON	MA138
		THE CRESCENT, SALFORD	MA137
		TRAFFORD ROAD	MA136
Salisbury	2011	ALDERBURY	BR072
		AMESBURY	BR071
		ARMY 158 PROVOST PSU	BR068

PS scheme name	PS scheme code	Police station name	Police station ID
		BULFORD MILITARY CAMP	BR073
		MOD LARKHILL	BR069
		SALISBURY	BR070
		SALISBURY NON-POLICE STATION	BR910
Sandwell	3010	OLD HILL	BM139
		OLDBURY	BM138
		SANDWELL	BM137
		SANDWELL NON-POLICE STATION	BM909
		SMETHWICK	BM136
		TIPTON	BM135
		WEDNESBURY	BM134
		WEST BROMWICH	BM133
Scarborough/Whitby	1209	SCARBOROUGH	LS041
		SCARBOROUGH/WHITBY NON-POLICE STATION	LS908
		WHITBY	LS042
Scunthorpe	1202	BARTON UPON HUMBER	LS006
		BRIGG	LS005
		EPWORTH	LS007
		SCUNTHORPE	LS004
		SCUNTHORPE NON-POLICE STATION	LS901
Sedgemoor/Taunton Deane	2005	BRIDGEWATER	BR036
		BURNHAM-ON-SEA	BR035
		CHEDDAR	BR034
		DULVERTON	BR039
		MINEHEAD	BR038
		TAUNTON	BR041
		WELLINGTON, TAUNTON	BR040
		WILLITON	BR037
Sedgemore/Taunton Dane	2005	SEDGEMORE/TAUNTON DEANE NON-POLICE STATION	BR904
Sheffield	1215	ATTERCLIFFE	LS082

Police station scheme codes

PS scheme name	PS scheme code	Police station name	Police station ID
		BTP SHEFFIELD RAILWAY STATION	LS074
		DEEPCAR	LS076
		ECCLESFIELD	LS080
		HACKENTHORPE (NOT FOUND)	LS079
		HAMMERTON ROAD	LS078
		MOSS WAY	LS083
		SHEFFIELD BRIDGE STREET	LS075
		SHEFFIELD NON-POLICE STATION	LS914
		WEST BAR GREEN	LS081
		WOODSEATS	LS077
Shrewsbury	3007	BAYSTON HILL (SHREWSBURY)	BM100
		BISHOPS CASTLE	BM078
		BTP SHREWSBURY RAILWAY STATION	BM097
		GOBOWEN (SHREWSBURY)	BM099
		LUDLOW	BM064
		MARKET DRAYTON	BM104
		OSWESTRY	BM098
		RAF COSFORD	BM113
		RAF SHAWBURY	BM112
		SHREWSBURY	BM101
		SHREWSBURY NON-POLICE STATION	BM906
		WEM	BM103
		WHITCHURCH, CHESHIRE	BM270
Skegness	8009	ALFORD (SKEGNESS)	NT070
		HORNCASTLE	NT069
		LOUTH	NT067
		MABLETHORPE	NT066
		RAF CONINGSBY	NT071
		SKEGNESS	NT068
		SKEGNESS NON-POLICE STATION	NT908

PS scheme name	PS scheme code	Police station name	Police station ID
Skipton, Settle & Ingleton	1208	INGLETON	LS040
		SETTLE	LS039
		SKIPTON	LS038
		SKIPTON, SETTLE & INGLETON NON-POLICE STATION	LS907
Slough (East Berkshire)	1138	ASCOT	RD034
		BRACKNELL	RD035
		BURNHAM	RD033
		CROWTHORNE	RD032
		LANGLEY	RD031
		MAIDENHEAD	RD030
		SLOUGH	RD029
		SLOUGH (EAST BERKSHIRE) NON-POLICE STATION	RD906
		WINDSOR	RD028
		WOKINGHAM	RD027
Solihull	3015	BIRMINGHAM INT AIRPORT	BM202
		CASTLE BROMWICH	BM200
		CHADWICK END	BM281
		CHELMSLEY WOOD	BM203
		HM CUSTOMS BIRMINGHAM AIRPORT	BM199
		HM CUSTOMS PARK HOUSE SOLIHULL	BM279
		HOCKLEY HEATH	BM280
		SHIRLEY, WEST MIDS	BM201
		SOLIHULL	BM198
		SOLIHULL NON-POLICE STATION	BM914
		SOLIHULL NORTH	BM204
South Durham	1004	BARNARD CASTLE	NE017
		BISHOP AUKLAND	NE016
		CROOK	NE015
		NEWTON AYCLIFFE	NE014

Police station scheme codes

PS scheme name	PS scheme code	Police station name	Police station ID
		SOUTH DURHAM NON-POLICE STATION	NE903
		SPENNYMOOR	NE013
South East Northumberland	1008	ASHINGTON	NE029
		BEDLINGTON	NE030
		BLYTH	NE028
		CRAMLINGTON	NE027
		MORPETH	NE026
		PONTELAND	NE025
		SOUTH EAST NORTHUMBERLAND NON-POLICE STATION	NE907
South East Surrey	7010	CATERHAM	BG058
		DORKING	BG057
		HORLEY	BG056
		LEATHERHEAD	BG053
		OXTED	BG055
		REDHILL	BG059
		REIGATE	BG054
		SOUTH EAST SURREY NON-POLICE STATION	BG911
South London	1325	BATTERSEA	LN163
		EARLSFIELD	LN164
		LAVENDER HILL	LN165
		PUTNEY	LN166
		ROEHAMPTON	LN167
		SOUTH LONDON NON-POLICE STATION	LN923
		TOOTING	LN168
		WANDSWORTH	LN169
South Tyneside	1012	JARROW	NE046
		SOUTH SHIELDS	NE045
		SOUTH TYNESIDE NON-POLICE STATION	NE914

PS scheme name	PS scheme code	Police station name	Police station ID
South West Hants (Southampton)	1145	BITTERNE	RD083
		EASTLEIGH	RD082
		FORDINGBRIDGE	RD081
		HYTHE (SOUTHAMPTON)	RD085
		LYMINGTON	RD080
		LYNDHURST	RD079
		MOD MILITARY PORT, MARCHWOOD	RD084
		NETLEY	RD078
		NEW MILTON	RD077
		PORTSWOOD	RD076
		RINGWOOD	RD075
		ROMSEY	RD074
		SHIRLEY, HANTS	RD040
		SOUTH WEST HANTS (SOUTHAMPTON) NON-POLICE STATION	RD911
		SOUTHAMPTON CENTRAL	RD073
		TOTTON	RD072
		WEST END	RD071
Southport	5002	AINSDALE	LV029
		SOUTHPORT	LV028
		SOUTHPORT NON-POLICE STATION	LV903
St Albans	9020	HARPENDEN	EA079
		HATFIELD	EA082
		LONDON COLNEY	EA078
		POTTER'S BAR	EA152
		ST ALBANS	EA081
		ST ALBANS NON-POLICE STATION	EA919
		WELWYN GARDEN CITY	EA080
St Helens	5004	COLLEGE STREET, ST HELENS	LV030
		ST HELENS NON-POLICE STATION	LV904

Police station scheme codes 267

PS scheme name	PS scheme code	Police station name	Police station ID
Stafford/Cannock & Rugeley	3002	ARMITAGE	BM224
		AUDLEY	BM282
		BREWOOD	BM026
		CANNOCK	BM025
		CHESLYN HAY	BM024
		ECCLESHALL	BM020
		HEDNESFORD	BM023
		HILTON	BM022
		M6 MOTORWAY (DOXEY)	BM019
		MADELEY	BM016
		PENKRIDGE	BM223
		RAF STAFFORD	BM028
		RUGELEY	BM021
		STAFFORD	BM018
		STAFFORD/CANNOCK & RUGELEY NON-POLICE STATION	BM901
		STONE	BM017
Staines	7012	STAINES	BG061
		STAINES NON-POLICE STATION	BG912
		SUNBURY	BG060
Stansted	9014	HM CUSTOMS STANSTED AIRPORT	EA052
		SAFFRON WALDEN	EA053
		STANSTED AIRPORT	EA054
		STANSTED NON-POLICE STATION	EA913
Stevenage & North Hertfordshire	9019	BALDOCK	EA150
		BUSHEY (BARNET)	EA151
		HITCHIN	EA077
		LETCHWORTH	EA076
		ROYSTON, HERTS	EA074
		STEVENAGE	EA075
		STEVENAGE & NORTH HERTFORDSHIRE NON-POLICE STATION	EA918

PS scheme name	PS scheme code	Police station name	Police station ID
Stockport	6009	BREDBURY	MA125
		CHEADLE HEATH	MA128
		CHEADLE HULME	MA127
		HAZEL GROVE	MA124
		MARPLE	MA212
		REDDISH	MA123
		STOCKPORT	MA126
		STOCKPORT NON-POLICE STATION	MA908
Stoke On Trent/Leek	3001	ABBEY HULTON	BM285
		BIDDULPH	BM014
		BRITISH RAIL (NOT FOUND)	BM005
		BTP STOKE-ON-TRENT	BM015
		BUCKNALL	BM004
		BURSLEM	BM011
		CHEADLE	BM013
		ENDON	BM259
		HANLEY	BM010
		KEELE	BM283
		KIDSGROVE	BM009
		LEEK	BM012
		LONGTON	BM008
		MEIR	BM284
		NEWCASTLE UNDER LYME	BM001
		NORTHERN AREA CUSTODY FACILITY	BM029
		NORTON GREEN	BM003
		STOKE	BM007
		STOKE-ON-TRENT/LEEK NON-POLICE STATION	BM900
		TRENTHAM	BM002
		TUNSTALL	BM006
		WARSLOW	BM258

Police station scheme codes 269

PS scheme name	PS scheme code	Police station name	Police station ID
		WATERHOUSES	BM257
		WERRINGTON	BM256
Stroud	2016	CIRENCESTER	BR106
		DURSLEY	BR104
		FAIRFORD	BR105
		NAILSWORTH	BR103
		STROUD	BR107
		STROUD NON-POLICE STATION	BR915
Sudbury & Hadleigh/ Bury St Edmunds/ Haverhill/Newmarket	9030	BRANDEN	EA130
		BRANDON	EA131
		BURY ST EDMUNDS	EA140
		CLARE	EA133
		ELMSWELL	EA139
		HADLEIGH	EA135
		HAVERHILL	EA142
		HORINGER	EA138
		IXWORTH	EA137
		MILDENHALL	EA129
		NEWMARKET	EA128
		RAF HONNINGTON	EA136
		STOWMARKET	EA141
		SUDBURY	EA134
		SUDBURY & HADLEIGH / BURY ST EDMUNDS / HAVERHILL / NEWMARKET NON-POLICE STATION	EA929
Sunderland/ Houghton Le Spring	1013	HOUGHTON-LE-SPRING	NE051
		SUNDERLAND / HOUGHTON LE SPRING NON-POLICE STATION	NE911
		SUNDERLAND CENTRAL	NE049
		SUNDERLAND NORTH	NE048
		SUNDERLAND WEST	NE047
		WASHINGTON	NE050

PS scheme name	PS scheme code	Police station name	Police station ID
Sutton	1326	SUTTON	LN170
		SUTTON NON-POLICE STATION	LN924
		WALLINGTON	LN171
		WORCESTER PARK	LN172
Swale	7004	EASTLING (FAVERSHAM)	BG031
		FAVERSHAM	BG035
		HM CUSTOMS SHEERNESS	BG034
		SELLING (HERNE BAY)	BG036
		SHEERNESS	BG033
		SITTINGBOURNE	BG032
		SWALE NON-POLICE STATION	BG905
Swansea	4027	CLYDACH	WA137
		COCKETT	WA136
		GORSEINON	WA135
		MORRISTON	WA134
		MUMBLES	WA132
		PONTARDAWE	WA130
		REYNOLDSTONE	WA129
		SKETTY	WA133
		SWANSEA CENTRAL	WA131
		SWANSEA NON-POLICE STATION	WA926
Swindon	2013	GABLECROSS	BR095
		HIGHWORTH	BR089
		MARLBOROUGH	BR088
		RAF HOSP WROUGHTON	BR090
		RAF LYNEHAM PSU	BR091
		SWINDON CENTRAL	BR093
		SWINDON NON-POLICE STATION	BR912
		SWINDON WESTLEA (CLOSED)	BR094
		WOOTON BASSETT	BR092
Tameside	6016	ASHTON-UNDER-LYNE	MA175
		DENTON	MA172

PS scheme name	PS scheme code	Police station name	Police station ID
		HYDE	MA174
		STALYBRIDGE	MA173
		TAMESIDE NON-POLICE STATION	MA915
Teeside	1002	BILLINGHAM	NE006
		COULBY NEWHAM	NE009
		GUISBOROUGH	NE002
		MIDDLESBOROUGH	NE008
		NORTH ORMESBY	NE005
		REDCAR	NE004
		SOUTH BANK	NE003
		STOCKTON-ON-TEES	NE007
		TEESIDE NON-POLICE STATION	NE901
Teignbridge/Torbay	2022	ASHBURTON	BR190
		BOVEY TRACEY	BR189
		BRIXHAM	BR191
		BUCKFASTLEIGH	BR188
		CHUDLEIGH	BR187
		DARTMOUTH	BR198
		DAWLISH WARREN	BR186
		KINGSBRIDGE	BR197
		KINGSKERSWELL	BR185
		KINGSTEIGNTON	BR181
		MORETONHAMPSTEAD	BR180
		NEWTON ABBOT	BR184
		PAIGNTON, TORBAY	BR192
		SOUTH BRENT	BR196
		TEIGNBRIDGE	BR179
		TEIGNBRIDGE / TORBAY NON-POLICE STATION	BR921
		TEIGNMOUTH	BR183
		TORQUAY	BR182
		TORQUAY (SOUTH HAMS)	BR195

PS scheme name	PS scheme code	Police station name	Police station ID
		TORQUAY (TORBAY) (NOT FOUND)	BR 193
		TOTNES	BR 194
Telford	3008	BRIDGNORTH	BM 105
		DONNINGTON	BM 109
		MALLINSGATE (TELFORD)	BM 111
		MUCH WENLOCK	BM 107
		OAKENGATES	BM 108
		RMP DONNINGTON	BM 286
		SHIFNAL	BM 106
		TELFORD NON-POLICE STATION	BM 907
		WELLINGTON	BM 110
Thames	1327	ARBOUR SQUARE	LN 173
		BETHNAL GREEN	LN 174
		BOW	LN 175
		BRICK LANE	LN 176
		ISLE OF DOGS	LN 177
		LEMAN STREET	LN 178
		LIMEHOUSE	LN 179
		POPLAR	LN 180
		THAMES NON-POLICE STATION	LN 925
Tower Bridge	1328	CAMBERWELL	LN 181
		HM CUSTOMS DORSET HOUSE (LONDON)	LN 182
		PECKHAM	LN 183
		ROTHERHITHE	LN 184
		TOWER BRIDGE	LN 185
		TOWER BRIDGE NON-POLICE STATION	LN 926
		WALWORTH	LN 186
Trafford	6010	ALTRINCHAM	MA 132
		BROADHEATH (TRAFFORD)	MA 133
		MANCHESTER AIRPORT	MA 122

Police station scheme codes 273

PS scheme name	PS scheme code	Police station name	Police station ID
		PARTINGTON	MA129
		STRETFORD	MA131
		TRAFFORD NON-POLICE STATION	MA909
		URMSTON	MA130
Tynedale & Hexham	1015	BELLINGHAM	NE061
		CORBRIDGE	NE060
		HALTWHISTLE	NE059
		HEXHAM	NE058
		PRUDHOE	NE057
		TYNEDALE & HEXHAM NON-POLICE STATION	NE913
Uxbridge	1329	HAYES	LN187
		HEATHROW AIRPORT, MET	LN205
		NORTHWOOD (RUISLIP)	LN188
		RAF NORTHOLT	LN189
		RAF UXBRIDGE	LN190
		RUISLIP	LN191
		UXBRIDGE	LN192
		UXBRIDGE NON-POLICE STATION	LN927
		WEST DRAYTON	LN193
Vale of Glamorgan	4020	BARRY	WA098
		CARDIFF AIRPORT	WA099
		COWBRIDGE	WA097
		PENARTH	WA096
		RAF ST ATHAN	WA100
		VALE OF GLAMORGAN NON-POLICE STATION	WA919
Wakefield	1223	NORMANTON, WAKEFIELD	LS128
		OSSETT	LS127
		WAKEFIELD	LS126
		WAKEFIELD NON-POLICE STATION	LS922
Walsall	3013	ALDRIDGE	BM154
		BLOXWICH	BM159

PS scheme name	PS scheme code	Police station name	Police station ID
		BROWNHILLS	BM158
		DARLASTON	BM157
		WALSALL	BM156
		WALSALL NON-POLICE STATION	BM912
		WILLENHALL	BM155
Waltham Forest	1330	CHINGFORD	LN194
		LEYTON	LN195
		LEYTONSTONE	LN196
		WALTHAM FOREST NON-POLICE STATION	LN928
		WALTHAMSTOW	LN197
Warrington/Halton	6002	NORTHERN AREA (RUNCORN)	MA019
		RISLEY (WARRINGTON)	MA018
		RUNCORN (CLOSED)	MA014
		SANKEY	MA017
		STOCKTON HEATH	MA016
		WARRINGTON (CLOSED)	MA015
		WARRINGTON / HALTON NONPOLICE STATION	MA901
		WIDNES (CLOSED)	MA013
Watford	9021	BOREHAMWOOD	EA153
		OXHEY	EA083
		RICKMANSWORTH	EA084
		WATFORD	EA085
		WATFORD CENTRAL (NOT FOUND)	EA086
		WATFORD NON-POLICE STATION	EA920
West Berkshire (Newbury Etc.)	1139	HUNGERFORD	RD064
		LAMBOURNE	RD063
		NEWBURY	RD062
		PANGBOURNE	RD065
		THATCHAM	RD061

Police station scheme codes 275

PS scheme name	PS scheme code	Police station name	Police station ID
		WEST BERKSHIRE (NEWBURY ETC.) NON-POLICE STATION	RD908
West Kent (Tonbridge)	7007	CRANBROOK	BG041
		SEVENOAKS	BG040
		TONBRIDGE	BG039
		TUNBRIDGE WELLS	BG038
		WEST KENT (TONBRIDGE) NON-POLICE STATION	BG907
		WESTERHAM (SEVENOAKS)	BG037
West London	1331	BTP HAMMERSMITH RAIL STATION	LN198
		FULHAM	LN199
		HAMMERSMITH	LN200
		SHEPHERDS BUSH	LN201
		WEST LONDON NON-POLICE STATION	LN929
Weston-Super-Mare	2006	RAF WESTON-SUPER-MARE	BR042
		WESTON-SUPER-MARE	BR043
		WESTON-SUPER-MARE NON-POLICE STATION	BR905
Whitehaven/ Workington	6007	ABBEYTOWN	MA095
		ALLONBY	MA094
		BOTHEL	MA093
		BRIGHAM	MA092
		BROUGHTON MOOR	MA091
		CLEATOR MOOR	MA076
		COCKERMOUTH	MA098
		CROSBY	MA090
		DEARHAM	MA089
		DISTINGTON	MA082
		EGREMONT	MA077
		FLIMBY	MA088
		GREAT BROUGHTON	MA100
		GREAT CLIFTON	MA101

PS scheme name	PS scheme code	Police station name	Police station ID
		GT CLIFTON	MA086
		KESWICK	MA099
		MARYPORT	MA097
		MEALSGATE	MA075
		PARTON	MA081
		SEASCALE	MA080
		SEATON, CUMBRIA	MA085
		SIDDICK	MA084
		ST BEES	MA079
		THORNHILL	MA078
		WHITEHAVEN	MA083
		WHITEHAVEN / WORKINGTON NON-POLICE STATION	MA906
		WORKINGTON	MA096
Wigan	6014	ASHTON-IN-MAKERFIELD	MA161
		GOLBORNE	MA164
		HINDLEY	MA160
		INCE-IN-MAKERFIELD	MA159
		LEIGH, MANCHESTER	MA163
		ORRELL	MA158
		PEMBERTON	MA157
		STANDISH	MA156
		TYLDESLEY	MA162
		WIGAN (HARROGATE STREET)	MA155
		WIGAN NON-POLICE STATION	MA913
Wimbledon	1332	MITCHAM	LN202
		WIMBLEDON	LN203
		WIMBLEDON NON-POLICE STATION	LN930
Wirral	5006	BEBINGTON	LV041
		BIRKENHEAD	LV040
		BROMBOROUGH	LV034
		HESWALL	LV039

PS scheme name	PS scheme code	Police station name	Police station ID
		HOYLAKE	LV038
		LAIRD STREET	LV031
		LARTON	LV042
		MORETON	LV032
		ROCK FERRY	LV033
		UPTON	LV037
		WALLASEY	LV036
		WEST FLOAT	LV035
		WIRRAL NON-POLICE STATION	LV905
Wolverhampton & Seisdon	3011	BILSTON (NOT FOUND)	BM146
		BIRMINGHAM ROAD	BM142
		BTP WOLVERHAMPTON RAILWAY STATION	BM140
		CODSALL	BM290
		DUNSTALL ROAD	BM141
		KINVER	BM289
		RED LION STREET	BM143
		SEISDON	BM291
		TETTENHALL	BM145
		WEDNESFIELD	BM144
		WOLVERHAMPTON & SEISDON NON-POLICE STATION	BM910
		WOLVERHAMPTON CENTRAL	BM147
		WOMBOURNE	BM027
Worcester	3009	ALFRICK	BM117
		ASHPERTON	BM300
		BADSEY	BM305
		BECKFORD	BM129
		BREDON	BM128
		BRETFORTON	BM304
		BROADHEATH (WORCESTER)	BM297
		BROADWAS	BM122

PS scheme name	PS scheme code	Police station name	Police station ID
		BROADWAY	BM127
		CRADLEY	BM116
		CROPTHORNE	BM126
		CROWLE	BM121
		DRAKES BROUGHTON	BM303
		DROITWICH	BM118
		EVESHAM	BM125
		FERNHILL HEATH	BM296
		HALLOW	BM295
		HARVINGTON	BM092
		HM CUSTOMS DROITWICH	BM306
		KEMPSEY	BM120
		LEIGH SYNTON	BM299
		LITTLETON	BM124
		LOWER MOOR	BM302
		MALVERN	BM115
		OFFENHAM	BM301
		OMBERSLEY	BM307
		PERSHORE	BM123
		POWICK	BM294
		STRENSHAM	BM132
		UPTON-ON-SEVERN	BM298
		WARNDON	BM293
		WELLAND	BM114
		WHITTINGTON	BM292
		WORCESTER	BM119
		WORCESTER NON-POLICE STATION	BM908
		WORCESTER, HINDLIP HALL	BM131
Worksop & East Retford	8015	CARLTON IN LINDRICK	NT111
		HARWORTH	NT110
		RETFORD	NT109

PS scheme name	PS scheme code	Police station name	Police station ID
		WORKSOP	NT108
		WORKSOP & EAST RETFORD NON-POLICE STATION	NT914
Worthing	7017	ARUNDEL	BG092
		LITTLEHAMPTON	BG091
		SHOREHAM	BG090
		STEYNING	BG089
		WORTHING	BG088
		WORTHING NON-POLICE STATION	BG918
Wrexham	4018	CORWEN	WA082
		LLANGOLLEN	WA081
		OVERTON	WA080
		RHOSLLANERCHROGOG	WA079
		RUABON	WA078
		WREXHAM	WA077
		WREXHAM NON-POLICE STATION	WA917
York/Selby	1211	BTP YORK RAILWAY STATION	LS046
		SELBY	LS048
		YORK	LS047
		YORK/SELBY NON-POLICE STATION	LS910

APPENDIX E

Magistrates' court codes

Editors' note: courts have been re-organised and many courts closed.

London Courts

Court name	ID
[HOUNSLOW PSD] BRENTFORD	C2769
ACTON	C2723
BALHAM HIGH ROAD	C6686
BALHAM HIGH ROAD YOUTH	C6013A
BARKING	C2814
BARNET	C2725
BELMARSH (GREENWICH PSA)	C2643B
BEXLEY	C2728
BOW STREET	C2641
BRENT (WILLESDEN)	C2762
BRENTFORD	C2769A
BROMLEY	C2727
CAMBERWELL GREEN	C2656
CITY OF LONDON (JUSTICE ROOMS)	C2631
CLERKENWELL (COURT CLOSED)	C2642
CROYDON	C2732
EALING	C2734
FELTHAM	C2769B
GREENWICH	C2643

Court name	ID
GREENWICH & LEWISHAM	C6643
GREENWICH & LEWISHAM YOUTH	C6013C
GREENWICH, LEWISHAM & SOUTHWARK YOUTH	C6656
HAMPSTEAD	C2740
HARROW	C2760
HAVERING	C1837
HENDON	C2741
HIGHBURY CORNER (EAST CENTRAL)	C2663
HIGHGATE (HARINGEY)	C2742
HILLINGDON	C2766
HORSEFERRY ROAD (CITY OF WESTMINSTER)	C2660
INNER LONDON JUVENILE COURTS	C6013
KINGSTON	C2812
LAMBETH & WANDSWORTH YOUTH COURTS	C6649
MARLBOROUGH STREET (CLOSED)	C2644
MARYLEBONE (CLOSED)	C2646

282 Criminal Costs: legal aid costs in the criminal courts / Appendix E

Court name	ID
NORTH AND NORTH EAST LONDON YOUTH COURTS	C6650
REDBRIDGE	C2815
REDBRIDGE YOUTH	C6815
RICHMOND (SURREY)	C2768
SOUTH WESTERN (LAVENDER HILL)	C2649
SOUTHWARK	C6693
SOUTHWARK YOUTH	C6013B
STRATFORD (CLOSED)	C2721
STRATFORD YOUTH	C2722
SUTTON	C2733
THAMES	C2650
TOTTENHAM (ENFIELD)	C2757
TOWER BRIDGE	C2651
WALTHAM FOREST	C2813
WALTON STREET	C2657
WEST LONDON MAGISTRATES' COURT (HAMMERSMITH)	C2658
WEST LONDON YOUTH COURT	C6658
WIMBLEDON	C2763
WOOLWICH	C2653

National courts

Court Name	ID
(SKIPTON PSD)	C2538
[BEDWELLTY PSD]	C3201
[CROWBOROUGH PSD]	C1598
[DERBY & SOUTH DERBYSHIRE PSD]	C1427
[DONCASTER PSD]	C2771
[EAST GWENT PSD]	C3208
[KEIGHLEY PSD]	C2979
[MID SUSSEX PSD]	C2932

Court Name	ID
[NEWCASTLE UPON TYNE PSD]	C2851
[ABERCONWY PSD]	C3237
[BAINTON, WILTON, HOLME BEACON PSD]	C1905
[BLACKB'N/DARWEN/ RIBBLE VAL.]	C2012
[BOURNEMOUTH & CHRISTCHURCH]	C1514
[BRAINTREE]	C1617
[BROMSGROVE & REDDITCH PSD]	C1840
[CENTRAL BUCKINGHAMSHIRE PSD]	C1129
[CITY OF SALFORD PSD]	C1747
[DICKERING & NTH HOLDERN PSD]	C1904
[ELLOES DIV]	C2076
[FURNESS & DISTRICT PSD]	C1398
[LLIW VALLEY]	C3358
[MARKET HARBORO' & LUTT'WORTH]	C2051
[N'CASTLE/LYME & P'HILL PSD]	C2797
[NORTH DORSET PSD]	C1507
[NORTH EAST HAMPSHIRE PSD]	C1780
[NORTH WEST HAMPSHIRE PSD]	C1781
[NORTH WEST SUFFOLK PSD]	C2862
[NTH GLOUCESTERSHIRE PSD]	C1696
[NTH TYNESIDE PSD]	C2852
[OXFORD PSD]	C2777
[PONTEFRACT PSD]	C2994
[SOUTH ANGLESEY PSD]	C3232
[SOUTH NORFOLK PSD]	C1446

Court Name	ID
[STH TYNESIDE PSD]	C2853
[SWANSEA PSD]	C3360
[TAMESIDE PSD]	C1748
[THAME & HENLEY PSD]	C2778
[THANET PSD]	C1968
[WEST NORFOLK PSD]	C1447
ABERGAVENNY	C3208A
ABERGELE	C3052B
ABERTILLERY	C3201B
ABERYSTWYTH	C3135A
ABINGDON	C2681
ABINGDON (AB/DID/WANT)	C2774A
ALDERSHOT (NORTH EAST HANTS)	C1780C
ALFRETON	C1429B
ALNWICK	C2347
ALSTON (COURT CLOSED)	C1384B
ALTON	C1780A
ALTON & PETERSFIELD	C1778
AMERSHAM (C. BUCKS)	C1129C
AMPTHILL	C1050
ANDOVER	C1781A
ARUNDEL	C2927
ASHBOURNE	C1428A
ASHBY-DE-LA-ZOUCH (COALVILLE)	C2047
ASHFORD AND TENTERDEN (PSD DELETED)	C1952
ASHFORD (CHANNEL)	C1957C
ASHTON-UNDER-LYNE (TAMESIDE)	C1748A
ATHERSTONE & COLESHILL	C2894

Court Name	ID
AXMINSTER	C1493A
AYLESBURY	C1125
AYLESBURY (C. BUCKS)	C1129A
BAKEWELL	C1428B
BANBURY/CHIPPING NORTON	C2702
BANGOR	C3222
BARNARD CASTLE	C1582B
BARNSLEY	C2770
BARNSTAPLE	C1494A
BARROW WITH BOOTLE	C1380
BARROW WITH BOOTLE (FURNESS)	C1398A
BASILDON	C5610
BASILDON (MID-SOUTH ESSEX)	C1610
BASINGSTOKE	C1781B
BATH & WANSDYKE	C1022
BATLEY & DEWSBURY	C2996
BATTLE & RYE	C1606A
BEACONSFIELD (WICKHAM/B'FIELD)	C1130A
BEAUMARIS	C3232A
BECCLES	C6816
BEDALE	C2543B
BEDFORD	C1051
BERWICK-ON-TWEED	C2348
BEVERLEY	C1925
BEVERLEY & THE WOLDS	C1942
BEXHILL	C1606B
BICESTER	C2671
BICESTER, OXON	C2776
BIDEFORD & GREAT TORRINGTON	C1477
BIGGLESWADE	C1052

Magistrates' court codes 283

Court Name	ID
BINGLEY	C2979B
BIRMINGHAM	C2908
BISHOP AUCKLAND	C1582A
BISHOP'S STORTFORD	C1875
BLACKBURN	C1995
BLACKBURN (B'BURN/ DAR/RIB.VAL)	C2012A
BLACKPOOL	C1996
BLACKWOOD	C3201D
BLANDFORD & STURMINSTER	C1512
BLANDFORD FORUM (CENT.DORSET)	C1515A
BLAYDON	C2850B
BODMIN	C1279
BOLTON	C1731
BOSTON	C2073
BOURNE & STAMFORD	C2074
BOURNEMOUTH	C1501
BOURNEMOUTH (B&C DIV)	C1514A
BRACKNELL (FOREST)	C1066
BRADFORD	C2978
BRAINTREE	C1631
BRECON	C3350A
BRENTWOOD	C1611
BRIDGNORTH	C3274
BRIDLINGTON	C1904A
BRIDLINGTON	C1941
BRIDPORT	C1502
BRIDPORT (WEST DORSET)	C1516A
BRIGHTON	C1597
BRIGHTON (BRIGHTON & HOVE)	C1604A

Court Name	ID
BRISTOL	C1013
BROMSGROVE (CLOSED)	C1846
BROMSGROVE (COURT CLOSED)	C1840A
BROUGH	C1901A
B'STAPLE & S. MOLTON PSD]	C1494
BUCKINGHAM (C. BUCKS)	C1129B
BURNLEY	C1997
BURNLEY (BURNLEY & PENDLE)	C2011A
BURNLEY, PENDLE AND ROSSENDALE	C2014
BURTON-UPON-TRENT	C2780
BURY	C1732
CAERNARFON & GWYRFAI	C3234
CAISTOR	C2056
CALDER (HALIFAX)	C2984
CALDERDALE	C2997
CAMBERLEY	C2846C
CAMBRIDGE	C1165
CANNOCK	C2781
CANNOCK & SEISDON MAGISTRATES' COURT	C2859
CANTERBURY AND ST AUGUSTINE	C1953
CARDIFF	C3348
CARDIGAN	C3135B
CARLISLE	C1364
CARLISLE AND DISTRICT	C1322
CARMARTHEN	C3138
CASTLEFORD	C2994B
CENTRAL & SOUTH WEST STAFFORDSHIRE PSA	C2799
CENTRAL DEVON PSA	C1292

Magistrates' court codes 285

Court Name	ID
CENTRAL HERTFORDSHIRE	C1892
CEREDIGION	C3135
CEREDIGION GANOL (PSD DELETED)	C3134
CHANNEL PSA	C1957
CHEADLE	C2796B
CHELMSFORD/WITHAM (MID-NORTH)	C1612
CHELTENHAM	C1672
CHELTENHAM (N. GLOS)	C1696A
CHEPSTOW	C3208C
CHERTSEY	C2846A
CHESHUNT (EAST HERTFORDSHIRE)	C1877
CHESHUNT (EAST HERTFORDSHIRE)	C1888A
CHESTER	C1173
CHESTER, ELLESMERE PORT & NESTON	C1188
CHESTERFIELD (TAPTON LANE)	C1432
CHESTERFIELD (BRIMIMINGTON ROAD)	C1418B
CHESTERFIELD (WEST BARS)	C1418
CHESTER-LE-STREET	C1576
CHICHESTER AND DISTRICT	C2936
CHIPPENHAM (NORTH WILTSHIRE)	C3022
CHORLEY	C1998
CHRISTCHURCH	C1503
CHRISTCHURCH (B&C DIV)	C1514B
CIRENCESTER	C1689
COLCHESTER (TOWN HALL)	C1613B

Court Name	ID
COLCHESTER/HARWICH (NORTH EAST ESSEX)	C1613
COLWYN (CLWYD)	C3052A
COMMUNITY JUSTICE CENTRE – MERSEYSIDE	C9000
CONGLETON	C1187A
CONWY	C3062
CONWY AND LLANDUDNO	C3237A
CORBY	C2321
CORWEN	C3051C
COVENTRY	C2910
CRAWLEY	C2929
CREWE AND NANTWICH	C1187B
CROMER	C1444B
CROWBOROUGH	C1598A
CROWBOROUGH (MARK CROSS)	C1598B
CROWBOROUGH (LEWES & CROBORO')	C1607A
CULLOMPTON	C1478
CWMBRAN	C3208B
CYNON VALLEY	C3262
DACORUM	C1878
DARLINGTON	C1577
DARTFORD	C1954
DARTFORD & GRAVESHAM (GRAVESEND)	C1969
DARWEN	C2000
DARWEN (B'BURN/DAR/RIB.VAL)	C2012B
DAVENTRY	C2322
DE BRYCHEINIOG	C3350
DE CEREDIGION (PSD DELETED)	C3136
DE MALDWYN	C3352

Court Name	ID
DENBIGH	C3061C
DENBIGHSHIRE	C3061
DERBY (BOLD LANE)	C1427C
DERBY (DERWENT STREET)	C1427A
DERWENTSIDE (CONSETT)	C1578
DEVIZES	C3025
DIDCOT (AB/DID/WANT)	C2774B
DIDCOT AND WANTAGE	C2718
DINEFWR	C3140
DISS	C1446A
DOLGELLAU	C3239
DONCASTER	C2771A
DORCHESTER	C1504
DORCHESTER (WEST DORSET)	C1516B
DORKING	C2847B
DOVER (CHANNEL)	C1957A
DOVER AND EAST KENT (PSD DELETED)	C1955
DRAYTON DIVISION	C3275
DRIFFIELD	C1905A
DROITWICH (SOUTH WORCESTERSHIRE)	C1843A
DROXFORD	C1783A
DUDLEY	C2911
DUNHEVED AND STRATTON	C1284
DUNMOW	C1615
DUNMOW AND SAFFRON WALDON	C1632
DUNSTABLE	C1053
DURHAM	C1579
DWYFOR	C3236

Court Name	ID
DYFFRYN CLWYD (PSD DELETED)	C3053
EASINGTON (PETERLEE)	C1580
EASINGWOLD	C2544
EAST BERKSHIRE PSA (SLOUGH)	C1072
EAST CAMBRIDGESHIRE (ELY)	C5166
EAST CAMBS	C1166
EAST CORNWALL PSA	C1289
EAST DORSET PSA	C1522
EAST GRINSTEAD	C2932B
EAST HERTFORDSHIRE PSA	C1888
EAST OXFORDSHIRE	C2719A
EAST PENWITH (CAMBORNE)	C1263
EAST POWDER	C1264
EAST RETFORD	C2553
EASTBOURNE (EASTB'NE & H'SHAM)	C1605A
EASTLEIGH (SOUTHAMPTON)	C1775B
EBBW VALE	C3201C
ECCLES (CITY OF SALFORD)	C1747A
EDEN PSA (PENRITH)	C1324
ELLESMERE PORT	C1176A
ELLOES (LONG SUTTON)	C2076B
ELLOES (SPALDING)	C2076A
ELY	C1166A
EPPING	C1616
EPSOM	C2845A
EPWORTH	C1928A
EVESHAM (SOUTH WORCEST[ER]SHIRE)	C1843B
EXETER & WONFORD	C1497

Magistrates' court codes

Court Name	ID
EXMOUTH	C1480
FAKENHAM	C1447B
FALMOUTH AND KERRIER	C1283
FAREHAM (SOUTH HAMPSHIRE)	C1783
FARNHAM	C2848A
FAVERSHAM & SITTINGBOURNE	C1967
FELIXSTOWE (DEBEN)	C2861A
FLEETWOOD	C2009A
FLINT	C3054
FLINTSHIRE	C3059
FLYDE COAST PSA (BLACKPOOL/WYRE)	C1992
FOLKESTONE (CHANNEL)	C1957B
FOREST OF DEAN (COLEFORD)	C1695
FROME	C2715D
GAINSBOROUGH	C2075
GATESHEAD	C2850
GATESHEAD	C2850A
GILLINGHAM	C1507B
GILLINGHAM (CENTRAL DORSET)	C1515B
GLOSSOP	C1421
GLOUCESTER	C1692
GODSTONE	C2847C
GOGLEDD PRESELI (PSD DELETED)	C3141
GOOLE	C1928B
GOOLE AND HOWDENSHIRE	C1928
GOSFORTH	C2851B
GOSFORTH YOUTH (NEWCASTLE UPON TYNE)	C6851

Court Name	ID
GRANTHAM	C2077
GRAVESHAM	C1958
GRAYS (SOUTH WEST ESSEX)	C1626
GREAT YARMOUTH	C1443
GRIMSBY & CLEETHORPES	C1940
GUILDFORD	C2848B
GWENT	C3210
GWYNEDD PSA	C3244
HAILSHAM (EASTB'NE & HAILSHAM)	C1605B
HARLOW/EPPING (NORTH WEST ESSEX)	C1619
HARROGATE (PSD)	C2527
HARTLEPOOL	C1247
HARWICH	C1620
HASTINGS (HASTINGS & ROTHER)	C1606C
HAVERHILL (PSD DELETED)	C2825
HAVERHILL AND SUDBURY	C2864
HAWARDEN	C3055
HAWARDEN YOUTH	C7055
HAYWARDS HEATH	C2932A
HEBBURN	C2853B
HENLEY (THAME/ HENLEY)	C2778B
HEREFORD (HEREFORDSHIRE)	C1841A
HERTFORD (EAST HERTFORDSHIRE)	C1888B
HIGH PEAK (BUXTON)	C1422
HIGH PEAK PSA	C1430
HINCKLEY	C2050A
HONITON	C1493B

Court Name	ID
HORNCASTLE	C2078A
HORNSEA (COURT CLOSED)	C1904B
HORSHAM	C2930
HOUGHTON-LE-SPRING	C2854A
HOVE	C1602
HOVE (BRIGHTON & HOVE)	C1604B
HOWDEN (COURT CLOSED)	C1901B
HUDDERSFIELD	C2987
HULL & HOLDERNESS (KINGSTON UPON HULL)	C1943
HUNSTANTON	C1447C
HUNTINGDON	C1168A
HUNTINGDON DIVISION	C1168
HUYTON	C2266A
HYNDBURN	C2010
HYTHE	C1779A
ILKESTON	C1429A
INGLETON	C2538B
IPSWICH	C2830
ISLE OF WIGHT	C1945
ISLES OF SCILLY	C1268
IVYBRIDGE	C1496B
KEIGHLEY	C2979A
KENDAL AND LONSDALE	C1382
KESWICK	C1369
KETTERING	C2323
KIDSGROVE	C2797C
KINGS LYNN	C1447D
KINGSBRIDGE	C1496A
KINGSTON UPON HULL	C1933
KIRKBY	C2266B
LANCASTER	C2002

Court Name	ID
LANGBAURGH EAST	C1248
LEEDS	C2988
LEEDS	C2992
LEEDS	C6988
LEEK	C2784
LEEK	C2796A
LEICESTER	C2048A
LEIGH	C1743
LEIGHTON BUZZARD	C1054
LEOMINSTER (HEREFORDSHIRE)	C1841B
LEWES	C1603
LEWES (LEWES & CROWBORO')	C1607B
LEYBURN	C2545B
LICHFIELD	C2785
LINCOLN DISTRICT	C2079
LIVERPOOL	C2267
LLANDRINDOD WELLS	C3352C
LLANDUDNO	C3061A
LLANELLI	C3122
LLANGEFNI	C3232C
LLANGEFNI	C3238A
LLANGOLLEN	C3051A
LLIW VALLEY	C3360B
LONG ASHTON	C1023A
LOUGHBOROUGH	C2049
LOUTH	C2078B
LOWESTOFT	C2863A
LUDLOW	C3276
LUTON & SOUTH BEDFORDSHIRE	C1055
LUTTERWORTH	C2051A
LWR RHYMNEY VALLEY (CAERPHILLY)	C3263

Magistrates' court codes

Court Name	ID
LYMINGTON	C1779B
LYTHAM	C2001
MACCLESFIELD	C1178A
MACHYNLLETH (PSD DELETED)	C3330
MAIDENHEAD	C1068
MALDON & WITHAM	C1630
MALTON	C2546A
MANCHESTER	C1733
MANSFIELD	C2566
MARGATE (THANET)	C1968A
MARKET DRAYTON	C3275A
MARKET HARBOROUGH	C2051B
MARKET RASEN	C2081
MARKET STREET	C2851A
MARKET WEIGHTON	C1905C
MATLOCK	C1428C
MEDWAY (CHATHAM)	C1961
MELTON, BELVOIR AND RUTLAND	C2045
MENAI BRIDGE	C3232B
MENDIP PSA	C2715
MERTHYR TYDFIL	C3264
MID HERTFORDSHIRE (ST ALBANS)	C1883
MID KENT (MAIDSTONE)	C1959
MID WARWICKSHIRE (WARWICK)	C2903
MIDDLETON	C1735
MID-HERTFORDSHIRE	C1890
MID-STAFFORDSHIRE DIVISION	C2795
MILDENHALL	C2821
MILDENHALL (NW SUFFOLK)	C2862A

Court Name	ID
MILTON KEYNES	C1124
MISKIN	C3265
MOLD	C3056
MONMOUTH	C3208D
MORLEY	C2989
N.COTSWOLD	C1696C
NEATH	C3359A
NEATH PORT TALBOT PSA	C3359
NEW FOREST	C1779E
NEW FOREST (LYNDHURST)	C1779
NEWARK & SOUTHWELL	C2567
NEWBURY (WEST BERKS)	C1075
NEWCASTLE AND OGMORE	C3266
NEWCASTLE UNDER LYME	C2797A
NEWCASTLE-UNDER-LYME	C2786
NEWMARKET (CAMBS)	C1166B
NEWMARKET (NW SUFFOLK)	C2862B
NEWMARKET (SUFF)	C2823
NEWPORT	C3205
NORTH ANGLESEY	C3229
NORTH AVON	C1021
NORTH COTSWOLD	C1694
NORTH DEVON PSA	C1291
NORTH DURHAM PSA	C1583
NORTH EAST SUFFOLK MAGISTRATES' COURT	C2863
NORTH HERTFORDSHIRE	C1889
NORTH LINCOLNSHIRE (SCUNTHORPE)	C1903A
NORTH LONSDALE	C1372

Court Name	ID
NORTH PEMBROKESHIRE	C3139
NORTH SHIELDS	C2852A
NORTH SOMERSET (WOODSPRING)	C1023
NORTH STAFFORDSHIRE (STOKE-ON-TRENT)	C2791
NORTH STAFFORDSHIRE MAGISTRATES' COURT	C2798
NORTH WALSHAM	C1444A
NORTH WEST GWENT	C3209
NORTH WEST WILTSHIRE PSA	C3026
NORTH WITCHFORD	C1167A
NORTHALLERTON	C2543C
NORTHAMPTON	C2325
NORTHERN OXFORDSHIRE PSA (BANBURY)	C2775
NORTHWICH	C1179A
NORWICH	C1445
NOTTINGHAM	C2568
NRTH SEFTON	C6269
NTH & E. SURREY DIVISION	C2845
NTH & E. SURREY DIVISION	C2849
NTH. LONSDALE	C1398B
NTH. WEST SURREY DIVISION	C2846
NUNEATON	C2896
OKEHAMPTON	C1495A
OLDHAM	C1734
ORMSKIRK	C2003
OSWESTRY	C3277
OTLEY	C2990B
OXFORD CT.	C2777A
PENRITH (EDEN PSA)	C1384A

Court Name	ID
PENWITH (PENZANCE)	C1272
PETERBOROUGH	C1162
PETERSFIELD	C1780B
PICKERING	C2546B
PIREHILL NORTH	C2797B
PLYMOUTH	C1484
PLYMOUTH DISTRICT PSA	C1290
POCKLINGTON	C1905B
PONTEFRACT	C2994A
PONTYPOOL	C3208E
POOLE	C1505
PORT TALBOT	C3359B
PORTSMOUTH (SOUTH EAST HAMPSHIRE)	C1782
PRESTATYN	C3061B
PRESTON	C2005
PUDSEY	C2990A
PWLLHELI	C3231
PYDAR (NEWQUAY)	C1274
RADNORSHIRE & N. BRECKNOCK	C3351
RAMSGATE (THANET)	C1968B
READING (READING AND SONNING)	C1076
REDDITCH	C1840B
REEDLEY (BURNLEY & PENDLE)	C2011B
REIGATE	C2847A
RHUDDLAN (PRESTATYN) (PSD DELETED)	C3057
RIBBLE VALLEY (B'BURN/ DAR/RV)	C2012C
RICHMOND (N. YORKS)	C2545A
RINGWOOD	C1779C
RIPON LIBERTY	C2534

Magistrates' court codes

Court Name	ID
ROCHDALE	C1736
ROCHFORD & SOUTHEND-ON-SEA	C5629
ROSSENDALE	C2006
ROTHERHAM	C2772
RUGBY DIVISION	C2897
RUGELEY	C2788
RUNCORN	C1177A
RUTLAND (PSD DELETED)	C2046
RYE	C1595B
S. THAMESIDE	C1748B
SAFFRON WALDON	C1623
SALFORD	C1738
SALFORD (CITY OF SALFORD)	C1747B
SALISBURY	C3023
SAXMUNDHAM	C2863C
SAXMUNDHAM	C6831
SCARBOROUGH	C2536
SE STAFFORDSHIRE (LICHFIELD & TAMWORTH)	C2860
SEDGEFIELD (NEWTON AYCLIFFE)	C1581
SEDGEMOOR	C2706
SEISDON	C2789
SELBY	C2537
SETTLE	C2538C
SEVENOAKS (WEST KENT)	C1963A
SEVERNMINSTER (KIDDERMINSTER)	C1842A
SHAFTESBURY	C1513
SHEFFIELD	C2773
SHERBORNE (WEST DORSET)	C1516C

Court Name	ID
SHERBOURNE	C1507A
SHREWSBURY	C3279
SKEGNESS	C2082
SKIPTON	C2538A
SKYRACK & WETHERBY	C2991
SLEAFORD	C2080
SOLIHULL	C2916
SOUTH AND MIDDLE HOLDERNESS (WITHERNSEA)	C1902A
SOUTH CHESHIRE	C1187
SOUTH DEVON PSA	C1293
SOUTH DURHAM PSA	C1584
SOUTH EAST CORNWALL	C1280
SOUTH EAST NORTHUMBERLAND	C2349
SOUTH EAST SUFFOLK	C2866
SOUTH EAST SURREY	C2856
SOUTH EAST SURREY (REDHILL)	C2856A
SOUTH EAST WILTSHIRE PSA	C3027
SOUTH GLOUCESTERSHIRE	C1693
SOUTH HAMS (TOTNES)	C1496C
SOUTH HEREFORDSHIRE	C1841C
SOUTH LAKELAND PSA (KENDAL/STH CUMBRIA)	C1323
SOUTH LAKES	C1381
SOUTH MOLTON	C1494B
SOUTH OXON [ABINGDON/DIDCOT/ WANTAGE]	C2774
SOUTH PEMBROKESHIRE	C3142
SOUTH RIBBLE (LEYLAND)	C2007

Court Name	ID
SOUTH SEFTON (BOOTLE)	C2270
SOUTH SHIELDS	C2853A
SOUTH SOMERSET	C2714
SOUTHAMPTON	C1775A
SOUTHAMPTON.	C1775
SOUTHEND ON SEA (SOUTH EAST ESSEX)	C1629
SOUTHERN DERBYSHIRE PSA	C1431
SOUTHPORT AND CROSBY	C2269A
SPROATLEY	C1902B
ST HELENS	C2268
ST. EDMUNDSBURY & STOWMARKET	C2865
ST. EDMUNDSBURY (PSD DELETED)	C2832
STAFF. MOORLANDS DIVISION PSD	C2796
STAFFORD	C2790
STAFFORD	C2795A
STAINES & SUNBURY	C2845B
STEYNING	C2934
STH. WARWICKSHIRE (STRATFORD)	C2902
STH. EAST SURREY DIVISION	C2847
STH. WEST SURREY DIVISION	C2848
STOCKPORT	C1739
STOCKTON HEATH	C1180B
STOKESLEY	C2543D
STOURBRIDGE	C2913
STOURBRIDGE & HALESOWEN	C2912
STOWMARKET (PSD DELETED)	C2833

Court Name	ID
SUDBURY (PSD DELETED)	C2828
SUNDERLAND	C2855
SUSSEX (CENTRAL) PSA (BRIGHTON)	C2950
SUSSEX (EASTERN) PSA (EASTBOURNE)	C2948
SUSSEX (NRTH) (CRAWLEY/HORSHAM/ MID-SSX)	C2947
SUSSEX (WESTERN) (WORTHING)	C2949
SUTTON COLDFIELD	C2909
SWADLINCOTE	C1427B
SWAFFHAM & DEREHAM	C1442A
SWANSEA	C3360A
SWINDON	C3015
TAMWORTH	C2793
TAUNTON & WEST SOMERSET	C2709
TAVISTOCK	C1495B
TEESSIDE	C1249
TEIGNBRIDGE (NEWTON ABBOT)	C1488
TELFORD	C3282
TENBY MAGISTRATES COURT	C3142B
TENDRING	C1625
TEWKESBURY (N. GLOS)	C1696B
THAME (THAME & HENLEY)	C2778A
THETFORD	C1442B
THIRSK	C2543A
THORNE	C2771B
TIVERTON	C1489
TONBRIDGE	C1965B
TORBAY (TORQUAY)	C1490

Magistrates' court codes

Court Name	ID
TOSELAND	C1168B
TOWCESTER	C2327
TRAFFORD (SALE)	C1742
TREDEGAR	C3201A
TROWBRIDGE	C3024
TRURO & SOUTH POWDER	C1282
TUNBRIDGE WELLS	C1966A
TYNEDALE	C2346
UPPER RHYMNEY VALLEY	C3267
USK	C3208F
UTTOXETER	C2795D
VALE OF GLAMORGAN	C3349
WAKEFIELD	C2995
WALSALL	C2918
WALSALL & ALDRIDGE	C2917
WANTAGE (AB/DID/WANT)	C2774C
WAREHAM	C1509
WAREHAM (DORSET)	C1515C
WARLEY	C2914
WARRINGTON (ARPLEY ST)	C1180C
WARRINGTON (WINMARLEIGH ST)	C1180A
WARWICKSHIRE PSA (NUNEATON/RUGBY)	C2904
WASHINGTON	C2854B
WATFORD	C1886
WELLINGBOROUGH	C2328
WELLS	C2715B
WELSHPOOL	C3346
WELSHPOOL	C3352B
WEST ALLERDALE AND KESWICK	C1325

Court Name	ID
WEST ALLERDALE (WORKINGTON)	C1379
WEST BROMWICH	C2915
WEST CORNWALL PSA	C1288
WEST DORSET PSA	C1523
WEST HERFORDSHIRE (WATFORD/DACORUM)	C1893
WEST KENT	C1963
WEST MALLING	C1965A
WEST SOMERSET (MINEHEAD)	C2711
WEST SUFFOLK	C2867
WESTON-SUPER-MARE	C1023B
WEYMOUTH & PORTLAND	C1510
WHITBY STRAND	C2540
WHITCHURCH	C3275B
WHITEHAVEN	C1375
WHITLEY BAY	C2852C
WIDNES	C1177B
WIGAN	C1746
WIGAN AND LEIGH (ACTIVE 01/01/03–) 1/0	C1749
WIGTON	C1376
WIMBORNE	C1511
WIMBORNE (CENTRAL DORSET)	C1515D
WINCHESTER	C1781C
WINDSOR	C1074
WIRRAL	C2271
WIRRAL JUVENILE	C6271
WISBECH	C1167B
WITNEY, OXON.	C2779
WOKING	C2846B
WOLVERHAMPTON	C2919
WOODSTOCK	C2701

Court Name	ID
WORCESTER (SOUTH WORCESTERSHIRE)	C1843D
WORCESTER (SOUTH WORCESTSHIRE)	C1843C
WORKSOP	C2560
WORKSOP & RETFORD PSA	C2569
WORTHING	C2935
WORTHING AND DISTRICT	C2937

Court Name	ID
WREXHAM MAELOR	C3058
WYCOMBE (WYCOMBE & B'FIELD)	C1130B
YNYS MON/ANGLESEY	C3238
YORK	C2541
YSTRADGYNLAIS	C3350B
YSTRADGYNLAIS (PSD DELETED)	C3340

APPENDIX F

Prison ID codes

If the location you provide advice at is not included on this list please use the code for the nearest prison.

Prison location	Code
ACKLINGTON	AKCM
ALBANY	ALCM
ALTCOURSE	ACAM
ASHFIELD	ASKM
ASHWELL	AWCM
ASKHAM GRANGE	AGDF
AYLESBURY	AYIM
BEDFORD	BFBM
BELMARSH	BAAM
BIRMINGHAM	BMBM
BLANTYRE HOUSE	BHCM
BLUNDESTON	BDCM
BRINSFORD	BSAM
BRISTOL	BLAM
BRIXTON	BXBM
BRONZEFIELD	BZAF
BUCKLEY HALL	BCCM
BULLINGDON	BNAM
BULLWOOD HALL	BUCM
BURE	BRCM
CAMP HILL	CHCM
CANTERBURY	CYCM
CARDIFF	CFBM

Prison location	Code
CASTINGTON	CSAM
CHANNINGS WOOD	CWCM
CHELMSFORD	CDAM
COLDINGLEY	CLCM
COOKHAM WOOD	CKLM
DARTMOOR	DACM
DEERBOLT	DTIM
DONCASTER	DNAM
DORCHESTER	DRAM
DOVEGATE	DGCM
DOVER(IRC)	DVAM
DOWNVIEW	DWBF
DRAKE HALL	DHDF
DURHAM	DMBM
EAST SUTTON PARK	ESDF
EASTWOOD PARK	EWBF
EDMUNDS HILL	NECM
ELMLEY	EYAM
ERLESTOKE	EECM
EVERTHORPE	EVCM
EXETER	EXAM
FEATHERSTONE	FSCM
FELTHAM	FMAM

295

Prison location	Code	Prison location	Code
FORD	FDDM	LINCOLN	LIBM
FOREST BANK	FBAM	LINDHOLME(IRC)	LHAM
FOSTON HALL	FHBF	LITTLEHEY	LTCM
FRANKLAND	FKCM	LIVERPOOL	LPBM
FULL SUTTON	FNCM	LONG LARTIN	LLCM
GARTH	GHCM	LOW NEWTON	LNBF
GARTREE	GTCM	LOWDHAM GRANGE	LGCM
GLEN PARVA	GPAM	MAIDSTONE	MSCM
GLOUCESTER	GLBM	MANCHESTER	MRBM
GRENDON	GNCM	MOORLAND (CLOSED)	MDCM
GUYS MARSH	GMCM	MOORLAND (OPEN)	HDDM
HASLAR(IRC)	HRAM	MORTON HALL	MHCF
HAVERIGG	HVCM	MOUNT	MTCM
HEWELL	HEBM	NEW HALL	NHBF
HIGHDOWN	HOAM	NORTH SEA CAMP	NSDM
HIGHPOINT SOUTH	HPCM	NORTHALLERTON	NNIM
HINDLEY	HIIM	NORWICH	NWAM
HOLLESLEY BAY	HBDM	NOTTINGHAM	NMBM
HOLLOWAY	HYBF	ONLEY	ONCM
HOLME HOUSE	HHBM	PARC	PRAM
HULL	HLAM	PARKHURST	PKCM
HUNTERCOMBE	HCLM	PENTONVILLE	PVBM
KENNET	KTCM	PETERBOROUGH	PBBM
KINGSTON	PTCM	PORTLAND	PDIM
KIRKHAM	KMDM	PRESCOED	UKDM
KIRKLEVINGTON	KVCM	PRESTON	PNBM
LANCASTER CASTLE	LACM	RANBY	RNCM
LANCASTER FARMS	LFAM	READING	RDAM
LATCHMERE HOUSE	LMCM	RISLEY	RSCM
LEEDS	LEBM	ROCHESTER	RCIM
LEICESTER	LCBM	RYE HILL	RHCM
LEWES	LWAM	SEND	SDCF
LEYHILL	LYDM	SHEPTON MALLET	SMCM

Prison location	Code	Prison location	Code
SHREWSBURY	SYBM	WANDSWORTH	WWBM
SPRING HILL	GNDM	WARREN HILL	WIKM
STAFFORD	SFCM	WAYLAND	WLCM
STANDFORD HILL	EHDM	WEALSTUN	WECM
STOCKEN	SKCM	WELLINGBOROUGH	WBCM
STOKE HEATH	SHIM	WERRINGTON	WNLM
STYAL	STCF	WETHERBY	WYKM
SUDBURY	SUDM	WHATTON	WTVM
SWALESIDE	SLCM	WHITEMOOR	WRCM
SWANSEA	SWBM	WINCHESTER	WCBM
SWINFEN HALL	SNCM	WOLDS	WOCM
THORN CROSS	TCDM	WOODHILL	WHAM
USK	UKVM	WORMWOOD	WSBM
VERNE	VECM	WYMOTT	WMCM
WAKEFIELD	WDCM		

APPENDIX G

Crown Court litigators' offence classes[1]

Offence	Contrary to	Year and chapter
Class A: Homicide and related grave offences		
Murder	Common law	
Manslaughter	Common law	
Soliciting to commit murder	Offences against the Person Act 1861 s4	1861 c100
Child destruction	Infant Life (Preservation) Act 1929 s1(1)	1929 c34
Infanticide	Infanticide Act 1938 s1(1)	1938 c36
Causing explosion likely to endanger life or property	Explosive Substances Act 1883 s2	1883 c3
Attempt to cause explosion, making or keeping explosives etc.	Explosive Substances Act 1883 s3	As above
Class B: Offences involving serious violence or damage, and serious drugs offences		
Endangering the safety of an aircraft	Aviation Security Act 1982 s2(1)(b)	1982 c36
Racially-aggravated arson (not endangering life)	Crime and Disorder Act 1998 s30(1)	1998 c37
Kidnapping	Common law	
False imprisonment	Common law	
Aggravated criminal damage	Criminal Damage Act 1971 s1(2)	1971 c48
Aggravated arson	Criminal Damage Act 1971 s1(2), (3)	As above
Arson (where value exceeds £30,000)	Criminal Damage Act 1971 s1(3)	As above
Possession of firearm with intent to endanger life	Firearms Act 1968 s16	1968 c27

---

1   Criminal Legal Aid (Remuneration) Regulations 2013 SI No 435 Sch 2.

Offence	Contrary to	Year and chapter
Use of firearm to resist arrest	Firearms Act 1968 s17	As above
Possession of firearm with criminal intent	Firearms Act 1968 s18	As above
Possession or acquisition of certain prohibited weapons etc.	Firearms Act 1968 s5	As above
Aggravated burglary	Theft Act 1968 s10	1968 c60
Armed robbery	Theft Act 1968 s8(1)	As above
Assault with weapon with intent to rob	Theft Act 1968 s8(2)	As above
Blackmail	Theft Act 1968 s21	As above
Riot	Public Order Act 1986 s1	1986 c64
Violent disorder	Public Order Act 1986 s2	As above
Contamination of goods with intent	Public Order Act 1986 s38	As above
Causing death by dangerous driving	Road Traffic Act 1988 s1	1988 c52
Causing death by careless driving while under the influence of drink or drugs	Road Traffic Act 1988 s3A	As above
Aggravated vehicle taking resulting in death	Theft Act 1968 s12A	1968 c60
Causing danger to road users	Road Traffic Act 1988 s22A	1988 c52
Attempting to choke, suffocate, strangle etc.	Offences against the Person Act 1861 s21	1861 c100
Causing miscarriage by poison, instrument	Offences against the Person Act 1861 s58	As above
Making threats to kill	Offences against the Person Act 1861 s16	As above
Wounding or grievous bodily harm with intent to cause grievous bodily harm etc.	Offences against the Person Act 1861 s18	As above
Endangering the safety of railway passengers	Offences against the Person Act 1861, ss32, 33, 34	As above
Impeding persons endeavouring to escape wrecks	Offences against the Person Act 1861 s17	As above
Administering chloroform, laudanum etc.	Offences against the Person Act 1861 s22	As above
Administering poison etc. so as to endanger life	Offences against the Person Act 1861 s23	As above
Cruelty to persons under 16	Children and Young Persons Act 1933 s1	1933 c12

Offence	Contrary to	Year and chapter
Aiding and abetting suicide	Suicide Act 1961 s2	1961 c60
Prison mutiny	Prison Security Act 1992 s1	1992 c25
Assaulting prison officer whilst possessing firearm etc.	Criminal Justice Act 1991 s90	1991 c53
Producing or supplying a Class A or B drug	Misuse of Drugs Act 1971 s4	1971 c38
Possession of a Class A or B drug with intent to supply	Misuse of Drugs Act 1971 s5(3)	As above
Manufacture and supply of scheduled substances	Criminal Justice (International Co-Operation) Act 1990 s12	1990 c5
Fraudulent evasion of controls on Class A and B drugs	Customs and Excise Management Act 1979 s170(2)(b), (c)	1979 c2
Illegal importation of Class A and B drugs	Customs and Excise Management Act 1979 s50	As above
Offences in relation to proceeds of drug trafficking	Drug Trafficking Act 1994, ss49, 50 and 51	1994 c37
Offences in relation to money laundering investigations	Drug Trafficking Act 1994, ss52 and 53	As above
Practitioner contravening drug supply regulations	Misuse of Drugs Act 1971, ss12 and 13	1971 c38
Cultivation of cannabis plant	Misuse of Drugs Act 1971 s6	As above
Occupier knowingly permitting drugs offences etc.	Misuse of Drugs Act 1971 s8	As above
Activities relating to opium	Misuse of Drugs Act 1971 s9	As above
Drug trafficking offences at sea	Criminal Justice (International Co-operation) Act 1990 s18	1990 c5
Firing on Revenue vessel	Customs and Excise Management Act 1979 s85	1979 c2
Making or possession of explosive in suspicious circumstances	Explosive Substances Act 1883 s4(1)	1883 c3
Causing bodily injury by explosives	Offences against the Person Act 1861 s28	1861 c100
Using explosive or corrosives with intent to cause grievous bodily harm	Offences against the Person Act 1861 s29	As above
Hostage taking	Taking of Hostages Act 1982 s1	1982 c28
Offences against international protection of nuclear material	Nuclear Material (Offences) Act 1983 s2	1983 c18

Offence	Contrary to	Year and chapter
Placing explosives with intent to cause bodily injury	Offences against the Person Act 1861 s30	1861 c100
Membership of proscribed organisations	Terrorism Act 2000 s11	2000 c11
Support or meeting of proscribed organisations	Terrorism Act 2000 s12	As above
Uniform of proscribed organisations	Terrorism Act 2000 s13	As above
Fund-raising for terrorism	Terrorism Act 2000 s15	As above
Other offences involving money or property to be used for terrorism	Terrorism Act 2000 ss16–18	As above
Disclosure prejudicing, or interference of material relevant to, investigation of terrorism	Terrorism Act 2000 s39	As above
Weapons training	Terrorism Act 2000 s54	As above
Directing terrorist organisation	Terrorism Act 2000 s56	As above
Possession of articles for terrorist purposes	Terrorism Act 2000 s57	As above
Unlawful collection of information for terrorist purposes	Terrorism Act 2000 s58	As above
Incitement of terrorism overseas	Terrorism Act 2000 s59	As above
Concealing criminal property	Proceeds of Crime Act 2002 s327	2002 c29
Involvement in arrangements facilitating the acquisition, retention, use or control of criminal property	Proceeds of Crime Act 2002 s328	As above
Acquisition, use or possession of criminal property	Proceeds of Crime Act 2002 s329	As above
Failure to disclose knowledge or suspicion of money laundering: regulated sector	Proceeds of Crime Act 2002 s330	As above
Failure to disclose knowledge or suspicion of money laundering: nominated officers in the regulated sector	Proceeds of Crime Act 2002 s331	As above
Failure to disclose knowledge or suspicion of money laundering: other nominated officers	Proceeds of Crime Act 2002 s332	As above
Tipping off	Proceeds of Crime Act 2002 s333	As above

Offence	Contrary to	Year and chapter
Disclosure under sections 330, 331, 332 or 333 of the Proceeds of Crime Act 2002 otherwise than in the form and manner prescribed	Proceeds of Crime Act 2002 s339(1A)	As above
Causing or allowing the death of a child	Domestic Violence, Crime and Victims Act 2004 s5	2004 c28
Class C: Lesser offences involving violence or damage, and less serious drugs offences		
Racially-aggravated assault	Crime and Disorder Act 1998 s29(1)	1998 c37
Racially-aggravated criminal damage	Crime and Disorder Act 1998 s30(1)	1998 c37
Robbery (other than armed robbery)	Theft Act 1968 s8(1)	1968 c60
Unlawful wounding	Offences against the Person Act 1861 s20	1861 c100
Assault occasioning actual bodily harm	Offences against the Person Act 1861 s47	As above
Concealment of birth	Offences against the Person Act 1861 s60	As above
Abandonment of children under two	Offences against the Person Act 1861 s27	As above
Arson (other than aggravated arson) where value does not exceed £30,000	Criminal Damage Act 1971 s1(3)	1971 c48
Criminal damage (other than aggravated criminal damage)	Criminal Damage Act 1971 s1(1)	As above
Possession of firearm without certificate	Firearms Act 1968 s1	1968 c27
Carrying loaded firearm in public place	Firearms Act 1968 s19	As above
Trespassing with a firearm	Firearms Act 1968 s20	As above
Shortening of shotgun or possession of shortened shotgun	Firearms Act 1968 s4	As above
Shortening of smooth bore gun	Firearms Amendment Act 1988 s6(1)	1988 c45
Possession or acquisition of shotgun without certificate	Firearms Act 1968 s2	1968 c27
Possession of firearms by person convicted of crime	Firearms Act 1968 s21(4)	As above
Acquisition by or supply of firearms to person denied them	Firearms Act 1968 s21(5)	As above

Offence	Contrary to	Year and chapter
Dealing in firearms	Firearms Act 1968 s3	As above
Failure to comply with certificate when transferring firearm	Firearms Act 1968 s42	As above
Permitting an escape	Common law	
Rescue	Common law	
Escaping from lawful custody without force	Common law	
Breach of prison	Common law	
Harbouring escaped prisoners	Criminal Justice Act 1961 s22	1961 c39
Assisting prisoners to escape	Prison Act 1952 s39	1952 c52
Fraudulent evasion of agricultural levy	Customs and Excise Management Act 1979 s68A(1) and (2)	1979 c2
Offender armed or disguised	Customs and Excise Management Act 1979 s86	As above
Making threats to destroy or damage property	Criminal Damage Act 1971 s2	1971 c48
Possessing anything with intent to destroy or damage property	Criminal Damage Act 1971 s3	As above
Child abduction by connected person	Child Abduction Act 1984 s1	1984 c37
Child abduction by other person	Child Abduction Act 1984 s2	As above
Bomb hoax	Criminal Law Act 1977 s51	1977 c45
Producing or supplying class C drug	Misuse of Drugs Act 1971 s4	1971 c38
Possession of a class C drug with intent to supply	Misuse of Drugs Act 1971 s5(3)	As above
Fraudulent evasion of controls on class C drugs	Customs and Excise Management Act 1979 s170(2)(b), (c)	1979 c2
Illegal importation of class C drugs	Customs and Excise Management Act 1979 s50	As above
Possession of class A drug	Misuse of Drugs Act 1971 s5(2)	1971 c38
Failure to disclose knowledge or suspicion of money laundering	Drug Trafficking Offences Act 1986 s26B	1986 c32
Tipping-off in relation to money laundering investigations	Drug Trafficking Offences Act 1986 s26C	As above
Assaults on officers saving wrecks	Offences against the Person Act 1861 s37	1861 c100

Offence	Contrary to	Year and chapter
Attempting to injure or alarm the sovereign	Treason Act 1842 s2	1842 c51
Assisting illegal entry or harbouring persons	Immigration Act 1971 s25	1971 c77
Administering poison with intent to injure etc.	Offences against the Person Act 1861 s24	1861 c100
Neglecting to provide food for or assaulting servants etc.	Offences against the Person Act 1861 s26	As above
Setting spring guns with intent to inflict grievous bodily harm	Offences against the Person Act 1861 s31	As above
Supplying instrument etc. to cause miscarriage	Offences against the Person Act 1861 s59	As above
Failure to disclose information about terrorism	Terrorism Act 2000 s19	2000 c11
Circumcision of females	Prohibition of Female Circumcision Act 1985 s1	1985 c38
Breaking or injuring submarine telegraph cables	Submarine Telegraph Act 1885 s3	1885 c49
Failing to keep dogs under proper control resulting in injury	Dangerous Dogs Act 1991 s3	1991 c65
Making gunpowder etc. to commit offences	Offences against the Person Act 1861 s64	1861 c100
Stirring up racial hatred	Public Order Act 1986, ss18–23	1986 c64
Class D: Sexual offences and offences against children		
Administering drugs to obtain intercourse	Sexual Offences Act 1956 s4	1956 c69
Procurement of a defective	Sexual Offences Act 1956 s9	As above
Incest other than by man with a girl under 13	Sexual Offences Act 1956 ss10 and 11	As above
Gross indecency between male of 21 or over and male under 16	Sexual Offences Act 1956 s13	As above
Indecent assault on a woman	Sexual Offences Act 1956 s14	As above
Indecent assault on a man	Sexual Offences Act 1956 s15	As above
Abuse of position of trust	Sexual Offences (Amendment) Act 2000 s3	2000 c44
Man living on earnings of prostitution	Sexual Offences Act 1956 s30	1956 c69
Woman exercising control over prostitute	Sexual Offences Act 1956 s31	As above

Offence	Contrary to	Year and chapter
Living on earnings of male prostitution	Sexual Offences Act 1967 s5	1967 c60
Incitement to commit incest	Criminal Law Act 1977 s54	1977 c45
Ill-treatment of persons of unsound mind	Mental Health Act 1983 s127	1983 c20
Abduction of unmarried girl under 18 from parent	Sexual Offences Act 1956 s19	1956 c69
Abduction of defective from parent	Sexual Offences Act 1956 s21	As above
Procuration of girl under 21	Sexual Offences Act 1956 s23	As above
Permitting defective to use premises for intercourse	Sexual Offences Act 1956 s27	As above
Causing or encouraging prostitution of defective	Sexual Offences Act 1956 s29	As above
Sexual assault	Sexual Offences Act 2003 s3	2003 c42
Causing sexual activity without penetration	Sexual Offences Act 2003 s4	As above
Engaging in sexual activity in the presence of a child	Sexual Offences Act 2003 s11	As above
Causing a child to watch a sexual act	Sexual Offences Act 2003 s12	As above
Child sex offence committed by person under 18	Sexual Offences Act 2003 s13	As above
Meeting child following sexual grooming	Sexual Offences Act 2003 s15	As above
Abuse of trust: sexual activity with a child	Sexual Offences Act 2003 s16	As above
Abuse of position of trust: causing a child to engage in sexual activity	Sexual Offences Act 2003 s17	As above
Abuse of trust: sexual activity in the presence of a child	Sexual Offences Act 2003 s18	As above
Abuse of position of trust: causing a child to watch sexual activity	Sexual Offences Act 2003 s19	As above
Engaging in sexual activity in the presence of a person with a mental disorder	Sexual Offences Act 2003 s32	As above
Causing a person with a mental disorder to watch a sexual act	Sexual Offences Act 2003 s33	As above
Engaging in sexual activity in the presence of a person with a mental disorder	Sexual Offences Act 2003 s36	As above

Offence	Contrary to	Year and chapter
Causing a person with a mental disorder to watch a sexual act	Sexual Offences Act 2003 s37	As above
Care workers: sexual activity in presence of a person with a mental disorder	Sexual Offences Act 2003 s40	As above
Care workers: causing a person with a mental disorder to watch a sexual act	Sexual Offences Act 2003 s41	As above
Causing or inciting prostitution for gain	Sexual Offences Act 2003 s52	As above
Controlling prostitution for gain	Sexual Offences Act 2003 s53	As above
Administering a substance with intent	Sexual Offences Act 2003 s61	As above
Committing offence with intent to commit sexual offence	Sexual Offences Act 2003 s62	As above
Trespass with intent to commit sexual offence	Sexual Offences Act 2003 s63	As above
Sex with adult relative	Sexual Offences Act 2003 ss64, 65	As above
Exposure	Sexual Offences Act 2003 s66	As above
Voyeurism	Sexual Offences Act 2003 s67	As above
Intercourse with an animal	Sexual Offences Act 2003 s69	As above
Sexual penetration of a corpse	Sexual Offences Act 2003 s70	As above
Class E: Burglary etc.		
Burglary (domestic)	Theft Act 1968 s9(3)(a)	1968 c60
Going equipped to steal	Theft Act 1968 s25	As above
Burglary (non-domestic)	Theft Act 1968 s9(3)(b)	As above
Classes F, G and K: Other offences of dishonesty		
The following offences are always in class F		
Destruction of registers of births etc.	Forgery Act 1861 s36	1861 c98
Making false entries in copies of registers sent to register	Forgery Act 1861 s37	As above
Possession (with intention) of false identity documents	Identity Cards Act 2006 s25(1)	2006 c15
Possession (with intention) of apparatus or material for making false identity documents	Identity Cards Act 2006 s25(3)	As above

Offence	Contrary to	Year and chapter
Possession (without reasonable excuse) of false identity documents or apparatus or material for making false identity documents	Identity Cards Act 2006 s25(5)	As above
The following offences are always in class G		
Undischarged bankrupt being concerned in a company	Insolvency Act 1986 s360	1986 c45
Counterfeiting notes and coins	Forgery and Counterfeiting Act 1981 s14	1981 c45
Passing counterfeit notes and coins	Forgery and Counterfeiting Act 1981 s15	As above
Offences involving custody or control of counterfeit notes and coins	Forgery and Counterfeiting Act 1981 s16	As above
Making, custody or control of counterfeiting materials etc.	Forgery and Counterfeiting Act 1981 s175	As above
Illegal importation: counterfeit notes or coins	Customs and Excise Management Act 1979 s50	1979 c2
Fraudulent evasion: counterfeit notes or coins	Customs and Excise Management Act 1979 s170(2)(b), (c)	As above
The following offences are in class G if the value involved exceeds £30,000, class K if the value exceeds £100,000 and in class F otherwise		
VAT offences	Value Added Tax Act 1994 s72(1–8)	1994 c23
Fraudulent evasion of duty	Customs and Excise Management Act 1979 s170(1)(b)	1979 c2
Theft	Theft Act 1968 s1	1968 c60
Removal of articles from places open to the public	Theft Act 1968 s11	As above
Abstraction of electricity	Theft Act 1968 s13	As above
Obtaining property by deception	Theft Act 1968 s15	As above
Obtaining pecuniary advantage by deception	Theft Act 1968 s16	As above
False accounting	Theft Act 1968 s17	As above
Handling stolen goods	Theft Act 1968 s22	As above
Obtaining services by deception	Theft Act 1978 s1	1978 c31
Evasion of liability by deception	Theft Act 1978 s2	As above
Illegal importation: not elsewhere specified	Customs and Excise Management Act 1979 s50	1979 c2

Crown Court litigators' offence classes

Offence	Contrary to	Year and chapter
Counterfeiting Customs documents	Customs and Excise Management Act 1979 s168	As above
Fraudulent evasion: not elsewhere specified	Customs and Excise Management Act 1979 s170(2)(b), (c)	As above
Forgery	Forgery and Counterfeiting Act 1981 s1	1981 c45
Copying false instrument with intent	Forgery and Counterfeiting Act 1981 s2	As above
Using a false instrument	Forgery and Counterfeiting Act 1981 s3	As above
Using a copy of a false instrument	Forgery and Counterfeiting Act 1981 s4	As above
Custody or control of false instruments etc.	Forgery and Counterfeiting Act 1981 s5	As above
Offences in relation to dies or stamps	Stamp Duties Management Act 1891 s13	1891 c38
Counterfeiting of dies or marks	Hallmarking Act 1973 s6	1973 c43
Fraud by false representation	Fraud Act 2006 s2	2006 c35
Fraud by failing to disclose information	Fraud Act 2006 s3	As above
Fraud by abuse of position	Fraud Act 2006 s4	As above
Possession etc. of articles for use in frauds	Fraud Act 2006 s6	As above
Making or supplying articles for use in frauds	Fraud Act 2006 s7	As above
Participating in fraudulent business carried on by sole trader etc.	Fraud Act 2006 s9	As above
Obtaining services dishonestly	Fraud Act 2006 s11	As above
Class H: Miscellaneous other offences		
Breach of a sexual harm prevention order or interim sexual harm prevention order	Sexual Offences Act 2003 s103I	2003 c42
Breach of a sexual risk order or interim sexual risk order	Sexual Offences Act 2003 s122H	As above
Breach of a criminal behaviour order	Anti-social Behaviour, Crime and Policing Act 2014	2014 c12
Racially-aggravated public order offence	Crime and Disorder Act 1998 s31(1)	1988 c37

Offence	Contrary to	Year and chapter
Racially aggravated harassment/ putting another in fear of violence	Crime and Disorder Act 1998 s32(1)	As above
Having an article with a blade or point in a public place	Criminal Justice Act 1988 s139	1988 c33
Breach of harassment injunction	Protection from Harassment Act 1997 s3(6)	1997 c40
Putting people in fear of violence	Protection from Harassment Act 1997 s4(1)	As above
Breach of restraining order	Protection from Harassment Act 1997 s5(5)	As above
Being drunk on an aircraft	Air Navigation Order 2005 article 75	SI 2005/1970
Possession of offensive weapon	Prevention of Crime Act 1953 s1	1953 c14
Affray	Public Order Act 1986 s3	1986 c64
Assault with intent to resist arrest	Offences against the Person Act 1861 s38	1861 c100
Unlawful eviction and harassment of occupier	Protection from Eviction Act 1977 s1	1977 c43
Obscene articles intended for publication for gain	Obscene Publications Act 1964 s1	1964 c74
Gross indecency between males (other than where one is 21 or over and the other is under 16)	Sexual Offences Act 1956 s13	1956 c69
Solicitation for immoral purposes	Sexual Offences Act 1956 s32	As above
Buggery of males of 16 or over otherwise than in private	Sexual Offences Act 1956 s12	As above
Acts outraging public decency	Common law	
Offences of publication of obscene matter	Obscene Publications Act 1959 s2	1959 c66
Keeping a disorderly house	Common law; Disorderly Houses Act 1751 s8	1751 c36
Indecent display	Indecent Displays (Control) Act 1981 s1	1981 c42
Presentation of obscene performance	Theatres Act 1968 s2	1968 c54
Procurement of intercourse by threats etc.	Sexual Offences Act 1956 s2	1956 c69
Causing prostitution of women	Sexual Offences Act 1956 s22	As above

Crown Court litigators' offence classes

Offence	Contrary to	Year and chapter
Detention of woman in brothel or other premises	Sexual Offences Act 1956 s24	As above
Procurement of a woman by false pretences	Sexual Offences Act 1956 s3	As above
Procuring others to commit homosexual acts	Sexual Offences Act 1967 s4	1967 c60
Trade description offences (9 offences)	Trade Descriptions Act 1968, ss1, 8, 9, 12, 13, 14	1968 c29
Misconduct endangering ship or persons on board ship	Merchant Shipping Act 1970 s27	1970 c36
Obstructing engine or carriage on railway	Malicious Damage Act 1861 s36	1861 c97
Offences relating to the safe custody of controlled drugs	Misuse of Drugs Act 1971 s11	1971 c38
Possession of Class B or C drug	Misuse of Drugs Act 1971 s5(2)	As above
Wanton or furious driving	Offences against the Person Act 1861 s35	1861 c100
Dangerous driving	Road Traffic Act 1988 s2	1988 c52
Forgery and misuse of driving documents	Public Passenger Vehicles Act 1981 s65	1981 c14
Forgery of driving documents	Road Traffic Act 1960 s233	1960 c16
Forgery etc. of licences and other documents	Road Traffic Act 1988 s173	1988 c52
Mishandling or falsifying parking documents etc.	Road Traffic Regulation Act 1984 s115	1984 c27
Aggravated vehicle taking	Theft Act 1968 s12A	1968 c60
Forgery, alteration, fraud of licences etc.	Vehicle Excise and Registration Act 1994 s44	1994 c22
Making off without payment	Theft Act 1978 s3	1978 c31
Agreeing to indemnify sureties	Bail Act 1976 s9(1)	1976 c63
Sending prohibited articles by post	Post Office Act 1953 s11	1953 c36
Impersonating Customs officer	Customs and Excise Management Act 1979 s13	1979 c2
Obstructing Customs officer	Customs and Excise Management Act 1979 s16	As above
Class I: Offences against public justice and similar offences		
Conspiring to commit offences outside the United Kingdom	Criminal Justice (Terrorism and Conspiracy) Act 1998 s5	1998 c40

Offence	Contrary to	Year and chapter
Perverting the course of public justice	Common law	
Perjuries (7 offences)	Perjury Act 1911 ss 1–7(2)	1911 c6
Corrupt transactions with agents	Prevention of Corruption Act 1906 s1	1906 c34
Corruption in public office	Public Bodies Corrupt Practices Act 1889 s1	1889 c69
Embracery	Common law	
Offences of bribing another person	Bribery Act 2010 s1	2010 c23
Offences relating to being bribed	Bribery Act 2010 s2	As above
Bribery of foreign public officials	Bribery Act 1010 s6	As above
Fabrication of evidence with intent to mislead a tribunal	Common law	
Personation of jurors	Common law	
Concealing an arrestable offence	Criminal Law Act 1967 s5	1967 c58
Assisting offenders	Criminal Law Act 1967 s4(1)	As above
False evidence before European Court	European Communities Act 1972 s11	1972 c68
Personating for purposes of bail etc.	Forgery Act 1861 s34	1861 c98
Intimidating a witness, juror etc.	Criminal Justice and Public Order Act 1994 s51(1)	1994 c33
Harming, threatening to harm a witness, juror etc.	Criminal Justice and Public Order Act 1994 s51(2)	As above
Prejudicing a drug trafficking investigation	Drug Trafficking Act 1994 s58(1)	1994 c37
Giving false statements to procure cremation	Cremation Act 1902 s8(2)	1902 c8
False statement tendered under section 9 of the Criminal Justice Act 1967	Criminal Justice Act 1967 s89	1967 c80
Making a false statement to obtain interim possession order	Criminal Justice and Public Order Act 1994 s75(1)	1994 c33
Making false statement to resist making of interim possession order	Criminal Justice and Public Order Act 1994 s75(2)	As above
False statement tendered under section 5B of the Magistrates' Courts Act 1980	Magistrates' Courts Act 1980 s106	1980 c43
Making false statement to authorised officer	Trade Descriptions Act 1968 s29(2)	1968 c29

Crown Court litigators' offence classes 313

Offence	Contrary to	Year and chapter
Class J: Serious sexual offences		
Rape	Sexual Offences Act 1956 s1(1)	1956 c69
Sexual intercourse with girl under 13	Sexual Offences Act 1956 s5	As above
Sexual intercourse with girl under 16	Sexual Offences Act 1956 s6	As above
Sexual intercourse with defective	Sexual Offences Act 1956 s7	As above
Incest by man with a girl under 13	Sexual Offences Act 1956 s10	As above
Buggery of person under 16	Sexual Offences Act 1956 s12	As above
Indecency with children under 14	Indecency with Children Act 1960 s1(1)	1960 c33
Taking, having etc. indecent photographs of children	Protection of Children Act 1978 s1	1978 c37
Assault with intent to commit buggery	Sexual Offences Act 1956 s16	1956 c69
Abduction of woman by force	Sexual Offences Act 1956 s17	As above
Permitting girl under 13 to use premises for sexual intercourse	Sexual Offences Act 1956 s25	As above
Allowing or procuring child under 16 to go abroad to perform	Children and Young Persons Act 1933 ss25, 26	1933 c12
Sexual intercourse with patients	Mental Health Act 1959 s128	1959 c72
Abduction of unmarried girl under 16 from parent	Sexual Offences Act 1956 s20	1956 c69
Permitting girl under 16 to use premises for intercourse	Sexual Offences Act 1956 s26	As above
Causing or encouraging prostitution of girl under 16	Sexual Offences Act 1956 s28	As above
Rape	Sexual Offences Act 2003 s1	2003 c42
Assault by penetration	Sexual Offences Act 2003 s2	As above
Causing sexual activity with penetration	Sexual Offences Act 2003 s4	As above
Rape of child under 13	Sexual Offences Act 2003 s5	As above
Assault of child under 13 by penetration	Sexual Offences Act 2003 s6	As above
Sexual assault of child under 13	Sexual Offences Act 2003 s7	As above
Causing a child under 13 to engage in sexual activity	Sexual Offences Act 2003 s8	As above
Sexual activity with a child	Sexual Offences Act 2003 s9	As above

Offence	Contrary to	Year and chapter
Causing a child to engage in sexual activity	Sexual Offences Act 2003 s10	As above
Arranging child sex offence	Sexual Offences Act 2003 s14	As above
Sexual activity with a child family member, with penetration	Sexual Offences Act 2003 s25	As above
Inciting a child family member to engage in sexual activity	Sexual Offences Act 2003 s26	As above
Sexual activity with a person with a mental disorder	Sexual Offences Act 2003 s30	As above
Causing or inciting a person with a mental disorder to engage in sexual activity	Sexual Offences Act 2003 s31	As above
Offering inducement to procure sexual activity with a person with a mental disorder	Sexual Offences Act 2003 s34	As above
Inducing person with mental disorder to engage in sexual activity	Sexual Offences Act 2003 s35	As above
Care workers: sexual activity with a person with a mental disorder	Sexual Offences Act 2003 s38	As above
Care workers: inciting person with mental disorder to engage in sexual act	Sexual Offences Act 2003 s39	As above
Paying for sexual services of a child	Sexual Offences Act 2003 s47	As above
Causing or inciting child prostitution or pornography	Sexual Offences Act 2003 s48	As above
Controlling a child prostitute	Sexual Offences Act 2003 s49	As above
Facilitating child prostitution	Sexual Offences Act 2003 s50	As above
Trafficking into UK for sexual exploitation	Sexual Offences Act 2003 s57	As above
Trafficking within UK for sexual exploitation	Sexual Offences Act 2003 s58	As above
Trafficking out of UK for sexual exploitation	Sexual Offences Act 2003 s59	As above
Trafficking for sexual exploitation	Sexual Offences Act 2003 s59A	As above
Class K: Other offences of dishonesty (high value)		
Class K Offences are listed under Class F and G.		

APPENDIX H

Mark-ups for litigators

(1) Defendant uplifts

Total number of defendants represented by litigator	Percentage uplift to total fee
2–4	20%
5+	30%

(2) Retrials and transfers

Scenario	Percentage of the total fee	Case type used to determine total fee	Claim period
Cracked trial before retrial, where there is no change of litigator	25%	Cracked trial	
Retrial where there is no change of litigator	25%	Trial	
Up to and including plea and case management hearing transfer (original litigator)	25%	Cracked trial	
Up to and including plea and case management hearing transfer – guilty plea (new litigator)	100%	Guilty plea	
Up to and including plea and case management hearing transfer – cracked trial (new litigator)	100%	Cracked trial	
Up to and including plea and case management hearing transfer – trial (new litigator)	100%	Trial	

Scenario	Percentage of the total fee	Case type used to determine total fee	Claim period
Before trial transfer (original litigator)	75%	Cracked trial	
Before trial transfer – cracked trial (new litigator)	100%	Cracked trial	
Before trial transfer – trial (new litigator)	100%	Trial	
During trial transfer (original litigator)	100%	Trial	Claim up to and including the day before the transfer
During trial transfer (new litigator)	50%	Trial	Claim for the full trial length
Transfer after trial or guilty plea and before sentencing hearing (original litigator)	100%	Trial, Cracked trial or Guilty plea as appropriate	Claim for the full trial length, excluding the length of the sentencing hearing
Transfer after trial or guilty plea and before sentencing hearing (new litigator)	10%	Trial	Claim for one day or for the length of the sentencing hearing if longer than one day
Transfer before retrial (original litigator)	25%	Cracked trial	
Transfer before cracked retrial (new litigator)	50%	Cracked trial	
Transfer before retrial (new litigator)	50%	Trial	Claim for the full retrial length
Transfer during retrial (original litigator)	25%	Trial	Claim up to and including the day before the transfer
Transfer during retrial (new litigator)	50%	Trial	Claim for the full retrial length
Transfer after retrial or cracked retrial and before sentencing hearing (original litigator)	25%	Trial or Cracked trial as appropriate	Claim for the full retrial length, excluding the length of the sentencing hearing
Transfer after retrial or cracked retrial and before sentencing hearing (new litigator	10%	Trial	Claim for one day or for the length of the sentencing hearing if longer than one day.

APPENDIX I

Advocates' rate bands and graduated fee tables[1]

Introduction
Fees depend on the banding of the case in accordance with table B published by the Ministry of Justice (Banding of offences in the Advocates' Graduated fee scheme (AGFS)), which should be read in conjunction with table A below
- Where the band within which an offence described in Table B falls depends on the facts of the case; the band within which the offence falls is to be determined by reference to Table A.
- In Table A and Table B, 'category' is used to provide a broad, overarching description for a range of similar offences which fall within a particular group or range of bands.

PART ONE
These figures apply where a representation order is dated on or after 1 April 2018 until 30 December 2018.

CATEGORIES OF OFFENCES

Category	Description	Bands
1	Murder/ Manslaughter	**Band 1.1**: Killing of a child (16 years old or under); killing of two or more persons; killing of a police officer, prison officer or equivalent public servant in the course of their duty; killing of a patient in a medical or nursing care context; corporate manslaughter; manslaughter by gross negligence; missing body killing. **Band 1.2**: Killing done with a firearm; defendant has a previous conviction for murder; body is dismembered (literally), or destroyed by fire or other means by the offender; the defendant is a child (16 or under). **Band 1.3**: All other cases of murder. **Band 1.4**: All other cases of manslaughter.

[1] Criminal Legal Aid (Remuneration) Regulations 2013 SI No 435 Sch 1 as amended.

2	Terrorism	**Band 2.1**: Terrorist murder (S63B Terrorism Act 2000); Explosive Substances Act 1883 offences – especially S2&3; preparation for terrorism, S5 Terrorism Act 2000, disseminating terrorist publications, S2 Terrorism Act 2006; possession of material for the purpose of terrorism, S57 Terrorism Act 2000. **Band 2.2**: All other terrorist offences.
3	Serious Violence	**Band 3.1**: Attempted murder of a child, two or more persons, police officer, nursing/medical contact or any violent offence committed with a live firearm. **Band 3.2**: All other attempted murder. **Band 3.3**: S18. **Band 3.4** All other serious violence (unless standard, or specified in Band 3.5) **Band 3.5**: s20 Offences Against the Persons Act cases, s47 cases (Actual Bodily Harm), and Threats to Kill.
4	Sexual Offences (children)	**Band 4.1**: Rape / Assault by penetration. **Band 4.2**: Sexual Assault. **Band 4.3**: All other offences (unless standard).
5	Sexual Offences (adult)	**Band 5.1**: Rape / Assault by penetration. **Band 5.2**: Sexual Assault. **Band 5.3**: All other offences (unless standard).
6	Dishonesty (to include Proceeds of Crime and Money Laundering)	**Band 6.1**: Over £10m or over 20,000 pages. **Band 6.2**: Over £1m or over 10,000 pages. **Band 6.3**: Over £100,000. **Band 6.4**: Under £100,000. **Band 6.5**: Under £30,000.
7	Property Damage Offences	**Band 7.1**: Arson with intent to endanger life/reckless as to endanger life. **Band 7.2**: Simple arson and criminal damage over £30,000. **Band 7.3**: All other offences (unless standard).
8	Offences Against the Public Interest	**Band 8.1**: All offences against the public interest (unless standard).
9	Drugs Offences	**Band 9.1**: Importation S3 Misuse of Drugs Act/S170 Customs and Excise Management Act Or over 5,000 pages of evidence; Or weight over: 5kg heroin or cocaine 10,000 ecstasy tablets 250,000 squares of LSD

			Band 9.2: Class B: Importation S3 Misuse of Drugs Act / S170 Customs and Excise Management Act; Or over 5,000 pages of evidence; Or weight over: 20kg amphetamine 200kg cannabis 5kg ketamine **Band 9.3:** Class C: Importation S3 Misuse of Drugs Act / S170 Customs and Excise Management Act; Or over 5,000 pages of evidence **Band 9.4:** Class A: 1,000 pages of evidence; Or weight over: 1kg Heroin or Cocaine 2,000 ecstasy tablets 2,5000 squares of LSD **Band 9.5:** Class B: 1,000 pages of evidence; Or weight over: 4kg of amphetamine 40kg of cannabis 1kg ketamine **Band 9.6:** Class C: 1,000 pages of evidence **Band 9.7:** All other drugs cases of any class (unless standard).
10	Driving Offences		**Band 10.1**: Death and serious injury by driving cases (unless standard).
11	Burglary & Robbery		**Band 11.1**: Aggravated burglary, burglary with intent to GBH or rape, and armed robbery. **Band 11.2**: Indictable only burglary; other robberies.
12	Firearms Offences		**Band 12.1**: Possession or supply of a firearm/ammunition with any ulterior intent or any offence for which the maximum penalty is life imprisonment. **Band 12.2**: Minimum sentence offence. **Band 12.3**: All other offences (unless standard).

13	Other offences against the person	**Band 13.1:** Kidnapping; false imprisonment; blackmail (unless standard).
14	Exploitation / human trafficking offences	**Band 14.1:** All exploitation / human trafficking offences (unless standard).
15	Public Order Offences	**Band 15.1:** Riot and prison mutiny/riot. **Band 15.2:** Violent disorder. **Band 15.3:** Affray.
16	Regulatory Offences	**Band 16.1:** Health and Safety or environmental cases involving one or more fatalities or defined by the HSE or EA as a category or Stage 1 "major incident"; Death of a child; A major accident at a site regulated by the Control of Major Accident Hazards Regulations 1999 (as amended); large scale explosion. **Band 16.2:** Health and Safety or environmental cases not falling within Band 1 but involving: Serious and permanent personal injury/disability and/or widespread Destruction of property (other than that owned or occupied by the defendant) Extensive pollution/irreparable damage to the environment Toxic gas release (e.g. carbon monoxide, chlorine gas) Cases involving incidents governed by mining/railways/ aviation legislation **Band 16.3:** All other offences (unless standard)
17	Standard Cases	**Band 17.1:** Standard cases
		Those cases not falling under the above categories of offence will be defined as 'Standard Cases'.
For each category, there will be set fees, stated in the Regulations, for the category of advocate (QC, Junior, Led Junior), and type of fee.		

TABLES OF FEES[2]
These italicised figures apply where a representation order is dated on or after 1 April 2018 until 30 December 2016

BASIC ADVOCACY FEES FOR JUNIOR OR LED JUNIOR				
Category of Offence	Junior or led Junior	Junior or led Junior	Junior or led Junior	Junior or led Junior
	Guilty Plea or Early Cracked Trial	Cracked Trial in Final Third	Trial	Daily Refresher
1.1	£4,250	£7,225	£8,500	£575
1.2	£2,125	£3,615	£4,250	£575
1.3	£1,275	£2,170	£2,550	£575
1.4	£1,065	£1,805	£2,125	£575
2.1	£4,250	£7,225	£8,500	£575
2.2	£1,275	£2,170	£2,550	£575
3.1	£1,750	£2,975	£3,500	£500
3.2	£1,000	£1,700	£2,000	£500
3.3	£500	£850	£1,000	£500
3.4	£375	£640	£750	£500
3.5	£300	£510	£600	£325
4.1	£1,000	£1,700	£2,000	£525
4.2	£700	£1,190	£1,400	£500
4.3	£500	£850	£1,000	£475
5.1	£900	£1,530	£1,800	£525
5.2	£700	£1,190	£1,400	£500
5.3	£500	£850	£1,000	£475
6.1	£4,000	£6,800	£8,000	£525
6.2	£2,500	£4,250	£5,000	£500
6.3	£1,000	£1,700	£2,000	£400
6.4	£375	£640	£750	£350
6.5	£325	£555	£650	£325
7.1	£700	£1,190	£1,400	£500
7.2	£400	£680	£800	£450
7.3	£375	£640	£750	£400
8.1	£600	£1,020	£1,200	£500

2 The tables, in this form, are the work of Paul Beaumont whose help we gratefully acknowledge.

BASIC ADVOCACY FEES FOR JUNIOR OR LED JUNIOR

Category of Offence	Junior or led Junior Guilty Plea or Early Cracked Trial	Junior or led Junior Cracked Trial in Final Third	Junior or led Junior Trial	Junior or led Junior Daily Refresher
9.1	£2,500	£4,250	£5,000	£525
9.2	£2,000	£3,400	£4,000	£525
9.3	£1,500	£2,550	£3,000	£450
9.4	£1,000	£1,700	£2,000	£450
9.5	£800	£1,360	£1,600	£450
9.6	£600	£1,020	£1,200	£400
9.7	£400	£680	£800	£350
10.1	£1,100	£1,870	£2,200	£525
11.1	£600	£1,020	£1,200	£450
11.2	£340	£575	£675	£360
12.1	£1,000	£1,700	£2,000	£500
12.2	£600	£1,020	£1,200	£500
12.3	£400	£680	£800	£500
13.1	£650	£1,105	£1,300	£500
14.1	£750	£1,275	£1,500	£550
15.1	£700	£1,190	£1,400	£500
15.2	£375	£640	£750	£400
15.3	£300	£510	£600	£325
16.1	£1,100	£1,870	£2,200	£550
16.2	£800	£1,360	£1,600	£500
16.3	£500	£850	£1,000	£500
17.1	£275	£470	£550	£300

Advocates' rate bands and graduated fee tables 323

	BASIC ADVOCACY FEES FOR LEADING JUNIOR			
Category of Offence	Leading Junior	Leading Junior	Leading Junior	Leading Junior
	Guilty Plea or Early Cracked Trial	Cracked Trial in Final Third	Trial	Daily Refresher
1.1	£6,375	£10,840	£12,750	£865
1.2	£3,190	£5,420	£6,375	£865
1.3	£1,915	£3,250	£3,825	£865
1.4	£1,595	£2,710	£3,190	£865
2.1	£6,375	£10,840	£12,750	£865
2.2	£1,915	£3,250	£3,825	£865
3.1	£2,625	£4,465	£5,250	£750
3.2	£1,500	£2,550	£3,000	£750
3.3	£750	£1,275	£1,500	£750
3.4	£565	£955	£1,125	£750
3.5	£450	£765	£900	£490
4.1	£1,500	£2,550	£3,000	£790
4.2	£1,050	£1,785	£2,100	£750
4.3	£750	£1,275	£1,500	£715
5.1	£1,350	£2,295	£2,700	£790
5.2	£1,050	£1,785	£2,100	£750
5.3	£750	£1,275	£1,500	£715
6.1	£6,000	£10,200	£12,000	£790
6.2	£3,750	£6,375	£7,500	£750
6.3	£1,500	£2,550	£3,000	£600
6.4	£565	£955	£1,125	£525
6.5	£490	£830	£975	£490
7.1	£1,050	£1,785	£2,100	£750
7.2	£600	£1,020	£1,200	£675
7.3	£565	£955	£1,125	£600
8.1	£900	£1,530	£1,800	£750

BASIC ADVOCACY FEES FOR LEADING JUNIOR

Category of Offence	Leading Junior	Leading Junior	Leading Junior	Leading Junior
	Guilty Plea or Early Cracked Trial	Cracked Trial in Final Third	Trial	Daily Refresher
9.1	£3,750	£6,375	£7,500	£790
9.2	£3,000	£5,100	£6,000	£790
9.3	£2,250	£3,825	£4,500	£675
9.4	£1,500	£2,550	£3,000	£675
9.5	£1,200	£2,040	£2,400	£675
9.6	£900	£1,530	£1,800	£600
9.7	£600	£1,020	£1,200	£525
10.1	£1,650	£2,805	£3,300	£790
11.1	£900	£1,530	£1,800	£675
11.2	£505	£860	£1,015	£540
12.1	£1,500	£2,550	£3,000	£750
12.2	£900	£1,530	£1,800	£750
12.3	£600	£1,020	£1,200	£750
13.1	£975	£1,660	£1,950	£750
14.1	£1,125	£1,915	£2,250	£825
15.1	£1,050	£1,785	£2,100	£750
15.2	£565	£955	£1,125	£600
15.3	£450	£765	£900	£490
16.1	£1,650	£2,805	£3,300	£825
16.2	£1,200	£2,040	£2,400	£750
16.3	£750	£1,275	£1,500	£750
17.1	£415	£705	£825	£450

Advocates' rate bands and graduated fee tables

BASIC ADVOCACY FEES FOR QC				
Category of Offence	QC	QC	QC	QC
	Guilty Plea or Early Cracked Trial	Cracked Trial in Final Third	Trial	Daily Refresher
1.1	£8,500	£14,450	£17,000	£1,150
1.2	£4,250	£7,225	£8,500	£1,150
1.3	£2,550	£4,335	£5,100	£1,150
1.4	£2,125	£3,615	£4,250	£1,150
2.1	£8,500	£14,450	£17,000	£1,150
2.2	£2,550	£4,335	£5,100	£1,150
3.1	£3,500	£5,950	£7,000	£1,000
3.2	£2,000	£3,400	£4,000	£1,000
3.3	£1,000	£1,700	£2,000	£1,000
3.4	£750	£1,275	£1,500	£1,000
3.5	£600	£1,020	£1,200	£650
4.1	£2,000	£3,400	£4,000	£1,050
4.2	£1,400	£2,380	£2,800	£1,000
4.3	£1,000	£1,700	£2,000	£950
5.1	£1,800	£3,060	£3,600	£1,050
5.2	£1,400	£2,380	£2,800	£1,000
5.3	£1,000	£1,700	£2,000	£950
6.1	£8,000	£13,600	£16,000	£1,050
6.2	£5,000	£8,500	£10,000	£1,000
6.3	£2,000	£3,400	£4,000	£800
6.4	£750	£1,275	£1,500	£700
6.5	£650	£1,105	£1,300	£650
7.1	£1,400	£2,380	£2,800	£1,000
7.2	£800	£1,360	£1,600	£900
7.3	£750	£1,275	£1,500	£800
8.1	£1,200	£2,040	£2,400	£1,000

BASIC ADVOCACY FEES FOR QC				
Category of Offence	QC	QC	QC	QC
	Guilty Plea or Early Cracked Trial	Cracked Trial in Final Third	Trial	Daily Refresher
9.1	£5,000	£8,500	£10,000	£1,050
9.2	£4,000	£6,800	£8,000	£1,050
9.3	£3,000	£5,100	£6,000	£900
9.4	£2,000	£3,400	£4,000	£900
9.5	£1,600	£2,720	£3,200	£900
9.6	£1,200	£2,040	£2,400	£800
9.7	£800	£1,360	£1,600	£700
10.1	£2,200	£3,740	£4,400	£1,050
11.1	£1,200	£2,040	£2,400	£900
11.2	£675	£1,150	£1,350	£720
12.1	£2,000	£3,400	£4,000	£1,000
12.2	£1,200	£2,040	£2,400	£1,000
12.3	£800	£1,360	£1,600	£1,000
13.1	£1,300	£2,210	£2,600	£1,000
14.1	£1,500	£2,550	£3,000	£1,100
15.1	£1,400	£2,380	£2,800	£1,000
15.2	£750	£1,275	£1,500	£800
15.3	£600	£1,020	£1,200	£650
16.1	£2,200	£3,740	£4,400	£1,100
16.2	£1,600	£2,720	£3,200	£1,000
16.3	£1,000	£1,700	£2,000	£1,000
17.1	£550	£940	£1,100	£600

Fees for confiscation hearings

	Fee for QC (£)	Fee for Leading Junior (£)	Fee for Junior Alone (£)	Fee for Led Junior (£)
1. Daily and half daily rates				
Half daily rate	260	195	130	130
Daily rate	497	346	238	238

	Fee for QC (£)	Fee for Leading Junior (£)	Fee for Junior Alone (£)	Fee for Led Junior (£)
2. Pages of evidence				
51–250	649	541	433	324
251–500	973	811	649	486
501–750	1,298	1,081	865	649
751–1000	1,946	1,622	1,298	973
3. Preparation hourly rates				
	74	56	39	39

Fixed fees

Category of work	Paragraph providing for fee	Fee for QC (£)	Fee for Leading Junior (£)	Fee for Led Junior or Junior alone (£)
Standard appearance	12(2)	180 per day	135 per day	90 per day
PTPH	19A	250 per day	190 per day	125 per day
Further case management hearing	19A	£200 per day	£150 per day	£100 per day
Abuse of process hearing	13(1)(a) and 13(3)	497 full day	346 full day	238 full day
		260 half day	195 half day	130 half day
Hearings relating to disclosure	13(1)(b), 13(1)(c) and 13(3)	497 full day	346 full day	238 full day
		260 half day	195 half day	130 half day
Hearings relating to the admissibility of evidence	13(1)(d) and 13(3)	497 full day	346 full day	238 full day
		260 half day	195 half day	130 half day
Ground rules hearings	13(1)(da) and (3)	497 full day	346 full day	238 full day
		260 half day	195 half day	130 half day
Hearings on withdrawal of guilty plea	13(1)(e) and 13(3)	497 full day	346 full day	238 full day
		260 half day	195 half day	130 half day
Senetncing hearings	15	250 per day	190 per day	125 p[er day
Deferred sentencing hearing	15(2)	324 per day	238 per day	173 per day
Ineffective trial payment	16	300 per day	300 per day	300 per day
Special preparation	17	74 per hour	56 per hour	39 per hour
Wasted preparation	18	74 per hour	56 per hour	39 per hour

Category of work	Paragraph providing for fee	Fee for QC (£)	Fee for Leading Junior (£)	Fee for Led Junior or Junior alone (£)
Conferences and views	19	80 per hour	60 per hour	40 per hour
Appeals to the Crown Court against conviction	20(1)	500 per day	375 per day	250 per day
Appeals to the Crown Court against sentence	20(1)	300 per day	225 per day	150 per day
Proceedings relating to breach of an order of the Crown Court	20(1)	216 per day	151 per day	108 per day
Committal for sentence	20(1)	300 per day	225 per day	150 per day
Adjourned appeals, committals for sentence and breach hearings	20(2)	173 per day	130 per day	87 per day
Bail applications, mentions and other applications in appeals, committals for sentence and breach hearings	20(3)	173 per day	130 per day	87 per day
Second and subsequent days of an application to dismiss	22(6)	497 full day	346 full day	238 full day
		260 half day	195 half day	130 half day
Noting brief	24	108 per day	108 per day	108 per day
Hearing for mitigation of sentence	34	260 per day	173 per day	108 per day

PART TWO

These figures apply where a representation order is dated on or after 31st December 2018.

CATEGORIES OF OFFENCES

Category	Description	Bands
1	Murder/ Manslaughter	**Band 1.1**: Killing of a child (16 years old or under); killing of two or more persons; killing of a police officer, prison officer or equivalent public servant in the course of their duty; killing of a patient in a medical or nursing care context; corporate manslaughter; manslaughter by gross negligence; missing body killing. **Band 1.2**: Killing done with a firearm; defendant has a previous conviction for murder; body is dismembered (literally), or destroyed by fire or other means by the offender; the defendant is a child (16 or under). **Band 1.3**: All other cases of murder. **Band 1.4**: All other cases of manslaughter.
2	Terrorism	**Band 2.1**: Terrorist murder (S63B Terrorism Act 2000); Explosive Substances Act 1883 offences – especially S2&3; preparation for terrorism, S5 Terrorism Act 2000, disseminating terrorist publications, S2 Terrorism Act 2006; possession of material for the purpose of terrorism, S57 Terrorism Act 2000. **Band 2.2**: All other terrorist offences.
3	Serious Violence	**Band 3.1**: Attempted murder of a child, two or more persons, police officer, nursing/medical contact or any violent offence committed with a live firearm. **Band 3.2**: All other attempted murder. **Band 3.3**: S18. **Band 3.4** s20 Offences Against the Persons Act cases and other serious violence offences specified in Table B. **Band 3.5**: s47 cases (Actual Bodily Harm), Threats to Kill and other serious violence offences specified in Table B.
4	Sexual Offences (children) – defendant or victim a child at the time of offence.	**Band 4.1**: Rape/Assault by penetration. **Band 4.2**: Sexual Assault. **Band 4.3**: All other offences (unless standard).
5	Sexual Offences (adult)	**Band 5.1**: Rape/Assault by penetration. **Band 5.2**: Sexual Assault. **Band 5.3**: All other offences (unless standard).

6	Dishonesty (to include Proceeds of Crime and Money Laundering)	**Band 6.1**: Over £10m or over 20,000 pages. **Band 6.2**: Over £1m or over 10,000 pages. **Band 6.3**: Over £100,000. **Band 6.4**: Under £100,000. **Band 6.5**: Under £30,000.
7	Property Damage Offences	**Band 7.1**: Arson with intent to endanger life/ reckless as to endanger life. **Band 7.2**: Simple arson and criminal damage over £30,000. **Band 7.3**: All other offences (unless standard).
8	Offences Against the Public Interest	**Band 8.1**: All offences against the public interest (unless standard).
9	Drugs Offences	**Band 9.1:** Class A: Importation S3 Misuse of Drugs Act / S170 Customs and Excise Management Act Or over 5,000 pages of evidence; Or weight over: 5kg heroin or cocaine 10,000 ecstasy tablets 250,000 squares of LSD **Band 9.2:** Class B: Importation S3 Misuse of Drugs Act / S170 Customs and Excise Management Act; Or over 5,000 pages of evidence; Or weight over: 20kg amphetamine 200kg cannabis 5kg ketamine **Band 9.3:** Class C: Importation S3 Misuse of Drugs Act / S170 Customs and Excise Management Act; Or over 5,000 pages of evidence **Band 9.4:** Class A: 1,000 pages of evidence; Or weight over: 1kg Heroin or Cocaine 2,000 ecstasy tablets 2,5000 squares of LSD

			Band 9.5:
			Class B:
			1,000 pages of evidence;
			Or weight over:
			4kg of amphetamine
			40kg of cannabis
			1kg ketamine
			Band 9.6:
			Class C:
			1,000 pages of evidence
			Band 9.7:
			All other drugs cases of any class (unless standard).
10		Driving Offences	**Band 10.1:** Death and serious injury by driving cases (unless standard).
11		Burglary & Robbery	**Band 11.1:** Aggravated burglary, burglary with intent to GBH or rape, and armed robbery.
			Band 11.2: other burglary and robbery.
12		Firearms Offences	**Band 12.1:** Possession or supply of a firearm/ammunition with any ulterior intent or any offence for which the maximum penalty is life imprisonment.
			Band 12.2: Minimum sentence offence.
			Band 12.3: All other offences (unless standard).
13		Other offences against the person	**Band 13.1:** Kidnapping; false imprisonment; blackmail (unless standard).
14		Exploitation/human trafficking offences	**Band 14.1:** All exploitation/human trafficking offences (unless standard).
15		Public Order Offences	**Band 15.1:** Riot and prison mutiny/riot.
			Band 15.2: Violent disorder.
			Band 15.3: Affray.
16		Regulatory Offences	**Band 16.1:** Health and Safety or environmental cases involving one or more fatalities or defined by the HSE or EA as a category or Stage 1 "major incident";
			Death of a child;
			A major accident at a site regulated by the Control of Major Accident Hazards Regulations 1999 (as amended); large scale explosion.
			Band 16.2: Health and Safety or environmental cases not falling within Band 1 but involving:
			Serious and permanent personal injury/disability and/or widespread
			Destruction of property (other than that owned or occupied by the defendant)

		Extensive pollution/irreparable damage to the environment
		Toxic gas release (e.g. carbon monoxide, chlorine gas)
		Cases involving incidents governed by mining/railways/aviation legislation
		Band 16.3: All other offences (unless standard)
17	Standard Cases	**Band 17.1:** Standard cases
		Those cases not falling under the above categories of offence will be defined as 'Standard Cases'.

For each category, there will be set fees, stated in the Regulations, for the category of advocate (QC, Junior, Led Junior), and type of fee.

BASIC ADVOCACY FEES FOR JUNIOR OR LED JUNIOR

Category of Offence	Junior or led Junior	Junior or led Junior	Junior or led Junior	Junior or led Junior
	Guilty Plea or Early Cracked Trial	Cracked Trial in Final Third	Trial	Daily Refresher
1.1	£4,295	£7,295	£8,585	£580
1.2	£2,150	£3,650	£4,295	£580
1.3	£1,290	£2,190	£2,575	£580
1.4	£1,075	£1,825	£2,145	£580
2.1	£4,295	£7,295	£8,585	£580
2.2	£1,290	£2,190	£2,575	£580
3.1	£1,770	£3,005	£3,535	£505
3.2	£1,010	£1,715	£2,020	£505
3.3	£600	£1,020	£1,200	£505
3.4	£425	£725	£850	£505
3.5	£375	£640	£750	£400
4.1	£1,010	£1,715	£2,020	£530
4.2	£785	£1,330	£1,565	£505
4.3	£760	£1,290	£1,515	£480
5.1	£950	£1,615	£1,900	£530
5.2	£710	£1,205	£1,415	£505
5.3	£505	£860	£1,010	£480
6.1	£4,245	£7,210	£8,485	£530
6.2	£3,850	£6,545	£7,700	£505

6.3	£1,430	£2,425	£2,855	£405
6.4	£505	£860	£1,010	£400
6.5	£405	£690	£810	£400
7.1	£710	£1,205	£1,415	£505
7.2	£405	£690	£810	£455
7.3	£380	£645	£760	£405
8.1	£605	£1,030	£1,210	£505

BASIC ADVOCACY FEES FOR JUNIOR OR LED JUNIOR

Category of Offence	Junior or led Junior Guilty Plea or Early Cracked Trial	Junior or led Junior Cracked Trial in Final Third	Junior or led Junior Trial	Junior or led Junior Daily Refresher
9.1	£2,930	£4,980	£5,860	£530
9.2	£2,020	£3,435	£4,040	£530
9.3	£1,515	£2,575	£3,030	£455
9.4	£1,325	£2,255	£2,650	£455
9.5	£810	£1,375	£1,615	£455
9.6	£605	£1,030	£1,210	£405
9.7	£405	£690	£810	£400
10.1	£1,110	£1,885	£2,220	£530
11.1	£700	£1,190	£1,400	£455
11.2	£400	£680	£800	£400
12.1	£1,060	£1,800	£2,120	£505
12.2	£660	£1,120	£1,315	£505
12.3	£455	£775	£910	£505
13.1	£900	£1,530	£1,800	£505
14.1	£1,165	£1,975	£2,325	£555
15.1	£810	£1,375	£1,615	£505
15.2	£700	£1,190	£1,400	£405
15.3	£425	£725	£850	£400
16.1	£1,110	£1,885	£2,220	£555
16.2	£810	£1,375	£1,615	£505
16.3	£505	£860	£1,010	£505
17.1	£365	£615	£725	£400

BASIC ADVOCACY FEES FOR LEADING JUNIOR				
Category of Offence	Leading Junior	Leading Junior	Leading Junior	Leading Junior
	Guilty Plea or Early Cracked Trial	Cracked Trial in Final Third	Trial	Daily Refresher
1.1	£6,440	£10,945	£12,880	£870
1.2	£3,220	£5,475	£6,445	£870
1.3	£1,930	£3,285	£3,865	£870
1.4	£1,610	£2,735	£3,220	£870
2.1	£6,440	£10,945	£12,880	£870
2.2	£1,930	£3,285	£3,865	£870
3.1	£2,650	£4,505	£5,305	£760
3.2	£1,515	£2,575	£3,030	£760
3.3	£900	£1,530	£1,800	£760
3.4	£640	£1,085	£1,275	£760
3.5	£565	£955	£1,125	£600
4.1	£1,515	£2,575	£3,030	£795
4.2	£1,175	£1,995	£2,350	£760
4.3	£1,135	£1,930	£2,275	£720
5.1	£1,425	£2,425	£2,850	£795
5.2	£1,060	£1,805	£2,125	£760
5.3	£760	£1,290	£1,515	£720
6.1	£6,365	£10,820	£12,730	£795
6.2	£5,775	£9,820	£11,550	£760
6.3	£2,140	£3,640	£4,285	£610
6.4	£760	£1,290	£1,515	£600
6.5	£610	£1,035	£1,215	£600
7.1	£1,060	£1,805	£2,125	£760
7.2	£610	£1,035	£1,215	£685
7.3	£570	£970	£1,140	£610
8.1	£910	£1,545	£1,815	£760

Advocates' rate bands and graduated fee tables

\	BASIC ADVOCACY FEES FOR LEADING JUNIOR			
Category of Offence	Leading Junior	Leading Junior	Leading Junior	Leading Junior
	Guilty Plea or Early Cracked Trial	Cracked Trial in Final Third	Trial	Daily Refresher
9.1	£4,395	£7,470	£8,790	£795
9.2	£3,030	£5,150	£6,060	£795
9.3	£2,275	£3,865	£4,545	£685
9.4	£1,990	£3,380	£3,975	£685
9.5	£1,210	£2,060	£2,425	£685
9.6	£910	£1,545	£1,815	£610
9.7	£610	£1,035	£1,215	£600
10.1	£1,665	£2,830	£3,330	£795
11.1	£1,050	£1,785	£2,100	£685
11.2	£600	£1,020	£1,200	£600
12.1	£1,590	£2,705	£3,180	£760
12.2	£985	£1,675	£1,975	£760
12.3	£685	£1,160	£1,365	£760
13.1	£1,350	£2,295	£2,700	£760
14.1	£1,745	£2,965	£3,490	£835
15.1	£1,210	£2,060	£2,425	£760
15.2	£1,050	£1,785	£2,100	£610
15.3	£640	£1,085	£1,275	£600
16.1	£1,665	£2,830	£3,330	£835
16.2	£1,210	£2,060	£2,425	£760
16.3	£760	£1,290	£1,515	£760
17.1	£545	£925	£1,090	£600

BASIC ADVOCACY FEES FOR QC				
Category of Offence	QC	QC	QC	QC
	Guilty Plea or Early Cracked Trial	Cracked Trial in Final Third	Trial	Daily Refresher
1.1	£8,585	£14,595	£17,170	£1,160
1.2	£4,295	£7,300	£8,590	£1,160
1.3	£2,575	£4,380	£5,150	£1,160
1.4	£2,145	£3,645	£4,290	£1,160
2.1	£8,585	£14,595	£17,170	£1,160
2.2	£2,575	£4,380	£5,150	£1,160
3.1	£3,535	£6,010	£7,070	£1,010
3.2	£2,020	£3,435	£4,040	£1,010
3.3	£1,200	£2,040	£2,400	£1,010
3.4	£850	£1,445	£1,700	£1,010
3.5	£750	£1,275	£1,500	£800
4.1	£2,020	£3,435	£4,040	£1,060
4.2	£1,565	£2,660	£3,130	£1,010
4.3	£1,515	£2,575	£3,030	£960
5.1	£1,900	£3,230	£3,800	£1,060
5.2	£1,415	£2,405	£2,830	£1,010
5.3	£1,010	£1,715	£2,020	£960
6.1	£8,485	£14,425	£16,970	£1,060
6.2	£7,700	£13,090	£15,400	£1,010
6.3	£2,855	£4,855	£5,710	£810
6.4	£1,010	£1,715	£2,020	£800
6.5	£810	£1,375	£1,620	£800
7.1	£1,415	£2,405	£2,830	£1,010
7.2	£810	£1,375	£1,620	£910
7.3	£760	£1,290	£1,520	£810
8.1	£1,210	£2,055	£2,420	£1,010

Advocates' rate bands and graduated fee tables 337

BASIC ADVOCACY FEES FOR QC				
Category of Offence	QC	QC	QC	QC
	Guilty Plea or Early Cracked Trial	Cracked Trial in Final Third	Trial	Daily Refresher
9.1	£5,860	£9,960	£11,720	£1,060
9.2	£4,040	£6,870	£8,080	£1,060
9.3	£3,030	£5,150	£6,060	£910
9.4	£2,650	£4,505	£5,300	£910
9.5	£1,615	£2,745	£3,230	£910
9.6	£1,210	£2,055	£2,420	£810
9.7	£810	£1,375	£1,620	£800
10.1	£2,220	£3,775	£4,440	£1,060
11.1	£1,400	£2,380	£2,800	£910
11.2	£800	£1,360	£1,600	£800
12.1	£2,120	£3,605	£4,240	£1,010
12.2	£1,315	£2,235	£2,630	£1,010
12.3	£910	£1,545	£1,820	£1,010
13.1	£1,800	£3,060	£3.600	£1,010
14.1	£2,325	£3,955	£4,650	£1,110
15.1	£1,615	£2,745	£3,230	£1,010
15.2	£1,400	£2,380	£2,800	£810
15.3	£850	£1,445	£1,700	£800
16.1	£2,220	£3,775	£4,440	£1,110
16.2	£1,615	£2,745	£3,230	£1,010
16.3	£1,010	£1,715	£2,020	£1,010
17.1	£725	£1,235	£1,450	£800

Fixed Fees	Junior/Led Junior	Leading Junior	QC
Standard Appearance	£91	£136	£182
Sentencing	£126	£192	£253
PTPH	£126	£192	£253
FCMH	£101	£152	£202
Committal for Sentence	£152	£227	£303

Fixed Fees	Junior/Led Junior	Leading Junior	QC
Appeal to CC against sentence	£250	£373	£498
Appeal to CC against conviction	£330	£496	£661
Conferences and Views (hourly)	£40.40 p/h	£60.60 p/h	£80.80 p/h
Breach of Crown Court Order	£109	£153	£218
Abuse of Process – Full Day	£240	£349	£502
Abuse of Process Half Day	£131	£197	£263
Disclosure Hearings Full Day	£240	£349	£502
Disclosure Hearings – Half Day	£131	£197	£263
Admissibility of Evidence Hearings – Full day	£240	£349	£502
Admissibility of Evidence Hearings – Half Day	£131	£197	£263
Ground Rules Hearings – Full day	£240	£349	£502
Ground Rules Hearings – Half day	£131	£197	£263
Hearings on withdrawal of guilty plea – FD	£240	£349	£502
Hearings on withdrawal of guilty plea – HD	£131	£197	£263
2nd and subsequent days of an application to dismiss – Full Day	£240	£349	£502
2nd and subsequent days of an application to dismiss – Half Day	£131	£197	£263
Adjourned Appeals, committals for sentence and breach hearings	£88	£131	£175
Bail applications, mentions and other applications in appeal, committals for sentence and breach hearings	£88	£131	£175
Deferred Sentence Hearing	£175	£240	£327
Ineffective Trial Hearings	£380	£380	£380
Special Preparation	£39.39 p/h	£56.56 p/h	£74.74 p/h
Wasted Preparation	£39.39 p/h	£56.56 p/h	£74.74 p/h
Noting Brief	£109	£109	£109
Hearing for Mitigation of Sentence	£109	£109	£109

Fees for confiscation Hearings

	Fee for QC	Fee for Leading Junior	Fee for Junior alone	Fee for Led Junior
Daily Rates	£502.00	£349.00	£240.00	£240.00
Half Daily Rates	£263.00	£197.00	£131.00	£131.00
Pages of Evidence				
51–250	£655.00	£546.00	£437.00	£327.00
251–500	£983.00	£819.00	£655.00	£491.00
501–750	£1,311.00	£1,092.00	£874.00	£655.00
751–1000	£1,965.00	£1,638.00	£1,311.00	£983.00
Preparation @ Hourly Rates	£74.74	£56.56	£39.39	£39.39

APPENDIX J

Crown Court hourly rates and Court of Appeal fees[1]

Litigators' fees for special preparation and confiscation and for proceedings in the Court of Appeal
These fees apply to all cases with a representation order dated on or after 1 April 2016.

For proceedings in the Court of Appeal the appropriate officer must allow fees for work by litigators at the following prescribed rates –

Class of work	Grade of fee earner	Rate	Variations
Preparation	Senior solicitor	£48.36 per hour	£50.87 per hour for a litigator whose office is situated within the City of London or a London borough
	Solicitor, legal executive or fee earner of equivalent experience	£41.06 per hour	£43.12 per hour for a litigator whose office is situated within the City of London or a London borough
	Trainee or fee earner of equivalent experience	£27.15 per hour	£31.03 per hour for a litigator whose office is situated within the City of London or a London borough
Advocacy	Senior solicitor	£58.40 per hour	
	Solicitor	£51.10 per hour	
Attendance at court where more than one representative assigned	Senior solicitor	£38.55 per hour	
	Solicitor, legal executive or fee earner of equivalent experience	£31.03 per hour	

1 Criminal Legal Aid (Remuneration) Regulations 2013 SI No 435 Sch 3.

342 Criminal Costs: legal aid costs in the criminal courts / Appendix J

Class of work	Grade of fee earner	Rate	Variations
	Trainee or fee earner of equivalent experience	£18.71 per hour	
Travelling and waiting	Senior solicitor	£22.58 per hour	
	Solicitor, legal executive or fee earner of equivalent experience	£22.58 per hour	
	Trainee or fee earner of equivalent experience	£11.41 per hour	
Routine letters written and routine telephone calls		£3.15 per item	£3.29 per item for a litigator whose office is situated within the City of London or a London borough

In respect of any item of work, the appropriate officer may allow fees at less than the relevant prescribed rate specified in the table following sub-paragraph (1) where it appears to the appropriate officer reasonable to do so having regard to the competence and despatch with which the work was done.

Advocates' fees for proceedings in the Court of Appeal

These fees apply to all cases with a representation order dated on or after 1 April 2013.

(1) Subject to sub-paragraph 9(4), for proceedings in the Court of Appeal the appropriate officer must allow fees for work by advocates at the following prescribed rates –

Junior counsel

Types of proceedings	Basic fee	Full day refresher	Subsidiary fees			
			Attendance at consultation, conferences and views	Written work	Attendance at pre-trial reviews, applications and other appearances	
All appeals	Maximum amount: £545 per case	Maximum amount: £178.75 per day	£33.50 per hour, minimum amount: £16.75	Maximum amount: £58.25 per item	Maximum amount: £110 per appearance	

QC

Types of proceedings	Basic fee	Full day refresher	Subsidiary fees			
			Attendance at consultation, conferences and views		Written work	Attendance at pre-trial reviews, applications and other appearances
All appeals	Maximum amount: £5,400 per case	Maximum amount: £330.50 per day	£62.50 per hour, minimum amount: £32		Maximum amount: £119.50 per item	Maximum amount: £257.50 per appearance

(2) Where an hourly rate is specified in the table following sub-paragraph (1), the appropriate officer must determine any fee for such work in accordance with that hourly rate, provided that the fee determined must not be less than the minimum amount specified.

(3) Where a refresher fee is claimed in respect of less than a full day, the appropriate officer must allow such fee as appears to the appropriate officer reasonable having regard to the fee which would be allowable for a full day.

(4) Where it appears to the appropriate officer, taking into account all the relevant circumstances of the case, that owing to the exceptional circumstances of the case the amount payable by way of fees in accordance with the table following sub-paragraph (1) would not provide reasonable remuneration for some or all of the work the appropriate officer has allowed, the appropriate officer may allow such amounts as appear to the appropriate officer to be reasonable remuneration for the relevant work.

APPENDIX K

Very high cost cases (VHCC) payment rates

These rates apply to all cases with a representation order dated on or after 2 December 2013.

Payment rates

Preparation (hourly rates)

	Category 1 (£)	Category 2 (£)	Category 3 (£)	Category 4 (£)	Standard rates (£)
Litigator					
Level A	101.50	79.10	63.70	63.70	39.03
Level B	88.90	70.00	55.30	55.30	33.08
Level C	58.80	45.50	35.70	35.70	24.05
Pupil/junior[1]	31.50	25.20	21.00	21.00	
Barrister					
QC	101.50	79.10	63.70	63.70	
Leading junior	88.90	70.00	55.30	55.30	
Led junior	63.70	51.10	42.70	42.70	
Junior alone	70	57.40	49.00	49.00	
2nd led junior	44.10	35.00	30.10	30.10	
Solicitor advocate					
Leading level a	101.50	79.10	63.70	63.70	
Led level A	88.90	70	55.30	55.30	
Leading level B	88.90	70	55.30	55.30	
Led level B	72.80	60.20	46.20	46.20	
Level A alone	91.70	76.30	61.60	61.60	
Level B alone	79.10	66.50	52.50	52.50	
Second advocate	44.10	35.00	30.10	30.10	

Advocacy

Advocacy rates for advocates are paid per hearing or per day depending upon the duration of the court sitting time. Advocacy rates are non-category specific.

	Preliminary hearing (£)	Half day (£)	Full day (£)
QC	79.10	166.60	333.20
Leading junior	60.20	136.50	273.00
Led junior	40.60	88.20	176.40
Junior alone	46.90	100.10	199.50
Second led junior	23.80	44.80	89.60
Noting junior	20.30	38.50	76.30

Attendance at court with advocate (hourly rates for litigators)

Level A	£29.58
Level B	£23.80
Level C	£14.35

Travelling and waiting

£25 per hour regardless of Litigator Level or Advocacy role. Travel limited to 4 hours in one day.

Mileage

£0.45 per mile

1) This is to cover situations where the scope of Legal Aid funding cannot be amended to provide for a second junior counsel but the VHCC Supervisor determines that to achieve value for money certain items of work should be done by a third counsel.
2) Solicitor-Advocates will be paid the appropriate rate for a leading junior, a led junior, or a junior alone.

APPENDIX L

Experts' fees and rates[1]

These rates apply to all cases with a representation order dated on or after 2 December 2013.

Expert	Non-London Hourly Rate or Fixed Fee (£)	London Hourly Rate or Fixed Fee (£)	Comments
A&E consultant	100.80	108	
Accident reconstruction	72	54.40	
Accountant	64	64	
Accountant (General staff)	40	40	
Accountant (manager)	86.40	86.40	
Accountant (Partner)	115.20	115.20	
Anaesthetist	108	72	
Architect	79.20	72	
Back calculations	144 fixed fee	151.20 fixed fee	
Benefit expert	72	72	
Cardiologist	115.20	72	
Cell telephone site analysis	72	72	
Child psychiatrist	108	72	
Child psychologist	100.80	72	
Computer expert	72	72	
Consultant engineer	72	54.40	
Dentist	93.60	72	
Dermatologist	86.40	72	
Disability consultant	54.40	54.40	

1 Criminal Legal Aid (Remuneration) Regulations 2013 SI No 2803.

Expert	Non-London Hourly Rate or Fixed Fee (£)	London Hourly Rate or Fixed Fee (£)	Comments
DNA (per person) – testing of sample	252 per test	252 per test	
DNA (per person) – preparation of report	72	72	
Doctor (GP)	79.20	72	
Drug expert	72	72	
Employment consultant	54.40	54.40	
Enquiry agent	25.60	18.40	
ENT surgeon	100.80	72	
Facial mapping	108	72	
Fingerprint expert	72	37.60	
Fire investigation	72	54.40	
Firearm expert	72	72	
Forensic scientist	90.40	72	
General surgeon	108	72	
Geneticist	86.40	72	
GP (records report)	50.40 fixed fee	72 fixed fee	
Gynaecologist	108	72	
Haematologist	97.60	72	
Handwriting expert	72	72	
Interpreter	28	25	
Lip reader / Signer	57.60	32.80	
Mediator	100.80	100.80	
Medical consultant	108	72	
Medical microbiologist	108	72	
Medical report	79.20	72	
Meteorologist	100.80	144 fixed fee	
Midwife	72	72	
Neonatologist	108	72	
Neurologist	122.40	72	
Neuropsychiatrist	126.40	72	
Neuroradiologist	136.80	72	
Neurosurgeon	136.80	72	

Experts' fees and rates

Expert	Non-London Hourly Rate or Fixed Fee (£)	London Hourly Rate or Fixed Fee (£)	Comments
Nursing expert	64.80	64.80	
Obstetrician	108	72	
Occupational therapist	54.40	54.40	
Oncologist	112	72	
Orthopaedic surgeon	115.20	72	
Paediatrician	108	72	
Pathologist	122.40	432 fixed fee	
Pharmacologist	97.60	72	
Photographer	25.60	18.40	
Physiotherapist	64.80	64.80	
Plastic surgeon	108	72	
Process server	25.60	18.40	
Psychiatrist	108	72	
Psychologist	93.60	72	
Radiologist	108	72	
Rheumatologist	108	72	
Risk assessment expert	50.40	50.40	
Speech therapist	79.20	72	
Surgeon	108	72	
Surveyor	40	40	
Telecoms expert	72	72	
Toxicologist	108	72	
Urologist	108	72	
Vet	72	72	
Voice recognition	93.60	72	

APPENDIX M

Prescribed proceedings fees

These figures apply to cases with a representation order dated on or after 1 April 2016.

13.1 Representation in Prescribed Proceedings in a Magistrates' Court is at the same rate as for magistrates' court work in chapter 3 and appendix O.

13.2 Representation in prescribed Proceedings in the Crown Court

	London (£)	National (£)
Routine letters written and telephone calls per item	3.70	3.56
Preparation hourly rate	47.95	45.35
Advocacy hourly rate	56.89	56.89
Travelling and waiting hourly rate	24.00	24.00

13.3 Representation in Prescribed Proceedings in the High Court or a county court

	London (£)	National (£)
Routine letters out per item	6.84	6.02
Routine telephone calls per item	3.79	3.33
All other preparation work hourly rate	68.44 (72.54 where Provider's office is in London)	60.23 (63.88 where Provider's office is in London)
Attending counsel in conference or at the trial or hearing of any summons or application at court or other appointment – hourly rate	33.76	29.66
Attending without counsel at the trial or hearing of any cause or the hearing of any summons or other application at court or other appointment – hourly rate	68.44	60.23
Travelling and waiting hourly rate	30.34	26.65

The fees payable to Assigned Counsel for representation in the High Court or a county court in proceedings prescribed as criminal proceedings under section 14(h) of the [Legal Aid, Sentencing and Punishment of Offenders Act 2012] are subject to the limits specified for the magistrates' court.

APPENDIX N

Crime Lower police station fees

These figures apply to all matters commencing on or after 1 April 2016.

Police station attendance – fixed fees and escape fee thresholds

Criminal Justice System Area	Scheme	Fixed Fee (£)	Escape Fee Threshold (£)
Cleveland	Hartlepool	131.40	405.40
	Teesside	135.96	417.03
Durham	Darlington	154.54	463.62
	South Durham	152.39	468.28
	Durham	177.94	554.48
	Derwentside	171.63	514.90
	Easington	166.99	512.54
Northumbria	South East Northumberland	148.33	444.98
	Newcastle upon Tyne	137.79	424.01
	Gateshead	142.90	428.69
	North Tyneside	140.53	431.02
	South Tyneside	133.23	410.05
	Sunderland/Houghton Le Spring	148.74	458.97
	Berwick & Alnwick	177.03	545.17
	Tynedale & Hexham	154.21	475.28

354 Criminal Costs: legal aid costs in the criminal courts / Appendix N

Criminal Justice System Area	Scheme	Fixed Fee (£)	Escape Fee Threshold (£)
Avon & Somerset	Avon North & Thornbury	177.94	561.49
	Bath & Wansdyke	193.37	580.10
	Mendip/Yeovil & South Somerset	216.67	650.02
	Bristol	159.98	479.94
	Sedgemore/Taunton Dane	181.59	615.06
	Weston-Super-Mare	180.95	542.85
Dorset	Central Dorset	182.50	547.50
	Bournemouth & Christchurch	145.22	435.67
	Poole East Dorset	153.30	470.60
	Bridport West Dorset/ Weymouth & Dorchester	146.00	438.00
Wiltshire	Salisbury	174.29	535.84
	Chippenham/Trowbridge	187.94	563.82
	Swindon	171.55	528.86
Gloucestershire	Cheltenham	157.86	486.92
	Gloucester	155.13	477.61
	Stroud	177.94	547.50
Devon & Cornwall	Barnstaple	173.96	521.88
	Exeter	154.54	463.62
	Plymouth	179.40	538.19
	East Cornwall	198.93	675.64
	Carrick/Kerrier (Camborne)/Penwith	177.94	563.82
	Teignbridge/Torbay	163.17	489.25
Staffordshire	Stoke on Trent/Leek	177.94	563.82
	Stafford/Cannock & Rugeley	177.94	547.50
	Lichfield & Tamworth/ Burton Upon Trent/ Uttoxeter	172.46	531.18
Warwickshire	Leamington/Nuneaton/ Rugby	178.61	535.84

Criminal Justice System Area	Scheme	Fixed Fee (£)	Escape Fee Threshold (£)
West Mercia	Hereford/Leominster	155.32	465.95
	Kidderminster/Redditch	198.81	596.42
	Shrewsbury	166.08	510.22
	Telford	172.46	531.18
	Worcester	180.95	542.85
West Midlands	Sandwell	176.11	540.52
	Wolverhampton & Seisdon	176.11	540.52
	Dudley & Halesowen	173.18	519.55
	Walsall	177.94	549.83
	Birmingham	177.94	566.14
	Solihull	187.16	561.49
	Coventry	153.77	461.30
Dyfed Powys	Amman Valley	177.94	570.80
	Carmarthen East Dyfed	201.92	605.75
	Llanelli	138.70	426.34
	Brecon & Radnor	203.47	610.41
	Mid Wales	155.32	465.95
	North Ceredigion/South Ceredigion	204.24	612.73
	Pembrokeshire	166.99	514.90
Gwent	East Gwent	169.73	521.88
	Newport	166.99	512.54
	Lower Rhymney Valley/ North Bedwellty/South Bedwellty	177.94	556.81
North Wales	Bangor & Caernarfon	189.49	568.47
	Colwyn Bay	173.38	533.51
	Denbighshire	188.71	566.14
	Dolgellau	188.71	566.14
	Mold & Hawarden	177.94	554.48
	North Anglesey	197.26	591.77
	Pwllheli	133.57	400.72
	Wrexham	161.53	484.59

Criminal Justice System Area	Scheme	Fixed Fee (£)	Escape Fee Threshold (£)
South Wales	Cardiff	177.94	587.11
	Vale of Glamorgan	208.13	624.40
	Cynon Valley	177.94	563.82
	Mid Glamorgan & Miskin	177.94	587.11
	Merthyr Tydfil	177.94	582.46
	Port Talbot	219.00	740.88
	Newcastle & Ogmore	177.94	596.42
	Neath	180.68	612.73
	Swansea	171.55	528.86
Merseyside	Bootle & Crosby	162.43	498.58
	Southport	135.91	407.72
	Liverpool	179.40	538.19
	St Helens	153.30	472.96
	Knowsley	165.16	507.89
	Wirral	157.86	484.59
Cheshire	Crewe & Nantwich/ Sandbach & Congleton/ Macclesfield	176.11	540.52
	Warrington/Halton	154.54	463.62
	Chester/Vale Royal (Northwich)	160.76	482.27
Cumbria	Barrow in Furness	153.77	461.30
	Kendal & Windermere	183.28	549.83
	Penrith/Carlisle	173.18	519.55
	Whitehaven/Workington	143.67	431.02
Greater Manchester	Manchester	177.94	587.11
	Stockport	167.74	503.23
	Trafford	177.94	559.16
	Salford	177.94	570.80
	Bolton	164.64	493.93
	Bury	159.98	479.94
	Wigan	170.07	510.22
	Rochdale/Middleton	169.30	507.89
	Tameside	156.04	479.94
	Oldham	137.46	412.38

Crime Lower police station fees

Criminal Justice System Area	Scheme	Fixed Fee (£)	Escape Fee Threshold (£)
Lancashire	Burnley/Rossendale	162.31	486.92
	Blackburn/Accrington/Ribble Valley	177.94	580.10
	Blackpool	126.58	379.75
	Fleetwood	129.69	389.08
	Lancaster	159.20	477.61
	Chorley/Ormskirk/South Ribble & Leyland	174.73	524.20
	Preston	142.90	428.69
Kent	Dartford & Gravesend	232.98	698.94
	Ashford & Tenterden/Dover/Folkestone	205.31	696.61
	Medway	205.02	615.06
	Swale	243.07	729.22
	Maidstone & West Malling	216.67	650.02
	Canterbury/Thanet	177.94	603.43
	West Kent (Tonbridge)	208.13	624.40
Surrey	Guildford & Farnham	179.76	610.41
	North West Surrey (Woking)	196.19	666.31
	South East Surrey	207.14	703.59
	Epsom	209.88	712.93
	Staines	240.90	815.42
Sussex	Brighton & Hove & Lewes	183.41	622.04
	Chichester & District	162.43	498.58
	Crawley/Horsham	228.32	684.95
	Hastings	142.35	438.00
	Worthing	164.25	505.56
	Eastbourne	173.18	519.55
Derbyshire	East Derbyshire (Ripley)/Ilkeston	206.57	619.72
	Ashbourne/Matlock/High Peak (Buxton)	190.27	570.80
	Chesterfield	177.84	533.51
	Derby/Swadlincote	177.94	570.80

Criminal Justice System Area	Scheme	Fixed Fee (£)	Escape Fee Threshold (£)
Leicestershire	Ashby & Coalville/ Loughborough/Melton Mowbray	181.72	545.17
	Leicester	177.94	552.15
	Hinckley/Market Harborough	201.92	605.75
Lincolnshire	Boston, Bourne, Stamford	173.38	533.51
	Skegness	156.09	468.28
	Lincoln/Gainsborough	161.53	484.59
	Grantham & Sleaford	159.69	491.57
Nottinghamshire	Mansfield	160.60	493.93
	Newark	180.17	540.52
	Nottingham	179.40	538.19
	Worksop & East Retford	170.64	524.20
Northamptonshire	Corby (Kettering)/ Wellingborough	157.65	472.96
	Northampton	170.85	512.54
Bedfordshire	Bedford	167.90	517.22
	Luton	177.94	601.07
Cambridgeshire	Cambridge	162.43	500.91
	Ely	177.94	575.45
	Huntingdon	173.18	519.55
	March & Wisbech	171.63	514.90
	Peterborough	142.90	428.69
Essex	Basildon	177.94	549.83
	Brentwood	249.11	845.72
	Braintree	198.93	673.32
	Clacton & Harwich/ Colchester	177.94	563.82
	Grays	232.69	789.80
	Harlow & Loughton	232.69	789.80
	Stansted	257.33	873.67
	Rayleigh/Southend on Sea	166.97	500.91
	Chelmsford/Witham	176.11	542.85

Crime Lower police station fees 359

Criminal Justice System Area	Scheme	Fixed Fee (£)	Escape Fee Threshold (£)
Hertfordshire	Dacorum (Hemel Hempstead)	209.88	710.57
	Bishop's Stortford/East Hertfordshire	254.59	864.34
	Stevenage & North Hertfordshire	236.34	801.46
	St. Albans	214.44	702.25
	Watford	210.79	715.25
Norfolk	Cromer & North Walsham	184.33	624.40
	Great Yarmouth	168.52	505.56
	Kings Lynn & West Norfolk	164.64	493.93
	Norwich & District	169.30	507.89
	Diss/Thetford	175.20	538.19
	Dereham	198.01	670.99
Suffolk	Lowestoft/Beccles & Halesworth/Aldeburgh	169.30	507.89
	Felixstowe/Ipswich & District/Woodbridge	172.41	517.22
	Sudbury & Hadleigh/Bury St. Edmunds/Haverhill/ Newmarket	177.94	552.15
Thames Valley	Abingdon, Didcot & Witney (South Oxfordshire)	208.96	708.25
	Aylesbury	198.81	596.42
	High Wycombe & Amersham	190.71	647.69
	Milton Keynes	165.16	507.89
	Bicester/North Oxon (Banbury)	194.36	659.33
	Oxford	194.36	659.33
	Reading	188.71	566.14
	Slough (East Berkshire)	208.96	708.25
	West Berkshire (Newbury etc.)	174.73	524.20

Criminal Justice System Area	Scheme	Fixed Fee (£)	Escape Fee Threshold (£)
Hampshire	Aldershot/Petersfield (North East Hampshire)	199.84	677.97
	Andover/Basingstoke/Winchester (North West Hampshire)	210.46	631.38
	Isle of Wight	171.63	514.90
	Portsmouth/Waterlooville (South East Hampshire)	176.29	528.86
	Gosport & Fareham	215.11	645.34
	Southampton (South West Hampshire)	198.81	596.42
Humberside	Grimsby & Cleethorpes	134.35	403.04
	Scunthorpe	144.18	444.98
	Hull	153.30	470.60
	Beverley/Bridlington	177.94	587.11
	Goole	182.50	617.39
North Yorkshire	Northallerton & Richmond	191.82	575.45
	Harrogate & Ripon	184.05	552.15
	Skipton, Settle & Ingleton	177.94	547.50
	Scarborough/Whitby	152.39	468.28
	Malton & Rydale	146.78	440.33
	York/Selby	159.69	491.57
South Yorkshire	Barnsley	158.78	489.25
	Doncaster	153.30	470.60
	Rotherham	162.43	500.91
	Sheffield	166.99	514.90
West Yorkshire	Halifax	173.96	521.88
	Huddersfield	146.78	440.33
	Dewsbury	159.20	477.61
	Bradford	135.96	419.36
	Keighley & Bingley	153.30	470.60
	Leeds	144.18	442.65
	Pontefract & Castleford	141.34	424.01
	Wakefield	139.61	428.69

Crime Lower police station fees 361

Criminal Justice System Area	Scheme	Fixed Fee (£)	Escape Fee Threshold (£)
London	Barking	224.48	761.85
	Bexley	200.75	680.30
	Bishopsgate	234.51	794.45
	Brent	219.00	740.88
	Brentford	222.65	754.84
	Bromley	211.70	717.58
	Camberwell Green	219.00	743.20
	Central London	237.25	803.78
	Clerkenwell/Hampstead	221.74	750.18
	Croydon	216.26	731.54
	Ealing	229.95	780.67
	Enfield	218.09	738.55
	Greenwich/Woolwich	208.96	708.25
	Haringey	225.39	764.17
	Harrow	219.00	743.20
	Havering	204.40	691.96
	Heathrow	274.66	931.93
	Hendon/Barnet	220.83	747.86
	Highbury Corner	229.95	778.16
	Kingston-Upon-Thames	228.13	773.48
	Newham	219.91	745.53
	Old Street	219.00	743.20
	Redbridge	225.39	764.17
	Richmond-Upon-Thames	240.90	815.42
	South London	229.95	778.16
	Sutton	218.09	738.55
	Thames	218.09	738.55
	Tower Bridge	232.69	789.80
	Uxbridge	210.79	715.25
	Waltham Forest	204.40	694.28
	West London	235.43	799.10
	Wimbledon	223.56	757.19

APPENDIX O

Magistrates' court fees and Crown Court fees for non-indictable cases

These figures apply to all cases with a representation order dated on or after 1 April 2016.

This table sets out the fees and fee limits for the standard fee payment scheme for representation in a magistrates' court.

Higher and lower standard fees table

	Lower Standard Fee (£)	Lower Standard Fee Limit (£)	Higher Standard Fee (£)	Higher Standard Fee Limit (£)
Designated area standard fees				
Category 1A	248.71	272.34	471.81	471.85
Category 1B	202.20	272.34	435.64	471.85
Category 2	345.34	467.84	723.35	779.64
Undesignated area standard fees				
Category 1A	194.68	272.34	412.30	471.85
Category 1B	158.27	272.34	380.70	471.85
Category 2	279.45	467.84	640.94	779.64

Representation in a magistrates' court

Hourly rates (for recording time and to determine whether the lower or higher standard fee limit has been reached; and for claiming costs in cases which fall outside the standard fee payment scheme).

	All areas
Routine letters written and telephone calls per item	£3.56
Preparation hourly rate	£45.35
Advocacy hourly rate (including applications for bail and other applications to the court)	£56.89
Hourly rate for attendance at court where counsel is assigned (including conferences with counsel at court)	£31.03
Travelling and waiting hourly rate (only claimable where the undesignated area fees apply)	£24.00

Appeal against sentence	£155.32
Appeal against conviction	£349.47
Committal for sentence	£232.98
Contempt proceedings– involving a non-defendant (for defendants the work is covered by the normal fee). These proceedings should be distinguished from contempt in civil proceedings which are prescribed proceedings (see chapter 10)	£116.49
Breach of Crown Court order	£77.66
Hearing subsequent to sentence: Crime and Disorder Act 1998 s1CA (variation and discharge of orders under s1C)	£155.32
Powers of Criminal Courts (Sentencing) Act 2000 s155 (alteration of Crown Court sentence)	£155.32
Serious Organised Crime and Police Act 2005 s74 (assistance by defendant; review of sentence)	£155.32

APPENDIX P

Payments for assigned counsel

These figures apply to all cases with a representation order dated on or after 1 April 2016.

Subject to exception described in chapter 3
(1) The fees payable to Assigned Counsel for –
   (a) representation in a magistrates' court;
   (b) representation in the High Court Family Court or a county court in proceedings prescribed as criminal proceedings under section 14(h) of the [Legal Aid, Sentencing and Punishment of Offenders Act 2012]; and
   (c) representation in the High Court on an appeal by way of case stated.
(2) The fees payable to Assigned Counsel are subject to the limits specified in the table following this paragraph.

Payment for assigned counsel

	Junior counsel (£)	Queen's Counsel (£)
Basic fee for preparation, including for a pre-trial review and, where appropriate, the first day's hearing including, where they took place on that day, short conferences, consultations, applications and appearances (including bail applications, views and any other preparation).	maximum amount: 427.00	maximum amount: 4,056.00
Refresher daily fee (for any day or part of a day during which a hearing continued, including, where they took place on that day, short conferences, consultations, applications and appearances (including bail applications, views and any other preparation).	maximum amount: 147.00	maximum amount: 271.01
Subsidiary fees:		
Attendance at consultations, conferences and views not covered by the basic fee or the refresher fee.	26.69 per hour – minimum amount: 13.25	49.73 per hour – minimum amount: 25.55
Written work (on evidence, plea, appeal, case stated or other written work).	maximum amount: 46.77	maximum amount: 95.81
Attendance at pre-trial reviews, applications and other appearances (including bail applications and adjournments for sentence) not covered by the basic fee or the refresher fee.	maximum amount: 85.78	maximum amount: 187.06

Index

Administration issues 9.1–9.41
Advocacy 1.34
Advocacy assistance 2.67–2.71
  application to vary pre-charge bail 2.67
  armed forces custody hearing, on 2.67, 2.69
  magistrates' court, application to vary pre-charge police bail conditions 2.71
  warrant of further detention, on 2.67–2.70
  High Court or senior judge, before 2.70
Advocacy in Crown Court 5.189–5.307
  calculations 5.233–5.250
    cracked trials 5.237–5.243
    defendants unfit to plead or stand trial 5.248
    guilty pleas 5.235, 5.236
    mark-ups 5.244–5.247
    retrials 5.249, 5.250
    trials 5.233, 5.234
  confiscation proceedings 5.285–5.296
  cross-examination of witness 5.292
  disbursements 5.301, 5.302
  discharge of legal aid 5.300
  early discontinuance or dismissal 5.282
  fees 5.189
  indictable crime 5.204–5.232
    bail hearings 5.211, 5.212
    category of advocate 5.225
    defence elections for trial 5.204–5.207
    graduated fees 5.213
    length of trial 5.223
    main hearing: basic fee 5.226–5.232
    number of PPE 5.219–5.221
    offences banding 5.214–5.218
    preliminary hearings 5.209, 5.210
  mitigation only 5.292, 5.293
  non-indictable crime 5.191–5.203
    contempt of court 5.196
    escape provisions 5.199–5.202
    mark-ups 5.197
    normal fees 5.192
    prescribed proceedings 5.203
  payment and distribution of advocacy fee 5.303–5.307
  provision of written or oral advice 5.294
  special circumstances 5.282–5.300
  supplementary fees 5.251–5.281
    conferences 5.264–5.268
    hearings paid by daily and half daily fees 5.261
    interim hearings 5.255–5.257
    sentencing hearings 5.258–5.260
    special preparation 5.269–5.278
    views 5.264–5.268
    wasted preparation 5.239–5.281
    work paid by hourly rates 5.264–5.268
  warrants 5.295–5.299
Appeals 6.1–6.14, 9.1–9.7 *see also* Reviews
  Court of Appeal 9.7

Appeals *continued*
  crime lower 9.1–9.2
  Crown Court cases 9.3–9.6
  SCC 6.1–6.9
    extent 6.3, 6.5
    fees 6.6–6.9
    matter type claim codes 6.2

Bails to return 2.56, 2.57
Business day
  meaning 2.4
Business hours
  meaning 2.4

Checking transcripts 1.30
Civil proceedings 10.1–10.26
  barristers, provision for 10.32
  breach of civil injunction 10.23, 10.24
  criminal cases, related to 10.15–10.18
  injunctions 10.19–10.21
  matters where criminal law solicitors may act 10.25, 10.26
  prescribed proceedings 10.3–10.14
    Crown Court 10.8–10.14
    magistrates' court 10.7
    youth court 10.19
Copying 8.26, 8.27
Costs
  principles *see* Principles of costs
Counsel
  magistrates' court proceedings 3.45–3.50
Court duty solicitor 3.2–3.7
  attendance 3.2, 3.3
  claim code 3.6
  disbursements 3.5
  exclusion 3.7
  travel 3.4
Court of Appeal 6.10–6.13
  remuneration 6.12, 6.13
  representation orders 6.10, 6.11
Cracked trial
  Crown Court 5.71–5.75
Criminal investigations 2.1–2.74
  agreements under Serious Organised Crime and Police Act 2005 2.22
  attendance cases 2.30
  attendance upon witnesses 2.6–2.9
  business day and hours 2.4, 2.5
  cases outside fixed fees 2.63–2.71
    advocacy assistance 2.67–2.71
  cases where criminal defence direct initially involved 2.29
  claim codes 2.6
  claim rates
    cases where criminal defence direct initially involved 2.29
    criminal direct defence not involved 2.26
  claims 2.6
  conducted other than by constable 2.6–2.9
    claim codes 2.6
    claims 2.6
    payment 2.7
  constable, conducted by 2.10–2.12
    advice and assistance 2.10
    claim codes 2.12
    claims 2.11
  custody records 2.18
  definitions 2.1–2.5
  detainees under Terrorism Act 2000 Sch 7 2.23
  disbursements 2.72–2.74
    method of claiming 2.74
  duty solicitor cases, definition 2.46–2.47
  enhanced cases, definition 2.46–2.47
  escape provisions 2.58–2.62
    calculating value 2.62
    value of claim 2.58–2.61
  fixed fees 2.31–2.45
    attendance at police station 2.32–2.34
    claiming 2.40, 2.41
    claiming more than 2.40, 2.41
    limitation on claims 2.42–2.45
    sufficient benefit test 2.35, 2.36
  genuinely separate matters 2.16
  matter, definition of 2.14–2.21
  payment 2.7–2.9, 2.13–2.74
  restriction on number of claims by different firms on same matter 2.48–2.57

Index 369

RUI 2.56, 2.57
single occasion 2.16
telephone-only advice 2.24
telephone-only cases 2.27, 2.28
volunteers 2.20, 2.21
work types and definitions 2.1–2.5
Criminal matter type code table 2.2
Crown Court 5.1–5.307
  advocacy *see* Advocacy in Crown Court
  aggravated burglary 5.124
  allegations of dishonesty 5.123
  categorisation of case 5.50–5.78
  conspiracy 5.124
  cracked trial 5.71–5.75
  guilty plea 5.76–5.78
  litigators' graduated fees 5.96–5.188 *see also* Litigators' graduated fees
  litigation and advocates in cases sent to 5.3–5.95
  number of cases 5.84–5.95
  number of days at trial 5.79–5.83
  number of pages of prosecution evidence 5.24–5.49
  advocates 5.5
  ancillary applications 5.27
  duplication and use of different formats 5.45
  electronic service of pictorial or documentary exhibits 5.28–5.44
  formats 5.42
  LAA notes 5.22
  notice of additional evidence 5.10
  service 5.11–5.13
  statutory definition 5.27
  summary of definition 5.15–5.22
  unused material 5.26
  video and audio recordings 5.23–5.25
  offensive weapons 5.120
  overview 5.1, 5.2
  retrials 5.61–5.70
  robbery 5.119
  sexual offences 5.126
  trade mark offences 5.130
  trial 5.51–5.60

Dictating time 1.21
Disbursements 2.72–2.74, 8.1–8.45
  advocacy in the Crown Court 5.301, 5.302
  copying 8.26, 8.27
  court duty solicitor 3.5
  definition 8.1
  expenses 8.40–8.45
  experts 8.23–8.39
  forensic science laboratory charges 8.38, 8.39
  interim payments 9.26–9.29
  intermediaries 8.37
  interpreters 8.35, 8.36
  litigators' graduated fees 5.188
  Livenote 8.24
  mileage rate 8.11–8.12
  parking 8.11–8.22
  payments on account of 8.8–8.10
  prior authorities 8.2–8.7
  prison law 4.15–4.17
  private transport 8.13, 8.14
  reasonable expenses 8.40–8.45
  transcripts 8.23
  translators 8.35, 8.36
  travel costs 8.11–8.22
  witness expenses 8.40–8.45
Divisional Court 6.10–6.13
  remuneration 6.12, 6.13
  representation orders 6.10, 6.11
Duty solicitor cases
  definition 2.46, 2.47

Electronic service of pictorial or documentary exhibits 5.28–5.44
  case law 5.36–5.43
  Crown Court 5.28–5.44
  LAA guidance 5.44
  relevant circumstances 5.31
  Secretary of State for Justice v SVS Solicitors 5.32
Enhanced cases
  definition 2.46, 2.47
Enhancement 1.39–1.47
  exceptionalities 1.40
  percentage uplift 1.41–1.42
  rates 1.42

Enhancement *continued*
reasons for 1.43
relevant factors 1.46
Escape provisions 2.58–2.62
calculating value 2.62
value of claim 2.58–2.61
Ex post facto billing 1.8–1.13
Experts 8.28–8.39

Freestanding advice 2.1–2.74

Guilty plea
Crown Court 5.76–5.78

Hardship payments 9.39, 9.40

Injunctions 10.19–10.24
Interim payments 9.25–9.38
advocates, for 9.38
Crown Court advocates in case awaiting determination 9.30
Crown Court litigators 9.31–9.37
disbursements, of 9.26–9.29

Litigators' graduated fees 5.96–5.188
additional payments 5.165–5.183
armed robbery 5.119
calculation 5.154–5.160
confiscation proceedings 5.165–5.183
Crown Court 5.9–5.188
defence elections for trial 5.106
disbursements 5.188
discontinuances 5.161–5.164
dishonesty allegations 5.123
dismissals 5.161–5.164
escape provisions 5.165–5.183
evidence provision fee 5.186, 5.187
hourly rates 5.183
index of fee tables 5.96
indictable jurisdiction 5.106–5.153
length of trial 5.142, 5.143
number of defendants represented 5.144
offence classification 5.114–5.133
proportion of case on which litigator represented defendant 5.145–5.151

retrial fees 5.152
whether case in trial, cracked or guilty plea 5.140, 5.141
non-indictable jurisdiction 5.97–5.105
number of pages not exceeding cut-offs 5.157–5.160
offensive weapons 5.120
post trial work 5.97–5.105
PPE in excess of 10,000 5.134–5.139
representation in prescribed proceedings 5.105
retrials 5.185
special circumstances 5.184–5.188
special preparation 5.165–5.183
unused material in long cases 5.167
VHCC cases 5.153
warrant cases 5.184
Livenote 8.24

Magistrates' court proceedings 3.2–3.50
additional payments 3.40–3.44
costs with representation order 3.18–3.50
claims 3.21–3.24
payment 3.25–3.38
standard fee tables 3.39
costs without representation order 3.12–3.17
early cover 3.15, 3.16
initial advice 3.17
pre-order costs 3.13, 3.14
counsel 3.45–3.50
assigned 3.46–3.49
assigned, attendance upon 3.50
disbursements 3.44
enhancements 3.42, 3.43
payment 3.25–3.28
core costs of each case 3.34–3.38
correct category of case 3.31
excluded cases 3.26
how many cases 3.30
non-excluded cases 3.27–3.38
notes on categories 3.31

special rules on categories 3.31–3.33
standard fee tables 3.39
travel and waiting 3.40
unassigned counsel's preparation and advocacy 3.35
virtual courts 3.8–3.11

Overpayments 9.41

Preparation 1.17–1.33
dictating time 1.21
matters included 1.17–1.33
supervision 1.27
Principles of costs 1.1–1.38
reasonableness 1.6–1.13
Prison law 4.1–4.22
additional payments 4.13–4.17
disbursements 4.15–4.17
advice and assistance 4.10, 4.11
advice and assistance: sentence cases 4.3–4.5
advocacy assistance: disciplinary cases and parole board oral hearings 4.6–4.8
calculating core costs 4.9–4.12
disciplinary and parole hearings 4.12
fees available 4.3–4.8
number of cases 4.18–4.22
travel 4.13, 4.14
Profit costs 1.6

Reasonable, meaning 1.6–1.13
Reviews 6.1–6.14 *see also* Appeals
SCC 6.1–6.9
extent 6.3–6.5
fees 6.6–6.9
matter type claim codes 6.2
Routine letters 1.14–1.16
Routine telephone calls 1.14–1.16

Supervision 1.27
Supreme Court 6.14

Time limits 9.8–9.24
crime lower 9.8, 9.9
Crown Court cases 9.10
extensions 9.16–9.24
when time begins to run 9.11–9.15
cases where appeal lodged 9.12, 9.13
confiscation cases 9.11
retrials 9.14, 9.15
Time recording 1.2–1.5
Travel and waiting time 1.35–1.38

Very high cost criminal cases 5.153, 7.1–7.15
appointment 7.7
cases ceasing to be 7.14, 7.15
definition 7.1–7.3
individual case contracts 7.8
notification 7.4–7.6
remuneration 7.9–7.13
Virtual courts 3.8–3.11
fees 3.8

Waiting time 1.35–1.38
Work logs 1.2–1.5